ALGORITHMS FOR IMAGE PROCESSING AND COMPUTER VISION

ALGORITHMS FOR IMAGE PROCESSING AND COMPUTER VISION

J.R. Parker

WILEY COMPUTER PUBLISHING

John Wiley & Sons, Inc.
New York • Chichester • Brisbane • Toronto • Singapore • Weinheim

To Katrin

Publisher: Katherine Schowalter
Senior Editor: Marjorie Spencer
Managing Editor: Frank Grazioli
Electronic Products Associate Editor: Mike Green
Text Design & Composition: University Graphics, Inc.

Designations used by companies to distinguish their products are often claimed as trademarks. In all instances where John Wiley & Sons, Inc., is aware of a claim, the product names appear in initial capital or ALL CAPITAL LETTERS. Readers, however, should contact the appropriate companies for more complete information regarding trademarks and registration.

This text is printed on acid-free paper.

Library of Congress Cataloging-in-Publication Data:
Parker, James R.
    Algorithms for image processing and computer vision (with CD-ROM)
/author, James R. Parker.
        p.   cm.
    Includes bibliographical references.
    ISBN 0-471-14056-2 (pbk. : CD-ROM : alk. paper)
    1. Image processing—Digital techniques.   2. Computer vision.
3. Computer algorithms.   I. Title.
TA1637.P37 1996
621.36′7′028551—dc20   96-15598
                                                                                  CIP

Printed in the United States of America
10 9 8

CONTENTS

3

ADVANCED METHODS IN GREY-LEVEL SEGMENTATION 116

4

TEXTURE 150

5

SKELETONIZATION—THE ESSENTIAL LINE 176

6

IMAGE RESTORATION 220

7
WAVELETS 250

8
OPTICAL CHARACTER RECOGNITION 275

9
SYMBOL RECOGNITION 305

10
GENETIC ALGORITHMS AND EVOLUTIONARY COMPUTING 357

APPENDIX THE CD—WHERE DO I START? 387

INDEX 413

PREFACE

Humans obtain the vast majority of their sensory input through their visual system, and an enormous effort has been made to artificially enhance this sense. Eyeglasses, binoculars, telescopes, radar, infrared sensors, and photo-multipliers all function to improve our view of the world and the universe. Even radio telescopes, which have been thought of as "big ears," capture and amplify electromagnetic radiation, which is simply light at a different frequency, and so really are "big eyes." It was a logical step to apply computers to this task.

This book was inspired by my numerous scans though the Internet news groups related to image processing and computer vision. I noted that some requests appeared over and over again, sometimes answered and sometimes not, and wondered if it would be possible to answer the more frequently asked questions in book form, which would allow the development of some of the background necessary for a complete explanation. However, since I had just completed a book (*Practical Computer Vision Using C*) I was in no mood to pursue the issue. I continued to collect information from the Net, hoping to one day collate it into a sensible form.

This has now, I hope, been done.

Much of the mathematics in this book is actually necessary for the detailed understanding of the algorithms described. The previous book was relatively free of math, but more advanced methods require the motivation and justification that only mathematics can provide. In some cases, I have only scratched the surface, and have left a more detailed study for those willing to follow the references given at the ends of chapters. I have tried to select references that provide a range of approaches, from detailed and complex mathematical analyses to clear and concise exposition. However, in some cases, such as that of wavelets, there are very few clear descriptions, and none that do not require at least a university-level math course. Here I have attempted to describe the situation in an intuitive manner, sacrificing rigor (which can be found almost anywhere else) for as clear a description as possible (it is still difficult—sorry).

Most of the algorithms described here are implemented in C, and the source code is included on the accompanying CD. Also included are many of the images used as examples, and a set of data images of various types to be used by those without access to a camera and frame grabber. In particular, the source code for a version of the Canny edge detector is included, which, to the best of my knowledge, is the only one published.

Another unique element is the inclusion of a compiler for a simple programming language called MAX, in which the basic operations of digital morphology are available as operators, an in which an image is a built-in data type.

The chapter on thresholding provides 17 programs, each implementing a different thresholding algorithm, including adaptive algorithms. Many programs are also provided for segmenting images using texture.

The chapter on thinning provides code for the well-known Zhang-Suen algorithm, as well as a number of novel approaches.

However, I am most pleased with the chapter on restoration, not because it is the best available or the most complete—it is not. The reason is, that for many years I kept seeing the same sample images in many different references on image restoration, and I wondered if those were the only images for which the algorithms would work! When the software for this book began to work correctly I knew this was not true. The programs for restoration that have been included in chapter 6 are some of the very few that are available in print.

Chapter 8 includes programs for optical character recognition, including some handprinted digits. I make no pretense about providing a complete solution that is usable in all situations—I would have sold it for a fortune and retired, had that been the case. A cross-section of algorithms is discussed, and the problems have been described, if not solved. The problem of recognizing printed music is also mentioned.

Finally, I make an effort to merely introduce some of the issues and methods in the use of genetic algorithms, a relatively new area, for solving vision problems. This is a truly vast and sometimes difficult area, and to do it justice would require many volumes as large as this one. The effort here was simply to describe the problem and some of its aspects, mention some specific solutions to specific problems, and summarize some of the work in the field. Consider this to be a mere taste of what is a fascinating area of study.

One other novel aspect of this book is the inclusion of a complete C compiler; this is a port of the famous GNU C compiler to the IBM/PC. One serious problem with including source code with a book is that not everyone uses the same compiler, and so those using a different compiler from the author may feel left out. The GCC compiler included here should run on any 386 or better, and comes with a floating point emulator, DOS extender, VGA package, debugger, and source code.

Comments and mistakes (how likely is that?) can be communicated by E-mail to:

parker@cpsc.ucalgary.ca

Fixes to bugs and enhanced versions of the code on the CD will be posted to:

ftp.cpsc.ucalgary.ca

in pub/images/vision/book

where they can, at least for now, be retrieved by anonymous FTP.

Jim Parker
Calgary, Alberta, Canada
October 1996.

ACKNOWLEDGMENTS

Thanks should go to many people, at the very real risk of omitting some one and getting into trouble. Anton Colijn, Danny Dimian, Todd Reed, Patrick Ang, Jon Rokne, Emad Attia, and Don Molaro all helped by reading over some of the chapters. Terry Ingoldsby is to be mentioned for his development of the finely tailored FFT program included on the CD; so is Jef Poskanzer, who created the PBM/PGM/PNM formats which are the standard image file formats used throughout this book. Todd Reed produced the Lemon music recognition system. The port of the GNU C compiler to the PC is the work of D.J. Delorie.

I would also like to thank all of those people who sent me kind e-mail messages about my previous book—these gave me the courage and confidence I needed to do it all again.

Almost all of the images used in this book were created by me, using an IBM PC with a frame grabber and a Sony CCD camera. Credits for the few that were not acquired in this way are as follows:

Corel corporation made available the color image of the grasshopper on a leaf seen on the back cover and in Figure 2.32.

Thanks to Big Hill Veterinary Clinic in Cochrane, Alberta, Canada for the X-ray image seen in Figure 3.8c.

Finally, thanks to Dr. N. Wardlaw of the University of Calgary Department of Geology for the geological micropore image of Figure 2.15.

Most importantly, I need to thank my family: my wife Katrin, and children Adam, Bailey, and Maximilian. They all sacrificed time and energy so that this work could be completed. I appreciate it, and hope that the effort has been worthwhile.

1

ADVANCED EDGE-DETECTION TECHNIQUES:
The Canny and the Shen-Castan Methods

1.1   THE PURPOSE OF EDGE DETECTION

Edge detection is one of the most commonly used operations in image analysis, and there are probably more algorithms in the literature for enhancing and detecting edges than for any other single subject. The reason for this is that edges form the outline of an object. An edge is the boundary between an object and the background, and indicates the boundary between overlapping objects. This means that if the edges in an image can be identified accurately, all of the objects can be located and basic properties such as area, perimeter, and shape can be measured. Since computer vision involves the identification and classification of objects in an image, edge detection is an essential tool.

A straightforward example of edge detection is illustrated in Figure 1.1. There are two overlapping objects in the original picture (a), which has a uniform grey background. The edge-enhanced version of the same image (b) has dark lines outlining the three objects. Note that there is no way to tell which parts of the image are background and which are object; only the boundaries between the regions are identified. However, given that the blobs in the image are the regions, it can be determined that the blob numbered 3 covers up a part of blob 2, and is therefore closer to the camera.

Edge detection is part of a process called *segmentation*—the identification of regions within an image. The regions that may be objects in Figure 1.1 have been isolated, and further processing may determine what kind of object each region represents. While in this example edge detection is merely a step in the segmen-

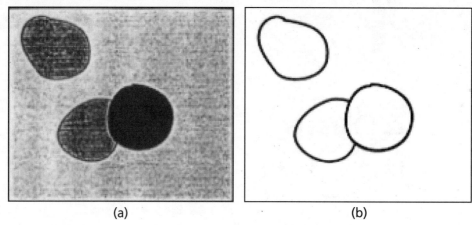

(a)   (b)

Figure 1.1 Example of edge detection. (a) Synthetic image with blobs on a grey background. (b) Edge-enhanced image showing only the outlines of the objects.

tation process, it is sometimes all that is needed, especially when the objects in an image are lines.

Consider the image in Figure 1.2, which is a photograph of a cross-section of a tree. The growth rings are the objects of interest in this image. Each ring represents a year of the tree's life, and the number of rings is therefore the same as the age of the tree. Enhancing the rings using an edge detector, as shown in Figure 1.2b, is all that is needed to segment the image into foreground (objects, which in this case are rings) and background (everything else).

Technically, *edge detection* is the process of locating the edge pixels, and *edge enhancement* will increase the contrast between the edges and the background so that the edges become more visible. In practice, the terms are used interchangeably, since most edge detection programs also set the edge pixel values to a specific grey level or color so that they can be easily seen. In addition, *edge tracing* is the process of following the edges, usually collecting the edge pixels into a list. This is done in a consistent direction, either clockwise or counterclockwise around the objects. Chain coding is one example of a method of edge tracing. The result is a nonraster representation of the objects, which can be used to compute shape measurements or otherwise identify or classify the object.

The remainder of this chapter will discuss the theory of edge detection, including a few traditional methods. Then two methods of special interest will be described and compared. These methods, the Canny edge detector and the Shen-Castan (or ISEF) edge detector, have received a lot of attention lately, and justifiably so. Both are based solidly on theoretical considerations, and both claim a degree of optimality; that is, both claim to be the best that can be done under

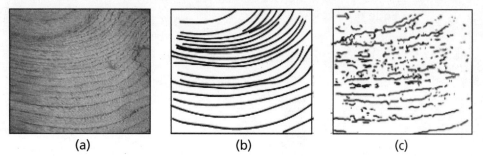

Figure 1.2 A cross-section of a tree. (a) Original grey-level image. (b) Ideal edge-enhanced image, showing the growth rings. (c) The edge enhancement that one might expect using a real algorithm.

certain specified circumstances. These claims will be examined, both in theory and in practice.

1.2   TRADITIONAL APPROACHES AND THEORY

Most good algorithms begin with a clear statement of the problem to be solved, and a cogent analysis of the possible method of solution and the conditions under which the methods will operate correctly. Using this paradigm to define an edge-detection algorithm means first defining what an edge is, then using this definition to suggest methods of enhancement.

As usual, there are a number of possible definitions of an edge, each being applicable in various specific circumstances. One of the most common and most general definitions is the *ideal step edge*, illustrated in Figure 1.3. In this one-dimensional example, the edge is simply a change in grey level occurring at one specific location. The greater the change in level, the easier the edge is to detect, but in the ideal case *any* level change can be seen quite easily.

The first complication occurs because of digitization. It is unlikely that the image will be sampled in such a way that all of the edges happen to correspond exactly with a pixel boundary. Indeed, the change in level may extend across some number of pixels (Figures 1.3b–d). The actual position of the edge is considered to be the center of the *ramp* connecting the low grey level to the high one. This is a ramp in the mathematical world only, since after the image has been made digital (sampled), the ramp has the jagged appearance of a staircase.

The second complication is the ubiquitous problem of *noise*. Due to a great many factors such as light intensity, type of camera and lens, motion, temperature, atmospheric effects, dust, and others, it is very unlikely that two pixels that correspond to precisely the same grey level in the scene will have the same level in the image. Noise is a random effect, and is characterizable only statistically. The

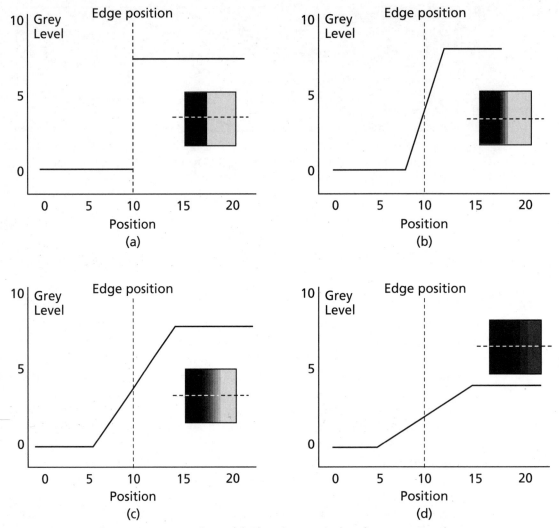

Figure 1.3 Step edges. (a) The change in level occurs exactly at pixel 10. (b) The same level change as before, but over four pixels centered at pixel 10. This is a *ramp* edge. (c) Same level change but over 10 pixels, centered at 10. (d) A smaller change over 10 pixels. The insert shows the way the image would appear, and the dotted line shows where the image was sliced to give the illustrated cross-section.

result of noise on the image is to produce a random variation in level from pixel to pixel, and so the smooth lines and ramps of the ideal edges are never encountered in real images.

Models of Edges

The step edge of Figure 1.3a is ideal because it is easy to detect: In the absence of noise, any significant change in grey level would indicate an edge. A step edge never really occurs in an image because: a) Objects rarely have such a sharp outline; b) A scene is never sampled so that edges occur exactly at the margins of a pixel; and c) Due to noise, as mentioned previously.

Noise will be discussed in the next section, and object outlines vary quite a bit from image to image, so let us concentrate for a moment on sampling. Figure 1.4a shows an ideal step edge and the set of pixels involved. Note that the edge occurs on the extreme left side of the white edge pixels. As the camera moves to the left by amounts smaller than one pixel width, the edge moves to the right. In Figure 1.4c the edge has moved by one half of a pixel, and the pixels along the edge now contain some part of the image that is black and some part that is white. This will be reflected in the grey level as a weighted average:

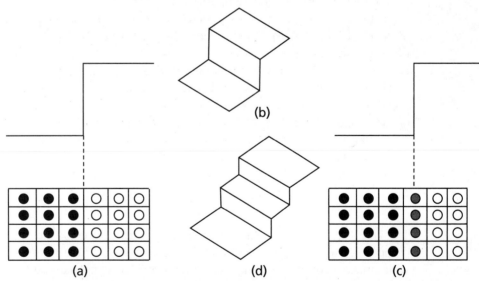

Figure 1.4 The effect of sampling on a step edge. (a) An ideal step edge. (b) Three-dimensional view of the step edge. (c) Step edge sampled at the center of a pixel, instead of on a margin. (d) The result, in three dimensions, has the appearance of a staircase.

$$v = \frac{(v_w a_w + v_b a_b)}{a_w + a_b} \qquad \text{(EQ 1.1)}$$

where v_w and v_b are the grey levels of the white and black regions, and a_w and a_b are the areas of the white and black parts of the edge pixel. For example, if the white level is 100 and the black level is 0, then the value of an edge pixel for which the edge runs through the middle will be 50. The result is a double step instead of a step edge.

If the effect of a blurred outline is to spread out the grey level change over a number of pixels, then the single stair becomes a *staircase*. The ramp is a model of what the edge must have originally looked like in order to produce a staircase, and so is an idealization; it is an interpolation of the data actually encountered.

Although the ideal step edge and ramp edge models were generally used to devise new edge detectors in the past, the model was recognized to be a simplification; newer edge-detection schemes incorporate noise into the model, and are tested on staircases and noise edges.

Noise

All image-acquisition processes are subject to noise of some type, so there is little point in ignoring it; the ideal situation (no noise) never occurs in practice. Noise cannot be predicted accurately because of its random nature, and cannot even be measured accurately from a noisy image, since the contribution to the grey levels of the noise can't be distinguished from the pixel data. However, noise can sometimes be characterized by its effect on the image, and is usually expressed as a probability distribution with a specific mean and standard deviation.

There are two types of noise that are of specific interest in image analysis. *Signal-independent* noise is a random set of grey levels, statistically independent of the image data; that is, added to the pixels in the image to give the resulting noisy image. This kind of noise occurs when an image is transmitted electronically from one place to another. If A is a perfect image and N is the noise that occurs during transmission, then the final image B is:

$$B = A + N \qquad \text{(EQ 1.2)}$$

A and N are unrelated to each other. The noise image N could have any statistical properties, but a common assumption is that it follows the normal distribution with a mean of zero and some measured or presumed standard deviation.

It is simple matter to create an artificially noisy image having known characteristics, and such images are very useful tools for experimenting with edge-detection algorithms. Figure 1.5 shows an image of a chessboard that has been subjected to various degrees of artificial noise. For a normal distribution with zero

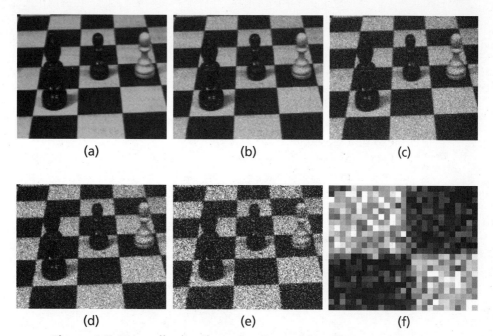

Figure 1.5 Normally distributed noise and its effect on an image. (a) Original image. (b) Noise having $\sigma = 10$. (c) Noise having $\sigma = 20$. (d) Noise having $\sigma = 30$. (e) Noise having $\sigma = 50$. (f) Expanded view of an intersection of four regions in the $\sigma = 50$ image.

mean, the amount of noise is specified by the standard deviation; values of 10, 20, 30, and 50 are shown in the figure.

For these images it is possible to obtain an estimate of the noise. The scene contains a number of small regions that should have a uniform grey level—the squares on the chess board. If the noise is consistent over the entire image, then the noise in any one square will be a sample of the noise in the whole image; and since the level is constant over the square, then any variation can be assumed to be caused by the noise alone. In this case, the mean and standard deviation of the grey levels in any square can be computed; the standard deviation of the grey levels will be close to that of the noise. To make sure that this is working properly, we can now use the mean already computed as the grey level of the square and compute the mean and standard deviation of the *difference of each grey level from the mean*; this new mean should be near to zero, and the standard deviation close to that of that noise (and to the previously computed standard deviation).

A program that does this appear in Figure 1.6. As a simple test, a black square and a white square were isolated from the image in Figure 1.5c and this program was used to estimate the noise. The results were:

```
/* Measure the Normally distributed noise in a small
region.
    Assume that the mean is zero.*/

#include <stdio.h>
#include <math.h>
#define MAX
#include "lib.h"
main (int argc, char *argv[])
{
    IMAGE im;
    int i,j,k;
    float x, y, z;
    double mean, sd;

    im = Input_PBM (argv[1]);
/* Measure */
    k = 0;
    x = y = 0.0;
    for (i=0; i<im->info->nr; i++)
     for (j=0; j<im->info->nc; j++)
     {
         x += (float)(im->data[i][j]);
         y += (float)(im->data[i][j]); *
(float)(im->data[i][j]);
         k += 1;
     }

/* Compute estimate — mean noise is 0 */
    sd = (double)(y — x*x/(float)k)/(float)(k—1);
    mean = (double) (x/(float)k);
    sd = sqrt(sd);
    printf ("Image mean is %10.5f Standard deviation is
%10.5f\n",
                    mean, sd);
```

Figure 1.6 A C program for estimating the noise in an image. The input image is sampled from the image to be measured, and must be a region that would ordinarily have a constant grey level.

```
/* Now assume that the uniform level is the mean, and
compute the mean and SD of the differences from that!*/
    x = y = z = 0.0;
    for (i=0; i<im->info->nr; i++)
     for (j=0; j<im->info->nc; j++)
     {
            z = (float)(im->data[i][j] - mean);
            x += z;
            y += z*z;
     }
    sd = (double)(y - x*x/(float)k)/(float)(k-1);
    mean = (double)(x/(float)k);
    sd = sqrt(sd);
    printf ("Noise mean is %10.5f Standard deviation is
%10.5f\n",
            mean, sd);
}
```

Figure 1.6 (continued)

Black region:
    Image mean is 31.63629 Standard deviation is 19.52933
    Noise mean is 0.00001 Standard deviation is 19.52933
White region:
    Image mean is 188.60692 Standard deviation is 19.46295
    Noise mean is −0.00000 Standard deviation is 19.47054

In both cases, the noise mean was very close to zero (although we have assumed this), and the standard deviation was very close to 20 (which was the value used to create the noisy image).

The second major type of noise is called *signal-dependent noise*. In this case the level of the noise value at each point in the image is a function of the grey level there. The grain seen in some photographs is an example of this sort of noise, and it is generally harder to deal with. Fortunately it is less often of importance, and becomes manageable if the photograph is sampled properly.

Figure 1.7 shows a step edge subjected to noise of a type that can be characterized by a normal distribution. This is an artificial edge generated by computer, so its exact location is known. It is difficult to see this in all of the random variations, but a good edge detector should be able to determine the edge position in even this situation.

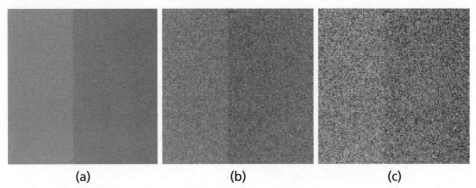

(a)   (b)   (c)

Figure 1.7 (a) A step edge subjected to Gaussian (normal distribution) noise. (b) Standard deviation is 10. (c) Standard deviation is 20. Note that the edge is getting lost in the random noise.

Returning, with less confidence, to the case of the ideal step edge, the question of how to identify the location of the edge remains. An edge (based on the previous discussion) is defined by a grey level or color contour. If this contour is crossed, then the level changes rapidly; following the contour leads to more subtle, possibly random, level changes. This leads to the conclusion that an edge has a measurable direction. Also, although it is by the large level change observed when crossing the contour that an edge pixel can first be identified, it is the fact that such pixels connect to form a contour that permits the separation of noise from edge pixels. Noise pixels also show a large change in level.

There are essentially three common types of operators for locating edges. The first type is a derivative operator designed to identify places where there are large intensity changes. The second resembles a template-matching scheme, where the edge is modeled by a small image showing the abstracted properties of a perfect edge. Finally, there are operators that use a mathematical model of the edge; the best of these use a model of the noise also, and make an effort to take it into account. Our interest is mainly in the latter types, but examples of the first two types will be explored first.

Derivative Operators

Since an edge is defined by a change in grey level, an operator that is sensitive to this change will operate as an edge detector. A derivative operator does this; one interpretation of a derivative is as the rate of change of a function, and the rate of change of the grey levels in an image is large near an edge and small in constant areas.

Since images are two-dimensional, it is important to consider level changes in many directions. For this reason, the partial derivatives of the image are used, with respect to the principal directions x and y. An estimate of the actual edge direction can be obtained by using the derivatives in x and y as the components of the actual direction along the axes, and computing the vector sum. The operator involved happens to be the *gradient*, and if the image is thought of as a function of two variables $\mathbf{A(x,y)}$ then the gradient is defined as:

$$\nabla A(x,y) \ = \ \left(\frac{\partial A}{\partial x}, \frac{\partial A}{\partial y} \right) \qquad \text{(EQ 1.3)}$$

which is a two-dimensional vector.

Of course, an image is not a function, and cannot be differentiated in the usual way. Because an image is discrete, we use *differences* instead; that is, the derivative at a pixel is approximated by the difference in grey levels over some local region. The simplest such approximation is the operator ∇_1:

$$\nabla_{x1}A(x,y) \ = \ A(x,y) \ - \ A(x-1,y)$$
$$\nabla_{y1}A(x,y) \ = \ A(x,y) \ - \ A(x,y-1) \qquad \text{(EQ 1.4)}$$

The assumption in this case is that the grey levels vary linearly between the pixels, so that no matter where the derivative is taken its value is the slope of the line. One problem with this approximation is that it does not compute the gradient at the point (x,y), but at $(x - \frac{1}{2}, y - \frac{1}{2})$. The edge locations would therefore be shifted by one half of a pixel in the $-x$ and $-y$ directions. A better choice for an approximation might be ∇_2:

$$\nabla_{x2}A \ = \ A(x+1,y) \ - \ A(x-1,y)$$
$$\nabla_{y2}A \ = \ A(x,y+1) \ - \ A(x,y-1) \qquad \text{(EQ 1.5)}$$

This operator is symmetrical with respect to the pixel (x,y), although it does not consider the value of the pixel at (x,y).

Whichever operator is used to compute the gradient, the resulting vector contains information about how strong the edge is at that pixel and what its direction is. The magnitude of the gradient vector is the length of the hypotenuse of the right triangle having sides ∇x and ∇y, and this reflects the strength of the edge, or *edge response*, at any given pixel. The direction of the edge at the same pixel is the angle that the hypotenuse makes with the axis.

Mathematically, the edge response is given by:

$$G_{mag} \ = \ \sqrt{\left(\frac{\partial A}{\partial x}\right)^2 + \left(\frac{\partial A}{\partial y}\right)^2} \qquad \text{(EQ 1.6)}$$

and the direction of the edge is approximately:

$$G_{dir} = \text{atan}\left(\frac{\dfrac{\partial A}{\partial y}}{\dfrac{\partial A}{\partial x}}\right) \qquad \text{(EQ 1.7)}$$

The edge magnitude will be a real number, and is usually converted to an integer by rounding. Any pixel having a gradient that exceeds a specified threshold value is said to be an edge pixel, and others are not. Technically, an edge detector will report the edge pixels only, while edge enhancement draws the edge pixels over the original image. This distinction will not be important in the further discussion. The two edge detectors evaluated here will use the middle value in the range of grey levels as a threshold.

At this point it would be useful to see the results of the two gradient operators applied to an image. For the purposes of evaluating all of the methods to be presented, a standard set of test images is suggested; the basic set appears in Figure 1.8, and noisy versions of these will also be used. Noise will be normal, and will have standard deviations of 3, 9, and 18. For edge gradients, of 18 grey levels, these correspond to signal-to-noise ratios of 6, 2, and 1. The appearance of the edge-enhanced test images will give a rough cue about how successful the edge-detection algorithm is.

In addition, it would be nice to have a numerical measure of how successful an edge-detection scheme is in an absolute sense. There is no such measure in general, but something usable can be constructed by thinking about the ways in which an edge detector can fail. First, an edge detector can report an edge where none exists; this can be due to noise, or simply poor design or thresholding, and is called a *false positive*. In addition, an edge detector could fail to report an edge pixel that does exist; this is a *false negative*. Finally, the position of the edge pixel could be wrong. An edge detector that reports edge pixels in their proper positions is obviously better than one that does not, and this must be measured somehow. Since most of the test images will have known numbers and positions of edge pixels, and will have noise of a known type and quantity applied, the application of the edge detectors to the standard images will give an approximate measure of their effectiveness.

One possible way to evaluate an edge detector, based on the above discussion, was proposed by Pratt (1978), who suggested the following function:

$$E_1 = \frac{\displaystyle\sum_{i=1}^{I_A}\left(\frac{1}{1 + \alpha d(i)^2}\right)}{\max\,(I_A, I_I)} \qquad \text{(EQ 1.8)}$$

where I_A is the number of edge pixels found by the edge detector, I_I is the actual number of edge pixels in the test image, and the function $d(i)$ is the distance

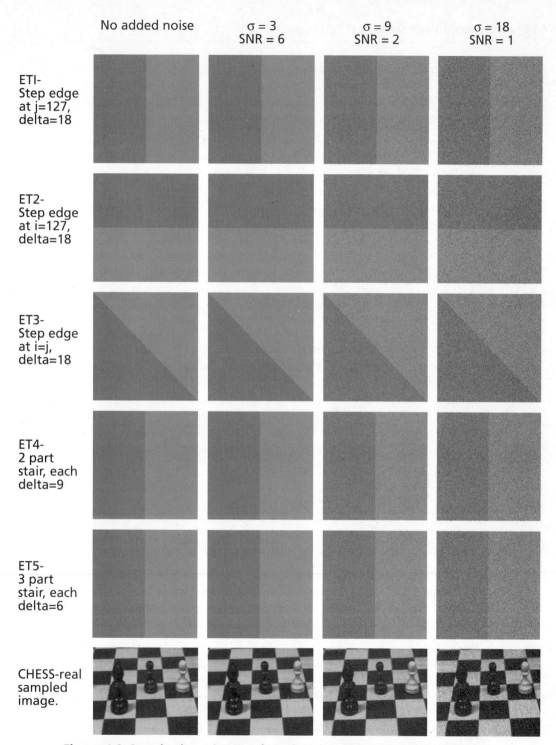

Figure 1.8 Standard test images for edge detector evaluation. There are three step edges and two stairs, plus a real sampled image; all have been subjected to normally distributed zero-mean noise with known standard deviations of 3, 9, and 18.

between the actual *ith* pixel and the one found by the edge detector. The value α is used for scaling, and should be kept constant for any set of trials. A value of ⅑ will be used here, as it was in Pratt's work. This metric is, as discussed previously, a function of the distance between correct and measured edge positions, but is only indirectly related to the false positives and negatives.

Kitchen and Rosenfeld (1981) also present an evaluation scheme, this one based on *local edge coherence*. It does not concern itself with the actual position of an edge, and so is a supplement to Pratt's metric. Instead, it measures how well the edge pixel fits into the local neighborhood of edge pixels. The first step is the definition of a function that measures how well an edge pixel is continued on the left; this function is:

$$L(k) = \begin{cases} a(d,d_k)a\left(\dfrac{k\pi}{4}, d + \dfrac{\pi}{2}\right) & \text{if neighbor k is an edge pixel} \\ 0 & \text{Otherwise} \end{cases} \qquad \text{(EQ 1.9)}$$

where d is the edge direction at the pixel being tested, d_0 is the edge direction at its neighbor to the right, d_1 is the direction of the upper-right neighbor, and so on counterclockwise about the pixel involved. The function a is a measure of the angular difference between any two angles:

$$a(\alpha, \beta) = \frac{\pi - |\alpha - \beta|}{\pi} \qquad \text{(EQ 1.10)}$$

A similar function measures directional continuity on the right of the pixel being evaluated:

$$R(k) = \begin{cases} a(d,d_k)a\left(\dfrac{k\pi}{4}, d - \dfrac{\pi}{2}\right) & \text{if neighbor k is an edge pixel} \\ 0 & \text{Otherwise} \end{cases} \qquad \text{(EQ 1.11)}$$

The overall continuity measure is taken to be the average of the best (largest) value of L(k) and the best value of R(k); this measure is called C.

Then a measure of thinness is applied. An edge should be a thin line, one pixel wide. Lines of a greater width imply that false positives exist, probably because the edge detector has responded more than once to the same edge. The thinness measure T is the fraction of the six pixels in the 3 × 3 region centered at the pixel being measured, not counting the center and the two pixels found by L(k) and R(k), that are edge pixels. The overall evaluation of the edge detector is:

$$E_2 = \gamma C + (1 - \gamma)T \qquad \text{(EQ 1.12)}$$

where γ is a constant: we will use the value 0.8 here.

We are now prepared to evaluate the two gradient operators. Each of the operators was applied to each of the 24 test images. Then both the Pratt and the KR metric were taken on the results, with the outcome for ∇_1 outlined in Table 1.1.

Table 1.1 Evaluation of the ∇_1 operator

Image	Evaluator	No Noise	SNR = 6	SNR = 2	SNR = 1
ET1	Eval 1	0.9650	0.5741	0.0510	0.0402
	Eval 2	1.0000	0.6031	0.3503	0.3494
ET2	Eval 1	0.9650	0.6714	0.0484	0.0392
	Eval 2	1.0000	0.6644	0.3491	0.3493
ET3	Eval 1	0.9726	0.7380	0.0818	0.0564
	Eval 2	0.9325	0.6743	0.3532	0.3493
ET4	Eval 1	0.4947	0.0839	0.0375	0.0354
	Eval 2	0.8992	0.3338	0.3473	0.3489
ET5	Eval 1	0.4772	0.0611	0.0365	0.0354
	Eval 2	0.7328	0.3163	0.34614	0.3485

The drop in quality for ET4 and ET5 is due to the operator giving a response to each step, rather than a single overall response to the edge. Our outcome for ∇_2 is outlined in Table 1.2.

This operator gave two edge pixels at each point along the edge, one in each region. As a result, each of the two pixels contributes to the distance to the actual edge. This duplication of edge pixels should have been penalized in one of the evaluations, but E1 does not penalize extra edge pixels as much as it does missing ones.

Table 1.2 Evaluation of the ∇_2 operator

Image	Evaluator	No Noise	SNR = 6	SNR = 2	SNR = 1
ET1	Eval 1	0.9727	0.8743	0.0622	0.0421
	Eval 2	0.8992	0.6931	0.4167	0.4049
ET2	Eval 1	0.9726	0.9454	0.0612	0.0400
	Eval 2	0.8992	0.6696	0.4032	0.4049
ET3	Eval 1	0.9726	0.9707	0.1000	0.0623
	Eval 2	0.9325	0.9099	0.4134	0.4058
ET4	Eval 1	0.5158	0.4243	0.0406	0.0320
	Eval 2	1.000	0.5937	0.4158	0.4043
ET5	Eval 1	0.5062	0.1963	0.0360	0.0316
	Eval 2	0.8992	0.4097	0.4147	0.4046

It is not possible to show all of the edge-enhanced images, since in this case alone there are 48 of them. Figure 1.9 shows a selection of the results from both operators; from these images and from the evaluations it can be concluded that ∇_2 is slightly superior, especially where the noise is higher.

Template-Based Edge Detection

The idea behind template-based edge detection is to use a small, discrete template as a model of an edge instead of using a derivative operator directly (as in the previous section) or a complex, more global model (as in the next section). The template can be either an attempt to model the level changes in the edge, or an attempt to approximate a derivative operator; the latter appears to be most common.

There is a vast array of template-based edge detectors. Two were chosen to be examined here simply because they provide the best sets of edge pixels while using a small template. The first of these is the Sobel edge detector, which uses templates in the form of convolution masks having the following values:

$$
\begin{matrix}
-1 & -2 & -1 \\
0 & 0 & 0 \\
1 & 2 & 1
\end{matrix} = S_y
\qquad
\begin{matrix}
-1 & 0 & 1 \\
-2 & 0 & 2 \\
-1 & 0 & 1
\end{matrix} = S_x
$$

One way to view these templates is as an approximation to the gradient at the pixel corresponding to the center of the template. Note that the weights on

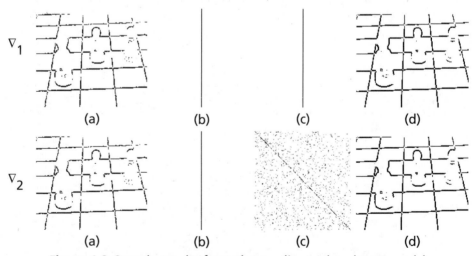

Figure 1.9 Sample results from the gradient edge detectors. (a) Chess image ($\sigma=3$). (b) ET1 image (SNR=6). (c) ET3 image (SNR=2). (d) Chess image ($\sigma=18$).

the diagonal elements is smaller than the weights on the horizontal and vertical. The x component of the Sobel operator is S_x, and the y component is S_y; considering these as components of the gradient means that the magnitude and direction of the edge pixel is given by Equations 1.6 and 1.7.

For a pixel at image coordinates (i,j), S_x and S_y can be computed by:

$$S_x = I[i-1][j+1]+2I[i][j+1]+I[i+1][j+1]-(I[i-1][j-1]+2I[i][j-1]$$
$$+I[i+1][j-1])$$

$$S_y = I[i+1][j+1]+2I[i+1][j]+I[i+1][j-1]-(I[i-1][j+1]+2I[i-1][j]$$
$$+I[i-1][j-1])$$

which is equivalent to applying the operator ∇_1 to each 2×2 portion of the 3×3 region, and then averaging the result. After S_x and S_y are computed for every pixel in an image, the resulting magnitudes must be thresholded. All pixels will have some response to the templates, but only the very large responses will correspond to edges. The best way to compute the magnitude is by using Equation 1.6, but this involves a square root calculation that is both intrinsically slow and requires the use of floating-point numbers. Optionally we could use the sum of the absolute values of S_x and S_y (that is: $|S_x| + |S_y|$) or even the largest of the two values. Thresholding could be done using almost any standard method. Sections 1.4 and 1.5 describe some techniques that are specifically intended for use on edges.

The second example of the use of templates is the one described by Kirsch, and was selected as an example here because these templates have a different motivation than Sobel's. For the 3×3 case the templates are:

$$
K0 = \begin{matrix} -3 & -3 & 5 \\ -3 & 0 & 5 \\ -3 & -3 & 5 \end{matrix} \quad
K1 = \begin{matrix} -3 & 5 & 5 \\ -3 & 0 & 5 \\ -3 & -3 & -3 \end{matrix} \quad
K2 = \begin{matrix} 5 & 5 & 5 \\ -3 & 0 & -3 \\ -3 & -3 & -3 \end{matrix} \quad
K3 = \begin{matrix} 5 & 5 & -3 \\ 5 & 0 & -3 \\ -3 & -3 & -3 \end{matrix}
$$

$$
K4 = \begin{matrix} 5 & -3 & -3 \\ 5 & 0 & -3 \\ 5 & -3 & -3 \end{matrix} \quad
K5 = \begin{matrix} -3 & -3 & -3 \\ 5 & 0 & -3 \\ 5 & 5 & -3 \end{matrix} \quad
K6 = \begin{matrix} -3 & -3 & -3 \\ -3 & 0 & -3 \\ 5 & 5 & 5 \end{matrix} \quad
K7 = \begin{matrix} -3 & -3 & -3 \\ -3 & 0 & 5 \\ -3 & 5 & 5 \end{matrix}
$$

These masks are an effort to model the kind of grey level change seen near an edge having various orientations, rather than an approximation to the gradient. There is one mask for each of eight compass directions. For example, a large response to mask K0 implies a vertical edge (horizontal gradient) at the pixel corresponding to the center of the mask. To find the edges, an image I is convolved with all of the masks at each pixel position. The response of the operator at a pixel is the *maximum* of the responses of any of the eight masks. The direction of the

Table 1.3 Evaluation of the Sobel Edge Detector

Image	Evaluator	No Noise	SNR = 6	SNR = 2	SNR = 1
ET1	Eval 1	0.9727	0.9690	0.1173	0.0617
	Eval 2	0.8992	0.8934	0.4474	0.4263
ET2	Eval 1	0.9726	0.9706	0.1609	0.0526
	Eval 2	0.8992	0.8978	0.4215	0.4255
ET3	Eval 1	0.9726	0.9697	0.1632	0.0733
	Eval 2	0.9325	0.9186	0.4349	0.4240
ET4	Eval 1	0.4860	0.4786	0.0595	0.0373
	Eval 2	0.7328	0.6972	0.4426	0.4266
ET5	Eval 1	0.4627	0.3553	0.0480	0.0355
	Eval 2	0.7496	0.6293	0.4406	0.4250

edge pixel is quantized into eight possibilities here, and is $\pi/4*i$ where i is the number of the mask having the largest response.

Both of these edges detectors were evaluated using the test images of Figure 1.8. The results are outlined in Table 1.3.

The results for the Kirsch operator are found in Table 1.4.

Figure 1.10 shows the response of these templates applied to a selection of the test images. Based on the evaluations and the appearance of the test images,

Table 1.4 Evaluation of the Kirsch Edge Detector

Image	Evaluator	No Noise	SNR = 6	SNR = 2	SNR = 1
ET1	Eval 1	0.9727	0.9727	0.1197	0.0490
	Eval 2	0.8992	0.8992	0.4646	0.4922
ET2	Eval 1	0.9726	0.9726	0.1517	0.0471
	Eval 2	0.8992	0.8992	0.4528	0.4911
ET3	Eval 1	0.9726	0.9715	0.1458	0.0684
	Eval 2	0.9325	0.9200	0.4708	0.4907
ET4	Eval 1	0.4860	0.4732	0.0511	0.0344
	Eval 2	0.7328	0.7145	0.4819	0.4907
ET5	Eval 1	0.4627	0.3559	0.0412	0.0339
	Eval 2	0.7496	0.6315	0.5020	0.4894

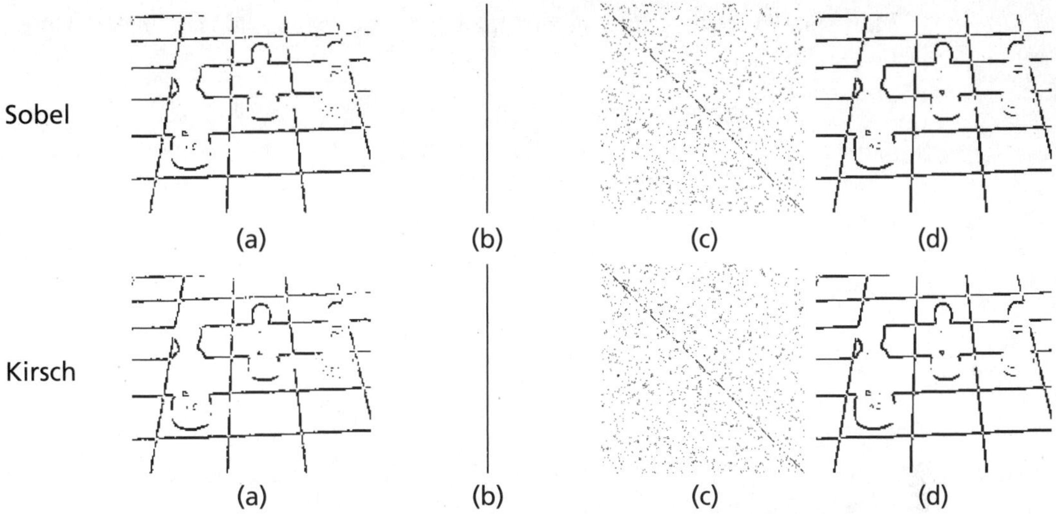

Sobel
(a)   (b)   (c)   (d)

Kirsch
(a)   (b)   (c)   (d)

Figure 1.10 Sample results from the template edge detectors.
(a) Chess image, noise $\sigma = 3$. (b) ET1, SNR=6. (c) ET3, SNR=2.
(d) Chess image, noise $\sigma = 18$.

the Kirsch operator appears to be the best of the two template operators, although the two are very close. Both template operators are superior to the simple derivative operators, especially as the noise increases.

It should be pointed out that in all cases studied so far there are unspecified aspects to the edge detection methods that will have an impact on their efficacy. Principal among these is the thresholding method used, but sometimes simple noise removal is done beforehand and edge thinning is done afterward. The model-based methods that follow generally include these features, sometimes as part of the edge model.

1.3   EDGE MODELS: MARR-HILDRETH EDGE DETECTION

In the late 1970s, David Marr attempted to combine what was known about biological vision into a model that could be used for machine vision. According to Marr,

> "... the purpose of early visual processing is to construct a primitive but rich description of the image that is to be used to determine the reflectance and illumination of the visible surfaces, and their orientation and distance relative to the viewer" (Marr 1980).

The lowest-level description he called the *primal sketch*, a major component of which are the edges.

Marr studied the literature on mammalian visual systems and summarized these in five major points:

1. In natural images, features of interest occur at a variety of scales. No single operator can function at all of these scales, so the result of operators at each of many scales should be combined.
2. A natural scene does not appear to consist of diffraction patterns or other wavelike effects, and so some form of local averaging (*smoothing*) must take place.
3. The optimal smoothing filter that matches the observed requirements of biological vision (smooth and localized in the spatial domain and smooth and band-limited in the frequency domain) is the *Gaussian*.
4. When a change in intensity (an edge) occurs, there is an extreme value in the first derivative or intensity. This corresponds to a *zero crossing* in the second derivative.
5. The orientation-independent differential operator of lowest order is the *Laplacian*.

Each of these points is either supported by the observation of vision systems or derived mathematically, but the overall grounding of the resulting edge detector is still a little loose. However, based on the five points above, an edge-detection algorithm can be stated as follows:

1. Convolve the image I with a two-dimensional Gaussian function.
2. Complete the Laplacian of the convolved image; call this L.
3. Edges pixels are those for which there is a zero crossing in L.

The results of convolutions with Gaussians having a variety of standard deviations are combined to form a single edge image. The standard deviation is a measure of scale in this instance.

The algorithm is not difficult to implement, although it is more difficult than the methods seen so far. A convolution in two dimensions can be expressed as:

$$I*G(i,j) = \sum_n \sum_m I(n,m)G(i - n, j - m)$$ (EQ 1.13)

The function G being convolved with the image is a two-dimensional Gaussian, which is:

$$G_\sigma(x,y) = \sigma^2 e^{\frac{-(x^2+y^2)}{\sigma^2}}$$ (EQ 1.14)

To perform the convolution on a digital image, the Gaussian must be sampled to create a small two-dimensional image. After the convolution, the Laplacian operator can be applied. This is:

$$\nabla^2 = \frac{\partial^2}{\partial x^2} + \frac{\partial^2}{\partial y^2}$$ (EQ 1.15)

and could be computed using differences. However, because order does not matter in this case, we could compute the Laplacian of the Gaussian analytically and sample that function, creating a convolution mask that can be applied to the image to yield the same result. The Laplacian of a Gaussian (LoG) is:

$$\nabla^2 G_\sigma = \left(\frac{r^2 - 2\sigma^2}{\sigma^4} \right) e^{\left(\frac{-r}{2\sigma^2} \right)}$$ (EQ 1.16)

where $r = \sqrt{x^2 + y^2}$. This latter approach is the one taken in the C code implementing this operator, which appears at the end of this chapter.

This program first creates a two-dimensional, sampled version of the Laplacian of the Gaussian (called lgau in the function marr) and convolves this in the obvious way with the input image (function convolution). Then the zero crossings are identified, and pixels at those positions are marked.

A zero crossing at a pixel P implies that the values of the two opposing neighboring pixels in some direction have different signs. For example, if the edge through P is vertical, then the pixel to the left of P will have a different sign than the one to the right of P. There are four cases to test: up/down, left/right, and the two diagonals. This test is performed for each pixel in the Laplacian of the Gaussian by the function zero_cross.

In order to ensure that a variety of scales are used, the program uses two different Gaussians, and selects the pixels that have zero crossings in both scales as output edge pixels. More than two Gaussians could be used, of course. The program accepts a standard deviation value σ as a parameter, either from the command line or from the parameter file marr.par. It then uses both $\sigma + 0.8$ and $\sigma - 0.8$ as standard deviation values, does two convolutions, locates two sets of zero

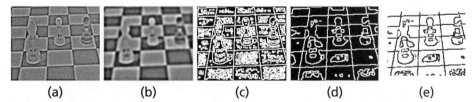

| (a) | (b) | (c) | (d) | (e) |

Figure 1.11 Steps in the computation of the Marr-Hildreth edge detector. (a) Convolution of the original image with the Laplacian of a Gaussian having $\sigma = 1.2$. (b) Convolution of the image with the Laplacian of a Gaussian having $\sigma = 2.8$. (c) Zero crossings found in (a). (d) Zero crossings found in (b). (e) Result, found by using zero crossings common to both.

crossings, and merges the resulting edge pixels into a single image. The program is called marr, and can be invoked as

```
marr input.pgm 2.0
```

which would read in the image file named input.pgm and apply the Marr-Hildreth edge-detection algorithm using 1.2 and 2.8 as standard deviations.

Figure 1.11 illustrates the steps in this process, using the chess image (no noise) as an example. Figures 1.11a and b show the original image after being convolved with the Laplacian of the Gaussians, having σ values of 1.2 and 2.8 respectively. Figures 1.11c and 1.11d are the responses from these two different values of σ, and Figure 1.11e shows the result of merging the edge pixels in these two images.

Figure 1.12 shows the result of the Marr-Hildreth edge detector applied to the all of the test images of Figure 1.8. In addition, the evaluation of this operator is shown in Table 1.5.

The evaluations above tend to be low. Because of the width of the Gaussian filter, the pixels that are a distance less than about 4σ from the boundary of the

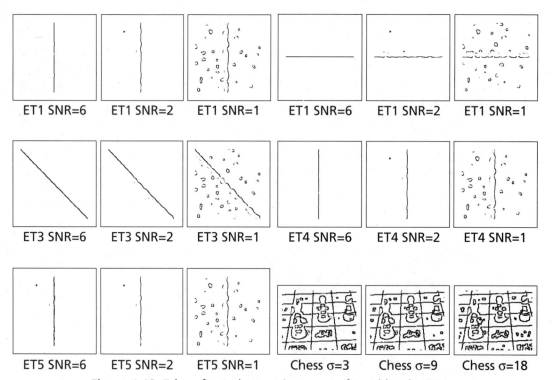

Figure 1.12 Edges from the test images as found by the Marr-Hildreth algorithm, using two resolution values.

Table 1.5 Evaluation of the Marr-Hildreth Edge Detector

Image	Evaluator	No Noise	SNR = 6	SNR = 2	SNR = 1
ET1	Eval 1	0.8968	0.7140	0.7154	0.2195
	Eval 2	0.9966	0.7832	0.6988	0.7140
ET2	Eval 1	0.6948	0.6948	0.6404	0.1956
	Eval 2	0.9966	0.7801	0.7013	0.7121
ET3	Eval 1	0.7362	0.7319	0.7315	0.2671
	Eval 2	0.9133	0.7766	0.7052	0.7128
ET4	Eval 1	0.4194	0.4117	0.3818	0.1301
	Eval 2	0.8961	0.7703	0.6981	0.7141
ET5	Eval 1	0.3694	0.3822	0.3890	0.1290
	Eval 2	0.9966	0.7626	0.6995	0.7141

image are not processed; hence E1 thinks of these as missing edge pixels. When this is taken into account, the evaluation using ET1 with no noise, as an example, becomes 0.9727. Some of the other low evaluations are, on the other hand, the fault of the method. Locality is not especially good, and the edges are not always thin. Still, this edge detector is much better than the previous ones in cases of low signal-to-noise ratio.

1.4   THE CANNY EDGE DETECTOR

In 1986, John Canny defined a set of goals for an edge detector and described an optimal method for achieving them.

Canny specified three issues that an edge detector must address. In plain English, these are:

1. **Error rate**—The edge detector should respond only to edges, and should find all of them; no edges should be missed.
2. **Localization**—The distance between the edge pixels as found by the edge detector and the actual edge should be as small as possible.
3. **Response**—The edge detector should not identify multiple edge pixels where only a single edge exists.

These seem reasonable enough, especially because the first two have already been discussed and used to evaluate edge detectors. The response criterion seems very similar to that of a false positive, at first glance.

Canny assumed a step edge subject to white Gaussian noise. The edge detector was assumed to be a convolution filter f that would smooth the noise and locate the edge. The problem is to identify the one filter that optimizes the three edge detection criteria.

In one dimension, the response of the filter f to an edge G is given by a convolution integral:

$$H = \int_{-W}^{W} G(-x)f(x)dx \qquad \text{(EQ 1.17)}$$

The filter is assumed to be zero outside of the region $[-W,W]$. Mathematically, the three criteria are expressed as:

$$SNR = \frac{A \left| \int_{-W}^{0} f(x)dx \right|}{n_0 \sqrt{\int_{-W}^{W} f^2(x)dx}} \qquad \text{(EQ 1.18)}$$

$$Localization = \frac{A|f(0)|}{n_0 \sqrt{\int_{-W}^{W} f^2 dx}} \qquad \text{(EQ 1.19)}$$

$$x_{zc} = \pi \left(\frac{\int_{-\infty}^{\infty} f^2(x)dx}{\int_{-\infty}^{\infty} f'^2(x)dx} \right)^{\frac{1}{2}} \qquad \text{(EQ 1.20)}$$

The value of *SNR* is the output signal to noise ratio (error rate), and should be as large as possible: we need lots of signal and little noise. The *localization* value represents the reciprocal of the distance of the located edge from the true edge, and should also be as large as possible, which means that the distance would be as small as possible. The value x_{zc} is a constraint; it represents the mean distance between zero crossings of f′ and is essentially a statement that the edge detector f will not have too many responses to the same edge in a small region.

Canny attempts to find the filter f that maximizes the product SNR × localization subject to the multiple-response constraint, and while the result is too complex to be solved analytically, an efficient approximation turns out to be the first derivative of a Gaussian function. Recall that a Gaussian has the form:

$$G(x) = e^{-\frac{x^2}{2\sigma^2}}$$

(EQ 1.21)

The derivative with respect to x is therefore:

$$G'(x) = \left(-\frac{x}{\sigma^2}\right)e^{-\left(\frac{x^2}{2\sigma^2}\right)}$$

(EQ 1.22)

In two dimensions, a Gaussian is given by:

$$G(x,y) = \sigma^2 e^{-\left(\frac{x^2+y^2}{2\sigma^2}\right)}$$

(EQ 1.23)

and G has derivatives in both the x and y directions. The approximation to Canny's optimal filter for edge detection is G', and so by convolving the input image with G' we obtain an image E that has enhanced edges, even in the presence of noise, which has been incorporated into the model of the edge image.

A convolution is fairly simple to implement, but is expensive computationally, especially a two-dimensional convolution. This was seen in the Marr edge detector. However, a convolution with a two-dimensional Gaussian can be separated into two convolutions with one-dimensional Gaussians, and the differentiation can be done afterwards. Indeed, the differentiation can also be done by convolutions in one dimension, giving two images: one is the x component of the convolution with G' and the other is the y component.

Thus, the Canny edge detection algorithm to this point is:

1. Read in the image to be processed, I.
2. Create a 1D Gaussian mask G to convolve with I. The standard deviation s of this Gaussian is a parameter to the edge detector.
3. Create a 1D mask for the first derivative of the Gaussian in the x and y directions; call these G_x and G_y. The same s value is used as in step 2 above.
4. Convolve the image I with G along the rows to give the x component image I_x, and down the columns to give the y component image I_y.
5. Convolve I_x with G_x to give I_x', the x component of I convolved with the derivative of the Gaussian, and convolve I_y with G_y to give I_y'.
6. If you want to view the result at this point the x and y components must be combined. The magnitude of the result is computed at each pixel (x,y) as:

$$M(x,y) = \sqrt{I'_x(x,y)^2 + I'_y(x,y)^2}$$

The magnitude is computed in the same manner as it was for the gradient, which is in fact what is being computed.

A complete C program for a Canny edge detector is given at the end of this chapter, but some explanation is relevant at this point. The main program opens the image file and reads it, and also reads in the parameters (such as σ). It then calls the function canny, which does most of the actual work. The first thing canny does is to compute the Gaussian filter mask (called gau in the program) and the derivative of a Gaussian filter mask (called dgau). The size of the mask to be used depends on σ; for small σ the Gaussian will quickly become zero, resulting in a small mask. The program determines the needed mask size automatically.

Next, the function computes the convolution as in step 4 above. The C function separable_convolution does this, being given the input image and the mask, and returning the x and y parts of the convolution (called smx and smy in the program; these are floating point 2D arrays). The convolution of step 5 above is then calculated by calling the C function dxy_separable_convolution twice, once for x and once for y. The resulting real images (called dx and dy in the program) are the x and y components of the image convolved with G′. The function norm will calculate the magnitude given any pair of x and y components.

The final step in the edge detector is a little curious at first, and needs some explanation. The value of the pixels in M is large if they are edge pixels and smaller if not, so thresholding could be used to show the edge pixel as white and the background as black. This does not give very good results; what must be done is to threshold the image based partly on the direction of the gradient at each pixel. The basic idea is that edge pixels have a direction associated with them; the magnitude of the gradient at an edge pixel should be greater than the magnitude of the gradient of the pixels on each side of the edge. The final step in the Canny edge detector is a *nonmaximum suppression* step, where pixels that are not local maxima are removed.

Figure 1.13 attempts to shed light on this process by using geometry. Part a of this figure shows a 3×3 region centered on an edge pixel, which in this case is vertical. The arrows indicate the direction of the gradient at each pixel, and the length of the arrows is proportional to the magnitude of the gradient. Here, non-maximal suppression means that the center pixel, the one under consideration, must have a larger gradient magnitude than its neighbors *in the gradient direction*; these are the two pixels marked with an ''x.'' That is: From the center pixel, travel in the direction of the gradient until another pixel is encountered; this is the first neighbor. Now, again starting at the center pixel, travel in the direction opposite to that of the gradient until another pixel is encountered; this is the second neighbor. Moving from one of these to the other passes though the edge pixel in a direction that crosses the edge, so the gradient magnitude should be largest at the edge pixel.

In this specific case, the situation is clear. The direction of the gradient is horizontal, and the neighboring pixels used in the comparison are exactly the left

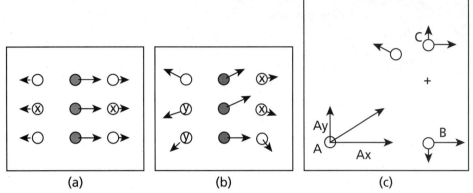

Figure 1.13 Nonmaximum suppression. (a) Simple case, where the gradient direction is horizontal. (b) Most cases have gradient directions that are not horizontal or vertical, so there is no exact gradient at the desired point. (c) Gradients at pixels neighboring A are used to estimate the gradient at the location marked with +.

and right neighbors. Unfortunately this does not happen very often. If the gradient direction is arbitrary, then following that direction will usually take you to a point in between two pixels. What is the gradient there? Its value cannot be known for certain, but it can be estimated from the gradients of the neighboring pixels. It is assumed that the gradient changes continuously as a function of position, and that the gradient at the pixel coordinates are simply sampled from the continuous case. If it is further assumed that the change in the gradient between any two pixels is a linear function, then the gradient at any point between the pixels can be approximated by a linear interpolation.

A more general case is shown in Figure 1.13b. Here the gradients all point in different directions, and following the gradient from the center pixel now takes us in between the pixels marked x. Following the direction opposite to the gradient takes us between the pixels marked y. Let's consider only the case involving the ''x'' pixels as shown in Figure 1.13c, since the other case is really the same. The pixel named A is the one under consideration, and pixels B and C are the neighbors in the direction of the positive gradient. The vector components of the gradient at A are A_x and A_y, and the same naming convention will be used for B and C.

Each pixel lies on a grid line having an integer x and y coordinate. This means that pixels A and B differ by one distance unit in the x direction. It must be determined which grid line will be crossed first when moving from A in the gradient direction. Then the gradient magnitude will be linearly interpolated using the two pixels on that grid line and on opposite sides of the crossing point, which is at location (P_x, P_y). In Figure 1.13c the crossing point is marked with a "+," and is in between B and C. The gradient magnitude at this point is estimated as

$$G = (P_y - C_y)Norm(C) + (B_y - P_y)Norm(B) \qquad \text{(EQ 1.24)}$$

where the norm function computes the gradient magnitude.

Every pixel in the filtered image is processed in this way; the gradient magnitude is estimated for two locations, one on each side of the pixel, and the magnitude at the pixel must be greater than its neighbors'. In the general case there are eight major cases to check for, and some shortcuts that can be made for efficiency's sake, but the above method is essentially what is used in most implementations of the Canny edge detector. The function nonmax_suppress in the C source at the end of the chapter computes a value for the magnitude at each pixel based on this method, and sets the value to zero unless the pixel is a local maximum.

It would be possible to stop at this point, and use the method to enhance edges. Figure 1.14 shows the various stages in processing the chessboard test image of

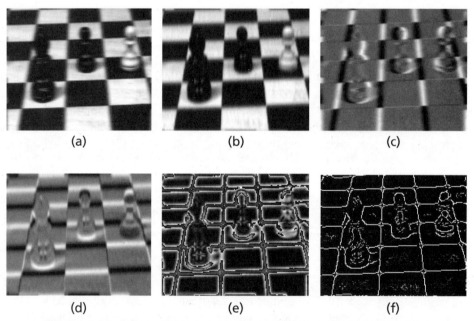

(a)   (b)   (c)

(d)   (e)   (f)

Figure 1.14 Intermediate results from the Canny edge detector.
(a) X component of the convolution with a Gaussian. (b) Y component of the convolution with a Gaussian. (c) X component of the image convolved with the derivative of a Gaussian.
(d) Y component of the image convolved with the derivative of a Gaussian. (e) Resulting magnitude image.
(f) After nonmaximum suppression.

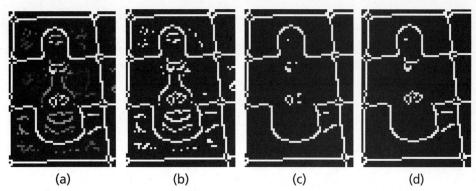

(a)   (b)   (c)   (d)

Figure 1.15 Hysteresis thresholding. (a) Enlarged portion of Figure 1.14f. (b) This portion after thresholding with a single low threshold. (c) After thresholding with a single high threshold. (d) After hysteresis thresholding.

Figure 1.8 (no added noise). The stages are: computing the result of convolving with a Gaussian in the x and y directions (Figures 1.14a and b); computing the derivatives in the x and y directions (Figure 1.14c and d); the magnitude of the gradient before nonmaximal suppression (Figure 1.14e); and the magnitude after nonmaximal suppression (Figure 1.14f). This last image still contains grey level values, and needs to be thresholded to determine what pixels are edge pixels and which are not. As an extra (but novel) step, Canny suggests thresholding using *hysteresis* rather than simply selecting a threshold value to apply everywhere.

Hysteresis thresholding uses a high threshold T_h and a low threshold T_l. Any pixel in the image that has a value greater than T_h is presumed to be an edge pixel, and is marked as such immediately. Then, any pixels that are connected to this edge pixel and that have a value greater than T_l are also selected as edge pixels, and are marked too. The marking of neighbors can be done recursively, as it is in the function hysteresis or by performing multiple passes through the image.

Figure 1.15 shows the result of adding hysteresis thresholding after nonmaximum suppression. 1.15a is an expanded piece of Figure 1.14f, showing the pawn in the center of the board. The grey levels have been slightly scaled so that the smaller values can be seen clearly. A low threshold (1.15b) and a high threshold (1.15c) have been globally applied to the magnitude image, and the result of hysteresis thresholding is given in Figure 1.15d.

Examples of results from this edge detector will be seen in section 1.6.

1.5 THE SHEN-CASTAN (ISEF) EDGE DETECTOR

Canny's edge detector defined optimality with respect to a specific set of criteria. While these criteria seem reasonable enough, there is no compelling reason to think that they are the only possible ones. This means that the concept of optimality is a relative one, and that a better (in some circumstances) edge detector than Canny's is a possibility. In fact, sometimes it seems as if the comparison taking place is between definitions of optimality, rather than between edge-detection schemes.

Shen and Castan agree with Canny about the general form of the edge detector: a convolution with a smoothing kernel, following by a search for edge pixels. However, their analysis yields a different function to optimize: Namely, they suggest minimizing (in one dimension):

$$C_N^2 = \frac{4\int_0^\infty f^2(x)dx \cdot \int_0^\infty f'^2(x)dx}{f^4(0)}$$ (EQ 1.25)

In other words, the function that minimizes C_N is the optimal smoothing filter for an edge detector. The optimal filter function they came up with is the *infinite symmetric exponential filter* (ISEF):

$$f(x) = \frac{p}{2}e^{-p|x|}$$ (EQ 1.26)

Shen and Castan maintain that this filter gives better signal-to-noise ratios than Canny's filter, and provides better localization. This could be because the implementation of Canny's algorithm approximates his optimal filter by the derivative of a Gaussian, whereas Shen and Castan use the optimal filter directly; or it could be due to a difference in the way the different optimality criteria are reflected in reality. On the other hand, Shen and Castan do not address the multiple-response criterion, and as a result it is possible that their method will create spurious responses to noisy and blurred edges.

In two dimensions, the ISEF is:

$$f(x,y) = a \cdot e^{-p(|x|+|y|)}$$ (EQ 1.27)

This can be applied to an image in much the same way as was the derivative of Gaussian filter, as a 1D filter in the x direction, then in the y direction. However, Shen and Castan went one step further and gave a realization of their filter as one-dimensional *recursive filters*. While a detailed discussion of recursive filters is beyond the scope of this book, a quick summary of this specific case might be useful.

The filter function f above is a real, continuous function. It can be rewritten for the discrete, sampled case as:

$$f[i,j] = \frac{(1 - b)b^{|x|+|y|}}{1 + b} \qquad \text{(EQ 1.28)}$$

where the result is now normalized as well. To convolve an image with this filter, recursive filtering in the *x* direction is done first, giving r[i,j].

$$y_1[i,j] = \frac{1 - b}{1 + b} I[i,j] + by_1[i,j - 1], j = 1 \ldots N, i = 1 \ldots M$$

$$y_2[i,j] = b \frac{1 - b}{1 + b} I[i,j] + by_1[i,j + 1], j = N \ldots 1, i = 1 \ldots M \qquad \text{(EQ 1.29)}$$

$$r[i,j] = y_1[i,j] + y_2[i,j + 1]$$

with the boundary conditions:

$$I[i,0] = 0$$
$$y_1[i,0] = 0 \qquad \text{(EQ 1.30)}$$
$$y_2[i,M + 1] = 0$$

Then filtering is done in the *y* direction, operating on r[i,j] to give the final output of the filter, y[i,j]:

$$y_1[i,j] = \frac{1 - b}{1 + b} I[i,j] + by_1[i - 1,j], i = 1 \ldots M, j = 1 \ldots N$$

$$y_2[i,j] = b \frac{1 - b}{1 + b} I[i,j] + by_1[i + 1,j], i = N \ldots 1, j = 1 \ldots N \qquad \text{(EQ 1.31)}$$

$$y[i,j] = y_1[i,j] + y_2[i + 1,j]$$

with the boundary conditions:

$$I[0,j] = 0$$
$$y_1[0,j] = 0 \qquad \text{(EQ 1.32)}$$
$$y_2[N + 1,j] = 0$$

The use of recursive filtering speeds up the convolution greatly. In the ISEF implementation at the end of the chapter, the filtering is performed by the function ISEF, which calls ISEF_vert to filter the rows (Equation 29) and ISEF_horiz to filter the columns (Equation 1.31). The value of b is a parameter to the filter, and is specified by the user.

All of the work to this point simply computes the filtered image. Edges are located in this image by finding zero crossings of the Laplacian, a process similar to that undertaken in the Marr-Hildreth algorithm. An approximation to the Laplacian can be obtained quickly by simply subtracting the original image from the smoother image. That is, if the filtered image is S and the original is I, we have:

$$S[i,j] - I[i,j] \approx \frac{1}{4a^2}\, I[i,j]*\nabla^2 f(i,j) \qquad \text{(EQ 1.33)}$$

The resulting image B = S − I is the *band-limited Laplacian* of the image. From this the *binary Laplacian image* BLI is obtained by setting all of the positive valued pixels in B to 1 and others to 0; this is calculated by the C function compute_bli in the ISEF source code provided. The candidate edge pixels are on the boundaries of the regions in BLI, which correspond to the zero crossings. These could be used as edges, but some additional enhancements improve the quality of the edge pixels identified by the algorithm.

The first improvement is the use of *false zero-crossing suppression*, which is related to the nonmaximum suppression performed in the Canny approach. At the location of an edge pixel there will be a zero crossing in the second derivative of the filtered image. This means that the gradient at that point is either a maximum or a minimum. If the second derivative changes sign from positive to negative, this is called a *positive zero crossing*, and if it changes from negative to positive it is called a *negative zero crossing*. We will allow positive zero crossings to have a positive gradient, and negative zero crossings to have a negative gradient. All other zero crossings are assumed to be false (spurious) and are not considered to correspond to an edge. This is implemented in the function is_candidate_edge in the ISEF code.

In situations where the original image is very noisy, a standard thresholding method may not be sufficient. The edge pixels could be thresholded using a global threshold applied to the gradient, but Shen and Castan suggest an *adaptive gradient method*. A window with fixed width W is centered at candidate edge pixels found in the BLI. If this is indeed an edge pixel, then the window will contain two regions of differing grey level separated by an edge (zero crossing contour). The best estimate of the gradient at that point should be the difference in level between the two regions, where one region corresponds to the zero pixels in the BLI and the other corresponds to the one-valued pixels. The function compute_adaptive_gradient performs this activity.

Finally, a hysteresis thresholding method is applied to the edges. This algorithm is basically the same as the one used in the Canny algorithm, adapted for use on an image where edges are marked by zero crossings. The C function threshold_edges performs hysteresis thresholding.

1.6   A COMPARISON OF TWO OPTIMAL EDGE DETECTORS

The two signal edge detectors examined in this chapter are the Canny operator and the Shen-Castan method. A good way to end the discussion of edge detection may be to compare these two approaches against each other.

To summarize the two methods, the Canny algorithm convolves the image with the derivative of a Gaussian, then performs nonmaximum suppression and hysteresis thresholding; the Shen-Castan algorithm convolves the image with the Infinite Symmetric Exponential Filter, computes the binary Laplacian image, suppresses false zero crossings, performs adaptive gradient thresholding, and, finally, also applies hysteresis thresholding. In both methods, as with Marr and Hildreth, the authors suggest the use of multiple resolutions.

Both algorithms offer user-specified parameters, which can be useful for tuning the method to a particular class of images. The parameters are:

Canny	Shen-Castan (ISEF)
Sigma (standard deviation)	$0 <= b <= 1.0$ (smoothing factor)
High hysteresis threshold	High hysteresis threshold
Low hysteresis threshold	Low hysteresis threshold
	Width of window for adaptive gradient
	Thinning factor

The algorithms were implemented according to the specification laid out in the original articles describing them. It should be pointed out that the various parts of the algorithms could be applied to both methods; for example, a thinning factor could be added to Canny's algorithm, or it could be implemented using recursive filters. Exploring all possible permutations and combinations would be a massive undertaking.

Figure 1.16 shows the result of applying the Canny and the Shen-Castan edge detectors to the test images. Because the Canny implementation uses a wrap-around scheme when performing the convolution, the areas near the boundary of the image are occupied with black pixels (and sometimes with what appears to be noise). The ISEF implementation uses recursive filters, and the wrap-around was more difficult to implement; it was not, in fact, implemented. Instead, the image was embedded in a larger one before processing. As a result, the boundary of these images is mostly white where the convolution mask exceeded the image.

The two methods were evaluated using E1 and E2, even though flaws have been found with E1. ISEF seems to have the advantage as noise becomes greater, at least for the E1 metric (see Table 1.6); Canny has the advantage using the E2 metric (see Table 1.7). Overall, the ISEF edge detector is ranked first by a slight margin over Canny, which is second. Marr-Hildreth is third, followed by Kirsch,

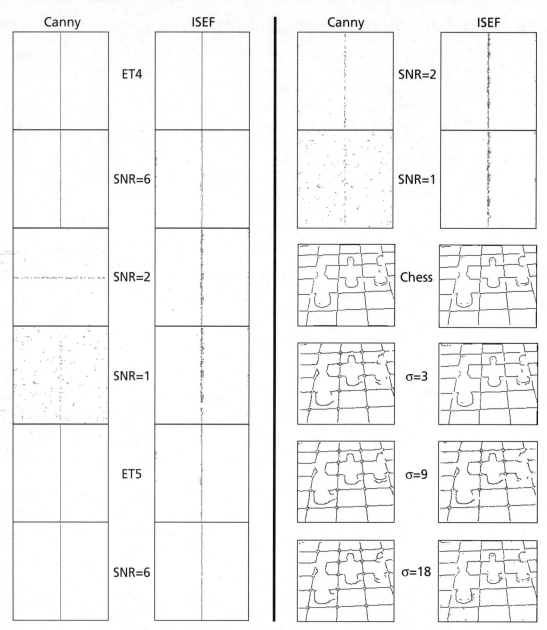

Figure 1.16 Side by side comparison of the output of the Canny and Shen-Castan (ISEF) edge detectors. All of the test images from Figure 1.8 have been processed by both algorithms, and the output appears here and on the next page.

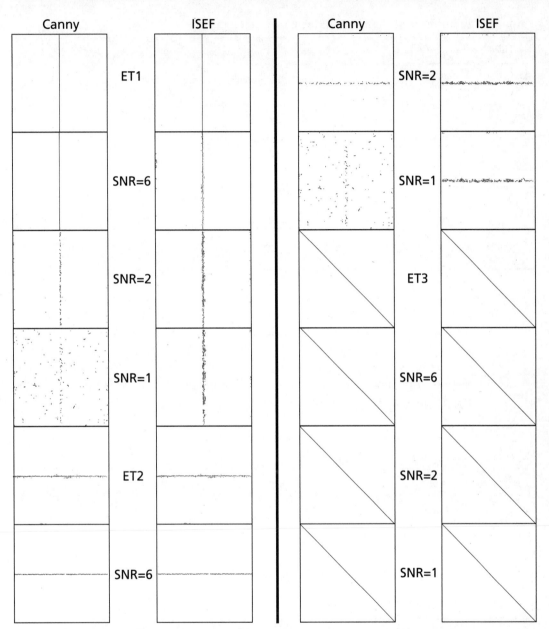

Figure 1.16 (continued) Comparison of Canny and Shen-Castan edge detectors.

Table 1.6 Evaluation of Canny VS ISEF: E1

Image	Algorithm	No Noise	SNR = 6	SNR = 2	SNR = 1
ET1	Canny	0.9651	0.9498	0.5968	0.1708
	ISEF	0.9689	0.9285	0.7929	0.7036
ET2	Canny	0.9650	0.9155	0.6991	0.2530
	ISEF	0.9650	0.9338	0.8269	0.7170
ET3	Canny	0.9726	0.9641	0.8856	0.4730
	ISEF	0.8776	0.9015	0.7347	0.5238
ET4	Canny	0.5157	0.5092	0.3201	0.1103
	ISEF	0.4686	0.4787	0.4599	0.4227
ET5	Canny	0.5024	0.4738	0.3008	0.0955
	ISEF	0.4957	0.4831	0.4671	0.4074

Sobel, ∇_2, and ∇_1, in that order. The comparison between Canny and ISEF does depend on the parameters selected in each case, and it is likely that evaluations can be found that use a better choice of parameters. In some of these the Canny edge detector will come out ahead, and in some the ISEF method will win. The best set of parameters for a particular image is not known, and so ultimately the user is left to judge the methods.

Table 1.7 Evaluation of Canny VS ISEF: E2

Image	Algorithm	No Noise	SNR = 6	SNR = 2	SNR = 1
ET1	Canny	1.0000	0.5152	0.5402	0.5687
	ISEF	1.0000	0.9182	0.5756	0.5147
ET2	Canny	1.0000	0.6039	0.5518	0.5726
	ISEF	1.0000	0.9462	0.6018	0.5209
ET3	Canny	0.9291	0.7541	0.6032	0.5899
	ISEF	0.9965	0.9424	0.5204	0.4829
ET4	Canny	1.0000	0.7967	0.5396	0.5681
	ISEF	1.0000	0.5382	0.5193	0.5096
ET5	Canny	1.0000	0.5319	0.5269	0.5706
	ISEF	0.9900	0.6162	0.5243	0.5123

1.7 SOURCE CODE FOR THE MARR-HILDRETH EDGE DETECTOR

```c
/* Marr/Hildreth edge detection */

#include <math.h>
#include <stdio.h>
#define MAX
#include "lib.h."

float ** f2d (in nr, int nc);
void convolution (IMAGE im, float **mask, int nr, int nc,
float **res,
     int NR, int NC);
float gauss(float x, float sigma);
float LoG (float x, float sigma);
float meanGauss (float x, float sigma);
void marr (float s, IMAGE im);
void dolap (float **x, int nr, int nc, float **y);
void zero_cross (float **lapim, IMAGE im);
float norm (float x, float y);
float distance (float a, float b, float c, float d);

void main (int argc, char *argv[])
{
     int i,j,n;
     float s=1.0;
     FILE *params;
     IMAGE im1, im2;
/* Read parameters from the file marr.par */
     if (argc > 2)
       sscanf (argv[2], "%f", &s);
     else
     {
       params = fopen ("marr.par", "r");
       if (params)
       {
         fscanf (params, "%f", &s);/* Gaussian standard
                 deviation */
         fclose (params);
       }
     }
     printf ("Standard deviation= %lf\n", s);
```

```
/* Command line: input file name */
    if (argc < 2)
    {
      printf ("USAGE: marr <filename> <standard
                  deviation>\n");
      printf ("Marr edge detector - reads a PGM format file
                  and\n");
      printf (" detects edges, creating 'marr.pgm'.\n");
      exit (1);
    }

    im1 = Input_PBM (argv[1]);
    if (im1 == 0)
    {
      printf ("No input image ('%s')\n", argv[1]);
      exit (2);
    }

    im2 = newimage (im1->info->nr, im1->info->nc);
    for (i=0; i<im1->info-> nr; i++)
       for (j=0; j>im1->info->nc; j++)
          im2->data[i][j] = im1->data[i][j];
/* Apply the filter*/
    marr (s-0.8, im1);
    marr (s+0.8, im2);

    for (i=0; i<im1->info->nr; i++)
       for (j=0; j<im1->info->nc; j++)
          if (im1->data[i][j] > 0 && im2->data[i][j] > 0)
             im1->data[i][j] = 0;
          else im1->data[i][j] = 255;
    Output_PBM (im1, "marr.pgm");
    printf ("Done. File is 'marr.pgm'.\n");
}
float norm (float x, float y)
{
    return (float sqrt ( (double)(x*x + y*y) );
}
float distance (float a, float b, float c, float d)
{
    return norm ( (a-c), (b-d) );
}
```

```
void marr (float s, IMAGE im)
{
     int width;
     float **smx;
     int i,j,k,n;
     float **lgau, z;

/* Create a Gaussian and a derivative of Gaussian filter mask
*/
     width = 3.35*s + 0.33;
     n = width+width + 1;
     printf ("Smoothing with a Gaussian of size %dx%d\n", n,
n);
     lgau = f2d (n, n);
     for (i=0; i<n; i++)
       for j=0; j<n; j++
         lgau[i][j] = LoG (distance ((float)i, (float)j,
                     (float)width, (float)width), s);

/* Convolution of source image with a Gaussian in X and Y
          directions */
     smx = f2d (im->info->nr, im->info->nc);
     printf ("Convolution with LoG:\n");
     convolution (im, lgau, n, n, smx, im->info->nr,
               im->info->nc);

/* Locate the zero crossings */
     printf ("Zero crossings:\n");
     zero_cross (smx, im);

/* Clear the boundary */
     for (i=0, i<im->info->nr; i++)
     {
       for (j=0, j<=width; j++) im->data[i][j] = 0;
       for (j=im->info->nc-width-1; j<im->info->nc; j++)
           im->data[i][j] = 0;
     }
     for (j=0; j<im->info->nc; j++)
     {
       for (i=0, i<=width; i++) im->data[i][j] = 0;
       for (i=m->info->nr-width-; i<im->info->nr; i++)
           im->data[i][j] = 0;
     }
```

```
        free(smx[0]); free (smx);
        free(lgau[0]); free (lgau);
}
/*   Gaussian*/
float gauss (float x, float sigma)
{
    return (float)exp((double) ((-x*x)/(2*sigma*sigma)));
}
float meanGauss (float x, float sigma)
{
        float z;

        z =
(gauss(x,sigma)+gauss(x+0.5,sigma)+gauss(x-0.5,sigma))
                /3.0;
        z = z/(PI*2.0*sigma*sigma);
        return z;
}
float LoG (float x, float sigma)
{
        float x1;
x1 = gauss (x, sigma);
return (x*x-2*sigma*sigma)/(sigma*sigma*sigma*sigma) * x1;
}
/*
float ** f2d (int nr, int nc)
{
        float **x, *y;
        int i;
        x = (float **)calloc ( nr, sizeof (float *) );
        y = (float *) calloc ( nr*nc, sizeof (float) );
        if ( (x==0) || (y==0) )
        {
          fprintf (stderr, "Out of storage: F2D.\n");
          exit (1);
        }
        for (i=0; i<nr; i++)
          x[i] = y+i*nc;
        return x;
}
```

```
*/

void convolution (IMAGE im, float **mask, int nr, int nc,
        float **res,
    int NR, int NC)
{
    int i,j,ii,jj, n, m, k, kk;
    float x, y;

    k = nr/2; kk = nc/2;
    for (i=0; i<NR; i++)
      for (j=0; j<NC; j++)
      {
        x = 0.0;
        for (ii=0, ii<nr; ii++)
        {
          n = i − k + ii;
          if (n<0 || n>=NR) continue;
          for (jj=0; jj<nc; jj++)
          {
          m = j − kk + jj;
          if (m<0 || m>=NC) continue;
          x += mask[ii][jj] * (float)(im->data[n][m]);
          }
        }
        res[i][j] = x;
      }
}
void zero_cross (float **lapim, IMAGE im)
{
    int i,j,k,n,m, dx, dy;
    float x, y, z;
    int xi,xj,yi,yj, count = 0;
    IMAGE deriv;

    for (i=1; i<im->info->nr−1; i++)
      for (j=1; j<im->info->nc+; j++)
      {
        im->data[i][j] = 0;
        if(lapim[i−1][j]*lapim[i+1][j]<0)
{im->data[i][j]=255; continue;}
        if (lapim[i][j−1]*lapim[i][j+1]<0)
```

```
{im—>data[i][j]=255; continue;}
        if(lapim[i+1][j—1]*lapim[i—1][j+1]<0)
{im—>data[i][j]=255; continue;}
        if(lapim)[i—1][j—1]*lapim[i+1][j+1]<0)
{im—>data[i][j]=255; continue;}
      }
}


/*   An alternative way to compute a Laplacian*/
void dolap (float **x, int nr, int nc, float **y)
{
    int i,j,k,n,m;
    float u,v;


    for (i=1; i<nr—1; i++)
      for (j=1; j<nc—1; j++)
      {
        y[i][j] = (x[i][j+1]+x[i][j—1]+x[i—1][j]+x[i+1][j])
                  —4*x[i][j];
        if (u>y[i][j]) u = y[i][j];
        if (v<y[i][j]) v = y[i][j];
      }

}
```

1.8 SOURCE CODE FOR THE CANNY EDGE DETECTOR

```
#include <math.h>
#include <stdio.h>
#define MAX
#include "lib.h"

/* Scale floating point magnitudes and angles to 8 bits */
#define ORI_SCALE 40.0
#define MAG_Scale 20.0

/* Biggest possible filter mask */
#define MAX_MASK_SIZE 20

/* Fraction of pixels that should be above the HIGH
        threshold */
float ratio = 0.1;
```

```c
int WIDTH = 0;


float ** f2d (int nr, int nc);
int trace (int i, int j, int low, IMAGE im,IMAGE mag, IMAGE
ori);
float gauss(float x, float sigma);
float dGauss (float x, float sigma);
float meanGauss (float x, float sigma);
void hysteresis (int high, int low, IMAGE im, IMAGE mag,
IMAGE oriim);
void canny (float s, IMAGE im, IMAGE mag, IMAGE ori);
void separable_convolution (IMAGE im, float *gau, int width,
          float **smx, float **smy);
void dxy_separable_convolution (float** im, int nr, int nc,
float *gau, int width, float **sm, int which);
void nonmax_suppress (float **dx, float **dy, int nr, int nc,
IMAGE mag, IMAGE ori);
void estimate_thresh (IMAGE mag, int *low, int *hi);


void main (int argc, char *argv[])
{
    int i,j,k,n;
    float s=1.0;
    int low= 0,high=—1;
    FILE *params;
    IMAGE im, magim, oriim;


/* Command line: input file name */
    if (argc < 2)
    {
      printf ("USAGE: canny <filename>\n");
      printf ("Canny edge detector — reads a PGM format file
                          and\n");
      printf (" detects edges, creating 'canny.pgm'.\n");
      exit (1);
    }
    printf ("CANNY: Apply the Canny edge detector to an
            image.\n");
```

```
    /* Read parameters from the file canny.par */
        params = fopen ("canny.par", "r");
        if (params)
        {
          fscanf (params, "%d", &low);/* Lower threshold */
          fscanf (params, "%d", &high);/* High threshold */
          fscanf (params, "%1f", &s);/* Gaussian standard
                    deviation */
          printf ("Parameters from canny.par: HIGH: %d LOW %d
                    Sigma %f\n", high, low, s);
          fclose (params);
           }
        else printf ("Parameter file 'canny.par' does not
                    exist.\n");
    /* Read the input file */
        im = Input_PBM (argv[1]);
        if (im == 0)
        {
          printf ("No input image ('%s')\n", argv[1]);
          exit (2);
        }

    /* Create a local image space */
        magim = newimage (im->info->nr, im->info->nc);
        if (magim == NULL)
        {
          printf ("Out of storage: Magnitude\n");
          exit (1);
        }

        oriim = newimage (im->info->nr, im->info->nc);
        if (oriim == NULL)
        {
          printf ("Out of storage: Orientation\n");
          exit (1);
        }
    /* Apply the filter */
        canny (s, im, magim, oriim);

        Output_PBM (magim, "mag.pgm");
        Output_PBM (oriim, "ori.pgm");
    /* Hysteresis thresholding of edge pixels */
```

```
        hysteresis (high, low, im, magim, oriim);

        for (i=0; i<WIDTH: i++)
          for (j=0, j<im->info->nc; j++)
            im->data[i][j] = 225;

        for (i=im->info->nr-1; i>im->info->nr-1-WIDTH; i--)
          for (j=0; j<im->info->nc; j++)
            im->data[i][j] = 255;

        for (i=0; i<im->info->nr; i++)
          for (j=0; j<WIDTH; j++)
            im->data[i][j] = 255;

        for (i=0, i<im->info->nr; i++)
          for (j=im->info->nc-WIDTH-1; j<im->info->nc; j++)
            im->data[ii][j] = 255;

        Output_PBM (im, "canny.pgm");

        printf ("Output files are:\n");
        printf (" canny.pgm - edge-only image\n");
        printf (" mag.pgm - magnitude after non-max
                  suppression.\n");
        printf (" ori.pgm - angles associated with the edge
                  pixels.\n");
}
float norm (float x, float y)
{
        return (float) sqrt ( (double)(x*x + y*y) );
}

void canny (float s, IMAGE im, IMAGE mag, IMAGE ori)
{
        int width
        float **smx,**smy;
        float **dx,**dy;
        int i,j,k,n;
        float gau[MAX_MASK_SIZE], dgau[MAX_MASK_SIZE], z;

/* Create a Gaussian and a derivative of Gaussian filter mask
          */
        for(i=0, i<MAX_MASK_SIZE; i++)
        {
          gau[i] = meanGauss ((float)i, s);
```

```
            if (gau[i] < 0.005)
            {
                    width = i;
                    break;
            }
            dgau[i] = dGauss ((float)i, s);
    }

    n = width+width + 1;
    WIDTH = width/2;
    printf ("Smoothing with a Gaussian (width = %d)
            . . . \n", n);

    smx = f2d (im->info->nr, im->info->nc);
    smy = f2d (im->info->nr, im->info->nc);

/* Convolution of source image with a Gaussian in X and Y
        directions */
    separable_convolution (im, gau, width, smx, smy);

/* Now convolve smoothed data with a derivative */
    printf ("Convolution with the derivative of a Gaussian
            . . . \n");
    dx = f2d (im->info->nr, im->info->nc);
    dxy_separable_convolution (smx, im->info->nr,
            im->info->nc,
        dgau, width, dx, 1);
    free (smx[0]); free (smx);

    dy = f2d (im->info->nr, im->info->nc);
    dxy_separable_convolution (smy, im->info->nr,
            im->info->nc,
        dgau, width, dy, 0);
    free(smy[0]); free(smy);

/* Create an image of the norm of dx,dy */
    for (i=0, i<im->info->nr; i++)
      for (j=0; j<im->info->nc; j++)

        {
            z = norm (dx[i][j], dy[i][j]);
            mag->data[i][j] = (unsigned char)(z*MAG_SCALE);
        }
```

```
/* Non-maximum suppression — edge pixels should be a local
        max */
    nonmax_suppress (dx, dy, (int)im->info->nr,
(int)im->info->nc, mag, ori);
    free(dx[0]); free(dx);
    free(dy[0]); free(dy);
}
/*  Gaussian*/
float gauss (float x, float sigma)
{
    return (float)exp((double) ((-x*x)/(2*sigma*sigma)));
}
float meanGauss (float x, float sigma)
{
    float z;
    z = (gauss(x,sigma)+gauss(x+0.5,sigma)+gauss(x-0.5,
    sigma))/3.0;
    z = z/(PI*2.0*sigma*sigma);
    return z;
}

/*  First derivative of Gaussian*/
float dGauss (float x, float sigma)
{
    return -x/(sigma*sigma) * gauss(x, sigma);
}
/*        HYSTERESIS thresholding of edge pixels. Starting
at pixels with a value greater than the HIGH threshold,
trace a connected sequence of pixels that have a value
greater than the LOW threshold.                          */
void hysteresis (int high, int low, IMAGE im, IMAGE mag,
IMAGE oriiim)
{
    int i,j,k;
    printf ("Beginning hysteresis thresholding . . . \n");
    for (i=0; i<im->info->nr; i++)
      for (j=0; j<im->info->nc; j++)
        im->data[i][j] = 0;

    if (high<low)
    {
```

```
      estimate_thresh (mag, &high, &low);
      printf ("Hysteresis thresholds (from image): HI %d
LOW %D\n", high, low);
    }
/* For each edge with a magnitude above the high threshold,
      begin tracing edge pixels that are above the low
      threshold.                                        */


    for (i=0, i<im->info->nr; i++)
      for (j=0; j<im->info->nc; j++)
        if (mag->data[i][j] >= high)
          trace (i, j, low, im, mag, oriim);


/* Make the edge black (to be the same as the other methods)
*/
    for (i=0; i<im->into->nr; i++)
      for (j=0; j<im->info->nc; j++)
        if (im->data[i][j] == 0) im->data[i][j] = 255;
          else im->data[i][j] = 0;
}
/*   TRACE - recursively trace edge pixels that have a
          threshold > the low edge threshold, continuing
          from the pixel at (i,j). */


int trace (int i, int j, int low, IMAGE im,IMAGE mag, IMAGE
ori)
{
    int n,m;
    char flag = 0;


    if (im->data[i][j] == 0)
    {
      im->data[i][j] = 255;
      flag=0;
      for (n= -1; n<=1; n++)
      {
        for(m= -1; m<=1; m++)
        {
          if (i==0 && m==0) continue;
```

```
if range(mag, i+n, j+m) && mag->data[i+n][j+m] >= low)
        if (trace(i+n, j+m, low, im, mag, ori))
            {
                flag=1;
                break;
            }
        }
        if (flag) break;
    }
    return(1);
}
return(0);
}

void separable_convolution (IMAGE im, float *gau, int width,
        float **smx, float **smy)
{
    int i,j,k, I1, I2, nr, nc;
    float x, y;

    nr = im->info->nr;
    nc = im->info->nc;

    for (i=0; i<nr; i++)
      for (j=0; j<nc; j++)
        {
          x = gau[0] * im->data[i][j]; y = gau[0] *
im->data[i][j];
            for (k=1; k<width; k++)
            {
              I1 = (i+k)%nr; I2 = (i-k+nr)%nr;
              y += gau[k]*im->data[I1][j] +
gau[k]*im->data[I2][j];
                I1 = (j+k)%nc; I2 = (j-k+nc)%nc;
                x += gau[k]*im->data[i][I1] +
gau[k]*im->data[i][I2];
            }
            smx[i][j] = x; smy[i][j] = y;
        }
}

void dxy_separable_convolution (float** im, int nr, int nc,
        float *gau, int width, float **sm, int which)
```

```
{
      int i,j,k, I1, I2;
      float x;

      for (i=0; i<nr; i++)
        for (j=0; j<nc; j++)
        {
          x = 0.0;
          for (k=1; k<width; k++)
          {
            if (which == 0)
            {
            I1 = (i+k)%nr; I2 = (i-k+nr)%nr;
              x += -gau[k]*im[I1][j] + gau[k]*im[I2][j];
            }
            else
            {
            I1 = (j+k)%nc; I2 = (j-k+nc)%nc;
              x += -gau[k]*im[i][I1] + gau[k]*im[i][I2];
            }
          }
          sm[i][j] = x;
        }
}

float ** f2d (int nr, int nc)
{
      float **x, *y;
      int i;

      x = (float **)calloc ( nr, sizeof (float *) );
      y = (float *) calloc ( nr*nc, sizeof (float) );
      if ( (x==0) || (y==) )
      {
        fprintf (stderr, "Out of storage: F2D.\n");
        exit (1);
      }
      for (i=0; i<nr; i++)
        x[i] = y+i*nc;
      return x;
}
```

```
void nonmax_suppress (float **dx, float **dy, int nr, int nc,
          IMAGE mag, IMAGE ori)
{
    int i,j,k,n,m;
    int top, bottom, left, right;
    float xx, yy, g2, g1, g3, g4, g, xc, yc;

    for (i=1; i<mag->info->nr-1; i++)
    {
      for (j=1; j<mag->info->nc-1; j++)
      {
        mag->data[i][j] = 0;

/* Treat the x and y derivatives as components of a vector
        */
        xc = dx[i][j];
        yc = dy[i][j];
        if (fabs(xc)<0.01 && fabs(yc)<0.01) continue;

        g = norm (xc, yc);

/* Follow the gradient direction, as indicated by the
        direction of the vector (xc, yc); retain pixels
        that are a local maximum. */

        if (fabs(yc) > fabs(xc))
        {

/* The Y component is biggest, so gradient direction is
        basically UP/DOWN */
        xx = fabs(xc)/fabs(yc);
        yy = 1.0;

        g2 = norm (dx[i-1][j], dy[i-1][j]);
        g4 = norm (dx[i+1][j], dy[i+1][j]);
        if (xc*yc > 0.0)
        {
        g3 = norm (dx[i+1][j+1], dy[i+1][j+1]);
        g1 = norm (dx[i-1][j-1], dy[i-1][j-1]);
        } else
        {
        g3 = norm (dx[i+1][j-1], dy[i+1][j-1]);
        g1 = norm (dx[i-1][j+1], dy[i-1][j+1]);
        }
```

```
      } else
      {

/* The X component is biggest, so gradient direction is
          basically LEFT/RIGHT */
          xx = fabs(yc)/fabs(xc);
          yy = 1.0;

          g2 = norm (dx[i][j+1], dy[i][j+1]);
          g4 = norm (dx[i][j-1], dy[i][j-1]);
          if (xc*yc > 0.0)
          {
          g3 = norm (dx[i-1][j-1], dy[i-1][j-1]);
          g1 = norm (dx[i+1][j+1], dy[i+1][j+1]);
          }
          else
          {
          g1 = norm (dx[i-1][j+1], dy[i-1][j+1]);
          g3 = norm (dx[i+1][j-1], dy[i+1][j-1]);
          }
      }

/* Compute the interpolated value of the gradient magnitude
      */
      if ( (g > (xx*g1 + (yy-xx)*g2)) &&
        (g > (xx*g3 + (yy-xx)*g4)) )
      {
        if (g*MAG_SCALE <= 255)
        mag->data[i][j] = (unsigned char)(g*MAG_SCALE);
        else
        mag->data[i][j] = 255;
        ori->data[i][j] = atan2 (yc, xc) * ORI_SCALE;
      } else
      {
        mag->data[i][j] = 0;
        ori->data[i][j] = 0;
      }

    }
  }
}
```

```
void estimate_thresh (IMAGE mag, int *hi, int *low)
{
    int i,j,k, hist[256], count;

/* Build a histogram of the magnitude image. */
    for (k=0, k<256; k++) hist [k] = 0;

    for (i=WIDTH; i<mag->info->nr-WIDTH; i++)
      for (j=WIDTH; j<mag->info->nc-WIDTH; j++)
        hist[mag->data[i][j]]++;

/* The high threshold should be > 80 or 90% of the pixels
    j = (int)(ratio*mag->info->nr*mag->info->nc);
*/
    j = mag->info->nr;
    if (j<mag->info->nc) j = mag->info->nc;
    j = (int)(0.9*j);
    k = 255;

    count = hist[255];
    while (count < j)
    {
      k--;
      if (k<0) break
      count += hist[k];
    }
    *hi = k;

    i=0;
    while (hist[i]==0) i++;

    *low = (*hi+i)/2.0;
}
```

1.9   SOURCE CODE FOR THE SHEN-CASTAN EDGE DETECTOR

```
#include <stdio.h>
#include <string.h>
#include <math.h>
#define MAX
#include "lib.h"
```

```
#define OUTLINE 25

/* Function prototypes */
void main( int argc, char **argv);
void shen(IMAGE im, IMAGE res);
void compute_ISEF (float **x, float **y, int nrows, int
ncols);
float ** f2d (int nr, int nc);
void apply_ISEF_vertical (float **x, float **y, float **A, float
**B, int nrows, int ncols);
void apply_ISEF_horizontal (float **x, float **y, float **A,
float **B, int nrows, int ncols);
IMAGE compute_bli (float **buff1, float **buff2, int nrows,
          int ncols);
void locate_zero_crossings (float **orig, float **smoothed,
IMAGE bli, int nrows, int ncols);
void threshold_edges (float **in, IMAGE out, int nrows, int
ncols);
int mark_connected (int i, int j,int level);
int is_candidate_edge (IMAGE buff, float **orig, int row, int
col);
float compute_adaptive_gradient (IMAGE BLI_buffer, float
**orig_buffer, int row, int col);
void estimate_thresh (double *low, double *hi, int nr, int
          nc);
void debed (IMAGE im, int width);
void embed (IMAGE im, int width);

/* globals for shen operator*/
double b = 0.9;        /* smoothing factor 0 < b < 1 */
double low_thresh=20, high_thresh=22;/* threshold for
hysteresis*/
double ratio = 0.99;
int window_size = 7;
int do_hysteresis = 1;
float **lap;    /* keep track of laplacian of image */
int nr, nc;      /* nrows, ncols */
IMAGE edges;     /* keep track of edge points (thresholded)
*/
int thinFactor;
```

```
void main(int argc, char **argv)
{
      int i,j,n,m;
      IMAGE im, res;
      FILE *params;

/* Command line args — file name, maybe sigma */
      if (argc < 2)
      {
        printf ("USAGE: shen <imagefile>\n");
        exit (1);
      }
      im = Input_PBM (argv[1]);
      if (im == 0)
      {
        printf ("Can't read input image from '%s'.\n",
argv[1]);
        exit (2);
      }

/* Look for parameter file */
      params = fopen ("shen.par", "r");
      if (params)
      {
        fscanf (params, "%1f", &ratio);
        fscanf (params, "%1f", &b);
        if (b<0) b = 0;
          else if (b>1.0) b = 1.0;
        fscanf (params, "%d", &window_size);
        fscanf (params, "%d", &thinFactor);
        fscanf (params, "%d", &do_hysteresis);

        printf ("Parameters:\n")
        printf (" %% of pixels to be above HIGH threshold:
                %7.3f-\n", ratio);
        printf (" Size of window for adaptive gradient :
                %3d\n", window_size);
        printf (" Thinning factor                      :
                %d\n", thinFactor);
        printf ("Smoothing factor                      :
                %7.4f\n", b);
```

```
        if (do_hysteresis) printf ("Hysteresis thresholding
                turned on.\n");
          else printf ("Hysteresis thresholding turned
                  off.\n");
        fclose (params);
      }
      else printf ("Parameter file 'shen.par' does not
exist.\n");

      embed (im, OUTLINE);

      res = newimage (im->info->nr, im->info->nc);
      shen (im, res);

      debed (res, OUTLINE);

      Output_PBM (res, "shen.pgm");
      printf ("Output file is 'shen.pgm'\n");
}

void shen (IMAGE im, IMAGE res)
{
      register int i,j;
      float **buffer;
      float **smoothed_buffer;
      IMAGE bli_buffer;

/* Convert the input image to floating point */
      buffer = f2d (im->info->nr, im->info->nc);
      for (i=0, i<im->info->nr; i++)
        for (j=0; j<im->info->nc; j++)
          buffer[i][j] = (float)(im->data[i][j]);

/* Smooth input image using recursively implemented ISEF
            filter */
      smoothed_buffer = f2d( im->info->nr, im->info->nc);
      compute_ISEF (buffer, smoothed_buffer, im->info->nr,
im->info->nc);

/* Compute bli image band-limited laplacian image from
            smoothed image */
      bli_buffer = compute_bli(smoothed_buffer,
                  buffer,im->info->nr,im->info->nc);
/* Perform edge detection using bli and gradient
            thresholding */
```

```
        locate_zero_crossings (buffer, smoothed_buffer,
                bli_buffer, im->info->nr, im->info->nc);
        free(smoothed_buffer[0]); free(smoothed_buffer);
        freeimage (bli_buffer);
        threshold_edges (buffer, res, im->info->nr,
                im->info->nc);
        for (i=0; i<im->info->nr; i++)
          for (j=0; j<im->info->nc; j++)
            if (res->data[i][j] > 0) res->data[i][j] = 0;
            else res->data[i][j] = 255;
        free(buffer[0]); free(buffer);
}


/*   Recursive filter realization of the ISEF
     (Shen and Castan CVIGP March 1992) */
void computer_ISEF (float **x, float **y, int nrows, int
        ncols)
{
      float **A, **B;
      A = f2d(nrows, ncols); /* store causal component */
      B = f2d(nrows, ncols); /* store anti-causal component
*/

/* first apply the filter in the vertical direction (to the
rows) */
      apply_ISEF_vertical (x, y, A, B, nrows, ncols);
/* now apply the filter in the horizontal direction (to the
columns) and */
/* apply this filter to the results of the previous one */
      apply_ISEF_horizontal (y, y, A, B, nrows, ncols);
   /* free up the memory */
      free (B[0]); free(B);
      free (A[0]); free(A);
}
void apply_ISEF_vertical (float **x, float **y, float **A, float
        **B, int nrows, int ncols)
{
      register int row, col;
      float b1, b2;
      b1 = (1.0 - b)/(1.0 + b);
      b2 = b*b1;
```

```
/* compute boundary conditions */
    for (col=0; col<ncols; col++)
    {

/* boundary exists for 1st and last column */
        A[0][col] = b1 * x[0][col];
        B[nrows-1][col] = b2 * x[nrows-1][col];
    }

/* compute causal component */
    for (row=1, row<nrows; row++)
      for (col=0, col<ncols; col++)
        A[row][col] = b1 * x[row][col] + b * A[row-1][col];

/* compute anti-causal component */
    for (row=nrows-2; row>=0; row--)
      for (col=0; col<ncols; col++)
        B[row][col] = b2 * x[row][col] + b * B[row+1][col];

/* boundary case for computing output of first filter */
    for (col=0; col<ncols-1; col++)
      y[nrows-1][col] = A[nrows-1][col];

/* now compute the output of the first filter and store in y
        */
/* this is the sum of the causal and anti-causal components
*/
    for (row=0; row<nrows-1; row++)
      for (col=0; col<ncols-1; col++)
        y[row][col] = A [row][col] + B[row+1][col];
}

void apply_ISEF_horizontal (float **x, float **y, float **A,
        float **B, int nrows, int ncols)
{
    register int row, col;
    float b1, b2;

    b1 = (1.0 - b)/(1.0 + b);
    b2 = b*b1;

/* compute boundary conditions */
    for (row=0; row<nrows; row++)
    {
      A[row][0] = b1 * x[row][0];
```

```
         B[row][ncols—1] = b2 * x[row][ncols—1];
    }
/* compute causal component */
    for (col=1; col<ncols; col++)
      for (row=0; row<nrows; row++)
        A[row][col] = b1 * x [row][col] + b * A
[row][col—1];
/* compute anti-causal component */
    for (col=ncols—2; col>=0; col——)
      for (row=0; row<nrows;row++)
        B[row][col] = b2 * x[row][col] + b * B[row][col+1];
/* boundary case for computing output of first filter */
    for (row=0; row<nrows; row++)
      y[row][ncols—1] = A[row][ncols—1];
/* now compute the output of the second filter and store in y
        */
/* this is the sum of the causal and anti-causal components
        */
    for (row=0; row<nrows; row++)
      for (col=0; col<ncols—1; col++)
        y[row][col] = A[row][col1] + B[row][col+1];
}
/* compute the band-limited laplacian of the input image */
IMAGE compute_bli (float **buff1, float **buff2, int nrows,
        int ncols)
{
    register int row, col;
    IMAGE bli_buffer;
    bli_buffer = newimage(nrows, ncols);
    for (row=0; row<nrows; row++)
      for (col=0; col<ncols; col++)
        bli_buffer—>data[row][col] = 0;
/* The BLI is computed by taking the difference between the
        smoothed image */
/* and the original image. In Shen and Castan's paper this
        is shown to */
/* approximate the band-limited laplacian of the image. The
        bli is then */
/* made by setting all values in the bli to 1 where the
        laplacian is */
```

```
/* positive and 0 otherwise. */
    for (row=0, row <nrows; row++)
      for (col=0; col<ncols; col++)
      {
          if (row<OUTLINE || row >= nrows—OUTLINE ||
col<OUTLINE || col >= ncols—OUTLINE) continue;
        bli_buffer—>data[row][col] =
          ((buff1[row][col] — buff2[row][col]) > 0.0);
      }
    return bli_buffer;
}
void locate_zero_crossings (float **orig, float **smoothed,
        IMAGE bli, int nrows, int ncols)
{
    register int row, col;
    for (row=0; row<nrows; row++)
    {
      for (col=0; col<ncols; col++)
      {

/* ignore pixels around the boundary of the image */
      if (row<OUTCOME || row >= nrows—OUTLINE ||
        col<OUTLINE || col >= ncols—OUTLINE)
      {
        orig[row][col] = 0.0;
      }

/* next check if pixel is a zero-crossing of the laplacian
      */
      else if (is_candidate_edge (bli, smoothed, row, col))
      {

/* now do gradient thresholding */
        float grad = compute_adaptive_gradient (bli,
              smoothed, row, col);
        orig[row][col] = grad;
      }
      else orig[row][col] = 0.0;
      }
    }
}
```

```
void threshold_edges (float **in, IMAGE out, int nrows, int
        ncols)
{
    register int i, j;

    lap = in;
    edges = out;
    nr = nrows;
    nc = ncols;

    estimate_thresh (&low_thresh, &high_thresh, nr, nc);
    if (!do_hysteresis)
      low_thresh = high_thresh;

    for (i=0; i<nrows; i++)
      for (j=0; j<ncols; j++)
        edges->data[i][j] = 0;

    for (i=0; i<nrows; i++)
      for (j=0; j<ncols; j++)
      {
          if (i<OUTLINE || i>= nrows-OUTLINE ||
                j<OUTLINE || j >= ncols-OUTLINE) continue;

/* only check a contour if it is above high_thresh */
          if ((lap[i][j]) > high_thresh)

/* mark all connected points above low thresh */
            mark_connected (i,j,0);
      }
    for (i=0; i<nrows; i++)/* erase all points which were
            255 */
        for (j=0; j<ncols; j++)
          if (edges->data[i][j] == 255) edges->data[i][j] =
0;
}

/*   return true if it marked something */
int mark_connected (int i, int j, int level)
{
        int notChainEnd;

    /* stop if you go off the edge of the image */
      if (i >= nr || i < 0 || j >= nc || j < 0) return 0);
```

```
    /* stop if the point has already been visited */
      if (edges->data[i][j] != 0) return 0);

  /* stop when you hit an image boundary */
      if (lap[i][j] == 0.0) return 0;

      if ((lap[i][j]) > low_thresh)
      {
         edges->data[i][j] = 1;
      }
      else
      {
         edges->data[i][j] = 255;
      }

      notChainEnd =0;

      notChainEnd = mark_connected(i ,j+1, level+1);
      notChainEnd = mark_connected(i ,j-1, level+1)
      notChainEnd = mark_connected(i+1,j+1, level+1)
      notChainEnd = mark_connected(i+1,j , level+1);
      notChainEnd = mark_connected(i+1,j-1, level+1);
      notChainEnd = mark_connected(i-1,j-1, level+1);
      notChainEnd = mark_connected(i-1,j , level+1);
      notChainEnd = mark_connected(i-1,j+1, level+1);

      if (notChainEnd && ( level > 0 ) )
      {
      /* do some contour thinning */
        if ( thinFactor > 0 )
        if ( ( level%thinFactor) != 0) )
        {
          /* delete this point */
          edges->data[i][j] = 255;
        }
      }

      return 1;
}

/* finds zero-crossings in laplacian (buff) orig is the
          smoothed image */
int is_candidate_edge (IMAGE buff, float **orig, int row, int
          col)
{
```

```
/* A positive z-c must have a positive 1st derivative, where
        positive z—c means the second derivative goes
        from + to — as we cross the edge */


    if (buff—>data[row][col] == 1 && buff—>data[row+1][col]
            == 0) /* positive z-c */
    {
       if (orig[row+1][col] — orig[row—1][col] > 0) return
1;
       else return 0;
    }
    else if (buff—>data[row][col] == 1 && buff—>data[row]
            [col+1] == 0 ) /* positive z-c */
    {
       if (orig[row][col+1] — orig[row][col—1] > 0) return
1;
       else return 0;
    }
    else if ( buff—>data[row][col] == 1 && buff—>
            data[row—1] [col] == 0) /* negative z-c */
    {
       if (orig[row+1][col] — orig[row—1][col] < 0) return
1;
       else return 0;
    }
    else if (buff—>data[row][col] == 1 &&
            buff—>data[row][col—1] == 0) /*negative z-c
              */
    {
       if (orig[row][col+1] — orig[row][col—1] < 0) return
1;
       else return 0;
    }
    else /* not a z—c */
      return 0;
}
float compute_adaptive-gradient (IMAGE BLI_buffer, float
        **orig_buffer, int row, int col)
{
    register int i, j;
```

```
    float sum_on, sum_off;
    float avg_on, avg_off;
    int num_on, num_off;

    sum_on = sum_off = 0.0;
    num_on = num_off = 0;

    for (i= (-window_size/2); i<=(window_size/2); i++)
    {
       for (j=(-window_size/2); j<=(window_size/2); j++)
       {
         if (BLI_buffer->data[row+1][col+j])
         {
            sum_on += orig_buffer[row+i][col+j];
            num_on++;
         }
         else
         {
            sum_off += orig_buffer[row+1][col+j];
            num_off++;
         }
       }
    }

    if (sum_off) avg_off = sum_off / num_off;
    else avg_off = 0;

    if (sum_on) avg_on = sum_on / num_on;
    else avg_on = 0;

    return (avg_off - avg_on);
}

void estimate_thresh (double *low, double *hi, int nr, int
         nc)
{
    float vmax, vmin, scale, x;
    int i,j,k, hist[256], count;
/* Build a histogram of the Laplacian image. */
    vmin = vmax = fabs ((float)(lap[20][20]));
    for (i=0; i<nr; i++)
      for (j= 0; j<nc; j++)
       {
           if (i<OUTLINE || i >= nr-OUTLINE ||
```

```
                              j<OUTLINE || j >= nc—OUTLINE) continue;
             x = lap[i][j];
             if (vmin > x) vmin = x;
             if (vmax < x) vmax = x;
          }
       for (k=0; k<256; k++) hist[k] = 0;

       scale = 256.0/(vmax—vmin + 1);

       for (i=0; i<nr; i++)
          for (j=0; j<nc; j++)
          {
             if (i<OUTLINE || i >= nr—OUTLINE ||
                    j<OUTLINE || j >= nc—OUTLINE) continue;
             x = lap[i][j];
             k = (int)((x — vmin)*scale);
             hist[k] += 1;
          }

/* The high threshold should be > 80 or 90% of the pixels */
       k = 255;
       j = (int)(ratio*nr*nc);
       count = hist[255];
       while (count < j)
       {
          k——;
          if (k<0) break;
          count += hist[k];
       }
       *hi = (double)k/scale + vmin ;
       *low = (*hi)/2;
}

void embed (IMAGE im, int width)
{
       int i,j,I,J;
       IMAGE new;
       width += 2;
       new = newimage (im—>info—>nr+width+width,
im—>info—>nc+width+width);
       for (i=0, i<new—>info—>nr; i++)
          for (j=0, j<new—>info—>nc; j++)
          {
```

```
          I = (i-width+im->info->nr)%im->info->nr;
          J = (j-width+im->info->nc)%im->info->nc;
          new->data[i][j] = im->data[I][J];
        }
      free (im->info);
      free(im->data[0]); free(im->data);
      im->info = new->info;
      im->data = new->data;
  }
  void debed (IMAGE im, int width)
  {
      int i,j;
      IMAGE old;
      width +=2
      old = newimage (im->info->nr-width-width,
  im->info->nc-width-width);
      for (i=0; i<old->info->nr-1; i++)
      {
        for (j=1; j<old->info->nc; j++)
        {
          old->data[i][j] = im->data[i+width][j+width];
          old->data[old->info->nr-1][j] = 255;
        }
        old->data[i][0] = 255;
      }
      free (im->info);
      free(im->data[0]); free(im->data);
      im->info = old->info;
      im->data = old->data;
  }
```

1.10 BIBLIOGRAPHY

Abdou, I. E. and W. K. Pratt. 1979. Quantitative Design and Evaluation of Enhancement/ Thresholding Edge Detectors. *Proceedings of the IEEE*. vol. 67. 5:753–763.

Canny, J. 1986. A Computational Approach to Edge Detection, *IEEE Transactions on Pattern Analysis and Machine Intelligence*, Vol. PAMI-8. (6):679–698.

Deutsch, E. S. and J. R. Fram. 1978. A Quantitative Study of Orientation Bias of Some Edge Detector Schemes. *IEEE Transactions on Computers*, Vol. C-27. (3):205–213.

Grimson, W.E.L. 1981. *From Images to Surfaces*. Cambridge, MA: MIT Press.

Kaplan, W. 1973. *Advanced Calculus* (2nd edition). Reading, MA: Addison Wesley.

Kirsch, R. A. 1971. Computer Determination of the Constituent Structure of Biological Images. *Computers and Biomedical Research*, 4:315–328.

Kitchen, L. and A. Rosenfeld. 1981. Edge Evaluation Using Local Edge Coherence. *IEEE Transactions on Systems, Man, and Cybernetics*. Vol. SMC-11. 9:597–605.

Marr, D. and E. Hildreth. 1980. Theory of Edge Detection. *Proceedings of the Royal Society of London*. Series B. Vol. 207. 187–217.

Nalwa, V. S. and T. O. Binford. 1986. On Detecting Edges. *IEEE Transactions on Pattern Analysis and Machine Intelligence*. Vol. PAMI-8. 6:699–714.

Prager, J. M. 1980. Extracting and Labeling Boundary Segments in Natural Scenes. *IEEE Transactions on Pattern Analysis and Machine Intelligence*. Vol. PAMI-2. 1:16–27.

Pratt, W. K. 1978. *Digital Image Processing*. New York, NY: John Wiley & Sons.

Shah, M., Sood, A., and R. Jain. 1986. Pulse and Staircase Edge Models. *Computer Vision, Graphics, and Image Processing*. Vol. 34. 321–343.

Shen, J. and S. Castan. 1992. An Optimal Linear Operator for Step Edge Detection. *Computer Vision, Graphics, and Image Processing: Graphical Models and Understanding*. Vol. 54. 2:112–133.

Torre, V. and T. A. Poggio. 1986. On Edge Detection. *IEEE Transactions on Pattern Analysis and Machine Intelligence*. Vol. PAMI-8. 2:147–163.

2

THE USE OF DIGITAL MORPHOLOGY

2.1 MORPHOLOGY DEFINED

To be completely precise, the word morphology means ''the form and structure of an object,'' or the arrangements and interrelationships between the parts of an object. Morphology is related to shape, and digital morphology is a way to describe or analyze the shape of a digital (most often raster) object.

The oldest uses of the word relate to language and to biology. In linguistics, morphology is the study of the structure of words, and this has been an area of study for a great many years. In biology, morphology relates more directly to the shape of an organism—the shape of a leaf can be used to identify a plant, and the shape of a colony of bacteria can be used to identify its variety. In each case, there is an intricate scheme for classification based on overall shape (elliptical, circular, etc.), type and degree of irregularities (convex, rough or smooth outline, etc.), and internal structures (holes, linear or curved features, etc.) that has been accumulated over many years of observation.

The science of digital morphology is relatively recent, since it is only recently that digital computers have made it practical. On the other hand, the mathematics behind it is simply set theory, which is a well studied area. The idea underlying digital morphology is that images consist of a set of picture elements (pixels) that collect into groups having a two-dimensional structure (shape). Certain mathematical operations on the set of pixels can be used to enhance specific aspects of the shapes so that they might be (for example) counted or recognized. Basic operations are *erosion*, in which pixels matching a given pattern are deleted from the image, and *dilation*, in which a small area about a pixel is set to a given pattern. However, depending on the type of image being processed—bilevel, grey level, or color—the definition of these operations changes, so each must be considered separately.

2.2   ELEMENTS OF DIGITAL MORPHOLOGY—BINARY OPERATIONS

Binary morphological operations are defined on bilevel images; that is, images that consist of either black or white pixels only. For the purpose of beginning the discussion, consider the image seen in Figure 2.1a. The set of black pixels form a square object. The object in Figure 2.1b is also square, but is one pixel larger in all directions. It was obtained from the previous square by simply setting all white neighbors of any black pixel to black. This amounts to a simple *binary dilation*, so named because it causes the original object to grow larger. Figure 2.1c shows the result of dilating Figure 2.1b by one pixel, which is the same as dilating Figure 2.1a by two pixels; this process could be continued until the entire image consisted entirely of black pixels, at which point the image would stop showing any change.

This is a very simple example of digital morphology, and one that can be implemented directly by first marking all white pixels having at least one black neighbor, and then setting all of the marked pixels to black. This is not, however, how morphological operators are usually implemented. In general the object is considered to be a mathematical set of black pixels; since each pixel is identified by its row and column indices, a pixel is said to be a point in two-dimensional space (E^2). The set of pixels comprising the object in Figure 2.1a can now be written as $\{(3,3)(3,4)(4,3)(4,4)\}$ if the upper left pixel in the image has the index $(0,0)$. This set is too awkward to write out in full all of the time, so it will simply be called A.

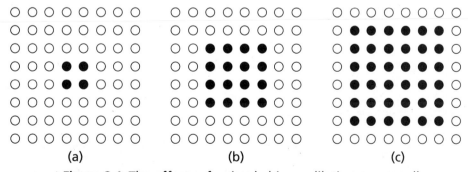

Figure 2.1 The effects of a simple binary dilation on a small object. (a) Original image. (b) Dilation of the original by 1 pixel. (c) Dilation of the original by 2 pixels (dilation of (b) by 1 pixel).

Binary Dilation

Now some definitions of simple set operations can be stated, with the goal being to define dilation in a more general fashion in terms of sets. The *translation* of the set A by the point x is defined, in set notation, as:

$$(A)_x = \{c | c = a + x, a \in A\} \qquad \text{(EQ 2.1)}$$

For example, if x were at (1,2) then the first (upper left) pixel in A_x would be (3,3) + (1,2) = (4,5); all of the pixels in A shift down by one row and right by two columns in this case. This is a translation in the same sense that is seen in computer graphics—a change in position by a specified amount.

The *reflection* of the set A is defined as:

$$\hat{A} = \{c | c = -a, a \in A\} \qquad \text{(EQ 2.2)}$$

This is really a rotation of the object A by 180 degrees about the origin. The *complement* of the set A is the set of pixels not belonging to A. This would correspond to the white pixels in the figure, or in the language of set theory:

$$A^c = \{c | c \notin A\} \qquad \text{(EQ 2.3)}$$

The *intersection* of two sets A and B is the set of elements (pixels) belonging to both A and B:

$$A \cap B = \{c | ((c \in A) \wedge (c \in B))\} \qquad \text{(EQ 2.4)}$$

The *union* of two sets A and B is the set of pixels that belong to either A or B, or to both:

$$A \cup G = \{c | (c \in A) \vee (c \in B)\} \qquad \text{(EQ 2.5)}$$

Finally, completing this collection of basic definitions, the *difference* between the set A and the set B is:

$$A - B = \{c | (c \in A) \wedge (c \notin B)\} \qquad \text{(EQ 2.6)}$$

which is the set of pixels that belong to A but not also to B. This is really just the intersection of A with the complement of B or $A \cap B^c$.

It is now possible to define more formally what is meant by a dilation. A dilation of the set A by the set B is:

$$A \oplus B = \{c | c = a + b, a \in A, b \in B\} \qquad \text{(EQ 2.7)}$$

where A represents the image being operated on, and B is a second set of pixels, a shape that operates on the pixels of A to produce the result; the set B is called a *structuring element*, and its composition defines the nature of the specific dilation. To explore this idea, let A be the set of Figure 2.1a, and let B be the set

{(0,0)(0,1)}. The pixels in the set C = A + B are computed using Equation 2.7, which can be rewritten in this case as:

$$A \oplus B = (A + \{(0,0)\}) \cup (A + \{(0,1)\}) \quad\quad\quad \text{(EQ 2.8)}$$

There are four pixels in the set A, and since any pixel translated by (0,0) does not change, those four will also be in the resulting set C after computing C = A + {(0,0)}:

$$(3,3) + (0,0) = (3,3) \quad (3,4) + (0,0) = (3,4)$$

$$(4,3) + (0,0) = (4,3) \quad (4,4) + (0,0) = (4,3)$$

The result of A + {(0,1)} is:

$$(3,3) + (0,1) = (3,4) \quad (3,4) + (0,1) = (3,5)$$

$$(4,3) + (0,1) = (4,4) \quad (4,4) + (0,1) = (4,5)$$

The set C is the result of the dilation of A using structuring element B, and consists of all of the pixels listed above (some of which are duplicates). Figure 2.2 illustrates this operation, showing graphically the effect of the dilation. The

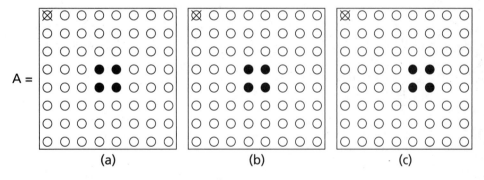

A =   (a)   (b)   (c)

B = 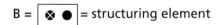 = structuring element

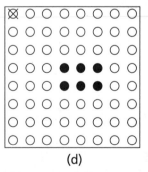

(d)

Figure 2.2 Dilation of the set A (Figure 2.1a) by the set B. (a) The two sets. (b) The set obtained by adding (0,0) to all element of A. (c) The set obtained by adding (0,1) to all elements of A. (d) The union of the two sets is the result of the dilation.

pixels marked with an "X," either white or black, represent the origin of each image. The location of the origin is really quite important. In the example above, if the origin of B were the rightmost of the two pixels the effect of the dilation would be to add pixels to the left of A, rather than to the right. The set B in this case would be $\{(0,-1)(0,0)\}$.

Moving back to the simple binary dilation that was performed in Figure 2.1, one question that remains is "What was the structuring element that was used?" Note that the object increases in size in all directions, and by a single pixel. From the example just completed it was observed that if the structuring element has a set pixel to the right of the origin, then a dilation that uses that structuring element "grows" a layer of pixels on the right of the object. To grow a layer of pixels in all directions, it seems to make sense to use a structuring element having one pixel on every side of the origin; that is, a 3×3 square with the origin at the center. This structuring element will be named simple in the ensuing discussion, and is correct in this instance (although it is not always easy to determine the shape of the structuring element needed to accomplish a specific task).

As a further example, consider the object and structuring element shown in Figure 2.3. In this case, the origin of the structuring element B_1 contains a white pixel, implying that *the origin is not included* in the set B_1. There is no rule against this, but it is more difficult to see what will happen, so the example will be done in detail. The image to be dilated, A_1, has the following set representation:

$$A_1 = \{(1,1)(2,2)(2,3)(3,2)(3,3)(4,4)\}.$$

The structuring element B_1 is:

$$B_1 = \{(0,-1)(0,1)\}.$$

The translation of A_1 by $(0,-1)$ yields

$$(A_1)_{(0,-1)} = \{(1,0)(2,1)(2,2)(3,1)(3,2)(4,3)\}$$

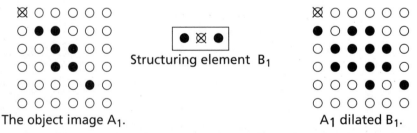

The object image A_1.

Structuring element B_1

A_1 dilated B_1.

Figure 2.3 Dilation by a structuring element that does not include the origin. Some pixels that are set in the original image are not set in the dilated image.

and the translation of A_1 by $(0,1)$ yields:

$$(A_1)_{(0,1)} = \{(1,2)(2,3)(2,4)(3,3)(3,4)(4,5)\}.$$

The dilation of A_1 by B_1 is the union of $(A)_{1(0,-1)}$ with $(A_1)_{(0,1)}$, and is shown in Figure 2.3. Notice that the original object pixels, those belonging to A_1, are not necessarily set in the result; $(1,1)$ and $(4,4)$, for example, are set in A_1 but not in $A_1 + B_1$. This is the effect of the origin not being a part of B_1.

The manner in which the dilation is calculated above presumes that a dilation can be considered to be the union of all of the translations specified by the structuring element; that is, as

$$A \oplus B = \bigcup_{b \in B} (A)_b \qquad \text{(EQ 2.9)}$$

Not only is this true, but because dilation is commutative, a dilation can also be considered to be the union of all translations of the structuring element by all pixels in the image:

$$A \oplus B = \bigcup_{a \in A} (B)_a \qquad \text{(EQ 2.10)}$$

This gives a clue concerning a possible implementation for the dilation operator. Think of the structuring element as a template, and move it over the image. When the origin of the structuring element aligns with a black pixel in the image, all of the image pixels that correspond to black pixels in the structuring element are marked, and will later be changed to black. After the entire image has been swept by the structuring element, the dilation calculation is complete. Normally the dilation is not computed in place; that is, where the result is copied over the original image. A third image, initially all white, is used to store the dilation while it is being computed.

Implementing Binary Dilation

The general implementation of dilation for bilevel images consists of two parts: a program that creates a dilated image given an input image and a structuring element, and a function that will do the same but that can be called from another function, and which will allow dilation to be incorporated into a larger imaging program. The program, which will be called BinDil, accepts three arguments from the command line:

```
BinDil input_file SE_file output_file
```

All three arguments are file names; *input_file* is the name of the image file that contains the image to be dilated; *SE_file* contains the data for the structuring element; and *output_file* is the name of the file that will be created to hold the resulting dilated image. Both the input file and the output file will be in PBM format, which will be discussed in Appendix C. The structuring element file has its own special format, since the location of the origin is needed. Because dilation is commutative, though, the structuring element should also be a PBM image. It was decided to add a small ''feature'' to the definition of a PBM file—if a comment begins with the string ''#origin,'' then the coordinates of the origin of the image will follow, first the column and then the row. Such a file is still a PBM image file, and can still be read in and displayed as such because the new specification occurs in a comment. If no origin is explicitly given, then it is assumed to be at (0,0).

Thus, the PBM file for the structuring element B_1 of Figure 2.3 would be:

```
P1
#origin 1 0
3 1
1 0 1
```

This file will be called B1.pbm; to perform the dilation seen in Figure 2.3 the call to BinDil would be:

```
BinDil A1.pbm B1.pbm A1dil.pbm
```

where the file Al.pbm contains the image A_1, and A1dil.pbm will be the file into which the dilated image will be written.

The program BinDil really does not do very much. It merely reads in the images and passes them to the function that does the work: the C function bin_dilate, defined as:

```
int bin_dilate (IMAGE im, SE p);
```

This function implements a dilation by the structuring element pointed to by p by moving the origin of p to each of the black pixel positions in the image im, and then copying the black pixels from p to the corresponding positions in the output image. Figure 2.4 shows this process, which is basically that specified in Equation 2.9, and which has a strong resemblance to a convolution.

As seen in Figures 2.5 and 2.6, the function bin_dilate looks through the data image for black pixels, calling dil_apply when it finds one—this function performs the actual copy from the current position of the structuring element to the output (dilated) image. A temporary image is used for the result, which is copied over the input image after the dilation is complete.

Binary Erosion

If dilation can be said to add pixels to an object, or to make it bigger, then erosion will make an image smaller. In the simplest case, a binary erosion will remove

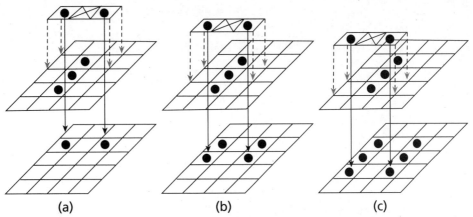

Figure 2.4 Dilating an image using a structuring element. (a) The origin of the structuring element is placed over the first black pixel in the image, and the pixels in the structuring element are copied into their corresponding positions in the result image. (b) Then the structuring element is placed over the next black pixel in the image and the process is repeated. (c) This is done for every black pixel in the image.

the outer layer of pixels from an object. For example, Figure 2.1b is the result of such a simple erosion process applied to Figure 2.1c. This can be implemented by marking all black pixels having at least one white neighbor, and then setting to white all of the marked pixels. The structuring element implicit in this implementation is the same 3×3 array of black pixels that defined the simple binary dilation.

In general, the erosion of image A by structuring element B can be defined as:

$$A \ominus B = \{c | (B)_c \subseteq A\} \qquad \text{(EQ 2.11)}$$

In other words, it is the set of all pixels c such that the structuring element B translated by c corresponds to a set of black pixels in A. That the result of an erosion is a subset of the original image seems clear enough; any pixels that do not match the pattern defined by the black pixels in the structuring element will not belong to the result. However, the manner in which the erosion removes pixels is not clear (at least at first), so a few examples are in order, and the statement above that the eroded image is a subset of the original is not necessarily true if the structuring element does not contain the origin.

First, a simple example. Consider the structuring element B = {(0,0)(1,0)} and the object image A = {(3,3)(3,4)(4,3)(4,4)}. The set A $\ominus$ B is the set of translations of B that align B over a set of black pixels in A. This means that not all translations need to be considered, but only those that initially place the origin of B at one of the members of A. There are four such translations:

```
void dil_apply (IMAGE im, SE p, int ii, int jj, IMAGE res)
{
     int i,j is,js, ie, je, k;
/* Find start and end pixel in IM */
     is = ii − p−>oi; js = jj − p−>oj;ie = is + p−>nr; je
               = js + p−>nc;
/* Place SE over the image from (is,js) to (ie,je). Set
          pixels in RES if the corresponding SE pixel is
          1; else do nothing. */
     for (i=is; i<ie; i++)
          for (j=js; j<je; j++)
          {
               if (range(im,i,j))
               {
                    k = (p−>data[i−is][j−js] == 1);
                    if (k>=0) res −>data[i][j] |= k;
}            }         }
int bin_dilate (IMAGE im, SE p)
{
     IMAGE tmp;
     int i,j;
/* Source image empty? */
     if (im==0)
     {
          printf ("Bad image in BIN_DILATE\n");
          return 0;
     }
/* Create a result image */
     tmp = newimage (im−>info−>nr, im−>info−>nc);
     if (tmp ==0)
     {
          print f ("Out of memory in BIN_DILATE.\n");
          return 0;
     }
     for (i=0, i<tmp−>info−>nr; i++)
          for (j=0; j<tmp−>info−>nc; j++)
               tmp−>data[i][j] = 0;
```

Figure 2.5 C source code for the dilation of a binary image by a binary structuring element.

```
/* Apply the SE to each black pixel of the input */
    for (i=0, i<im->info->nr; i++)
          for (j=0, j<im->info->nc; j++)
        if (im->data [i][j] == WHITE)
    dil_apply (im, p, i, j, tmp);
/* Copy result over the input */
    for (i=0; i<im->info->nr; i++)
          for (j=0; j<im->info->nc; j++)
              im->data[i][j] = tmp->data[i][j];

    /* Free the result image — it was a temp */
    freeimage (tmp);
    return 1;
    }
```

Figure 2.5 (continued)

$$B_{(3,3)} = \{(3,3)(4,3)\}$$

$$B_{(3,4)} = \{(3,4)(4,4)\}$$

$$B_{(4,3)} = \{(4,3)(5,3)\}$$

$$B_{(4,4)} = \{(4,4)(5,4)\}$$

In two cases, $B_{(3,3)}$ and $B_{(3,4)}$, the resulting (translated) set consists of pixels that are all members of A, and so those pixels will appear in the erosion of A by B. This example is illustrated in Figure 2.6.

Now consider the structuring element $B_2 = \{(1,0)\}$; in this case the origin is not a member of B_2. The erosion $A \ominus B$ can be computed as before, except that now the origin of the structuring element need not be correspond to a black pixel in the image. There are quite a few legal positions, but the only ones that result in a match are:

$$B_{(2,3)} = \{(3,3)\}$$

$$B_{(2,4)} = \{(3,4)\}$$

$$B_{(3,3)} = \{(4,3)\}$$

$$B_{(3,4)} = \{(4,4)\}$$

This means that the result of the erosion is $\{(2,3)(2,4)(3,3)(3,4)\}$, which is *not* a subset of the original.

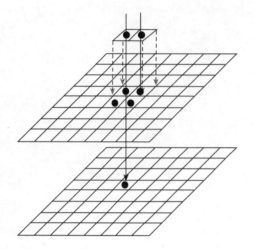

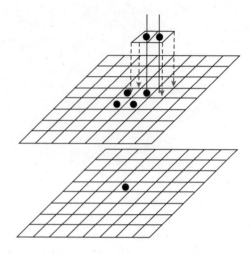

The structuring element is translated to the position of a black pixel in the image. In this case all members of the structuring element correspond to black image pixels, so the result is a black pixel.

Now the structuring element is translated to the next black pixel in the image, and there is one pixel that does not match. The result is a white pixel.

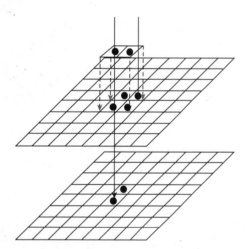

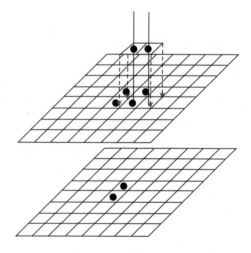

At the next translation there is another match so, again, the pixel in the output image that corresponds to the translated origin of the structuring element is set to black.

The final translation is not a match, and the result is a white pixel. The remaining image pixels are white and could not match the origin of the structuring element; they need not be considered.

Figure 2.6 Binary erosion using a simple structuring element.

It is important to realize that erosion and dilation are not inverse operations. Although there are some situations where an erosion will undo the effect of a dilation exactly, this is not true in general. Indeed, as will be observed later, this fact can be used to perform useful operations on images. However, erosion and dilation are *duals* of each other in the following sense:

$$(A \ominus B)^c = A^c \oplus \hat{B} \qquad \text{(EQ. 2.12)}$$

In more or less plain English, this says that the complement of an erosion is the same as a dilation of the complement image by the reflected structuring element. If the structuring element is symmetrical then reflecting it does not change it, and the implication of Equation 2.12 is that the complement of an erosion of an image is the dilation of the background, in the case where simple is the structuring element.

The proof of the erosion-dilation duality is fairly simple, and may yield some insights into how morphological expressions are manipulated and validated. The definition of erosion is:

$$A \ominus B = \{z | (B)_z \subseteq A\}$$

so the complement of the erosion is:

$$(A \ominus B)^c = \{z | (B_z) \subseteq A\}^c$$

If $(B)_z$ is a subset of A, then the intersection of $(B)_z$ with A is not empty:

$$(A \ominus B)^c = \{z | ((B)_z \cap A) \neq \emptyset\}^c$$

but the intersection with A^c will be empty:

$$= \{z | (B)_z \cap A^c = \emptyset\}^c$$

and the set of pixels not having this property is the complement of the set that does:

$$= \{z | ((B)_z \cap A^c) \neq \emptyset\}$$

By the definition of translation in Equation 2.1, if $(B)_z$ intersects A^c then

$$= \{z | b + z \in A^c, b \in B\}$$

which is the same thing as

$$= \{z | b + z = a, a \in A^c, b \in B\}$$

Now if $a = b + z$ then $z = a - b$:

$$= \{z | z = a - b, a \in A^c, b \in B\}$$

Finally, using the definition of reflection, if b is a member of B then −b is a member of the reflection of B:

$$= \{z | z = a + b,\, a \in A^c,\, b \in \hat{B}\}$$

which is the definition of $A^c \oplus \hat{B}$.

The erosion operation also brings up an issue that was not a concern about dilation; the idea of a ''don't care'' state in the structuring element. When using a strictly binary structuring element to perform an erosion, the member black pixels must correspond to black pixels in the image in order to set the pixel in the result, but the same is not true for a white (0) pixel in the structuring element. We don't care what the corresponding pixel in the image might be when the structuring element pixel is white.

Figure 2.7 gives some examples of erosions of a simple image by a collection of different structuring elements. The basic shape of the structuring elements is,

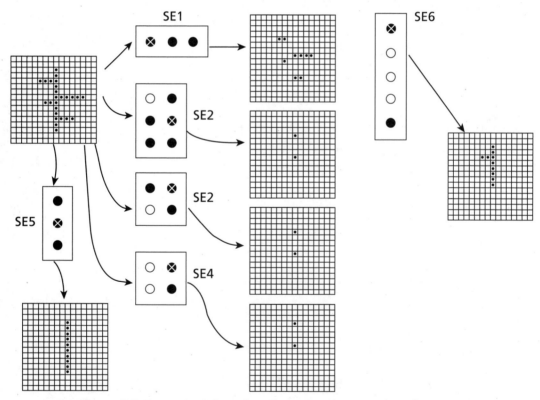

Figure 2.7 Examples of erosions by various structuring elements. The binary structuring elements are labelled SE1 through SE6.

in each case, identified if it appears in the data image. The intent of SE2, for example, is to identify "T" intersections of a vertical line with a horizontal line on the left, and SE3 and SE4 attempt to isolate corners. SE6 has three white pixels spacing apart two black ones; at first glance it might be used to locate horizontal lines spaced three pixels apart, but it will also respond to vertical line segments. This sort of unexpected (to the beginner) behavior leads to difficulties in designing structuring elements for specific tasks.

Figure 2.8 is a better illustration of the use of erosion elements in a practical sense. The problem is to design a structuring element that will locate the staff lines in a raster image of printed music. The basic problem is to isolate the symbols so that, once identified, the staff lines will be removed. The structuring element consists of five horizontal straight line segments separated by "don't care" pixels—the latter corresponds to whatever occupies the space between the staff lines: note heads, sharps, etc. In effect, these elements act as spacers, permitting the combination of five distinct structuring elements into one.

After an erosion by the structuring element, each short section of staff lines has been reduced to a single pixel. The staff lines can be regenerated by a dilation of the eroded image by the same structuring element (Figure 2.8d). If it is necessary to remove the staff lines, this can be done by subtracting this image from the original (Figure 2.8e). There are now gaps in the image where the lines used to be, but otherwise the music symbols are free of the lines. A further morphological step can fill in some of the gaps (Figure 2.8f).

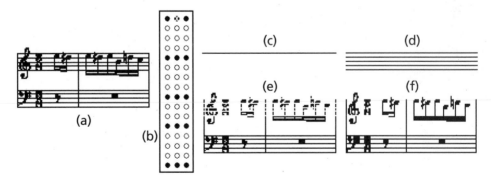

Figure 2.8 Morphological removal of staff lines from printed music. (a) The original image. (b) The structuring element. (c) Result of the erosion of (a) by (b). (d) Result of dilating again by the same structuring element. (e) Subtract (d) from (a). (f) Use a simple morphological operator to fill in the gaps.

Implementing Binary Erosion

As was done previously in the case of dilation, the implementation will consist of a program that creates an eroded image given an input image and a structuring element, and a function that does the actual work. The program is in the same style as BinDil, and is called BinErode:

```
BinErode input_file SE_file output_file
```

The PBM file for the structuring element of Figure 2.8b would be:

```
P1
#origin 1 0
3 16
1 1 1
0 0 0
0 0 0
0 0 0
1 1 1
0 0 0
0 0 0
0 0 0
1 1 1
0 0 0
0 0 0
1 1 1
0 0 0
0 0 0
0 0 0
1 1 1
```

This file will be called elise_SE.pbm; to perform the dilation seen in Figure 2.8 the call to the BinErode would be:

```
BinErode elise.pbm elise_SE.pbm out1.pbm
```

where the file elise.pbm contains the image 2.8a, and out1.pbm will be the file into which the dilated image will be written (Figure 2.8c). The C function bin_erode is implemented in a very similar manner to bin_dilate, and appears in Figure 2.9.

```
/* Apply an erosion step on one pixel of IM, result to RES
        */

void erode_apply (IMAGE im, SE p, int ii, int jj, IMAGE
        res)

{
    int i,j, is,js, ie, je, k, r;

    /* Find start and end pixel in IM */
    is = ii - p->oi; js = jj - p->oj;
    ie = is + p->nr; je = js + p->nc;

    /* Place SE over the image from (is,js) to (ie,je).
            Set pixels in RES
    if the corresponding pixels in the image agree. */
    r = 1;
    for (i=is; i<ie; i++)
        for (j=js; j<je; j++)
        {
            if (range(im,i,j))
            {
                k = p->data[i-is][j-js];
                if (k == 1 && im->data[i][j]==0) r =
                    0;
            } else if (p->data [i-is][j-js] != 0) r =
                0;
        }
        res->data[ii][jj] = r;
} }

int bin_erode (IMAGE im, SE p)
{
    IMAGE tmp;
    int i,j;

/* Create a result image */
    tmp = newimage (im->info->nr, im->info->nc);
    for (i=0; i<tmp->info->nr; i++)
        for (j=0; j<tmp->info->nc; j++)
            tmp->data[i][j] = 0;
```

Figure 2.9 Slightly shortened version of the C source code for bin_erode.
(See the CD Rom for the complete version.) Some error checking has been
removed for brevity.

```
/* Apply the SE to each black pixel of the input */
    for (i=0; i<im->info->nr; i++)
        for (j=0; j<im->info->nc; j++)
            erode_apply (im, p, i, j, tmp);
/* Copy result over the input */
    for (i=0; i<im->info->nr; i++)
        for (j=0; j<i->info->nc; j++)
            im->data[i][j] = tmp->data[i][j];

/* Free the result image — it was a temp */
    freeimage (tmp);
    return 1;
}
```

Figure 2.9 (continued)

Opening and Closing

The application of an erosion immediately followed by a dilation using the same structuring element is referred to as an *opening* operation. The name opening is a descriptive one, describing the observation that the operation tends to "open" small gaps or spaces between touching objects in an image. This effect is most easily observed when using the simple structuring element. Figure 2.10 shows an image having a collection of small objects, some of them touching each other. After an opening using simple the objects are better isolated, and might now be counted or classified.

Figure 2.10 also illustrates another, and quite common, using of opening: the removal of noise. When a noisy grey-level image is thresholded some of the noise pixels are above the threshold, and result in isolated pixels in random locations. The erosion step in an opening will remove isolated pixels as well as boundaries of objects, and the dilation step will restore most of the boundary pixels without restoring the noise. This process seems to be successful at removing spurious black pixels, but does not remove the white ones.

The example in Figure 2.8 is actually an example of opening, albeit with a more complex structuring element. The image was eroded (leaving only a horizontal line), and then dilated by the same structuring element, which is certainly an opening. What is being eroded in this case is all portions of the image that are not staff lines, which the dilation subsequently restores. The same description of the process applies to Figure 2.10: What is being eroded is all parts of the image that

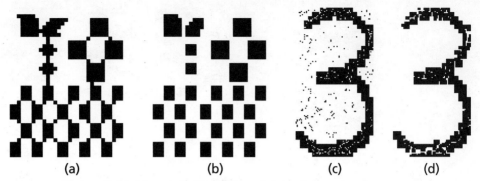

Figure 2.10 The use of opening. (a) An image having many connected objects. (b) Objects can be isolated by opening using the simple structuring element. (c) An image that has been subjected to noise. (d) The noisy image after opening showing that the black noise pixels have been removed.

are not small black squares, which are restored by the dilation, thus removing everything except that in which we are interested.

A *closing* is similar to an opening except that the dilation is performed first, followed by an erosion using the same structuring element. If an opening creates small gaps in the image, a closing will fill them, or ''close'' the gaps. Figure 2.11a shows a closing applied to the image of Figure 2.10d, which you may remember was opened in an attempt to remove noise. The closing removes much of the white pixel noise, giving a fairly clean image.

The same figure shows an application of a closing to reconnect broken features. Figure 2.11b is a section of a printed circuit board that has been thresholded. Noise somewhere in the process has resulted in the traces connecting the components being broken in a number of places. Closing this image (Figure 2.11c) fixes many of these breaks, but not all of them. It is important to realize that when using real images it is rare for any single technique to provide a complete and perfect solution to an image processing or vision problem. A more complete method for fixing the circuit board may use four or five more structuring elements, and two or three other techniques outside of morphology.

Closing can also be used for smoothing the outline of objects in an image. Sometimes digitization followed by thresholding can give a jagged appearance to boundaries; in other cases the objects are naturally rough, and it may be necessary to determine how rough the outline is. In either case, closing can be used. However, more than one structuring element may be needed, since the simple structuring element is only useful for removing or smoothing single pixel irregularities. Another possibility is repeated application of dilation followed by the same num-

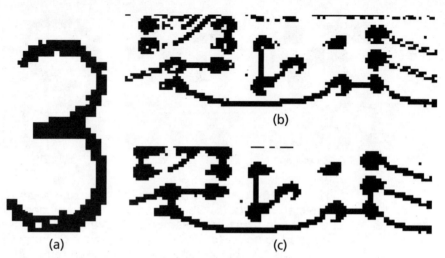

Figure 2.11 The closing operation. (a) The result of closing Figure 2.10d using the simple structuring element. (b) A thresholded image of a circuit board, showing broken traces. (c) The same image after closing, showing that most of the breaks have been repaired.

ber of erosions; N dilation/erosion applications should result in the smoothing of irregularities of N pixels in size.

First consider the smoothing application, and for this purpose Figure 2.11a will be used as an example. This image has been both opened and closed already, and another closing will not have any effect. However, the outline is still jagged, and there are still white holes in the body of the object. An opening of depth 2 (that is, two dilations followed by two erosions) gives Figure 2.12a. Note that the holes have been closed, and that most of the outline irregularities are gone. On opening of depth 3 very little change is seen (one outline pixel is deleted), and no further improvement can be hoped for. The example of the chess piece in the same figure shows more specifically the kind of irregularities introduced sometimes by thresholding, and illustrates the effect that closing can have in this case.

Most opening and closings use the simple structuring element in practice. The traditional approach to computing an opening of depth N is to perform N consecutive binary erosions followed by N binary dilations. This means that computing all of the openings of an image up to depth ten requires that 110 erosions or dilations be performed. If erosion and dilation are implemented in a naive fashion, this will require 220 passes through the image. The alternative is to save each of the ten erosions of the original image; each of these is then dilated by the proper number of iterations to give the ten opened images. The amount of storage required

(a)   (b)   (c)   (d)   (e)   (f)

Figure 2.12 Multiple closings for outline smoothing. (a) Glyph from Figure 2.11a after a depth 2 closing. (b) After a depth 3 closing. (c) A chess piece. (d) Thresholded chess piece showing irregularities in the outline and some holes. (e) Chess piece after closing. (f) Chess piece after a depth 2 closing.

for this latter option can be prohibitive, and if file storage is used the I/O time can be large also.

A fast erosion method is based on the *distance map* of each object, where the numerical value of each pixel is replaced by new value representing the distance of that pixel from the nearest background pixel. Pixels on a boundary would have a value of 1, being that they are one pixel width from a background pixel; pixels that are two widths from the background would be given a value of 2, and so on. The result has the appearance of a contour map, where the contours represent the distance from the boundary. For example, the object shown in Figure 2.13a has the distance map shown in Figure 2.13b. The distance map contains enough information to perform an erosion by any number of pixels in just one pass through the image; in other words, all erosions have been encoded into one image. This *globally eroded* image can be produced in just two passes through the original image, and a simple thresholding operation will give any desired erosion.

There is also a way, similar to that of global erosion, to encode all possible openings as one grey-level image, and all possible closings can be computed at the same time. First, as in global erosion, the distance map of the image is found. Then all pixels that do NOT have at least one neighbor nearer to the background and one neighbor more distant are located and marked: These will be called nodal pixels. Figure 2.13c shows the nodal pixels associated with the object of Figure 2.13a. If the distance map is thought of as a three-dimensional surface where the distance from the background is represented as height, then every pixel can be thought of as being the peak of a pyramid having a standardized slope. Those peaks that are not included in any other pyramid are the nodal pixels. One way to locate nodal pixels is to scan the distance map, looking at all object pixels; find the minimum (or MIN) and maximum (or MAX) value of all neighbors of the

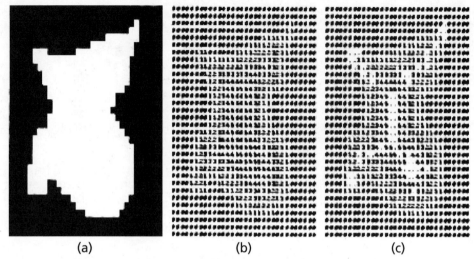

(a) (b) (c)

Figure 2.13 Erosion using a distance map. (a) A blob as an example of an image to be eroded. (b) The distance map of the blob image. (c) Nodal pixels in this image are shown as periods (".").

target pixel, and compute MAX-MIN. If this value is less than the maximum possible, which is 2 when using 8-distance, then the pixel is nodal.

To encode all openings of the object, a digital disk is drawn centered at each nodal point. The pixel values and the extent of the disk are equal to the value of the nodal pixel. If a pixel has already been drawn, then it will take on the larger of its current value or the new one being painted. The resulting object has the same outline as the original binary image, so the object can be recreated from the nodal pixels alone. In addition, the grey levels of this globally opened image represent an encoding of all possible openings. As an example, consider the disk shaped object in Figure 2.14a and the corresponding distance map of Figure 2.14b. There are nine nodal points: Four have the value 3, and the remainder have the value 5. Thresholding the encoded image yields an opening having depth equal to the threshold.

All possible closings can be encoded along with the openings if the distance map is changed to include the distance of background pixels from an object. Closings are coded as values less than some arbitrary central value (say, 128) and openings are coded as values greater than this central value.

As a practical case, let's consider an example from geology. To a geologist the pores that exist in oil-bearing (reservoir) rock are of substantial interest; it is in these pores that the oil resides. Porosity of reservoir rock can be measured by slicing the rock into thin sections after filling the pores with a colored resin. The

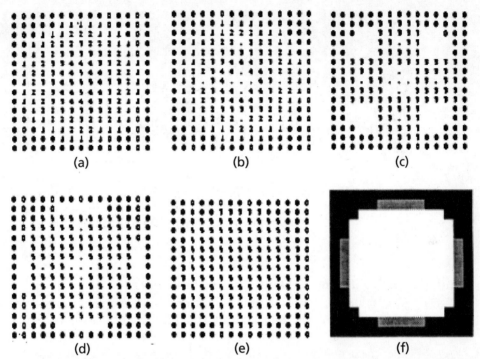

Figure 2.14 Global opening of a disk-shaped object. (a) Distance map of the original object. (b) Nodal pixels identified. (c) Regions grown from the pixels with value 3. (d) Regions grown from pixels with value 5. (e) Globally opened image. (f) Globally opened image drawn as pixels.

slices show microscopic features of grain and pore space, and one method of characterizing the shapes of the pores is to examine the differences between openings of increasing depth. Openings of higher orders are smoother than those of lower orders, and the difference between the order N opening and the order $N + 1$ opening is referred to as the *roughness* of order N. The histogram of the pixels in each opened pore image by order of roughness yields a *roughness spectrum*, which has been extensively applied to the classification of pore shape.

Figure 2.15 is a sample reservoir rock pore image having a size of 300×300 pixels. The results of opening using the distance encoded image are identical with the results from the traditional erode-dilate method, although all openings were found in only three passes through the image. Two sample openings are shown, with the deleted pixels shown in grey. The roughness spectrum can be calculated by repeatedly thresholding the image and counting the pixels remaining after each step, but there is an easier way. The roughness spectrum can now be found by simply computing the grey-level histogram of the globally opened image.

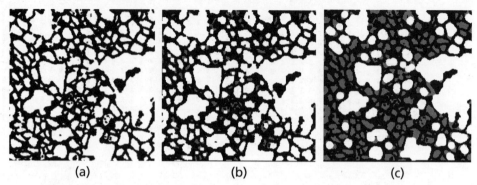

(a) (b) (c)

Figure 2.15 Computing the roughness of reservoir rock pores. (a) A pore image. (b) Opening of depth 3. Grey areas are pixels that have been changed. (c) Opening of depth 6.

A High-Level Programming Language for Morphology

Many of the tools needed for experimenting with morphology are provided in this chapter and on the accompanying CD in the form of C functions and procedures. However, their use requires a certain fluency in the C language, and any given experiment may involve a sequence of compilation/test/debug steps that can be time consuming. To avoid this, and to encourage experimentation with morphological techniques, a programming language named MAX (Morphology And eXperimentation) has been devised. MAX is a very simple language in the style of Pascal and Modula; its sole purpose is to evaluate morphological expressions.

To help explain the use of MAX, here is a simple program that reads in two images and copies them to new image files:

```
//Test of input and output in MAX.
//
image a, b;
begin
//Read in two images
   do a <<"a";
   do b <<"b";

//Copy them to new files.
   do b>>"copyb";
   do a>>"copya";
end;
```

The ''//'' characters being a comment, which extends to the end of the line. Any characters within a comment are ignored by the MAX compiler. The first statements in this program are declarations; all variables must be declared between the beginning of the file and the first begin statement. MAX recognizes only three types: IMAGE, which is used for both data and structuring elements interchangeably; INT, which is a traditional integer type; and PIXEL, which is a pair of integers that represent the row and column indices of a pixel in an image. Variables can be declared to be of any of these three types by stating the type name followed by a list of variables having that type. STRING constants are allowed in some cases, but there are no string variables.

The executable part of a MAX program is a sequence of statements enclosed by a begin at the beginning and an end at the end. A semicolon (;) separates each statement from the next in a statement sequence, except before an end statement. In the program above we see only one kind of statement: a DO. This is simply the word ''do'' followed by any legal expression, and permits the expression to be evaluated without assigning the value to anything.

The only operators seen above are ''<<'' (input) and ''>>'' (output), in this case applied to images. The expression (a<<''a'' reads an image in PBM file format from the file name ''a'' into the image variable a; if the string constant is the empty string '''', then standard input is used as the input file, and if the string is ''$1'' then the first command line argument is copied into the string, allowing a program to open dynamically specified file. In the program above, two images are read into variables. These are immediately written out again under different names: the output operator ''>>'' works in the same way as the input operator, creating a PBM image file from the specified image.

MAX has six different types of statement, designed to allow a great deal of flexibility in what kinds of morphological operations can be easily implemented. In summary, the legal statements are:

if (*expression*) then *statement*

If the expression evaluates to a nonzero integer (TRUE), then the statement that follows will be executed. The statement can be a sequence of statements enclosed by begin–end.

if (*expression*) then *statement1* else *statement2*

As above, but if the expression is 0 (FALSE) then *statement2* is executed.

loop . . . end

Repeat a sequence of code. When the end is reached, execution resumes from the statement following the loop statement. Statements within the loop must be separated by semicolons.

exit *N* when *expression*

Exit from a loop if the expression evaluates to a nonzero integer. If N is omitted, the exit branches to the statement following the end of the nearest enclosing loop. If $N = 2$, then we escape from the nearest two nested loops, and so on.

do *expression*

Evaluate the expression. Useful for input and output, mainly.

message *expression*

Print a message to standard output. If the expression is a string constant then that string is printed on the screen; integers and pixels can also be printed, and images will be printed as a two-dimensional array of integers as if they were structuring elements.

Assignment

The assignment operator is ``:=``. The type of the variable on the left of the assignment operator must agree with the expression on the right of it. If the expression is an image, the result of the assignment is a copy of that image.

For a small language there is quite an array of operators in MAX, and many of these can operate on all three possible data types. Table 2.1 is a convenient summary of all of the legal MAX operators.

Parentheses can be used in expressions to specify the order of evaluation. There is no precedence implicit in the operators other than that unary operators will be computed before binary ones, and evaluation is otherwise left to right.

There is a collection of test programs named t1.max through t30.max; any MAX program must have the *.max* suffix. Running a compiler is quite simple. The command:

```
MAX t1.max
```

will compile the program t1.max into C code file called t1.c. On some systems this will be automatically compiled into the object file t1.exe. In order for the C compilation to be successful, the files max.h and max-lib.o must be in the same working directory.

As a tool for education and as a test bed for morphological experimentation and testing of structuring elements, MAX is unique (if perhaps not perfect). For example, the program BinDil can now be written:

```
//Dilation using ++
image a, b;
begin
        do (a<<"$1")++(b<<"$2")>>"$3"
end;
```

Table 2.1 Legal MAX Operators

Operator	Left	Right	Result	Description
±±	image	image	image	Dilate LEFT by RIGHT. EG A++B.
−−	image	image	image	Erode LEFT by RIGHT. EG A−−B.
<=	image	image	int	Subset: Is LEFT a subset of RIGHT?
<=	int	int	int	Less than or equal to (integer).
>=	image	image	int	Subset: Is RIGHT a subset of LEFT?
>=	int	int	int	Greater or equal (integer).
>	image	image	int	Proper subset.
>	int	int	int	Greater than.
<	image	image	int	Proper subset.
<	int	int	int	Less than.
<>	image	image	int	Images not the same.
<>	int	int	int	Not equal.
<>	pixel	pixel	int	Not equal, pixels.
=	image	image	int	Are LEFT and RIGHT equal?
=	int	int	int	Integer equality.
=	pixel	pixel	pixel	Pixel equality.
=	image	int	int	Are all pixels in the image equal to the given integer?
−	image	image	image	Set difference, LEFT-RIGHT.
−	int	int	int	Integer subtraction.
−	pixel	pixel	pixel	Vector subtraction.
+	image	image	image	Union of images LEFT and RIGHT.
+	int	int	int	Integer addition.
+	pixel	pixel	pixel	Vector addition.
+	image	pixel	image	Add a pixel to an image (set value).
+	pixel	image	image	Add a pixel to an image (set value).
*	image	image	image	Intersection of LEFT and RIGHT.
*	int	int	int	Integer multiplication.
<<	image	string	image	Read an image from a PBM format file named by the string.
<<	int	string	int	Read an integer.
<<	pixel	string	pixel	Read a pixel (2 ints).
>>	image	string	image	Write an image to a PBM format file named by the string.
>>	int	string	int	Write an integer.
>>	pixel	string	pixel	Write a pixel (2 ints).
−>	image	pixel	image	Translate the image by the pixel.
<−	pixel	image	image	Translate the image by the pixel.
@	pixel	image	int	Membership: is the pixel in the image?

Table 2.1 (continued)

Operator	Left	Right	Result	Description
[]	[int, int]			Pixel generator. Result is the pixel whose ROW is the first int and whose column is the second.
.	image.rows			Each image has 4 attributes: number of rows and columns, and the row and column locations of the origin. These can be accessed by imagename.attrname.
.	image.cols			
.	image.origin_x			
.	image.origin_y			
.	pixel.row			
.	pixel.col			

Unary operators:
~		Set complement.
!		Allocate a new image like the given one.
#		The (integer) number of isolated pixels in an image.
−		Integer negation.

Image Generator:
{PIXEL1, PIXEL2, ''0110101 . . . ''}	Generates an image, whose size is given by PIXEL1, whose origin is given by PIXEL2, and whose pixels are specified by the string.

Figure 2.16 shows a MAX program for doing a dilation the hard way: By translating the structuring element to all pixel positions in the image being dilated and accumulating the union of all of these images (sets). From this point forward programs illustrating morphological operations will be written in MAX.

The "Hit And Miss" Transform

The hit and miss transform is a morphological operator designed to locate simple shapes within an image. It is based on erosion; this is natural, since the erosion of A by S consists only of those pixels (locations) where S is contained within A, or matches the set pixels in a small region of A. However, it also includes places where the background pixels in that region do not match those of S, and these locations would not normally be thought of as a match. What we need is an operation that matches both the foreground and the background pixels of S in A.

Matching the foreground pixels in S against those in A is a "hit," and is accomplished with a simple erosion $A \ominus S$. The background pixels in A are those found in A^c, and while we could use S^c as the background for S a more flexible approach is to specify the background pixels explicitly in a new structuring element T. A "hit" in the background is called a "miss," and is found by $A^c \ominus T$.

```
// MAX Program to perform a dilation the hard way.
//
int i,j;
image x, y, z;
begin
     i := 0; j = 0;
     y := !(x<<"$1");              // Allocate a result image like
                                                   x.
     do z<<"$2";                   // Read the structuring element.
     loop                          //For all indices i
     j :=0;
          loop                     // For all indices j
               if ([i,j] @ x) then // Is pixel i,j in the image?
                                   // Translate structuring element
                                                 by i,j
                                   // and OR the result (union)
                                               with y
                    y := y + (z->[i,j]);
               j := j + 1;         // Next j
               exit when j >= x.cols; // j exceeds maximum column?
          end;
          i := i + i;              // Next i
          exit when i >= y.rows;   //i exceeds max row?
     end;

     do y>>"$3";               // Output the result.
end;
```

Figure 2.16 MAX program to compute a dilation by repeated translations and unions.

We want the locations having both a "hit" and a "miss," which are the pixels:

$$A \otimes (S,T) = (A \ominus S) \cap (A^c \ominus T) \qquad \text{(EQ 2.13)}$$

As an example, let's use this transform to detect upper right corners. Figure 2.17a shows an image that could be interpreted as being two overlapping squares. A corner will be a right angle consisting of the corner pixel and the ones immediately below and to the left, as shown in Figure 2.17b. The figure also shows the "hit" portion of the operation (c), the complement of the image (d) and the structuring element used to model the background (e), the "miss" portion (f), and

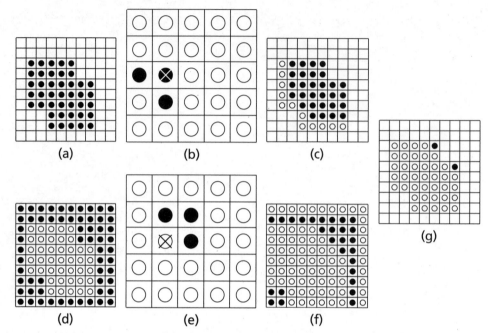

Figure 2.17 Illustration of the hit and miss transform. (a) The image to be examined. (b) Foreground structuring element for the location of upper right corners. (c) The erosion of (a) by (b)—the "hit" portion of the computation. (d) The complement of (a). (e) The background structuring element, showing that the three pixels to the upper right of the corner must be background pixels. (f) The erosion of (d) by (e), or the "miss" portion of the computation. (g) The intersection of (c) and (f)—the result, showing the location of each of the two upper right corners in the original image.

the result of the intersection of the "hit" and the "miss." The set pixels in the result both correspond to corners in the image.

Also notice that the background structuring element is *not* the complement of the foreground structuring element; indeed, if it had been, then the result would have been an empty image since there is no match to its peculiar shape in the complement image. The set pixels in the background structuring element are those that *must* be background pixels in the image in order for a match to take place. Overspecification of these pixels results in few matches, and underspecification results in too many. Careful selection, possibly through experimentation, is needed.

By the way, the upper and right pixels in Figure 2.17f are white because they correspond to locations where the structuring element 2.17e has black pixels placed outside of the bounds of the image. The complement operator produces an image of the same size as the image being complemented, although when using sets this would not be so. This problem can be avoided by copying the input image to a bigger image before doing the complement.

The MAX program that performs a hit and miss transform is:

```
//Hit and miss transform
image a, se1, se2;
begin
        do a<<"$1";
        se1 :={[5,5],[2,1],"0000000000110000100000000"};
        se2 :={[5,5],[2,1],"0000001100001000000000000"};

        a :=(a--se1)*(~a--se2);
        message a;
end;
```

Identifying Region Boundaries

The pixels on the boundary of an object are those that have at least one neighbor that belongs to the background. Because *any* background neighbor is involved it cannot be known in advance which neighbor to look for, and a single structuring element that would allow an erosion or dilation to detect the boundary can't be constructed. This is in spite of the fact that an erosion by the simple structuring element removes exactly these pixels!

On the other hand, this fact can be used to design a morphological boundary detector. The boundary can be stripped away using an erosion and the eroded image can then be subtracted from the original. This should leave only those pixels that were eroded; that is, the boundary. This can be formally written as:

$$Boundary = A - (A \ominus simple) \tag{EQ 2.14}$$

A MAX program for this is:

```
//Boundary extraction
image a, b, c;
begin
    do a <<"$1";
    b :={[3,3][1,1], "111111111"}; //SIMPLE structuring
                                    //element
    c :=(a-(a--b));
    message c;
    do c>> "boundary.pbm";
end;
```

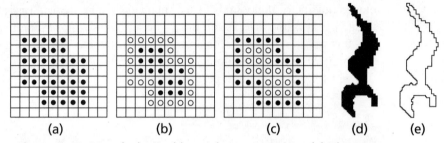

Figure 2.18 Morphological boundary extraction. (a) The squares image. (b) The squares image after an erosion by the simple structuring element. (c) Difference between the squares image and the eroded image: the boundary. (d) A musical quarter rest, scanned from a document. (e) The boundary of the quarter rest as found by this algorithm.

Figure 2.18 shows this method used to extract the boundaries of the "squares" image of Figure 2.17a. A larger example, that of a quarter rest scanned from a page of sheet music, also appears in the figure.

Conditional Dilation

There are occasions when it is desirable to dilate an object in such a way that certain pixels remain immune. If, for example, an object cannot occupy certain parts of an image, then a dilation of the object must not intrude into that area. In that case, a *conditional dilation* can be performed. The forbidden area of the image is specified as a second image in which the forbidden pixels are black (1). The notation for conditional dilation will be:

$$A \oplus (S_e, A') \tag{EQ 2.15}$$

where S_e is the structuring element to be used in the dilation, and A' is the image representing the set of forbidden pixels.

One place where this is useful is in segmenting an image. Determining a good threshold for grey-level segmentation can be difficult, as discussed later in Chapter 3. However, sometimes two bad thresholds can be used instead of one good one. If a very high threshold is applied to an image, then only those pixels that are certainly supposed to belong to an object will remain. Of course, a great many will be missed. Now a very low threshold can be applied to the original image, giving an image that has too many object pixels, but where the background is marked with some certainty. Then the following conditional dilation is performed:

$$R = I_{high} \oplus (\text{simple}, I_{low}) \tag{EQ 2.16}$$

The image R is now a segmented version of the original, and it is in some cases a superior result than could be achieved using any single threshold (Figure 2.19).

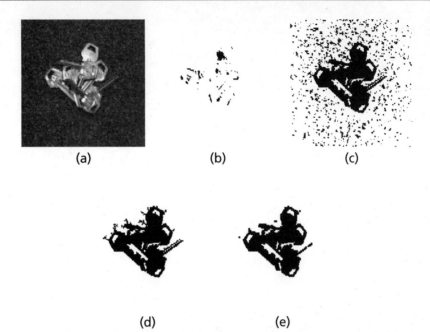

(a)   (b)   (c)

(d)   (e)

Figure 2.19 Conditional dilation. (a) Image of a pile of keys.
(b) Negative image resulting from use of a high threshold.
(c) Result of using a low threshold. (d) Conditional dilation of
(b) using the simple structuring element, conditional on (c).
(e) The result after being cleaned up—in this case by
using an opening.

The conditional dilation is computed in an iterative fashion. Using the notation
of Equation 2.15, let $A_0 = A$. Each step of the dilation is computed by:

$$A_i = (A_{i-1} \oplus S_e) \cap A' \qquad \text{(EQ 2.17)}$$

The process continues until $A_i = A_{i-1}$, at which point A_i is the desired dilation.
A MAX program for conditional dilation is:

```
//Conditional Dilation
image a,b,c,d;
begin
     do a << "$1";                  //Input image.
     do c << "$2";                  //Forbidden image.
     b :={[3,3],[1,1],"111111111"};//Simple structuring
//element.

     loop
         d :=(a++b)*c;
         exit when d=a;
         a :=d;
```

```
        end;
        do a >> "$3";
  end;
```

Another application of conditional dilation is that of filling a region with pixels, which is the inverse operation of boundary extraction. Given an outline of black pixels and a pixel inside of the outline, we are to fill the region with black pixels. In this case the forbidden image will consist of the boundary pixels; we want to fill the region up to the boundary, but never set a pixel that is outside. Since the outside pixels and the inside pixels have the same value, the boundary pixels are forbidden and the dilation continues until the inside region is all black. Then this image and the boundary image are combined to form the final result.

The conditional dilation is:

$$\text{Fill} = P \oplus (S_{cross}, A^c) \tag{EQ 2.18}$$

where P is an image containing only the seed pixel, which is any pixel known to be inside the region to be filled, and A is the boundary image for the region to be filled. S_{cross} is the cross-shaped structuring element seen in Figure 2.20b. The same figure shows the steps in the conditional dilation that fills the same boundary that was identified earlier in this section. The seed pixel used in the example is [3,3], but any of the white pixels inside the boundary could have been used.

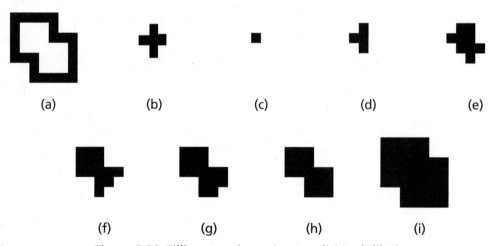

(a)   (b)   (c)   (d)   (e)

(f)   (g)   (h)   (i)

Figure 2.20 Filling a region using conditional dilation.
(a) The boundary of the region to
be filled. This is the boundary found in Figure 2.18. (b) The
structuring element. (c) The seed pixel, and iteration 0 of the
process. (d) After iteration 1. (e) After iteration 2. (f) After
iteration 3. (g) After iteration 4. (h) After iteration 5 the dilation is
complete. (i) Union of (h) with (a) is the result.

A MAX program for region filling requires the input of the coordinates of the seed pixel, which is the first time that integer input has been performed in a MAX program. It is:

```
//Fill a region with 1 pixels - Conditional Dilation
pixel p;
int i,j:
image a,b,c,d;
begin
 do a << "$1";
 message "FILL: Enter the coordinates of the seed pixel";
 do i << ""; do j << "";
 p :=[i,j];                  //SEED pixel.
 b :={[3,3],[1,1],"010111010"};
                        c :=!a+p;
 a := ~a;
 loop
      d :=(c++b)*a;
      exit when d=c;
      c :=d;
 end;
 do c+ ~a >> "$2";
end;
```

Counting Regions

As a final example of the uses of morphology in binary images, it is possible to count the number of regions in an image using morphological operators. This method was first discussed by Levialdi, and uses six different structuring elements. The first four are used to erode the image, and were carefully chosen so as not to change the connectivity of the regions being eroded. The last two are used to count isolated "1" pixels; in MAX this is done using the "#" operator, and so these structuring elements will not be needed.

Figure 2.21 shows the four structuring elements, named L1 through L4. The initial count of regions is the number of isolated pixels in the input image A, and the image of iteration 0 is A:

$$\text{count}_0 = \#A$$
$$A_0 = A$$

(EQ 2.19)

The image of the next iteration is the union of the four erosions of the current image:

$$A_{n+1} = (A_n \ominus L_1) \cup (A_n \ominus L_2) \cup (A_n \ominus L_3) \cup (A_n \ominus L_4) \quad \text{(EQ 2.20)}$$

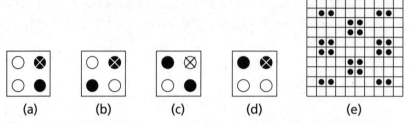

Figure 2.21 Counting 8-connected regions. (a)–(d) the structuring elements L1 through L4. (e) An example image having eight regions. The algorithm counts these correctly.

And the count for that iteration is the number of isolated pixels in that image:

$$\text{count}_{n+1} = \#A_{n+1} \qquad \text{(EQ 2.21)}$$

The iteration stops when A_n becomes empty (all 0 pixels). The overall number of regions is the sum of all of the values count$_i$. The MAX program that does this is:

```
//Count 8-connected regions.
image L1,L2,L3,L4,a,b;
int count;
begin
     L1 :={[2,2],[0,1],"0101"};
     L2 :={[2,2],[0,1],"0110"};
     L3 :={[2,2],[0,1],"1001"};
     L4 :={[2,2],[0,1],"1100"};
     do a << "$1";
     count :=0;
     loop
     count :=#a + count;
 b :=(a--L1) + (a--L2) + (a--L3) + (a--L4);
 exit when b = 0;
 a :=b;
 end;
     message "Number of 8 regions is"; message count; message;
end;
```

This program counts eight regions in Figure 2.21e, which is correct for 8-connected regions. It also counts two regions in Figure 2.10a, which is also correct, the algorithm for 4-connected regions is the same, but uses different structuring elements.

2.3 GREY-LEVEL MORPHOLOGY

The use of multiple grey levels introduces an enormous complication, both conceptually and computationally. A pixel can now have any integer value, so the nice picture of an image being a set disappears. There is also some question about what dilation, for example, should *mean* for a grey-level image. Rather than being strictly mathematical here we will take a more intuitive approach, in the hope that the result will make sense.

Consider the image of a line in Figure 2.22a. This is a bilevel image, and the dilation of this image by simple can be computed (Figure 2.22b). Now imagine that instead of having levels 0 and 1, the pixels in the line have the value 20 and the background is 0. What should a dilation of this new image by simple look like? The binary dilation spread out the line, as determined by the locations of the ''1'' pixels, making it three pixels wide instead of only one. The grey-level image should have a corresponding appearance after dilation, where the difference between the foreground and background pixels should be about the same as in the original and the line should be about three pixels wide. An example of how the dilated grey-level line (Figure 2.22c) might appear is given in Figure 2.22d.

This appears to be a reasonable analogue of dilation for the grey-level case, at least for a simple image. The image in Figure 2.22d was computed from Figure 2.22c in the following way:

$$(A \oplus S)[i,j] = \max\{A[i - r, j - c] +$$
$$S[r,c][i - r, j - c] \in A, [r,c] \in S\} \quad \text{(EQ 2.22)}$$

where S is the simple structuring element and A is the grey-level image to be dilated. This is one definition of a grey-scale dilation, and it can be computed as follows:

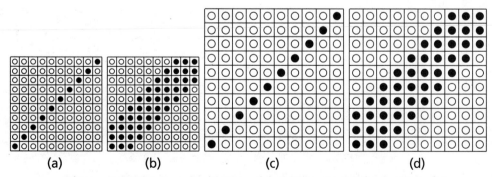

(a)   (b)   (c)   (d)

Figure 2.22 Grey-scale dilation. (a) A bilevel image of a line. (b) Binary dilation of (a) by simple. (c) A grey-scale image of a line; background is 0, line pixels have the value 20. (d) This is what the grey line should look like after a dilation.

1. Position the origin of the structuring element over the first pixel of the image being dilated.
2. Compute the sum of each corresponding pair of pixel values in the structuring element and the image.
3. Find the maximum value of all of these sums, and set the corresponding pixel in the output image to this value.
4. Repeat this process for each pixel in the image being dilated.

The values of the pixels in the structuring element are grey levels as well, and can be negative. Since negative-valued pixels can't be displayed, there are two possible ways to deal with negative pixels in the result; they could be set to 0 (underflow), or the entire image could have its levels shifted so that the smallest became 0 and the rest had the same values relative to each other as they did before. We choose the former approach for simplicity.

Given the definition of dilation in Equation 2.22, a possible definition for grey-scale erosion would be:

$$(A \ominus S)[i,j] = \min\{A[i - r, j - c] -$$
$$S[r,c][i - r, j - c] \in A, [r,c] \in S\} \quad \text{(EQ 2.23)}$$

This definition of erosion works because it permits the same duality between erosion and dilation that was proved in Section 2.2.

Figure 2.23 shows an application of grey-scale erosion and dilation to the image of keys first seen in Figure 2.19. The structuring element was simple made into grey levels. While it is not immediately clear why this operation is useful, the parallel with binary dilation and erosion is plain enough. Note, for instance, that dilation makes the small hole in the top of each key smaller, while the erosion made them larger.

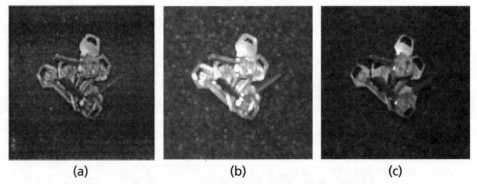

(a)   (b)   (c)

Figure 2.23 Grey-scale erosion and dilation. (a) Original.
(b) Dilated by simple. (c) Eroded by simple.

Opening and Closing

Opening and closing a grey-scale image is done in the same way as before, except that the grey-scale erosion and dilation operators are used; that is, an opening is a grey-scale erosion followed by a grey-scale dilation using the same structuring element, and a closing is vice versa. However, intuitively it is more useful to use a geometric model to see what is happening.

Consider a grey-level image to be a three-dimensional surface, where the horizontal (x) and vertical (y) axes are as before, and the depth (z) axis is given by the grey value of the pixel. A structuring element will also be a grey-level image, and in particular consider one that is spherical such as:

```
00000000000
00111211100
01122322110
01233433210
01235553210
02345654320
01235553210
01233433210
01122322110
00111211100
00000000000
```

Of course, this is only half of a sphere, and is only approximately spherical because of truncation error and sampling. Nonetheless, imagine this sphere being rolled over the underside of the surface represented by the image being opened. Whenever the center of the sphere is directly beneath an image pixel, the value of the opened image at that point is the highest (maximum) point achieved by any part of the sphere. The closing would be modeled by rolling the structuring element over the top of the surface and taking the lowest point on the sphere at all pixels as the value of the corresponding pixel in the closed image.

Figure 2.24 shows this process in two dimensions, as if viewing a cross section of the image. An opening, in this case, can be seen as a smoothing process that *decreases* the average level of the pixels, whereas closing appears to *increase* the levels. Figure 2.25 shows grey level opening and closing applied to the keys image of Figure 2.23.

One interesting application of opening and closing is in the visual inspection of objects. For example, when an object is cut or polished, there can be scratches left in the material. These become more visible if light is reflected off of the surface at a low angle and the object is seen from the side opposite the lighting source. Figure 2.26 shows an example of this, using a pair of disk guards from 3-½-inch-

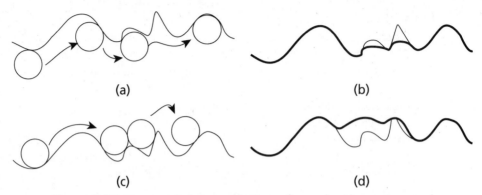

Figure 2.24 Geometric interpretation of grey level opening and closing. (a) A 'slice' through the image being opened, showing four positions of the structuring element. (b) The opened slice— the highest points of the circle at all pixels. (c) Rolling the circle over the top of the slice. (d) The closed slice—the lowest points of the circle at all pixels. These figures are approximations.

floppy disks. The guard on the right (2.26b) is scored, which can be seen clearly in the image.

The first step in the inspection process is to gain a good estimate of the location of the object being inspected. This is done by thresholding the image and then using the thresholded image as a mask: into an all-black image, copy those pixels from the original that correspond to a white pixel in the thresholded image (2.26d). The masked image is then closed using a circular structuring element with grey values. The result will be to raise the grey levels of the pixels in the defects to near that of the surrounding pixels, giving a clear image of the guard in the sampled

Figure 2.25 Examples of grey level opening and closing.
(a) Opened 'keys' image, using spherical structuring element.
(b) Closed 'keys' image using spherical structuring element.
(c) Opened using simple structuring element. (d) Closed using simple structuring element.

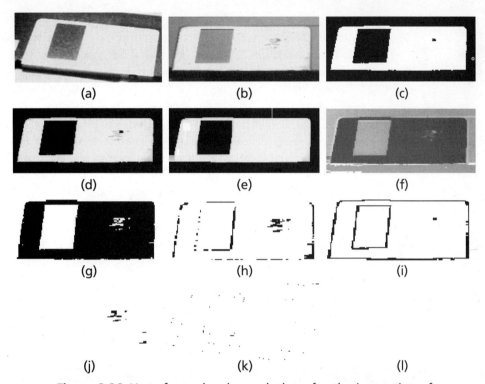

Figure 2.26 Use of grey-level morphology for the inspection of disk guards. (a) An acceptable disk guard. (b) A scored disk guard. (c) Image (b) after thresholding. (d) Thresholded image used as a mask to give an image showing mainly the guard. (e) Image (d) closed using a circle (rod). (f) Residual of images (b) and (d). (g) Thresholded version of the residual. (h) Image obtained by ANDing image (c) and image (g), showing some edges plus the defect in the guard. (i) Boundary of the thresholded guard image (c). (j) All pixels in ANDed image (j) that are near a boundary have been deleted. Remaining black pixels are potential defects. The same process applied to the 'good' guard image (a) showing (k) the ANDed image and (l) the image in (k) after removing edge pixels. No defects are reported here.

orientation. When the original is subtracted from this image, the defect will stand out in contrast to the guard (2.26f).

Thresholding will increase the contrast further, and the pixels that are white in both this image and the original thresholded image are of special interest (2.26h). Unfortunately, some of the pixels near the edges of the object(s) have been blurred a little, and so any pixels near the original boundary (as found by a morphological operation as well) are deleted, giving an image showing only potential defects as black pixels. As confirmation of this process, the image having no defects was also processed in the same way, and it shows no black pixels in the final image.

Many kinds of inspection tasks can be carried out in a similar way, including the inspection of paper for dirt, glass for bubbles, and wood and plastics for defects.

Smoothing

One possible smoothing operation involves a grey-level opening followed by a closing. This will remove excessively bright and excessively dark pixels from the image; such pixels can be the result of a noise process, but unfortunately might also be legitimate data values. The price to be paid for noise reduction is a general blurring of the image.

Figure 2.27a shows an image of a disk guard that has been subjected to Gaussian (normal distribution) noise with a standard deviation of 30. Figure 2.27c shows the result of morphological smoothing applied to this image; initially, it is not clear which image is to be preferred. However, the same two images after thresholding (Figures 2.27b and d) clearly demonstrate that the smoothing process eliminates much of the problem noise, which now shows up as a ''salt-and-pepper'' effect (and which would certainly create problems in later processing).

(a)   (b)

(c)   (d)

Figure 2.27 Grey-level smoothing. (a) Disk guard image subjected to Gaussian noise having a standard deviation of 30. (b) Thresholded version of (a) showing salt-and-pepper effect of thresholding the noise. (c) Image (a) after morphological smoothing. (d) Smoothed image after thresholding, showing less noise in the thresholded image.

The structuring element used to smooth the disk guard image was simple, but the choice would depend on the type of noise being cleaned up. One common problem is the appearance of *scan lines* in an image that was obtained by photographing a television or video screen. Figure 2.28 shows an example of this sort of structured noise. The structuring element was constructed by looking at the original noisy image in detail; the distance between scan lines was about nine pixels, and the grey values in the structuring element were chosen to be the differences between the grey level at the darkest point of the scan line and that of each of the following eight pixels in each column.

The result is surprisingly good. Figure 2.28c is the smoothed version of 2.28a, and while it is a little blurry, the scan-line noise has been significantly reduced; the same can be said for Figures 2.28d and 2.28e, which are the before and after versions of another sample taken from the same larger image.

Gradient

In Section 2.2 a method for identifying the boundaries of a bilevel object was discussed. The basic idea was to erode an image using the simple structuring element and then subtract the result from the original, leaving only the pixels that were eroded. This can be done with grey-level images too. The boundary detection operator can be expressed in the same manner as in Equation 2.14, and results in an operation not unlike *unsharp masking*, in which an average of a small (say, 3 × 3) region is subtracted from the original pixel at the center of the region. This procedure has an analog in photography.

Because the contrast is not as great in a grey-level image as in a bilevel one

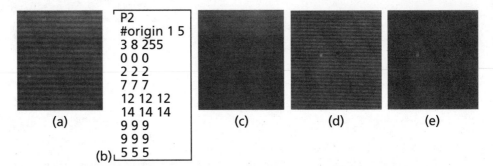

(a)

```
P2
#origin 1 5
3 8 255
0 0 0
2 2 2
7 7 7
12 12 12
14 14 14
9 9 9
9 9 9
5 5 5
```
(b)

(c)   (d)   (e)

Figure 2.28 Morphological smoothing used to reduce structured noise. (a) Small image section showing scan lines. (b) Structuring element used to reduce the scan lines. (c) Image (a) after smoothing. (d) A second example with scan lines. (e) Image (d) after smoothing with the element in (b).

the results of the boundary detection are not as good. However, an improvement can be achieved by using the formula:

$$G = (A \oplus S) - (A \ominus S) \qquad \text{(EQ 2.24)}$$

where S is a structuring element. Instead of subtracting the eroded image from the original, Equation 2.24 subtracts it from a dilated image. This increases the contrast and width of the extracted edges. Equation 2.24 is the definition of the morphological gradient, which detects edges in a manner than is less dependent on direction than is the usual gradient operator. Figure 2.29 shows both the boundary-detection algorithm (Equation 2.14) and the morphological gradient applied to the disk guard image. In all cases, the simple structuring element was used.

Segmentation of Textures

Closing removes dark detail, and opening will join dark regions. This suggests an application to textures, and the identification of regions in an image based on the textural pattern seen there. While this subject will be explored more fully in Chapter 4, a simple example at this point will probably not detract from later revelations.

If, for instance, one texture consists of small dark blots and another consists of larger dark blots, then closing by the size of the small blots will effectively remove them, but will leave some remnant of the larger ones. An opening by the size of

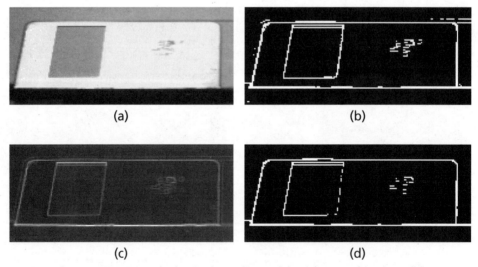

(a)

(b)

(c)

(d)

Figure 2.29 Morphological gradient. (a) Disk guard image. (b) Edges enhanced by the boundary extraction method of Equation 2.14 applied to grey-level images, then thresholded. (c) The morphological gradient. (d) Image (c) after thresholding.

the gaps between the large blots will join them into one large dark area. The boundary between the two regions should now be easy to identify.

An example of this can be seen in Figure 2.30. The original image has two regions filled with different textures; this image was created by a drawing package, so the textures repeat exactly, but this is not a requirement. Closing removes all traces of the smaller texture, and closing creates a solid black region where the larger texture had appeared. The morphological boundary extraction procedure can then be applied, giving a solid line along the margin between the two textures. The line is jagged wherever the boundary cuts a large blot in two, creating a small blot.

This method can be applied to a variety of textures, although some experimentation with structuring elements may be needed to achieve good results.

Size Distribution of Objects

The use of morphology for segmenting regions by texture suggests another application—the classification of objects by their size or shape. Since the use of

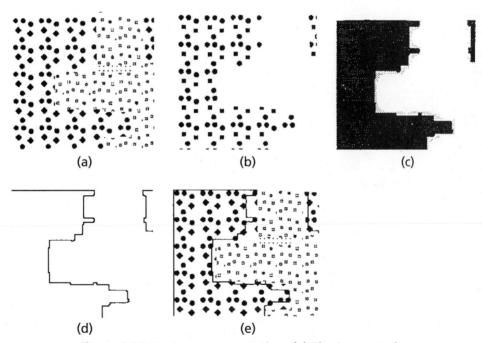

(a) (b) (c)

(d) (e)

Figure 2.30 Texture segmentation. (a) The image to be segmented. (b) After closing by the size of the small blots. (c) After further closing by the size of the spaces between the large texture blots. (d) The boundary seen in (c). (e) The boundary superimposed over the original texture image.

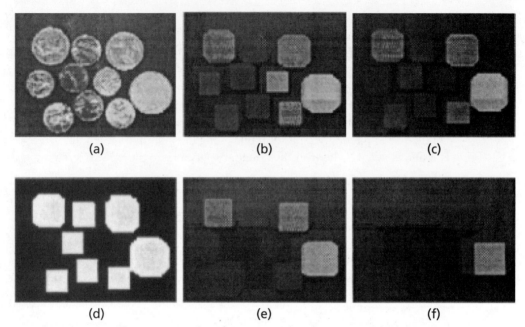

Figure 2.31 Classifying coins by their size. (a) The image containing coins to be classified. (b) After opening by a structuring element of radius 6. (c) After opening by radius 6.5. (d) Thresholded version of (c), showing that the dimes can be removed. (e) After opening by radius 8, showing that the pennies have been removed. (f) After opening by radius 10; the only coin remaining is the one-dollar coin.

shape would require quite a bit of experimenting with different structuring elements, size classification will be explored here. Quite a variety of objects are regularly classified according to their size, from biological objects under a microscope to eggs and apples. A ''grade A large'' egg, for example, should be noticeably bigger than a ''medium'' egg, and it should be possible to create a program for classifying eggs using grey-level morphology. However, since eggs are often graded using their weight, we will examine another case close to all of us—that of money.

As it happens, and not by accident, coins vary in size according to their value. A dime is the smallest, and a one-dollar coin is (if you can find one) the biggest. Figure 2.31a shows an image of a small collection of coins on a dark background. It is a mixture of U.S. and Canadian coins, since it was easy to obtain a Canadian one-dollar coin (called a *loon*).

Since a grey-level opening will decrease the level of an object, the image was opened with circular structuring elements of gradually increasing radius. At some

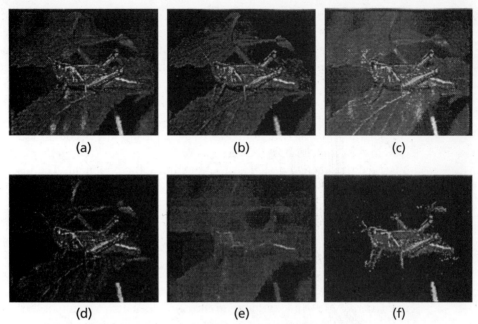

(a)   (b)   (c)

(d)   (e)   (f)

Figure 2.32 Color morphology. (a) Image of a grasshopper. (b) Red component of the RGB color image. (c) Green component. (d) Blue component. (e) Image resulting from closing the red and blue components and opening the green part. (f) Original image masked with the processed one, showing the insect.

point, when the radius of the structuring element exceeds that of the coin, the coin will be removed from the image. The radii actually used were those from 5 to 14; opening by a circular structuring element of radius 14 actually removes all coins, leaving a dark and empty image.

The first change is at radius 6.5 (diameter 13), where the dimes are reduced in level sufficiently that thresholding can delete them. An opening using a radius of 8 removes the pennies, allowing them to be counted.

Finally, an opening using a radius of 10 removes the quarters, leaving only the loon. By counting the regions that vanish after each iteration it should be possible to accumulate the total value of the coins in the image. In many countries the paper money also varies in size, allowing bills to be classified by size as well.

2.4 COLOR MORPHOLOGY

Color can be used in two ways. We can assume that the existence of three color components (red, green, and blue) is an extension of the idea of a grey level, or each color can be thought of as a separate domain containing new information. In either case, morphology is not commonly applied to color images, possibly because the construction of the structuring elements necessary to perform a particular task is really quite complex. Color morphology will only be touched on here through the use of a single example.

Figure 2.32a is a grey-level version of the color image on the back cover of this book; it shows an insect sitting on a leaf. Both the insect and the background are basically green, so automatically locating the insect could be a little tricky. On close examination of the three-color basis images (red, green, and blue), it is observed that there are slight variations in each component: The insect seems to be brighter in the red and blue images, whereas the background is brighter in the green image.

Closing the red and blue images should brighten the insect further, and opening the green image should suppress the background a little. A circular structuring element with a radius of four was used in each case. Following the closings and opening the three component images were recombined to form a single color image. The insect is now a bright pinkish color, and can be seen in sharp contrast to the darker green background. Figure 2.32e is a grey version of this color image, but the insect is still clearly present. Using this image as a mask of the original will give an isolated picture of the insect, or at least most of it, as seen in Figure 2.32f, and on the back cover, in color.

2.5 BIBLIOGRAPHY

Dougherty, E. R. 1992. *An Introduction to Morphological Image Processing*. Bellingham, WA: SPIE Press.

Dougherty, E. R. and C. R. Giardina. 1987. *Matrix Structured Image Processing*. Englewood Cliffs, NJ: Prentice-Hall.

Ehrlich, R., Crabtree, S. J., Kennedy, S. K., and R. L. Cannon. 1984. Petrographic Image Analysis, I. Analysis of Reservoir Pore Complexes. *Journal of Sedimentary Petrology*. Vol. 54. 4:1365–1378.

Giardina, C. R. and E. R. Dougherty. 1988. *Morphological Methods in Image and Signal Processing*. Englewood Cliffs, NJ: Prentice-Hall.

Gonzalez, R. C. and R. E. Woods. 1992. *Digital Image Processing*. Reading, MA: Addison-Wesley.

Haralick, R. M. and L. Shapiro. 1992. *Computer and Robot Vision* (Vol. 1). Reading, MA: Addison-Wesley.

Haralick, R. M., Sternberg, S. R., and X. Zhuang. 1987. Image Analysis Using Mathematical Morphology. *IEEE Transactions on Pattern Analysis and Machine Intelligence*. Vol. PAMI-9. 44:532–550.

Levialdi, S. 1972. On Shrinking Binary Picture Patterns, *Communications of the ACM*. Vol. 15. 1:7–10.

Meyer, H. and S. Beucher. 1990. Morphological Segmentation, *Journal of Visual Communication and Image Representation*, Vol. 1. 1:21–46.

Parker, J. R. and D. Horsley. Grey Level Encoding of Openings and Closings. *SPIE Vision Geometry II*. Boston: Sept. 9–10, 1993.

Schonfeld, D. and J. Goutsias. 1991. Optimal Morphological Pattern Restoration From Noisy Binary Images. *IEEE Transactions on Pattern Analysis and Machine Intelligence*. Vol. 13. 1:14–29.

Serra, J. 1982. *Image Analysis and Mathematical Morphology*. New York, NY: Academic Press.

Serra, J. 1988. *Image Analysis and Mathematical Morphology, Volume 2*. New York, NY: Academic Press.

Shih, F. Y. C. and O. R. Mitchell. 1989. Threshold Decomposition of Grey Scale Morphology into Binary Morphology. *IEEE Transactions on Pattern Analysis and Machine Intelligence*. Vol. 11. 1:31–42.

Sternberg, S. R. 1986. Grayscale Morphology. *Computer Vision, Graphics, and Image Processing*. Vol. 35. 333–335.

3

ADVANCED METHODS IN GREY-LEVEL SEGMENTATION

3.1 BASICS OF GREY-LEVEL SEGMENTATION

Grey-level segmentation, or *thresholding*, is a conversion between a grey-level image and a *bilevel* (or *monochrome*, or *black and white*) image. A bilevel image should contain all of the essential information concerning the number, position, and shape of objects while containing a lot less information. The essential reason for classifying pixels by grey level is that pixels with similar levels in a nearby region usually belong to the same object, and reducing the complexity of the data simplifies many recognition and classification procedures. Thresholding is almost essential before thinning, vectorization, and morphological operations.

The most common way to convert between grey-level and bilevel images is to select a single threshold value. All of the grey levels below this value will be classified as black (0), and those above will be white (1). The segmentation problem becomes one of selecting the proper value for the threshold T. What is being assumed here is that the pixels in an image I belong to one of two classes based on their grey level. The first class is the collection of black pixels, which will be given the value one, and for this class:

$$I(i,j) < T \qquad \text{(EQ 3.1)}$$

The other class consists of those pixels that will become white:

$$I(i,j) \geq T \qquad \text{(EQ 3.2)}$$

This assumption is only true in some real images because of noise and illumination effects. It is not generally true that a single threshold can be used to segment an image into objects and background regions, but it is true in enough useful cases to be used as an initial assumption. For example, documents scanned on any reasonable scanner these days can be thresholded into text and background with one threshold.

The threshold must be determined from the pixel values found in the image. Some measurement of a set of properties is made on the image, and from these (and from known characteristics of the image) the threshold is computed. One simple, but not especially good, example of this is the use of the mean grey level in the image as a threshold. This would cause about half of the pixels to become black and about half to become white. If this is appropriate, then it is an easy computation to perform. However, few images will be half black. The program that thresholds an image in this way appears on the CD, and is named thrmean.c. It takes two arguments: the first is the image to be thresholded, and the second is the name of the file in to which the thresholded image will be written.

Although fixing the percentage of black pixels at 50% is not a good idea, there are some image types that have a relatively fixed ratio of white to black pixels; text images are a common example. On a given page of text having known type styles and sizes, the percentage of black pixels should be approximately constant. For example, on a sample of ten pages from this book, the percentage of black pixels varied from 8.46% to 15.67%, with the smaller percentage being due to the existence of some equations on that page. Therefore, a threshold that would cause about 15% of the pixels to be black could be applied to this sort of image with the expectation of reasonable success.

An easy way to find a threshold of this sort is by using the histogram of the grey levels in the image. Given a histogram and the percentage of black pixels desired, determine the number of black pixels by multiplying the percentage by the total number of pixels. Then simply count the pixels in histogram bins, starting at bin 0, until the count is greater than or equal to the desired number of black pixels. The threshold is the grey level associated with last bin counted. This method appears on the CD as the program thrpct.c; the third argument to the program is the percentage of black pixels, where 50 would be 50% (as opposed to 0.5, which would be 0.5%). This method is quite old, and is sometimes called the *p-tile* method.

Using the histogram to select a threshold is a very common theme in thresholding. One observation that is frequently made is that when a threshold is obvious, it occurs at the low point between two peaks in the histogram. If the histogram has two peaks, then this selection for the threshold would appear to be a good one. The problem of selecting a threshold automatically now consists of two steps: locating the two peaks, and finding the low point between them.

Finding the first peak in the histogram is simple: It is the bin having the largest value. However, the second largest value is probably in the bin right next to the largest, rather than being the second peak. Because of this, locating the second peak is harder than it appears at first. A simple trick that frequently works well enough is to look for the second peak by multiplying the histogram values by the square of the distance from the first peak. This gives preference to peaks that are not close to the maximum. So, if the largest peak is at level j in the histogram, select the second peak as:

$$\max\{((k - j)^2 h[k])|(0 \le k \le 255)\} \qquad \text{(EQ 3.3)}$$

where h is the histogram, and there are 256 grey levels, 0..255. This method is implemented by the program called twopeaks.c.

A better way to identify the peaks in the histogram is to observe that they result from many observations of grey levels that should be approximately the same but for small disturbances (noise). If the noise is presumed to be normally distributed, then the peaks in the histogram could be approximated by Gaussian curves. Gaussians could be fit to the histogram, and the largest two used as the major peaks, the threshold being between them. This is an expensive proposition, with no promise of superior performance—we don't know how many Gaussians there are really, how near the means are to each other, or their standard deviations (still, see Section 3.2.).

Using Edge Pixels

An edge pixel must be near to the boundary between an object and the background, or between two objects: that is why it is an edge pixel. As a result, the levels of the edge pixels are likely to be more consistent. Because they will sometimes be inside the object and sometimes be a little outside due to sampling concerns, the histogram of the levels of the edge pixels will be more regular than the overall histogram.

This idea was used (Weszka 1974) to produce a thresholding method based on the digital Laplacian, which is a nondirectional edge-detection operator. The threshold is found by first computing the Laplacian of the input image. There are many ways to do this, but a simple one is to convolve the image with the mask:

```
0    1   0
1   -4   1
0    1   0
```

Now a histogram of the original image is found *considering only those pixels having large Laplacians*; those in the 85th percentile and above will do nicely. Those pixels having a Laplacian greater than 85% of their peers will have their grey level appear in the histogram, while all other pixels will not. Now the threshold is selected using the histogram thus computed.

Using a better approximation to the Laplacian should give better results, but in many cases this simple procedure will show an improvement over the previous methods. The C program on the CD that computes a threshold using this method is called thrlap.c, and requires that the third argument passed to the program be the percentage value used to select the Laplacian values.

Iterative Selection

Iterative selection (Ridler 1978) is a process in which an initial guess at a threshold is refined by consecutive passes through the image. It does not use the histogram, but instead thresholds the image into object and background classes repeatedly, using the levels in each class to improve the threshold.

The initial guess at the threshold is simply the mean grey level. This threshold is then used to collect statistics on the black and white regions obtained; the mean grey level for all pixels below the threshold is found and called T_b, and the mean level of the pixels greater than or equal to the initial threshold is called T_o. Now a new estimate of the threshold is computed as $(T_b + T_o)/2$, or the average of the mean levels in each pixel class, and the process is repeated using this threshold. When no change in threshold is found in two consecutive passes through the image, the process stops.

This is designed to work well in a hardware implementation, in which the initial estimate of a threshold assumes that the four corners of the image correspond to background regions and the rest of the image is used as an estimate of the object grey levels. However, in a software implementation, the same threshold can be computed using the histogram. This should be faster, since the histogram is a one-dimensional array of fixed small size.

Starting with the initial estimate of the threshold T_0, the *kth* estimate of the threshold is (Thrussel 1979):

$$T_k = \frac{\sum_{i=0}^{T_{k-1}} i \cdot h[i]}{2 \sum_{i=0}^{T_{k-1}} h[i]} + \frac{\sum_{j=T_{k-1}+1}^{N} j \cdot h[j]}{2 \sum_{j=T_{k-1}+1}^{N} h[j]} \qquad \text{(EQ 3.4)}$$

where h is the histogram of the grey levels in the image. Again, when $T_k = T_{k+1}$ then T_k is the proper threshold. This is the actual method used in the C code for the program thris.c, which implements the iterative selection algorithm.

The Method of Grey-Level Histograms

The thresholding methods that are based on selecting the low point between two histogram peaks use the concept that object pixels and background pixels have different mean levels, and are random numbers drawn from one of two normal distributions. These distributions also have their own standard deviations and variances, where variance is the square of the standard deviation.

If there are two groups of pixels in the image, as suggested, then it is a simple matter to compute the overall, or *total*, variance of the grey level values in the image, denoted by σ_t^2. For any given threshold t, it is also possible to separately compute the variance of the object pixels and of the background pixels; these represent the *within-class* variance values, denoted by σ_w^2. Finally, the variation of the mean values for each class from the overall mean of all pixels defines a *between-classes* variance, which will be denoted by σ_b^2. This is the beginning of a method in statistics called *analysis of variance*, but we will not go too much further with it here. The important issue is that an optimal (in some respects) threshold can be found by minimizing the ratio of the between-class variance to the total variance (Otsu 1978); in other words:

$$\eta(t) = \frac{\sigma_b^2}{\sigma_t^2}$$

(EQ 3.5)

defines the needed ratio, and the value of t that gives the smallest value for η is the best threshold. Since σ_t^2 is the overall variance it is easy to calculate from the image, as is the overall mean μ_T. The between class variance is calculated by:

$$\sigma_b^2 = \omega_0 \omega_1 (\mu_0 \mu_1)^2$$

(EQ 3.6)

where:

$$\omega_0 = \sum_{i=0}^{t} p_i \quad \omega_1 = 1 - \omega_0$$

(EQ 3.7)

and p_i is the probability of grey level i, or the histogram value at i divided by the total number of pixels. Also,

$$\mu_0 = \frac{\mu_t}{\omega_0} \quad \mu_1 = \frac{\mu_T - \mu_t}{1 - \omega_0} \quad \mu_t = \sum_{i=0}^{t} i \cdot p_i$$

(EQ 3.8)

All of these values are quite easy to calculate from the histogram of the image. Then $\eta(t)$ is computed for all possible values of t, and the t that gives the smallest η is the optimal threshold.

There is a program called thrglh.c on the CD that thresholds an image using this method. It is run in exactly the same way as thris.

Using Entropy

Entropy is a measure of information content. In information theory terms, assume that there are n possible symbols x (e.g., letters or digits) and that symbol i will occur with probability $p(x_i)$. Then the entropy associated with the source of the symbols X is

$$H(X) = - \sum_{i=1}^{n} p(x_i) \log(p(x_i)) \qquad \text{(EQ 3.9)}$$

where entropy is measured in bits/symbol.

An image can be thought of as a source of symbols, or grey levels. The entropy associated with the black pixels, having been thresholded using threshold t, is (Pun 1981):

$$H_b = - \sum_{i=0}^{t} p_i \log(p_i) \qquad \text{(EQ 3.10)}$$

where p_i is the probability of grey level i. Similarly, the entropy of the white pixels is:

$$H_w = - \sum_{i=t+1}^{255} p_i \log(p_i) \qquad \text{(EQ 3.11)}$$

for an image with levels 0–255. The suggested algorithm attempts to find the threshold t that maximizes $H = H_b + H_w$, which Pun shows to be the same as maximizing:

$$f(t) = \frac{H_t}{H_T} \frac{\log P_t}{\log(\max\{p_0, p_1, \ldots p_t\})}$$
$$+ \left[1 - \frac{H_t}{H_T} \right] \frac{\log(1 - P_t)}{\log(\max\{p_{t+1}, p_{t+2} \ldots, p_{255}\})} \qquad \text{(EQ 3.12)}$$

where

$$H_t = - \sum_{i=0}^{t} p_i \log p_i \qquad \text{(EQ 3.13)}$$

is the entropy of the black pixels as thresholded by t,

$$H_T = - \sum_{i=0}^{255} p_i \log p_i \qquad \text{(EQ 3.14)}$$

is the total entropy, and

$$P_t = \sum_{i=0}^{t} p_i \qquad \text{(EQ 3.15)}$$

is the cumulative probability up to the grey level t, or the probability that a given pixel will have a value less than or equal to t. These three factors can be computed from the grey-level histogram, and Equation 3.14 does not depend on t.

The program thrpun.c thresholds an image using this algorithm.

A variation on this theme (Kapur 1985) attempts to define an object probability distribution A and a background distribution B as follows:

$$A: \frac{p_0}{P_t}, \frac{p_1}{P_t}, \ldots, \frac{p_t}{P_t}$$

$$B: \frac{p_{t+1}}{1 - P_t}, \frac{p_{t+1}}{1 - P_t}, \ldots, \frac{p_{255}}{1 - P_t}$$

(EQ 3.16)

Now the entropy of the black and white pixels is computed in a similar way to Equations 3.10 and 3.11, but using these new distributions:

$$H_b = - \sum_{i=0}^{t} \frac{p_i}{P_t} \log\left(\frac{p_i}{P_t}\right)$$

(EQ 3.17)

$$H_w = - \sum_{i=t+1}^{255} \frac{p_i}{1 - P_t} \log\left(\frac{p_i}{1 - P_t}\right)$$

(EQ 3.18)

The optimal threshold is the value of t that maximizes $H = H_b(t) + H_w(t)$. To find this value, all thresholds between 0 and 255 are tried, and the one that gives the largest value of H is chosen. The C program thrkapur.c implements this algorithm.

Still another variation proposes to divide the grey levels into two parts so as to minimize the interdependence between them (Johannsen 1982). Without pursuing this in too much detail, the method amounts to minimizing $S_b(t) + S_w(t)$ where:

$$S_b(t) = \log\left(\sum_{i=0}^{t} p_i\right) + \frac{1}{\sum_{i=0}^{t} p_i}\left[E(p_t) + E\left(\sum_{i=0}^{t-1} p_i\right)\right]$$

(EQ 3.19)

and

$$S_w(t) = \log\left(\sum_{i=t}^{255} p_i\right) + \frac{1}{\sum_{i=t}^{255} p_i}\left[E(p_t) + E\left(\sum_{i=t+1}^{255} p_i\right)\right]$$

(EQ 3.20)

and where $E(x) = -x \log(x)$ is the entropy function. When implementing this algorithm, great care must be taken not to evaluate $S_b(t)$ and $S_w(t)$ for values of t where $p_t = 0$. As a detailed example of an entropy-based method, the C code for the function thr_joh is given in Figure 3.1. This is the function that does the bulk

```
void thr_joh (IMAGE im)
{
    int i, j, t= -1, start, end;
    float Sb, Sw, Pt[256], hist[256], F[256], Pq[256];
    unsigned char *p;

/* Histogram */
    histogram (im, hist);

/* Compute the factors */
    Pt[0] = hist[0]; Pq[0] = 1.0 - Pt[0];
    for (i=1; i<256; i++)
    {
     Pt[i] = Pt[i-1] + hist[i];
     Pq[i] = 1.0 - Pt[i-1];
    }

    start = 0; while (hist[start++] <= 0.0) ;
    end = 255; while (hist[end--] <= 0.0);

/* Calculate the function to be minimized at all levels */
    for (i=start; i<end; i++)
    {
     if (hist[i] <= 0.0) continue;
     Sb = (float)log((double)Pt[i]) + (1.0/Pt[i])*
               (entropy(hist[i])+entropy(Pt[i-1]));
     Sw = (float)log ((double)Pq[i]) + (1.0/Pq[i])*
               (entropy(hist[i]) + entropy(Pq[i+1]));
     F[i] = Sb+Sw;
     if (t<0) t = i;
     else if (F[i] < F[t]) t = i;
    }

/* Threshold */
    p = im->data[0];
    for (i=0; i<im->info->nr*im->info->nc; i++)
     if (*p < t) *p++ = 0;
     else*p++ = 255;
}
```

Figure 3.1 Source code for thr_joh, an entropy-based thresholding algorithm.

```
void histogram (IMAGE im, float *hist)
{
    int i;
    unsigned char *p;

    for (i=0; i<256; i++) hist[i] = 0.0;
    p = im->data[0];
    for (i=0; i<im->info->nc*im->info->nr; i++)
        hist[(*p++)] += 1.0;
    for (i=0; i<256; i++) hist[i] /=
        (float)im->info->nc*im->info;2>nr;
}

float entropy (float h)
{
    if (h > 0.0) return (-h * (float)log((double)(h)));
    else return 0.0;
}
```

Figure 3.1 (continued)

of the work for the program named thrjoh.c in implementing the algorithm outlined above.

Fuzzy Sets

In standard set theory, an element either belongs to a set or it does not. In a *fuzzy* set, an element x belongs to a set S with a particular probability u_x. When thresholding an image, we are attempting to classify pixels as belonging to either the set of background pixels or the set of object pixels, and the applicability of fuzzy sets to this problem seems apparent.

There have been a number of attempts to use fuzzy sets in image segmentation, but the one to be described here uses a measure of *fuzziness*, which is a distance between the original grey level image and the thresholded image (Huang 1995). By minimizing the fuzziness, the most accurate thresholded version of the image should be produced.

The first step is to determine the *membership function*, or the probability associated with the classification of each pixel as object or background. Let the average grey level of the background be μ_0 and that of the objects be μ_1. The smaller the difference between the level of any pixel x and the appropriate mean for its class, the greater will be the value of the membership function $u_x(x)$. A good membership function is:

$$u_x(x) = \begin{cases} \dfrac{1}{1 + |x - \mu_0|/C} & \text{if } x \le t \\[3mm] \dfrac{1}{1 + |x - \mu_1|/C} & \text{if } x > t \end{cases} \qquad \text{(EQ 3.21)}$$

for a given threshold t. C is a constant, and is the difference between the maximum and minimum grey levels. Any pixel x will be in either the background set or the object set depending on the relationship between the grey level of the pixel and the threshold t. For an object pixel ($x > t$), the degree to which it belongs to the object set is given by $u_x(x)$, which should be a value between ½ and 1.

Given the membership function, how is the degree of fuzziness of the segmentation measured for a given t? For example, if the original image is already bilevel, then a threshold of 0 should give exactly the same image back, and the fuzziness here should be zero. The maximum possible value of the fuzziness measure should probably be one. One way to measure fuzziness is based on the entropy of a fuzzy set (which is calculated using Shannon's function rather than as we have been doing). Shannon's function is:

$$H_f(x) = -x \log(x) - (1 - x) \log(1 - x) \qquad \text{(EQ 3.22)}$$

and so the entropy of the entire fuzzy set (the image) would be:

$$E(t) = \frac{1}{MN} \sum_g H_f(\mu_x(g))h(g) \qquad \text{(EQ 3.23)}$$

for all grey levels g, where N and M are the number of rows and columns, and h is the grey level histogram. This is a function of t because u_x is. Where $E(t)$ is a minimum, t is the appropriate threshold that minimizes fuzziness.

Another measure of fuzziness is based on the idea that for a normal set A there are no elements in common between A and its complement. For a fuzzy set, on the other hand, each element may belong to A and to A^c with certain probabilities. The degree to which A and its complement are indistinct is a measure of how fuzzy A is (Yager 1979). This can be calculated using the expression:

$$D_p(t) = \left[\sum_g |\mu_x(g) - \mu_{\bar{x}}(g)|^p \right]^{1/p} \qquad \text{(EQ 3.24)}$$

for levels g, where p is an integer and $\mu_{\bar{x}}(g) = 1 - \mu_x(g)$.

The value of p used defines a distance measure; $p = 2$ is used in the software here, which corresponds to a Euclidean distance.

Whichever fuzziness measure is used, an estimate for both μ_0 and μ_1 is needed. For a given threshold t we have:

$$\mu_0(t) = \frac{\sum_{g=0}^{t} g \cdot h(g)}{\sum_{g=0}^{t} h(g)} \qquad \text{(EQ 3.25)}$$

as the estimate of the background mean, and:

$$\mu_1(t) = \frac{\sum_{g=t+1}^{254} g \cdot h(g)}{\sum_{g=t+1}^{254} h(g)} \qquad \text{(EQ 3.26)}$$

as the estimate of the object mean, where both values depend on the threshold.

Now everything needed to minimize the fuzziness is known; simply try all possible thresholds t and select the one that yields the minimum value of the fuzziness measure. The C program thrfuz.c implements both measures described; the call

```
thrfuz sky.pgm thr.pgm ENTROPY
```

uses Equation 3.23 as the fuzziness metric, and the call

```
thrfuz sky.pgm thr.pgm YAGER
```

would use Equation 3.24.

Minimum Error Thresholding

The histogram of the image can be thought of as a measured probability density function of the two distributions (object pixels and background pixels). These are, as has been discussed, usually thought of as normal distributions, so the histogram is an approximation to

$$p(g) = \frac{1}{\sigma_1 \sqrt{2\pi}} e^{-((g-\mu_1)^2/2\sigma_1^2)} + \frac{1}{\sigma_2 \sqrt{2\pi}} e^{-((g-\mu_2)^2/2\sigma_2^2)} \qquad \text{(EQ 3.27)}$$

where σ_1 and μ_1 are the standard deviation and mean of one of the classes, and σ_2 and μ_2 are the standard deviation and mean of the other. After taking the log of both sides and rearranging, we get a quadratic equation that could be solved for g:

$$\frac{(g - \mu_1)^2}{\sigma_1^2} + \log \sigma_1 - 2\log P_1 = \frac{(g - \mu_2)^2}{\sigma_2^2}$$

$$+ \log \sigma_2 - 2\log P_2 \qquad \text{(EQ 3.28)}$$

However, the values of σ, μ, and P are not known, and they can be estimated only with some difficulty. Instead of that, Kittler and Illingworth (Kittler 1986) created a new criterion function to be minimized:

$$J(t) = 1 + 2(P_1(t) \log \sigma_1(t) + P_2(t) \log \sigma_2(t))$$

$$- 2(P_1(t) \log P_1(t) + P_2(t) \log P_2(t)) \qquad \text{(EQ 3.29)}$$

using formulas that should be starting to look familiar:

$$P_1(t) = \sum_{g=0}^{t} h(g) \qquad P_2(t) = \sum_{g=t+1}^{255} h(g) \qquad \text{(EQ 3.30)}$$

$$\mu_1(t) = \frac{\sum_{g=0}^{t} g \cdot h(g)}{P_1(t)} \qquad \mu_2(t) = \frac{\sum_{g=t+1}^{255} g \cdot h(g)}{P_2(t)} \qquad \text{(EQ 3.31)}$$

$$\sigma_1^2(t) = \frac{\sum_{g=0}^{t} h(g)(g - \mu_1(t))^2}{P_1(t)} \qquad \text{(EQ 3.32)}$$

$$\sigma_2^2(t) = \frac{\sum_{g=t+1}^{255} h(g)(g - \mu_2(t))^2}{P_2(t)} \qquad \text{(EQ 3.33)}$$

The value of t that minimizes $J(t)$ is the best threshold. This is often referred to as minimum error thresholding, and is implemented by the program thrme.c on the CD.

Sample Results from Single Threshold Selection

To this point 12 different threshold selection methods have been discussed, and it would be interesting to see how they compare by applying them to a set of sample images. Figure 3.2–3.4 show such a set, each having different properties that may present problems. Figure 3.2 is an example of an outdoor scene that will be re-examined later (Chapter 4) when discussing texture segmentation; this will be called the sky image. Figure 3.3 is a typical problem for grey-level segmentation, that being an image containing printed text. This will be called the pascal image. Finally, Figure 3.4 is a human face, which presents difficulties for many segmentation algorithms; it will be called the face image.

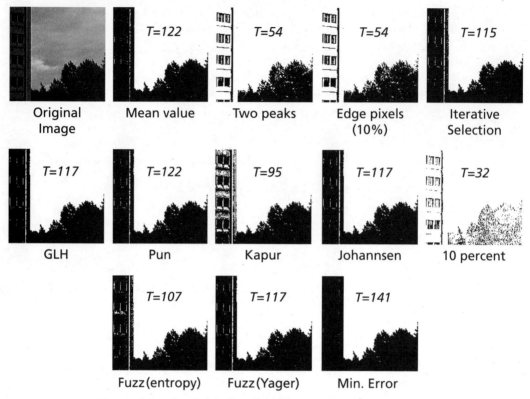

Figure 3.2 All twelve thresholding methods studied so far applied to the sky image.

Any discussion of the quality of the results would be subjective. Indeed, if a perfect quality measure were available, then it could be used as a thresholding algorithm. Still, it seems clear that the different methods perform well on different kinds of image. The minimum error method seems to deal best with the sky image, GLH with the pascal image, and Pun with the face image.

3.2 THE USE OF REGIONAL THRESHOLDS

So far in this discussion it has been presumed that the object pixels and the background pixels have non-overlapping grey levels. This need not be true, and leads to the conclusion that the selection of a single threshold for an image is not possible in all cases (perhaps not even in most). However, all that is needed is for the two classes of pixel not to overlap over each of a set of regions that collectively form the image. It may be that, for example, there is no single value that can threshold the entire image, but that there are *four* thresholds, each of which can threshold a

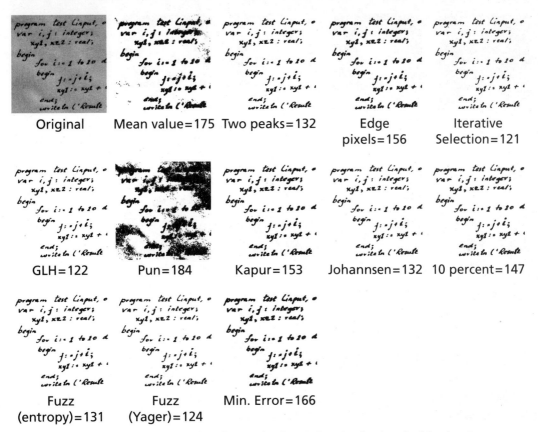

Figure 3.3 Sample results from the single threshold selection methods, using a handprinted text image (pascal).

quarter of the image. This situation still results in a segmentation of the whole image, but is simply more difficult to calculate.

The first issue with regional thresholds is the determination of how many regions are needed, and what the sizes of these regions are. Once that is done, it may be that any of the previously discussed algorithms can be used to give a threshold for each region, and the thresholding will simply be done in pieces. The number of regions can simply be dictated, by deciding to break up the original image to M subimages.

As an illustration, let's do an experiment. An image will be thresholded using iterative selection on overlapping 21×21 regions centered on each pixel. The threshold found in each region will be used only as a threshold on the pixel at the center, giving one threshold per pixel. There will, of course, be a 10-pixel-wide margin around the outside of the image that does not get thresholded, but that will

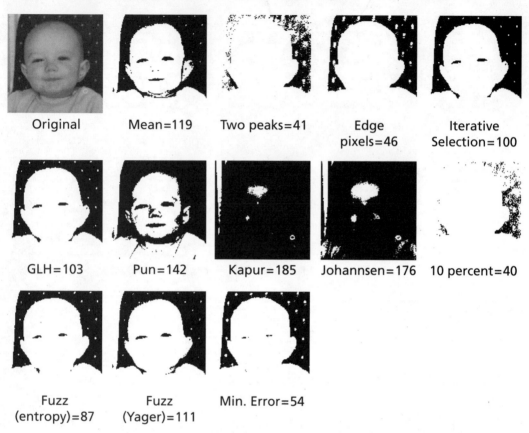

| Original | Mean=119 | Two peaks=41 | Edge pixels=46 | Iterative Selection=100 |

| GLH=103 | Pun=142 | Kapur=185 | Johannsen=176 | 10 percent=40 |

| Fuzz (entropy)=87 | Fuzz (Yager)=111 | Min. Error=54 |

Figure 3.4 Sample results from the single threshold selection methods, using an image of a human face (face). This is the most difficult of the three images to threshold.

be fixed later. What happens? The results for the sky image and the pascal image appear in Figure 3.5. (These images were created by the program thrmulis.c)

This is less than could be hoped for, but there is a simple explanation. The thresholding algorithm applied to each region attempts to divide the pixels into two groups, object and background, even when the region does not contain samples of both classes. When the region consists only of background pixels the algorithm tries too hard, and creates two classes where only one exists. It is therefore necessary, when using regional methods, to make sure that either each region contains a sample of both object and background pixels, or that no thresholding is attempted when only one pixel class exists.

Chow and Kaneko

This method (Chow 1972) divides the image into 49 overlapping regions, each one being 64 × 64 pixels; this division is for 256 × 256 pixel images, and is not

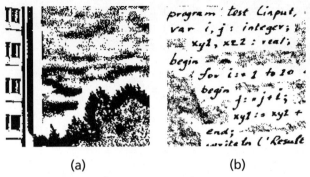

(a)   (b)

Figure 3.5 Using iterative selection to find a threshold for each pixel in the image. In all cases a square region of 21 × 21 pixels was used. (a) The sky image thresholded. (b) The pascal image thresholded. The method tries too hard to find object pixels, resulting in noise pixels being promoted to object pixels.

carved into stone. The histogram is found for each region, and a test of bimodality is performed. A bimodal histogram is presumed to have two classes of pixels represented, and a threshold will therefore exist between the two peaks. Each bimodal histogram then has a pair of Gaussian curves fit to it, using a least-squares method. This should more precisely locate the two peaks, allowing an "optimal" threshold to be selected for each region.

The thresholds for regions not having bimodal histograms are then interpolated from those regions that do, the assumption being that the region with the interpolated threshold is probably all background or all object, and a neighboring threshold will suffice. Finally, a pixel-by-pixel interpolation of the threshold values is done, giving every pixel in the image its own threshold. This algorithm historically forms the foundation of regional thresholding methods, and is frequently cited in the literature. Although it was originally devised for the enhancement of boundaries in heart X-rays (cineangiograms, actually) it is a very nice example of how to approach a vision problem.

A bimodal histogram can be expressed as the sum of two Gaussians, as expressed mathematically in Equation 3.27. We want to obtain the values for the mean, standard deviation, and scaling factor for each of the two Gaussians, and can do using a least-squares approach. First the histogram for the current window (a size of 16 × 16 was used) is found, and is smoothed in the following way:

$$F_s(i) = \frac{F(i - 2) + 2F(i - 1) + 3F(i) + 2F(i + 1) + F(i + 2)}{9} \qquad \text{(EQ 3.34)}$$

The smoothed version is less susceptible to noise than is the original. Now the histogram is divided into two parts at the lowest point in the smoothed version, which will be at index v. This assumption is that one of the Gaussians is to the left of this point, and the other is to the right of it. The initial parameters of each one can be estimated from the relevant portions of the histograms. The estimates are:

$$N_1 = \sum_{i=0}^{v} F(i) \qquad N_2 = \sum_{i=v+1}^{255} F(i) \qquad \text{(EQ 3.35)}$$

$$\mu_1 = \sum_{i=0}^{v} F(i) \cdot i \qquad \mu_2 = \sum_{i=v+1}^{255} F(i) \cdot i \qquad \text{(EQ 3.36)}$$

$$\sigma_1 = \sqrt{\frac{1}{N_1} \sum_{i=0}^{v} F(i) \cdot (i - \mu_1)^2} \qquad \text{(EQ 3.37)}$$

$$\sigma_2 = \sqrt{\frac{1}{N_2} \sum_{i=v+1}^{255} F(i) \cdot (i - \mu_2)^2} \qquad \text{(EQ 3.38)}$$

$$P_1 = \frac{\sigma_1 N_1}{\sum_{i=0}^{v} e^{-((i-\mu_1)^2/2\sigma_1^2)}} \qquad \text{(EQ 3.39)}$$

$$P_2 = \frac{\sigma_2 N_2}{\sum_{i=0}^{v} e^{-((i-\mu_2)^2/2\sigma_2^2)}} \qquad \text{(EQ 3.40)}$$

This is a slightly different form of Gaussian; the leftmost Gaussian is defined as:

$$G_1(x) = \frac{P_1}{\sigma_1} e^{-((x-\mu_1)^2/2\sigma_1^2)} \qquad \text{(EQ 3.41)}$$

and the rightmost is the same, but with subscript 2.

With these estimates used as our initial guess for the parameters of the two Gaussians, the sum of the squared residuals is minimized:

$$R(P_1,\mu_1,\sigma_1,P_2,\mu_2,\sigma_2) = \sum_{i=0}^{255} (G_1(i) + G_2(i) - F(i))^2 \qquad \text{(EQ 3.42)}$$

The original algorithm from 1972 used a FORTRAN program to do this, and this program is no longer available. However, the procedure powell from the book *Numerical Recipes in C* (Press 1988) seems to do an acceptable job in most cases. This procedure will minimize R by refining the estimates of the parameters. Since the *Numerical Recipes* code is not in the public domain, the source program for the Chow-Kaneko method was not included on the CD.

When the fit is complete, the bimodality of the two Gaussians is evaluated using four criteria. First, the means must differ by more than four grey levels ($\mu_2 - \mu_1$

> 4); the ratio of the standard deviations must be small, reflecting the fact that they are the same size within reasonable bounds ($0.05 < \sigma_1/\sigma_2 < 2.0$); and the ratio of the valley to peak must also be within a reasonable range. This last value is the smallest histogram value found between the two means divided by the smaller of the two values $F(\mu_1)$ and $F(\mu_2)$; its value should be less than 0.8.

If the histogram for the current window is not bimodal, then no threshold is selected for it. If it is bimodal, then the point of intersection between the two Gaussians is selected as the threshold. This point is found by solving the quadratic equation:

$$\left(\frac{1}{\sigma_2^2} + \frac{1}{\sigma_2^2}\right)t^2 + 2\left(\frac{\mu_2}{\sigma_2^2} - \frac{\mu_1}{\sigma_1^2}\right)t + 2\log\left(\frac{P_2\sigma_1}{P_1\sigma_2}\right) = 0 \qquad \text{(EQ 3.43)}$$

When two solutions exist, use the value of t that is between μ_1 and μ_2. In this way a threshold is chosen (or not) for each window. For each window not having a threshold, one is estimated from its neighbors, using a linear interpolation or simple weighting scheme. These are then smoothed by local weighted averaging using the following convolution-type mask:

$$
\begin{array}{ccc}
\frac{1}{\sqrt{2}} & 1 & \frac{1}{\sqrt{2}} \\[2mm]
1 & 2 & 1 \\[2mm]
\frac{1}{\sqrt{2}} & 1 & \frac{1}{\sqrt{2}}
\end{array}
$$

Finally, each pixel in the image is assigned a threshold estimated from the threshold of the surrounding four windows by linear interpolation. Figure 3.6 illustrates the situation for a pixel in between windows A, B, C, and D. For this case the threshold at the point P would be

$$T = \frac{bdT_A + bcT_B + adT_C + acT_D}{(a + b)(c + d)} \qquad \text{(EQ 3.44)}$$

The thresholds for pixels not having enough valid neighboring windows to perform an interpolation are simply taken from the nearest window having a threshold. This applies to pixels on the boundary of the image as well.

The algorithm outlined above is not exactly the Chow-Kaneko method, but is probably fairly close. It could be applied to the three test images of Figures 3.2–3.4 but this would not properly show off the advantages of multiple-region thresholding. Instead, an intensity gradient will be imposed on the images, as seen in Figure 3.7. A linear gradient, a Gaussian spot, and a sine-wave were superimposed over the existing images. The results, if thresholded using the best algorithm pre-

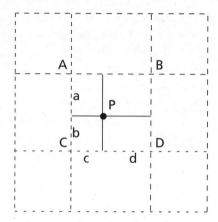

Figure 3.6 Linear interpolation of individual pixel thresholds. A, B, C, and D are the centers of adjacent windows, having thresholds T_a, T_b, T_c, and T_d. The distance a is the distance of the pixel P vertically to the point A; b is the distance from P vertically to C; c is the distance horizontally to C; and d is the distance horizontally to D.

viously found for that image, illustrate the problem resulting from using a single threshold.

Selecting one threshold per pixel or per region always takes longer than selecting a single threshold; sometimes substantially longer. Whether the results justify the extra time is something that must be judged on a case-by-case basis.

Modeling Illumination Using Edges

If the illumination falling on an object is known, then the task of segmenting the pixels belonging to the object is much simpler. This is because the intensity of a pixel in an image is proportional to the product of the illumination at that point and the color (reflectivity) of the object there. If the illumination gradient were known, then it could be factored out, leaving a relatively simple task of thresholding based only on the nature of the objects.

Figure 3.8 shows some images that have illumination problems, making them difficult to threshold. A single threshold will certainly not do the job for any of these images, and small regions will result in artifacts at the region boundaries. One threshold per pixel is best here, since any larger region may be subject to distortion through illumination effects. The method will decide what these threshold values are to be based on *local* properties of the image, specifically based on the levels of known object pixels. The confidence in the local threshold decreases with the distance from a known object pixel.

One approach to thresholding is based on the principle that objects in an image

(a)

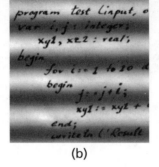

(b)

(c)

(d)

(e)

(f)

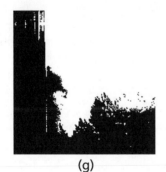

(g)

(h)

(i)

Figure 3.7 Badly illuminated images thresholded by Chow-Kaneko and by standard methods. (a–c) Show the original images with imposed illumination (sky, Gaussian; pascal, sine wave; face, linear). (d–f) The badly illuminated images thresholded using the best thresholding method from the previous trial. (g–i) The same images thresholded by Chow-Kaneko.

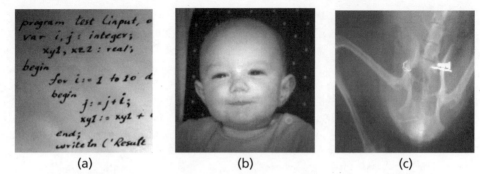

(a)   (b)   (c)

Figure 3.8 Difficult images to threshold, either due to illumination gradients or low contrast. (a) Pascal image with a linear illumination gradient. (b) The face image with a Gaussian gradient. (c) An X-ray image having generally low contrast, which is typical of X-rays.

provide the high spatial frequency component and illumination consists mainly of lower spatial frequencies. These two were multiplied together to produce the image. Another way to look at this is to say that the objects in an image will produce small regions with a relatively large intensity gradient (those being at the boundaries of objects), whereas other areas ought to have a relatively small gradient; this fact is used in many edge-enhancement algorithms. In this way a sample of the object pixels in an image can be found by looking for regions of high gradient and assuming that these pixels belong to an object that would appear as distinct in a thresholded picture.

This thresholding method involves first locating ''objects'' in an image by using the Shen-Castan edge detector (See Section 1.5) to locate pixels that belong to boundaries of objects. This edge detector has good localization properties, and a pixel that has been determined to be on an edge will be assumed to be a part of an object. The grey levels at edge pixels should be indicative of the levels elsewhere in object regions. A surface is produced that fits the levels at the edges, and this surface is presumed to give reasonable estimates of likely grey levels at object pixels that do not lie on an edge. Pixels significantly above this surface will be assumed to belong to the background, and those at or below it will belong to the object. This method is capable of thresholding images that have been produced in the context of variable illumination, and is called *Edge Level Thresholding* (ELT).

The method used to fit a surface to the edge points is a *moving least-squares* (MLS) scheme (Salkauskas 1981). This involves solving a weighted least-squares problem at each point in the plane. That is, if

$$J(x,y) = \sum_{i=1}^{N} w_i(x,y)(I(x_i,y_i) - S(x_i,y_i))$$

(EQ 3.45)

where N is the number of data points that are given by $I(x_i, y_i)$, $S(x,y) = ax + by + c$ and $w_i(x,y)$ are weights, then we find values for a, b, and c so that $J(x,y)$ is minimized at each point (x,y) in the plane. The weights depend on the evaluation points, and hence the requirement that we perform this minimization at each point.

The weight function $w_i(x,y)$ has several important properties. It essentially weights the data point (x_i, y_i) inversely according to its distance from the current evaluation point (x,y). If the data is further than some specified distance h from (x,y), we assume that it should have no bearing whatsoever on the height of the surface at that point, and so the weight is zero. Another parameter for the weight function, d, determines the fidelity of the surface to the data. When d is zero the weight is essentially infinite when the evaluation point is also a data point—the result is a surface that actually passes through all of the data, and this can lead to extreme fluctuations. As d increases toward 1, the fidelity increases and the surface relaxes, tending to average out fluctuations. When d = 1 our weight function is defined to be constant for all data, and no longer has compact support. The resulting surface is simply the standard least-squares planar approximation to the entire data set.

Since at every point we are looking for a least-squares plane, there is a rigid mathematical requirement that we have at least three data values in the disk of radius h centered at each point in the image. Without these, the linear system will be under-determined, and we won't be able to find a solution to the least-squares problem.

Others working on this problem have suggested methods for getting an approximation to the edge data, but these are all interpolants, and as we have previously mentioned, this is not necessarily desirable. One method described is a moving weighted average, which is simply an MLS method with $S(x,y) = a$. The resulting surface will have horizontal tangent planes or ''flat spots'' at each of the data points.

In addition, as the evaluation moves away from data, the value of the weighted average will tend to the actual mean of the data. This may cause unusual artifacts if the illumination gradient is actually linear. Figure 3.9 shows an example of weighted averages, restricted to the one-dimensional case. Figure 3.9b shows an example of the MLS method applied to the same data.

Implementation and Results

The ELT thresholding software consists of three major modules: the ISEF edge detector, the MLS surface fit, and the thresholding module. The function and sequence of execution is best described by using an example. Consider the image of Figure 3.8b, in which a bright Gaussian spot has been superimposed on the image of a map. The first step is edge detection by ISEF, and the result is shown in Figure 3.10a. Notice that clean edges are found even in the dark areas of the

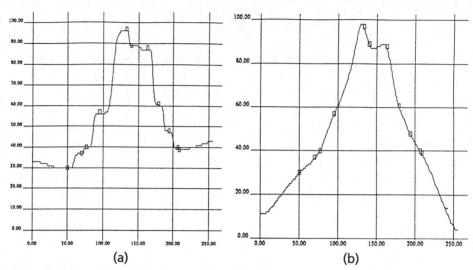

(a)   (b)

Figure 3.9 Weighted averaging VS moving least squares. (a) For a 1D sample, the weighted average method shows flat spots at each data point. (b) Moving least squares gives a smooth curve.

image. This is the secret of the ELT method: ISEF finds edges *very* well, and these edges are well localized.

Next, the grey levels at all edge pixels are used to form the basis of a surface, and the levels at the non-edge pixels are estimated from this surface, as found by the MLS procedure. For this case the surface is shown in Figure 3.10b as grey levels and in Figure 3.10c as a wire frame graphic. The value of the function at the edge pixels will be very near to the actual value of the corresponding image pixel, and will be assumed to be near to the value of non-edge object pixels as well. The final stage is a pass through the image, setting all pixels to zero if they are less than the value of the fit function +10, and setting them to MAX (255) otherwise. The results can be seen in Figures 3.10d–f.

In general, the results of ELT thresholding are better than other algorithms in situations of poor illumination, especially when compared to single-threshold methods. Standard methods give results that have large black areas where the illumination reaches low levels, and the objects can't be determined from the background. ELT permits widely varying thresholds across the image.

Comparisons

The ELT algorithm has been compared with other thresholding methods, and none has given the same results in widely varying illumination environments. A major problem is that ELT is quite slow at this time, taking many minutes to threshold even a 256 × 256 image. However, there are a few parameters to the algorithm

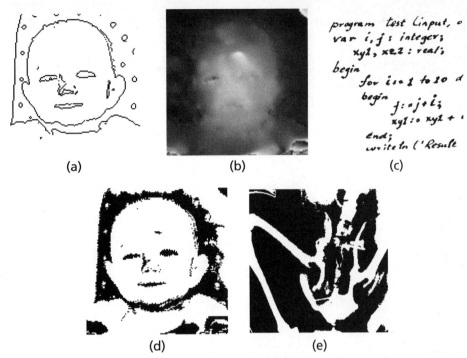

(a)   (b)   (c)

(d)   (e)

Figure 3.10 ELT example. (a) Shen-Castan edges for Figure 3.8b. (b) Surface fit to the edge pixels. (c) The thresholded version of Figure 3.8a. (d) Thresholded version of 3.8b. (f) Thresholded version of 3.8c.

that could be adjusted: for example, the MLS code used relies on a fixed value for the radius h for the entire image. This presents some problems, since in some regions a large radius is required so that we have at least three points, while in other areas the points are so dense that the same size disk will include hundreds of points.

3.3   RELAXATION METHODS

Relaxation is an iterative process. For the specific problem of image thresholding, the thresholds for any given iteration are computed as a function of those in the same neighborhood at the previous iteration. The scheme that will be followed is:

1. Create an initial guess at a segmentation for the image. Provide an estimate of the confidence in that guess at each pixel.
2. For each pixel, modify the segmentation and the confidence estimate based on the pixels in the local region; the surrounding eight pixels will do.

3. Repeat step 2 until the segmentation is complete. This might be when no further changes are seen in successive steps.

The confidence estimates have the appearance of probabilities, although they may not be accurate in that regard; all that matters is that they are fairly accurate with respect to the other pixels, especially those in the local neighborhood.

One way to find an initial classification is to use the mean grey level as a benchmark. A pixel greater than the mean has a probability of being white that is in proportion to the relative distance of its grey level from the level ¾ along the total range. For a pixel less than the mean we use ¼ of the grey level range. Thus, one possibility for the initial classification is (Rosenfeld 1981):

$$p_i^0 = \frac{1}{2} + \frac{1}{2} \frac{g_i - \mu}{max - \mu} \qquad \text{(EQ 3.46)}$$

This describes the situation for a pixel greater than the mean, where μ is the mean value, max is the largest grey level, and g_i is the grey level of pixel i. For pixels less than the mean we have:

$$q_i^0 = \frac{1}{2} + \frac{1}{2} \frac{\mu - g_i}{\mu - min} \qquad \text{(EQ 3.47)}$$

The value p_i^0 is the initial probability that pixel i is white, and q_i^0 is the probability that it is black. The superscript refers to the iteration, which is currently zero.

Now the problem is: Given that the probabilities of being white and black are known for a pixel and its neighborhood, how can the probabilities be refined so that they are driven to either end of the spectrum more clearly? Ideally these probabilities should become one or zero, giving a firm segmentation. What is needed is some measure of *compatibility*, which can be used to decide whether a particular classification is reasonable or not. For example, if a pixel is black and all of its neighbors are white, it would seem likely that the black pixel should become white. The compatibility of that pixel with its neighbors is low, suggesting a change.

Compatibility will be estimated by a function $C(i,c_1,j,c_2)$, which returns a measure, between -1 and 1, of how compatible pixel i (which is class c_1) is with pixel j (which is class c_2). For a thresholding problem there are only two classes, black or white, and for a small neighborhood the pixels i and j will be adjacent to each other. It is not possible to know for certain what this function should be, because it depends on probabilities found in the final thresholded image, and that is not known. However, a simple implementation would have $C = 1$ when $c_1 = c_2$, and $C = -1$ otherwise; that is, pixels are compatible if they agree.

Now, since there are two classes possible for any pixel, the average of these could be used as an overall compatibility between any two pixels:

$$Q_{ij} = C(i,c_1,j,\text{white})p_j + C(i,c_1,j,\text{black})q_j \qquad \text{(EQ 3.48)}$$

The compatibility of a region around the pixel i can be defined as the average compatibility of all eight neighbors:

$$Q_i(c_1) = \frac{1}{8} \sum_{j \in N} (C)(i,c_1,j,\text{white})p_j + C(i,c_1,j,\text{black})q_j \qquad \text{(EQ 3.49)}$$

for the one-pixel neighborhood N centered at i. This will be the net increment to p each time the probabilities are updated. However, to ensure that the p and q values remain positive, add 1 to Q. Then the values should be normalized over the region. This gives the following updating scheme:

$$p_i^{k+1} = \frac{p_i^k(1 + Q_i^k)}{p_i^k(1 + Q_i^k(\text{white})) + q_i^k(1 + Q_i^k(\text{black}))} \qquad \text{(EQ 3.50)}$$

where the superscript reflect the iteration number. A similar expression holds for the q values.

Each iteration of the relaxation process involves looking at all pixels in the image and updating the p (and q) values. Once a p becomes 0 or 1, it stays that way; thus, the initial classification is very important to the success of the method. In fact, the actual pixel values are never examined after the initial classification is complete; all further processing is performed on the probabilities.

Figure 3.11 shows some of the segmentations that result from the method, implemented directly from equations 3.46–3.50. These were created by the program relax.c, for which the source code can be found on the CD. It is clear,

(a)   (b)   (c)

Figure 3.11 Relaxation thresholding (a) The sky image. (b) The pascal image with sine-wave illumination. (c) The face image with linear illumination.

especially from the pascal image with sine-wave illumination, that something is wrong. Because a single mean for the whole image was used in the initial segmentation, the whole process gets off to a bad start. Areas that are too dark initially can never recover, except a little bit at the boundaries.

For this reason a modification was made to the program, which is found in the program relax2.c. In this version the initial classification is done using small regions of the image instead of the whole thing. The hope is that the more localized initial classification will now permit some of the illumination effects to be accounted for by the relaxation process. The results of this exercise can be seen in Figure 3.12. These images are a little better. It would appear that the relaxation approach, as implemented here, is quite sensitive to the initial classification.

Finally, as an illustration of the kind of experimentation that can be done, a new version of the relaxation program (called relax3.c on the CD) was devised. The function Q_i in Equation 3.49 does not make use of the actual grey levels in the image, and as a result the levels are never used after the initial classification is performed. This is changed in relax3.c so that the function Q_i returns a ''probability'' that is related to the difference in level of the two pixels involved. Pixels that are both supposed to be black in the segmented image should have levels that are near to each other; pixels that are supposed to be different should have differing levels.

Although the results are not significantly different from those of Figure 3.12, this version of the program was selected to appear in Figure 3.13 because it reflects an approach: Experimentation is to be encouraged. There are a great number of ways to update the probabilities, to weight the Q values, and to perform the initial classification. A good algorithm is soundly based in mathematics and good sense, but there is a lot of leeway in how it might be implemented.

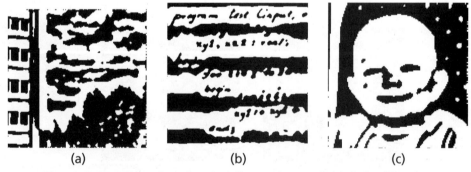

(a) (b) (c)

Figure 3.12 Relaxation thresholding, using an initial classification based on regional thresholds. These are better than those in Figure 3.11, but are not as good as some of the methods examined already.

```
/* Relaxation method 2 — Rosenfeld & Kak */

void thr_relax (IMAGE im)
{
        float res = 0.0, minres = 10000.0, **p, **q;
        int iter = 0, i, j, count = 0;

/* Space allocation */
        p = f2d (im—>info—>nr, im—>info—>nc);
        q = f2d (im—>info—>nr, im—>info—>nc);
        pp = f2d (im—>info—>nr, im—>info—>nc);
        qq = f2d (im—>info—>nr, im—>info—>nc);

/* Initial assignment of pixel classes */
        assign_class (im, p, q);

/* Relaxation */
        do
        {
          res = update (im, p, q);
          iter += 1;
          printf ("Iteration %d residual is %f\n", iter,
                    res);
          if (res < minres)
          {
                minres = res;
                count = 1;
          } else if (fabs(res—minres) < 0.0001)
          {
                if (count > 2) break;
                else count++;
          }
        } while (iter < 100 && res > 1.0);
        thresh (im, p, q);
}
/* Threshold */
void thresh (IMAGE im, float **p, float **q)
{
        int i,j;
        for (i=0; i<im—>info—>nr; i++)
          for (j=0; j<im—>info—>nc; j++)
            if (p[i][j] > q[i][j]) im—>data[i][j] = 0;
            else im—>data[i][j] = 255;
}

float R(IMAGE im, int r, int c, int rj, int cj, int 11, int 12)
{
        float xd = 0.0;
        xd = 1.0 — (im—>data[r][c] — im—>data[rj][cj])/256.0;
        if (11 == 12) return xd*0.9;
        return —(1.0—xd)*0.9;
}
```

Figure 3.13 C source code for the program relax3; it thresholds
an image using a relaxation method.

```
void assign_class (IMAGE im, float **p, float **q)
{
        int i,j;
        float ud2, y, z, u, lm2;

        for (i=0; i<im–>info–>nr; i++)/* Mean of local area
             */
          for (j=0, j<im–>info–>nc; j++)
          {
                meanminmax (im, i, j, &u, &z, &y);
                ud2 = 2.0*(u–z);
                lm2 = 2.0*(y–u);
                if (im–>data[i][j] <= u)
                {
                  p[i][j] = 0.5 + (u–im–>data[i][j])/ud2;
                  q[i][j] = 1.0–p[i][j];
                } else {
                  q[i][j] = (0.5 + (im–>data[i][j]–u)/lm2);
                  p[i][j] = 1.0–q[i][j];
                }
          }
}

void meanminmax (IMAGE im, int r, int c, float *mean, float *xmin, float
*xmax)
{
        int i,j, sum = 0, k=0;
        unsigned char *y;

        y = im–>data[0];
        *xmin = *xmax = im–>data[r][c];;
        for (i=r–10; i<=r+10; i++)
          for (j=c–10; j<=c+10; j++)
          {
            if (range(im, i, j) != 1) continue;
            if (*xmin > im–>data[i][j]) *xmin =im–>data[i][j];
            else if (*xmax < im–>data[i][j]) *xmax =im–>data[i][j];
            sum += im–>data[i][j];
            k++;
          }
        *mean = (float)sum/(float)(k);
}

float Q(IMAGE im, float **p, float **q, int r, int c, int class)
{
        int i, j;
        float sum = 0.0;

        for (i=r–1; i<=r+1; i++)
          for (j=c+1; j<=c+1; j++)
            if (i!=r || j!=c)
```

Figure 3.13 (continued)

```
                 sum += R(im, r, c, i, j,class, 0)*p[i][j] +
                        R(im, r, c, i, j,class, 1)*q[i][j];
        return sum|8.0;
}

float update (IMAGE im, float **p, float **q)
{
        float z, num, qw, pk, qb;
        int i,j;

        for (i=1; i<im->info->nr-1; i++)
          for (j=1; j<im->info->nc-i; j++)
          {
            qb = (1.0 + Q(im, p, q, i, j, 0));
            qw = (1.0 + Q(im, p, q, i, j, 1));
            pk = p[i][j]*qb + q[i][j]*qw;

            if (pk == 0.0)
            {
              continue;
            }

            pp[i][j] = p[i][j]*qb|pk;
            qq[i][j] = q[i][j]*qw|pk;
          }

        z = 0.0;
        for (i=1; i<im->info->nr-1; i++)
          for (j=1; j<im->info->nc-1; j++)
          {
                z += fabs(p[i][j]-pp[i][j]) + fabs(q[i][j]-qq[i][j]);
                p[i][j] = pp[i][j];
                q[i][j] = qq[i][j];
                qq[i] = pp[i][j] = 0.0;
          }
        return z;
{
```

Figure 3.13 (continued)

3.4 MOVING AVERAGES

The relaxation method has one serious drawback that has not been mentioned—it is very slow. If speed is a criterion of interest, then a method that uses *moving averages* is quite appealing (Wellner 1993). This algorithm yields one threshold per pixel very quickly, and gives surprisingly good segmentations. It is designed for images containing text (for example, scanned documents). In these cases the illumination can be expected to be good, as can the general image quality.

A moving average is just the mean grey level of the last n pixels seen. The image can be treated as a one-dimensional stream of pixels, which is common in C anyway, and the average can either be computed exactly or estimated via:

$$M_{i+1} = M_i - \frac{M_i}{n} + g_{i+1}$$ (EQ 3.51)

where M_{i+1} is the estimate of the moving average for pixel $i + 1$ having grey level g_{i+1} and M_i is the previous moving average (i.e., for pixel i).

Any pixel less than a fixed percentage of its moving average is set to black; otherwise it is set to white. To avoid a bias for one side of the image over the other, a novel scanning method called *boustrophedon*[1] scanning was employed.

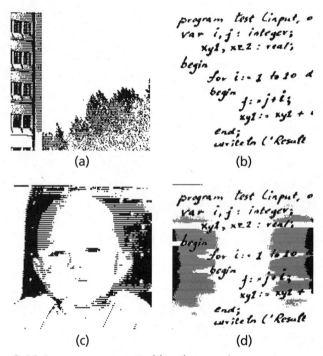

(a) (b)

(c) (d)

Figure 3.14 Images segmented by the moving average method. (a) The sky image. (b) The pascal image with superimposed sine-wave illumination. (c) The face image with linear illumination. (d) The pascal image with Gaussian illumination. This method works best on images of text, for which it was designed.

1. Greek, meaning ''as the ox plows.''

```
#define MAX
#include "lib.h"
void thrdd (IMAGE im);

void main (int argc, char *argv[])
{
    IMAGE data;

    if (argc < 3)
    {
      printf ("Usage: thrdd <input file> <output file>\n");
      exit (0);
    }
    data = Input_PBM (argv[1]);
    if (data == NULL)
    {
        printf ("Bad input file '%s'\n", argv[1]);
        exit(1);
    }
    thrdd (data);
    Output_PBM (data, argv[2]);
}
void thrdd (IMAGE im)
 {
        int NC, row, col, inc;
        float mean, s, sum;
        unsigned char *p;
        long N, i;

        N = (long)im->info->nc * (long)im->info->nr;
        NC = im->info->nc; s = (int)(float)(NC/Navg);
        sum = 127*s; row = col = 0; inc = 1;
        p = &(im->data[0][0]);

        for (i=0; i<N+1; i++) {
          if (col >= NC) {
             col = NC-1; row++; inc = -1;
             p = &(im->data[row][col]);
          } else if (col < 0)
```

Figure 3.15 Source code for the program thrdd.c; adaptive thresholding using a moving average.

```
    {
        col = 0; row++; inc = 1;
        p = &(im->data[row][col]);
    }
    sum = sum - sum/s + *p;
    mean = sum/s;
    if (*p < mean*(100-pct)/100.0) *p =
                0; else *p = 255;
    p += inc; col += inc;
    }
}
```

Figure 3.15 (continued)

This means traversing pixels in opposite directions in every other line. That is, the pixel following the last one in row i is the last one in row i + 1, followed by the second to last in row i + 1, and so on back to the start of row i + 1; this is followed by the start pixel in row i + 2, and so to the final one. This avoids the discontinuity at the end of the line that occurs with the usual C method of scanning a two-dimensional array.

The process begins with an estimate of the moving average; a value of 127 × n was selected, and this will only affect the first few pixels in the image. The value of *n* used is the number of columns divided by 8. Now Equation 3.51 is used to compute the moving average estimate for the next pixel (the first), which is used immediately as a threshold:

$$V = \begin{cases} 0 & \text{if } \left(g_i < \frac{M_i}{n}\right)\left(\frac{100 - pct}{100}\right) \\ 255 & \text{otherwise} \end{cases} \qquad \text{(EQ 3.52)}$$

where V is the threshold pixel and *pct* is the fixed percentage value; *pct* = 15 was used for the examples shown here.

A simple extension of this averages the current threshold with the one from the row above, allowing the vertical propagation of grey-level variations and illumination changes. This is not done in the program thrdd.c, which implements this scheme, but is an easy addition.

Figure 3.14 contains some of the images segmented by this method. The results are fairly good, at least until 3.14d. The white regions in the margins seems to have fooled it, at least in this case. Still, the program is very quick, and is 64 lines of C code (without the I/O functions), requiring at most two rows to be in memory at one time.

A likely pitfall is the fixed percentage value used to select the threshold from the mean. It is unlikely that a single value will be appropriate for use with a variety of image types. It does, however, seem highly appropriate for thresholding text, a function that it seems it was designed to perform.

Figure 3.15 gives the complete source code for thrdd.c.

3.5 BIBLIOGRAPHY

Bracho, R. and A. C. Sanderson. 1985. Segmentation of Images Based on Intensity Gradient Information. *Proceedings of the IEEE Computer Society Conference on Computer Vision and Pattern Recognition.* 341–347.

Huang L-K. and M-J. J. Wang. 1995. Image Thresholding by Minimizing the Measures of Fuzziness. *Pattern Recognition.* Vol. 28. 1:41–51.

Lancaster, P. and K. Salkauskas. 1981. Surfaces Generated by Moving Least Squares Methods. *Math. Comp.* 37:141–158.

Otsu, N. 1979. A Threshold Selection Method from Grey-level Histograms. *IEEE Transactions on Systems, Man, and Cybernetics.* Vol. 9. 1:377–393.

Parker, J. R. 1991. Grey Level Thresholding in Badly Illuminated Images. *IEEE Transactions on Pattern Analysis and Machine Intelligence.* Vol 13.

Perez, Arnulfo and R. C. Gonzalez. 1987. An Iterative Thresholding Algorithm for Image Processing. *IEEE Transactions on Pattern Analysis and Machine Intelligence.* Vol. PAMI-9. No. 6.

Press, W. H., Flannery, B. P., Teukolsky, S. A., and W. T. Vetterling. 1988. *Numerical Recipes in C.* Cambridge: Cambridge University Press.

Prewitt, J. M. S. 1970. Object Enhancement and Extraction. *Picture Processing and Psychopictorics.* (Lipkin and Rosenfeld Eds.). New York: Academic Press.

Ridler, T. W. and S. Calvard. 1978. Picture Thresholding Using an Iterative Selection Method. *IEEE Transactions on Systems, Man, and Cybernetics.* Vol. SMC-8. 8:630–632.

Sahoo, P. K., Soltani, S., Wong, A. K. C., and Y. C. Chen. 1988. A Survey of Thresholding Techniques. *Computer Vision, Graphics, and Image Processing.* Vol. 41. 233–260.

Salkauskas, K. and P. Lancaster. 1981. *Curve and Surface Fitting, An Introduction.* New York: Academic Press.

Thrussel, H. J. 1979. Comments on "Picture Thresholding Using an Iterative Selection Method." *IEEE Transactions on Systems, Man, and Cybernetics.* Vol. SMC-9. 5:311.

Wilson, R. and M. Spann. 1988. *Image Segmentation and Uncertainty.* New York: John Wiley & Sons Inc.

Yager, R. R. 1979. On the Measures of Fuzziness and Negation. Part 1: Membership in the Unit Interval. *Int. Journal of Gen. Sys.* Vol. 5. 221–229.

Yanowitz, S. D. and A. M. Bruckstein. A New Method for Image Segmentation. *Computer Vision, Graphics, and Image Processing.* 46:82–95.

4

TEXTURE

4.1 TEXTURE AND SEGMENTATION

When we look at a picture, we can easily connect regions having a similar grey or color value into objects. Indeed, we can even account for variations in level caused by illumination and distinguish those from changes caused by overlapping objects. The presence of *texture* complicates the issue, especially from a computer vision perspective.

While there is no agreement on a formal definition of texture, a major characteristic is the *repetition of a pattern or patterns over a region*. The pattern may be repeated exactly, or as a set of small variations on the theme, possibly a function of position. There is also a random aspect to texture that must not be ignored— the size, shape, color, and orientation of the elements of the pattern (sometimes called *textons*) can vary over the region. Sometimes the difference between two textures is contained in the degree of variation alone, or in the statistical distribution found relating the textons.

Figure 4.1 shows a small collection of textures, some natural and some artificial. The study of texture will be undertaken with the goal of segmenting regions rather than characterizing textures. That is, the very practical issue of determining which regions have texture A and which have texture B will be addressed. The result could be an image in which texture has been replaced by a unique grey level or color.

Texture is a property possessed by a region that is sufficiently large to demonstrate its recurring nature. A region cannot display texture if it is small compared with the size of a texton. This leaves us with a problem of scale, in addition to

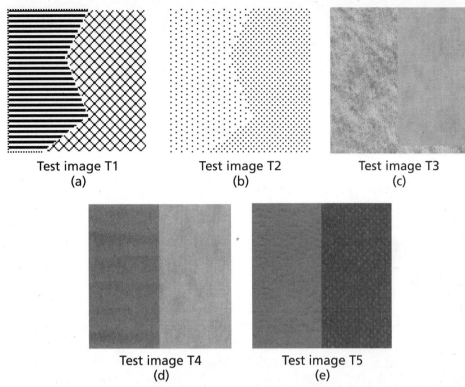

Test image T1
(a)

Test image T2
(b)

Test image T3
(c)

Test image T4
(d)

Test image T5
(e)

Figure 4.1 Some images displaying regions characterized by their texture. (a–b) Artificial textures, such as might be used on maps to delimit regions of interest. (c–e) Naturally occurring textures that delimit regions found in real scenes.

the other problems that texture presents. Indeed, the same texture at two different scales will be perceived as two different textures, provided that the scales are different enough. As the scales become closer together the textures are harder to distinguish, and at some point they become the same.

It is unlikely, given the preceding discussion, that any simple measure or operation will allow the segmentation of textured regions in a digital image. The lines drawn between textures are often arbitrary, a function of perception rather than mathematics. It is possible, on the other hand, that some combination of operations can yield reasonably good segmentations with a wide range of textures.

4.2   A SIMPLE ANALYSIS OF TEXTURE IN GREY-LEVEL IMAGES

A region having a particular texture, while having a wide variety in its grey levels, must have some properties that allow animal visual systems to identify them.

While the existence of texture elements is crucial, it is unlikely that a library of texture elements is maintained and recognized by any seeing creature. It is more likely that similarities and differences can be seen, and that a biological vision system can measure these and use them to delimit different textural regions.

One obvious way to delimit regions is by color or grey level alone. However, unlike grey-level segmentation, (in which each pixel is classed as white or black), the grey level associated with each pixel in a textured region could be the average (mean) level over some relatively small area. This area, which will be called a *window*, can be varied in size to capture a sample of the different scales to be found there.

The use of the average grey level is not recommended to distinguish between textures, but the use of a method this simple does help explain the general method that will be used to segment image regions according to texture. The use of windows of some sort is very common, since texture is only a concern in a region and not in individual pixels. As a result, the boundary between textured regions can only be determined to within a distance of about W pixels, where W is the width of the window.

Figure 4.2 illustrates this; here we are using mean grey levels to segment the image seen in Figure 4.1b. The method is: For each pixel in the image, replace it by the average of the levels seen in a region $W \times W$ pixels in size centered at that pixel. Now threshold the image into two regions using the new (average) levels. Figure 4.2a is the image of the mean grey levels and 4.2b is a thresholded version of this, showing the original boundary between the region superimposed. The exact location of the boundary between the regions depends on the threshold that is applied to the mean-level image. A reasonable threshold in this case is one

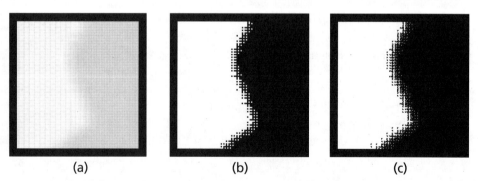

(a)   (b)   (c)

Figure 4.2 Windowing in texture segmentation. (a) Image consisting of mean grey levels in a 14 × 14 window about all pixels in Figure 4.1b. (b) A thresholding of this image showing two possible regions. (c) The region of uncertainty. The actual region boundary could be anywhere within the grey area.

that keeps the white region contiguous and on the left of the image, and keeps the black region contiguous and on the right. There is a range of reasonable thresholds, and the pixels that move from one region to the other as the threshold changes are those marked in grey in Figure 4.2c. This corresponds to the boundary between the regions, and is essentially an area of uncertainty. The actual boundary could be anywhere in the grey area, but is most likely in the middle.

The use of mean grey level seems to work well enough for the sample image, but this happens to be an exceptional case. It does not work at all well for any of the remaining sample images when they are normalized for grey level. On the other hand, using the standard deviation of the grey levels in a small window works a lot better. There seems to be more consistency in the *changes* in the levels than there is in the levels themselves. This does make some degree of sense: We have seen that even in the presence of varying illumination, the difference in level between local pixels remains nearly the same. In addition, if the texture elements are small objects with a different set of levels than the background, then the standard deviation in a small region tells us something about how many pixels in that region belong to textons and how many belong to the background.

Figure 4.3 shows the regions identified by using local standard deviations to segment textural areas. Figure 4.1a can be segmented by this method; in fact, so can all except 4.1d. Note that the precision with which the boundary between regions is known is still a function of the size of the window used. This will always be true, and so there is an advantage in using methods that permit the use of small windows.

The mean grey level and the standard deviation are known as statistical *moments*. The mean is related to the first moment, and the standard deviation depends on the second moment. There are others, and these could also be used to characterize textured areas. In general, we have:

$$M_n = \frac{\sum (x - \bar{x})^n}{N}$$

(EQ 4.1)

where N is the number of data points, and n is the order of the moment. Now the *skewness* can be defined as:

$$Sk = \frac{1}{N} \sum \left(\frac{(x - \bar{x})}{\sigma} \right)^3$$

(EQ 4.2)

and the *kurtosis* as:

$$Kurt = \frac{1}{N} \sum \left(\frac{(x - \bar{x})}{\sigma} \right)^4 - 3$$

(EQ 4.3)

These can be used in the same way as standard deviation: compute the statistic

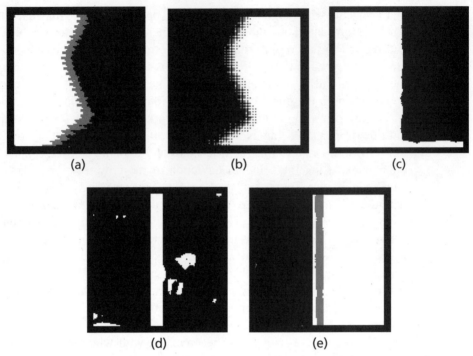

(a)   (b)   (c)

(d)   (e)

Figure 4.3 Use of standard deviation to segment the images of
Figure 4.1. Note that the standard deviation tends to be large
where the two textures meet.

over a window and let that be the value of the pixel at the center of the window,
then segment the resulting image. Rather large windows would be preferred, so
that a statistical sample is gathered.

A single C program (which is included on the companion CD) has been devised
for segmenting texture based on the preceding measures and on all of the methods
to be discussed in later sections. It is called simply text.c, and will produce an
output image that has been transformed by whatever segmentation algorithm is
specified on the command line. The general way that this program is invoked is
by:

```
text image.pgm KEYWORD
```

where KEYWORD is replaced by the name of one of the texture segmentation
algorithms. For example, to use the average grey level over a window the program
would be called as:

```
text image.pgm grey_level
```

The result in this case is a collection of image files for windows of size 13×13, 21×21, 29×29, 27×27 and 45×45; these files are in PGM format, and are named txt6.pgm, txt10.pgm, txt14.pgm, txt18.pgm, and txt22.pgm. The number in the file name refers to the number of pixels on each side of the pixel in the middle of the window. For the example above, each pixel in the resulting images represents the average level found in the window centered at that pixel. The other keywords for the simple statistical measures are sd_level (standard deviation), kurtosis, and skewness.

As more methods for texture segmentation are explored, these will be added to the text.c program, and the relevant keywords and other parameters needed will be explained. If the program is invoked without any parameters a short listing of the legal keywords will be printed on the screen as a reminder.

4.3 GREY-LEVEL CO-OCCURRENCE

The statistical texture measures described so far are easy to calculate, but do not provide any information about the repeating nature of the texture. For example, the texture seen on the left of Figure 4.1a consists of repeating horizontal lines. None of the measurements examined so far will reflect this property, and so a set of vertical lines with the same widths and separations will be indistinguishable from this texture, as would suitably constructed diagonal lines.

A *grey level co-occurrence matrix* (GLCM) contains information about the positions of pixels having similar grey level values. The idea is to scan the image and keep track of how often pixels that differ by Δz in value are separated by a fixed distance d in position. Normally the direction between the two pixels is also a concern, and this is implemented by having multiple matrices, one for each direction of interest. Usually there are four directions: horizontal, vertical, and the two diagonals. Therefore, for every value of d we have four images, each of which is 256×256 in size, for an original image with 256 levels of grey. This is really too much data, often more than there is in the original image. What is usually done is to analyze these matrices and compute a few simple numerical values that encapsulate the information. These values are often called *descriptors*, and eight of them will be examined here.

Collecting the value for the co-occurrence matrices is not especially difficult, but it is time-consuming. Consider the problem of determining the GLCM for an image I having 256 distinct levels of grey, in the horizontal direction and for $d = 2$. This matrix will be called M0, and M0$[i,j]$ will contain the number of pixels P1 and P2 in I for which P1 $= i$ and P2 $= j$ where P1 and P2 are separated by two pixels horizontally. The indices for M0 are grey levels, not rows or columns of the image.

This could be calculated in the following manner. Examine all pixels in the image I:

```
for (y=0; y<Nrows; y++)
      for (x=0, x<Ncolumns; x++)
      {
```

Let p1 be the grey level at pixel I[y,x] and let p2 be the grey level at the pixel I[y,x + d]:

```
p1 = I[y][x]; p2 = I[y][x+d];
```

These two levels are used as indices into the matrix M0 being constructed; increment the entry in M0.

```
M0[p1][p2] += 1;
```

Since M0 is symmetrical we could also increment the symmetrical element:

```
M0[p2][p1] += 1;
```

or we could merge the upper and lower triangles after M0 is constructed. When all of the pixels have been examined by this loop the matrix M0 is complete. A final pass through M0 is needed if normalized values are wanted. Dividing the elements of M0 by the number of pixels involved gives joint probabilities; specifically M0[i,j] will be the probability that a pixel having grey level i will have a pixel with level j a distance of d pixels away in the horizontal direction. A very similar process will create the other three matrices.

The artificial textures of Figure 4.1 a and b are ideally suited to be an example, since they are bilevel images: The color black has level 0, and the color white has level 255. If the 255 pixels are set to 1, then the GLCMs will be 2 × 2 matrices! For the horizontal line texture on the left of Figure 4.1a the line separation is 2 pixels; the co-occurrence matrices for $d = 1$ are:

Horizontal (0)		Vertical (90)	
0.5000	0.0000	0.2468	0.2532
0.0000	0.5000	0.2532	0.2468

and the diagonal matrices are the same as the vertical. These results make sense; since the lines are horizontal, there will be no black-to-white level changes in the horizontal direction. If you start on a black pixel, its horizontal neighbor will be black (Mat0[0][0] = 0.5) and from any white pixel the horizontal neighbor will be white (Mat0[1][1] = 0.5). For $d = 2$ the matrices are more interesting:

Horizontal (0)		Vertical (90)	
0.5000	0.0000	0.0000	0.5000
0.0000	0.5000	0.5000	0.0000

where, again, the diagonal matrices are the same as M90. This means that, no matter what the color of the pixel we start at, its neighbor two pixels away horizontally is the same color, and the neighbor two pixels away vertically is always the opposite color. This is an accurate characterization of the horizontal line texture.

As the number of grey levels in the image increases by a factor of 2, the co-occurrence matrices increase in size by a factor of 4. It very quickly becomes difficult to use the matrices directly, and so once again the use of statistics becomes important. Rather than measure the properties of the image directly, the co-occurrence matrices are measured and, as has been mentioned already, characterized by a selection of numerical descriptors. The mean and standard deviation have been used as descriptors for the image data, and could be used for the co-occurrence matrices as well. However, many descriptors have been tried, and some work better than others. Five of the more popular ones follow; then each one will be tested on the sample textures of Figure 4.1.

Maximum Probability

This is simple the largest entry in the matrix, and corresponds to the strongest response or the most likely transition. This could be the maximum in any of the matrices, or the maximum overall; in fact, there is useful information in simply knowing which matrix contains the maximum, since this will indicate an important direction for the texture being examined.

Moments

The order k *element difference moment* can be defined as:

$$Mom_k = \sum_i \sum_j (i - j)^k M[i,j] \qquad \text{(EQ 4.4)}$$

This descriptor has small values in cases where the largest elements in M are along the principal diagonal; this was the situation when analyzing Figure 4.1a. The opposite effect can be achieved using the *inverse moment*, which is computed as:

$$Mom_k^{-1} = \sum_i \sum_j \frac{M[i,j]}{(i - j)^k}, i \neq j \qquad \text{(EQ 4.5)}$$

Contrast

An estimate of contrast is given by the following expression:

$$C(k,n) = \sum_i \sum_j |i - j|^k M[i,j]^n \qquad \text{(EQ 4.6)}$$

When $k = n = 1$, which is the situation implemented by the software on the CD accompanying this book, this amounts to the expected value of the difference between two pixels.

Homogeneity

This value is given by:

$$G = \sum_i \sum_j \frac{M[i,j]}{1 + |i - j|} \qquad \text{(EQ 4.7)}$$

A small value of G means that the large values of M lie near the principal diagonal. G is very similar to Mom_1^{-1}.

Entropy

Entropy is calculated by:

$$H = -\sum_i \sum_j M[i,j]\log(M[i,j]) \qquad \text{(EQ 4.8)}$$

This is a measure of the information content of M. Large empty (featureless) spaces have little information content, whereas cluttered areas have a large information content.

Results from the GLCM Descriptors

The software that actually segments images using GLCM descriptors is very slow; one matrix must be computed for each window, followed by a calculation of the value for the descriptor—this yields a single pixel in the segmented image. Because of this, experimentation should be done using small images, smaller than the images in Figure 4.1. Each of these test images has been subjected to all five of the descriptors, and samples of the resulting segmented images appears in Figure 4.4.

The text.c program will compute the co-occurrence values described here. However, in addition to a keyword indicating which measure to apply, the co-occurrence calculation needs to be given a distance and a direction. These are specified after the keyword, and in that order; distance followed by direction. Distance is specified as the number of pixels; direction is an integer, having the value 0 for horizontal, 1 for 45 degrees, 2 for 90 degrees, and 3 for 135 degrees.

So, in order to segment the image t3.pgm using the entropy metric applied to the co-occurrence matrix for a distance of two pixels in the horizontal direction the command would be:

```
text t3.pgm entropy 2 0
```

Speeding Up the Texture Operators

Creating a co-occurrence matrix for each window is not only slow and memory intensive in practice, but is not even necessary—it is not the matrix that is needed,

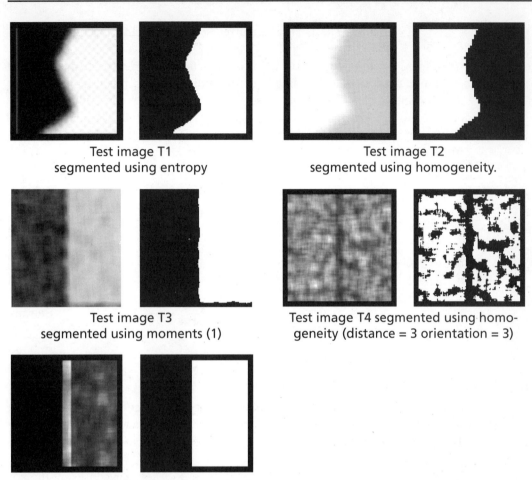

Test image T1
segmented using entropy

Test image T2
segmented using homogeneity.

Test image T3
segmented using moments (1)

Test image T4 segmented using homogeneity (distance = 3 orientation = 3)

Test image T5 segmented using contrast

Figure 4.4 Co-occurrence texture measures applied to the set of
test images of Figure 4.1. In all cases but one the distance was 2,
and the direction was horizontal.

but some measure (descriptor) that will be used to characterize it. Unser (1986)
devised a method for computing the statistics without actually creating the matrix.

The method is based on sum and difference histograms. The sum histogram S
depends on displacements d_x and d_y, and is the histogram of the sums of all pixels
d_x and d_y apart. For example, the pixel at (i,j) will be added to the pixel at $(i +
d_y, j + d_x)$ and the histogram bin corresponding to the sum is incremented. For a
256-level image, the sum histogram has bins 0 through 512. The difference histogram D is merely the histogram of the differences between pixels the specified
distance apart. Histogram D has bins -255 through $+255$ for an eight-bit image.

Now the histograms S and D are normalized so that the entries become probabilities.

The more common descriptors used to characterize co-occurrence matrices can be approximated using only these two histograms. This is much more efficient, since not only are the actual matrices not calculated, but the descriptors are now computed using two small one-dimensional arrays instead of a large two-dimensional array. Some of the descriptors that are efficiently found using sum and difference histograms are:

$$\mu = \frac{1}{2} \sum_i i \cdot S(i) \qquad \text{Mean}$$

$$\sum_j j^2 \cdot D(j) \qquad \text{Contrast}$$

$$\sum_j \frac{1}{1 + j^2} \cdot D(j) \qquad \text{Homogeneity}$$

$$- \sum_i S(i) \cdot \log(S(i)) - \sum_j D(j) \cdot \log(D(j)) \qquad \text{Entropy}$$

$$\sum_i S(i)^2 \cdot \sum_j D(j)^2 \qquad \text{Energy}$$

While these are approximations, they are good enough to be quite useful, and the speed up in the code is at least a factor of twenty. The C code that accomplishes this is called fast.c, and while perhaps not pretty, it enables texture analysis to be performed on a PC. Without the speedup, the use of co-occurrence matrices is not practical on small computers.

Fast.c accepts almost the same parameters as does text.c when using the co-occurrence measures. It recognizes the keywords average (mean of the window), stddev (standard deviation in the window), pmax (maximum value), contrast (as before), homo (homogeneity, as before), and a new measure energy, which is defined by the last definition in the list above. Most of the work is done by the procedure sdhist, which is given in Figure 4.5. This function is somewhat more opaque than the usual code shown here, but illustrates some of the methods that can be used to speed up image-analysis code. In particular, note the absence of any two-dimensional array references.

4.4 EDGES AND TEXTURE

If a collection of objects called textons forms a texture, then it should be possible to isolate individual textons and treat them as objects. It should be possible to locate the edges that result from the grey-level transitions along the boundary of

```
/* Compute the sum and difference histograms, and the mean
*/
void sdhist (IMAGE im, int d, WINDOW *w)
{
    int
ngl=256,p1=0,p2=0,i=0,j=0,k=0,l=0,r=0,t=0,b=0,id=0,
              nc;
    static float *Ps, *Pd;
    float sum=0.0;
    unsigned char *ptr1, *ptr2;

    nc = im->info->nc;

/* Allocate the matrix */
    if (Ps == 0)
    {
          Ps = (float *)calloc (ngl*2, sizeof(float));
          Pd = (float *)calloc (ngl*2, sizeof(float));
          Sum = Ps;
          Diff = Pd;
    }
    dir = (int)param[4];
    1 = w->left; r = w->right; t = w->top; b = w->bottom;

/* Compute the histograms for any of 4 directions */
    ptr2 = im->data[t];
    for (i = t; i < b; i++)
    {
          prt1 = ptr2+1; id = d*nc;
          for (j = 1; j < r; j++)
          {
                p1 = *ptr1;
                if (j+d < r && dir == 0)
                      p2 = *(ptr1+d);  /* Horizontal */
                else if (i+d < b && dir == 2)
                      p2 = *(ptr1+id);  /* Vertical */
                else if (i+d < b && j-d >= 1 && dir == 1)
                      p2 = *(ptr1 +id - d);  /* 45 degree
                                          diagonal */
```

Figure 4.5 Source code for the procedure that calculates the sum and difference histograms for a given window. The code has been designed to be relatively fast, rather than readable. Two-dimensional array references are absent, and most arrays are treated as pointers.

```
                    else if (i+d < b && j+d < r && dir == 3)
                        p2 = *(ptr1+id+d);    /*135 degree
                                    diagonal */
                    else { ptr1++; continue; }
                    k++, ptr1++; Ps[p1+p2]++;
Pd[p1-p2+ng1]++;
            }
        ptr2 += nc;
    }

/* Normalize */
    for (i=0; i<ng1+ng1; i++)
    {
        Ps[i] /= k;
        sum += Ps[i]*i;
        Pd[i] /= k;
    }
    Mean = sum/2.0;
}
```

Figure 4.5 (continued)

a texton. Moreover, since a texture will have large numbers of textons, there should be some property of the edge pixels that can be used to characterize the texture; this property may be a set of common directions, distances over which the edge pixels repeat, or simply a measure of the local density of the edge pixels.

A perfect example of this is the test image Figure 4.1a. The leftmost texture consists of repeated horizontal lines; it is to be expected that a large number of edge pixels having direction 0° will be found in this region. The neighboring texture, on the other hand, consists only of diagonal lines, and should have few (if any) edge pixels in this direction. Thus, edge pixel direction can be used in this case to segment the two regions.

The density of the edge pixels is probably the simplest edge-based metric, and is easy to calculate. A fast edge detector is applied to a window, and the number of edge pixels in that window is divided by the area to give the density. Any abrupt change in the edge-pixel density likely marks a boundary between two regions. Since it is usually a simple matter to extract directional information from an edge detector, this can be used to augment the edge density. Easy measurements to make include the mean x and y component of the gradient at the edge and the relative number of pixels whose principal direction is x or y.

Actual angles are harder to deal with since, depending on the window size, there can be a larger number of different angles. The histogram of the angles found in a window could characterize the texture there, but to compare a large number of N-dimensional histograms would be computationally intense. However, the spatial relationships between the pixels having particular angles, and for that matter edge pixels in general, convey a great deal of information. Why not compute the co-occurrence matrix of an edge-enhanced image? This will, in many circumstances, give a better result, in terms of discriminating ability, than using the co-occurrence matrix without edge enhancement (Dyer 1980; Davis 1981).

Figure 4.6 illustrates the use of edge information and co-occurrence statistics. The original image shows a few trees, a cloudy sky, and part of a building. The contrast measure of the grey-level co-occurrence matrix for this image (4.6b) could give a classification, but enhancing the edges first (4.6c) increases the contrast in edge-prone regions, such as the trees. The same contrast measure gives somewhat better results (4.6d) and was used to produce the final classification (4.6e). The region containing clouds is quite well marked as black in this image.

Noise smoothing before edge detection will reduce the number of spurious edge pixels, and will give better results in some instances. A Laplacian edge detector is less directional, and could be used in place of the Sobel edge detector in the software provided. Some of the more advanced edge detectors (e.g., Canny or ISEF) actually smooth too well, and respond to texture as if it were noise. The contrast of the image may have to be increased greatly before one of these methods could be used.

The text.c program cheats a little with respect to edges. Running text with the sobel keyword will result in an edge enhanced version of the original file being written to sobtxt.pgm. This file can then be used as input to fast.c or text.c, spec-

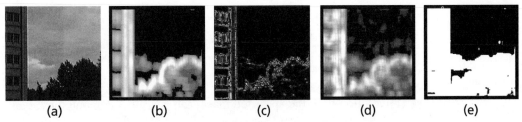

(a)   (b)   (c)   (d)   (e)

Figure 4.6 Using edges to enhance the results from co-occurrence matrices. (a) Original image. (b) Contrast of the co-occurrence matrix, distance 4 horizontal. (c) Edge enhanced image. (d) Contrast of the co-occurrence matrix of the edge image. (e) Classification based on (d).

ifying the desired co-occurrence operator. For example, Figure 4.6d was created in the following way:

```
text sky.pgm sobel
FAST sobtxt.pgm contrast 4 0
```

When the angles of the edge pixels are desired, specify sang as the keyword. The result, again, is a file sobtxt.pgm containing the scaled angles. The keywords dx and dy specify direction components in the x and y directions, and nx and ny as keywords yield the number of edges in each window having the largest component in the x or y direction.

4.5 ENERGY AND TEXTURE

There are many ways in which the energy content of an image could be calculated, depending on how energy is defined and what kind of image is at hand. One measure of the energy of a textured region was seen in Section 4.3, where an energy measure was computed from a co-occurrence matrix. Laws (1980) devised a collection of convolution masks specifically for the purpose of computing the energy in a texture. These have been used successfully for many years for texture segmentation, and are now a standard for comparison for new algorithms.

Although various sizes for the masks are possible, three of the five pixel masks are:

$$E5 = (-1, -2, 0, 2, 1)$$
$$L5 = (\ 1, 4, 6, 4, 1)$$
$$R5 = (\ 1, -4, 6, -4, 1)$$

These can be used in combination to create nine different two-dimensional convolution masks. If they are treated as vectors, then E5 × L5 gives a 5 × 5 matrix called E5L5 and having the value:

$$
\begin{array}{rrrrr}
-1 & -4 & -6 & -4 & -1 \\
-2 & -8 & -12 & -8 & -2 \\
0 & 0 & 0 & 0 & 0 \\
2 & 8 & 12 & 8 & 2 \\
1 & 4 & 6 & 4 & 1
\end{array}
$$

After the convolution with the specified mask, the energy is computed by:

$$E_n = \sum_r \sum_c |C(r,c)| \qquad \text{(EQ 4.9)}$$

where C is the convolved image. The size of the region used to determine the energy can vary; a 7 × 7 region seems to be quite common. If all nine masks that result from the combinations of E5, L5, and R5 are applied, the result is a nine-dimensional feature vector at each pixel of the image being analyzed. These vectors can be used with a statistical classifier (e.g., *K* nearest neighbor). In some cases only one or two of the energy values are sufficient.

At the boundary between two regions having different textures, this method (as well as many of the others we have seen) does not perform very well. The pixels near the boundary form a region of high variability that, statistically, has some properties of both adjoining regions. Sometimes this shows up in images as a thick black or white bar separating the regions, while other times it can be thresholded into one of the textures.

Something that has been suggested for use with the texture energy method specifically, but that has more general application, is to look carefully at the areas to the upper-left, upper-right, lower-left and lower-right of the window being processed. At the interior of a region these four areas should have statistically similar properties, but at the boundary between regions there will be variations observed. When this occurs, select the energy value for the region having the *smallest standard deviation*, this being most likely to be representative of the interior.

All nine of these energy operators are implemented by the text.c program. To apply an energy operator to an image, specify it as the keyword; for example,

```
text input.pgm E5E5
```

will apply the E5E5 operator to image.pgm, producing a file named txtN.pgm, where *N* is 6, 10, 14, 18, or 24 as before. The program creates the correct convolution mask and applies it to the input image, then determines the mean energy value for the window. The letters in the keyword must be specified in upper case. Figure 4.7 shows the result of each of the nine masks applied to test image t4.

4.6 SURFACES AND TEXTURE

There are some texture segmentation algorithms that are based on a view of the grey level image as a three-dimensional surface, where grey level is the third dimension. Depending on what sort of assumptions that are made concerning the nature of this surface, any number of descriptors can be devised. Two will be examined here, but the references give a few good pointers to other useful and interesting work.

Vector Dispersion

For the purposes of this algorithm, the texture image consists of a set of small planes, or facets. Each plane is really a small area of the image. The normal to

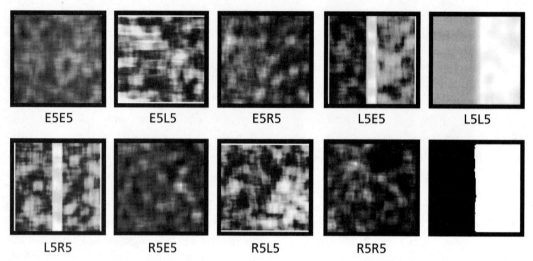

| E5E5 | E5L5 | E5R5 | L5E5 | L5L5 |

| L5R5 | R5E5 | R5L5 | R5R5 |

Figure 4.7 All energy convolution masks applied to the test image T4. The final image is the segmented version, using L5L5.

each plane is a vector, and for a region having many facets the variation in the direction of the normals may produce a measure that can characterize the texture in that region.

Figure 4.8 shows a 3 × 3 region of a grey level texture, in which the grey level is treated as a third dimension. The facets meet to form an edge every three pixels both horizontally and vertically, and do not overlap. Since a plane is a linear equation in two dimensions, it can be written in the form:

$$I(i,j) = \alpha i + \beta j + \gamma \qquad (EQ\ 4.10)$$

for image I over a small (3 × 3) area. The coefficients are easy to find using a least-squares best fit of a plane to the levels found in the small region of I. Details can be found in the math book of your choice, but the result is:

$$\alpha = \frac{\displaystyle\sum_{i=-1}^{1}\sum_{j=-1}^{1} i \cdot I(i,j)}{\sum \sum i^2} \qquad (EQ\ 4.11)$$

$$\beta = \frac{\displaystyle\sum_{i=-1}^{1}\sum_{j=-1}^{1} j \cdot I(i,j)}{\sum \sum j^2} \qquad (EQ\ 4.12)$$

$$\gamma = \frac{\displaystyle\sum_{i=-1}^{1}\sum_{j=-1}^{1} I(i,j)}{\sum \sum 1} \qquad (EQ\ 4.13)$$

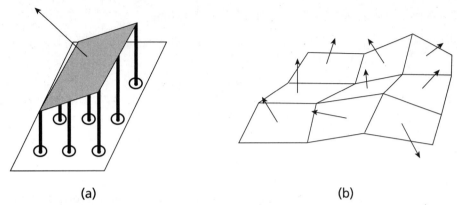

(a)   (b)

Figure 4.8 Vector dispersion. (a) Each facet is a small plane having an easily computed normal direction, indicated by the arrow. The posts supporting the facet represent the grey level at each of the nine pixels. (b) Texture metrics are computed over a local collection of facets, and represent how the directions of the normals are distributed about the local mean normal.

The coefficients α, β, and γ can be thought of as a vector. The normal vector is perpendicular to the plane, and the normalized form (i.e., length $= 1$) for the *i*th facet is

$$\begin{bmatrix} K_i \\ L_i \\ M_i \end{bmatrix} = \frac{1}{\sqrt{\alpha_i^2 + \beta_i^2 + 1}} \begin{bmatrix} \alpha_i \\ \beta_i \\ -1 \end{bmatrix} \qquad \text{(EQ 4.14)}$$

An estimate of the direction of the surface normal over the whole region can be obtained from the facet normals by simply averaging them. If it is assumed that the individual normals are measurements taken from the surface of a sphere, then the statistical distribution of the errors is related to $e^{\kappa \cos \theta}$, where θ is the error in the angle (Fish 1952). The value κ acts as a measure of precision, but in the case of the measurement of vector dispersion, a large κ value indicates a smooth texture, and values near zero indicate a rough texture. Given a set of normal vectors, the value of κ can be estimated by

$$\kappa = \frac{N - 1}{N - R} \qquad \text{(EQ 4.15)}$$

where R is found from the normal vectors:

$$R^2 = \left(\sum_{i=1}^{N} K_i \right)^2 + \left(\sum_{i=1}^{N} L_i \right)^2 + \left(\sum_{i=1}^{N} M_i \right)^2 \qquad \text{(EQ 4.16)}$$

This leaves us with the following algorithm:

1. For a given window into the image I, locate some number of nonoverlapping subregions.
2. For each subregion compute the coefficients of the plane, and from that compute the normal to the plane for that subregion; this is a vector (K_i, L_i, M_i).
3. Normalize the vectors from step 2, and then compute R using the vectors from all subregions.
4. Compute κ. This is the texture descriptor for this window. Repeat from step 1 for all windows in the image.

As usual, the κ value for the window centered at a pixel P will be the value of the pixel P in the segmented image. Thresholding the segmented image will still be needed.

Figure 4.9 shows this method applied to the test images seen in Figures 4.1c and 4.1e. When using the text.c program, simply specify the keyword vd. Figure 4.9 was created using the call:

```
text t3.pgm vd
```

Surface Curvature

The vector-dispersion method fits a plane to the pixels in a small area, which is really a first approximation to what is really there. A better approximation would be a polynomial surface, which can better conform to local variations in shape. A typical second-degree polynomial surface is defined by:

$$z(x,y) = a_{20}x^2 + a_{11}xy + a_{02}y^2 + a_{10}x + a_{01}y + a_{00} \qquad \text{(EQ 4.17)}$$

Curvature can be defined as the rate of change of the slope of the tangent to the surface at the point in question. Given this local approximation to the surface,

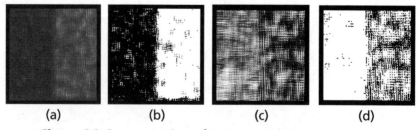

| (a) | (b) | (c) | (d) |

Figure 4.9 Segmentation of texture regions using vector dispersion. (a) Vector dispersion image obtained from Figure 4.1c. (b) Thresholded version, showing the two texture regions. (c) Vector dispersion image obtained from Figure 4.1e. (d) Thresholded version.

there are a number of surface curvature measures that might be useful for characterizing the surface (and therefore the texture) at that point. This would involve the following steps for each pixel in the region being evaluated:

1. Use least squares to fit a polynomial surface to the local pixel region.
2. Compute the derivatives of the surface at the specified point.
3. Use the derivatives, the slope of the tangent, to compute curvature.

Fortunately, this has been done for us by Peet and Sahota (Peet 1985). The values of a_{ij} are found in much the same way as were the values of α, β, and γ for vector dispersion. For a 3×3 region centered at $I(i,j)$ we have:

$$A_1 = \sum_{n=-1}^{1} \sum_{m=-1}^{1} I(i + n, j + m)$$

$$A_2 = \sum_{n=i-1}^{i+1} I(n, j + 1) - \sum_{n=i-1}^{i+1} I(n, j - 1)$$

$$A_3 = \sum_{m=j-1}^{j+1} I(i - 1, m) - \sum_{m=j-1}^{j+1} I(i + 1, m)$$

$$A_4 = \sum_{n=i-1}^{i+1} I(n, j - 1) + \sum_{n=i-1}^{i+1} I(n, j + 1)$$

$$A_5 = \sum_{m=j-1}^{j+1} I(i - 1, m) - \sum_{m=j-1}^{j+1} I(i + 1, m)$$

$$A_6 = I(i - 1, j + 1) + I(i + 1, j - 1) - I(i - 1, j - 1) - I(i + 1, j + 1)$$

The coefficients of the polynomial can now be expressed in terms of the A_i values:

$$a_{20} = A_4/2 - A_1/3$$
$$a_{11} = A_6/4$$
$$a_{02} = A_5/2 - A_1/3$$
$$a_{10} = A_2/6$$
$$a_{01} = A_3/6$$
$$a_{00} = 5A_1/9 - A_4/3 - A_5/3$$

This is the least-squares fit of the surface to the data. The curvature can be calculated given only a little more algebra motivated by differential geometry, but it is really quite simple to compute. The following values are parameters to the *first and second fundamental forms* of the surface:

$$E = 1 + a_{10}^2$$

$$F = a_{10}a_{01}$$

$$G = 1 + a_{01}^2$$

$$e = (2a_{20})/\sqrt{EG - F^2}$$

$$f = (2a_{11})/\sqrt{EG - F^2}$$

$$g = (2a_{02})/\sqrt{EG - F^2}$$

The minimum curvature at the point I(i,j) is given by:

$$k_1 = \frac{gE - 2Ff + Ge - \sqrt{gE + Ge - 2Ff)^2 - 4(eg - f^2)(EG - F^2)}}{2(EG - F^2)}$$

(EQ 4.18)

and the maximum curvature is:

$$k_2 = \frac{gE - 2Ff + Ge + \sqrt{gE + Ge - 2Ff)^2 - 4(eg - f^2)(EG - F^2)}}{2(EG - F^2)}$$

(EQ 4.19)

The *Gaussian curvature* is defined as the product of k_1 and k_2; that is, $k_3 = k_1 \times k_2$. The mean curvature k_4 is simply $(k_1 + k_2)/2$. Peet and Sahota define two other curvature measures, claimed to be better than $k_1 \ldots k_4$:

$$k_5 = \frac{(k2 - k1)}{2}$$

$$k_6 = \max(|k_1|,|k_2|)$$

(EQ 4.20)

Finally, from the sign of the expression $eg - f^2$ we can determine whether the point under consideration is a *saddle point* (<0), an *elliptic point* (>0) or a *parabolic point* (=0). The number of such points in each image window might provide some texture discrimination capability.

There are nine texture measures based on this discussion of surface curvature. Not all of these will be useful when applied to any particular image, but they are useful tools to have available. The text.c program implements each of these in the usual way; the algorithm names for the command line are: k_1, k_2, k_3, k_4, k_5, k_6, elliptic, parabolic, and saddle. Thus, the call

```
text t3.pgm saddle
```

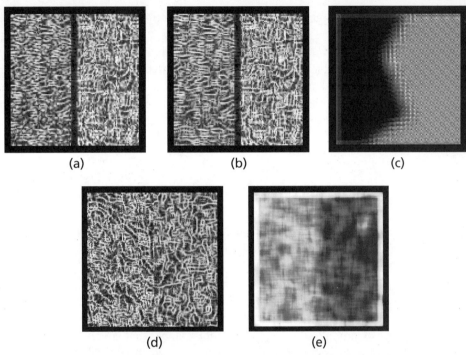

(a) (b) (c)

(d) (e)

Figure 4.10 Surface curvature measures. (a) K5 measured on test image T5. (b) K6 measured on T5. (c) Elliptic points found in windows in image T1. (d) K6 measured on T3. (e) Standard deviations of 13 × 13 windows of image (d).

will compute the number of saddle points in each window and create an image in which these values are the levels associated with each pixel. Figure 4.10 shows some of these measures applied to the test image.

4.7   FRACTAL DIMENSION

Fractal geometry can be used on occasion to discriminate between textures. The word ''fractal'' is really more of an adjective than a noun, and it refers to entities (especially sets of pixels) that display a degree of self-similarity at different scales. A mathematical straight line displays a high degree of self-similarity; any portion of the line is the same as any other, at any magnification.

The fractal dimension D of a set of pixels I is specified by the relationship:

$$1 = Nr^D \qquad \text{(EQ 4.21)}$$

where the image I has been broken up into N nonoverlapping copies of a basic shape, each one scaled by a factor of r from the original. It might be possible to measure D given a perfect synthetic image, but natural scenes with textures will not contain exact replicas of the basic shape. What we want is an estimate of D that can be calculated from a sampled raster representation. One such algorithm is the Differential Box Counting (DBC) algorithm (Sark 1992), and another uses the Hurst coefficient (Russ). Equation 4.21 can be rewritten as

$$ D = \frac{\log N}{\log\left(\frac{1}{r}\right)} \qquad \text{(EQ 4.22)} $$

From this it can be seen that there is a log-log relationship between N and r. If $\log(N)$ were plotted against $\log(r)$ the result should be a straight line whose slope is approximately D.

The Hurst coefficient is an approximation that makes use of this relationship. Consider Figure 4.11, in which a 7×7 pixel region is marked according to the distance of each pixel from the central pixel. There are eight groups of pixels, corresponding to the eight different distances that are possible. Within each group the largest difference in grey level is found; this is the same as subtracting the smallest grey level in the group from the largest.

The central pixel is ignored, and a straight line is fit to the log of the maximum difference (y coordinate) and the log of the distance from the central pixel (x coordinate). The slope of this line is the Hurst coefficient, and replaces the pixel at the center of the region.

As an example, consider the following 7×7 pixel region of an image:

85	70	86	92	60	102	202
91	81	98	113	86	119	189
96	86	102	107	74	107	194
101	91	113	107	83	118	198
99	68	107	107	76	107	194
107	94	93	115	83	115	198
94	98	98	107	81	115	194

The first step in computing the Hurst coefficient is to determine the maximum grey level difference for each distance class of pixels. Starting at the pixels at distance one or less from the center, the maximum level is 113 and the minimum is 83, for a difference of 30. The next class has the range $113 - 74 = 39$, and the distance $= 2$ class has a range of $118 - 74 = 44$.

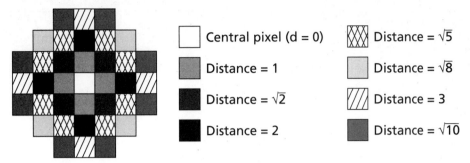

Figure 4.11 A 7 × 7 region for calculating the Hurst coefficient of the central pixel. There are eight classes of pixel, organized by their distance from the central pixel. The pixel at d = 0 is not really a class by itself.

Completing Table 4.1 gives:

Table 4.1 Hurst Coefficient Example Data

Class:	d=1	d=$\sqrt{2}$	d=2	d=$\sqrt{5}$	d=$\sqrt{8}$	d=3	d=$\sqrt{10}$
Number:	30	39	44	50	51	130	138

A line to be fit to this data using a log-log relationship, so the next step is to take the log of both the distance and the grey-level difference, as shown in Table 4.2:

Table 4.2 Hurst Coefficient Calculation Data

Ln(Distance):	0.000	0.347	0.693	0.805	1.040	1.099	1.151
Ln(Delta G):	3.401	3.664	3.784	3.912	3.932	4.868	4.927

Now a straight line is fit to the points, using a least-squares approach. The line in this case has the equation:

$$y = 1.145x + 3.229$$

The slope of this line, $m = 1.145$, is the Hurst coefficient. The graph of the raw data and the fit line can be seen in Figure 4.12.

Fractal dimension can be estimated using the text.c program as follows:

```
text t1.pgm fractal
```

The resulting image will be found in the file fractal.pgm.

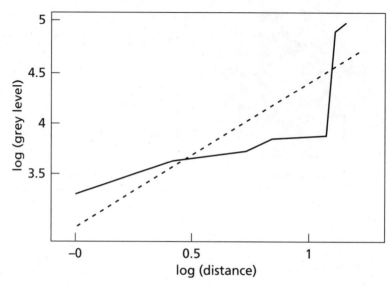

Figure 4.12 The straight-line fit to the log(distance) vs. log(grey-level change) data for the 7 × 7 region used as an example of the Hurst coefficient calculation. The slope of this line is the Hurst coefficient.

4.8 BIBLIOGRAPHY

Cohen, P., LeDinh, C. T., and V. Lacasse. 1989. Classification of Natural Textures by Means of Two Dimensional Masks. *IEEE Transactions on Acoustics, Speech, and Signal Processing*. Vol. 37. 1:125–128.

Derin, H. and W. S. Cole. 1986. Segmentation of Textured Images Using Gibbs Random Fields. *Computer Vision, Graphics, and Image Processing*. Vol. 35. 72–98.

Faugeras, O.D. (Ed.) 1983. *Fundamentals in Computer Vision*. Cambridge: Cambridge University Press.

Ferryanto, S. 1995. A Kolmogorov-Smirnov Type Statistic for Detecting Structural Changes of Textures. *Pattern Recognition Letters*. Vol. 16. 247–256.

Ganesan, L. and P. Bhattacharyya. 1995. A New Statistical Approach for Micro Texture Description. *Pattern Recognition Letters*. Vol. 16. 471–478.

Haralick, R. M. and L. G. Shapiro. 1992. *Computer and Robot Vision*. Reading, MA: Addison-Wesley.

Hsiao, J. Y. and A. A. Sawchuk. 1989. Unsupervised Image Segmentation Using Feature Smoothing and Probabalistic Relaxation Techniques. *Computer Vision, Graphics, and Image Processing*. Vol. 48. 1–21.

Jin, X. C., Ong, S. H., and Jaysooriah. 1995. A Practical Method for Estimating Fractal Dimension. *Pattern Recognition Letters*. Vol. 16. 457–464.

Julesz, B. 1981. Textons, the Elements of Texture Perception, and Their Interactions. *Nature*. Vol. 290. 12:91–97.

Laws, K. I. 1980. Rapid Texture Identification. *SPIE Image Processing for Missile Guidance*. 376–380.

Peet, F. G., and T. S. Sahota. 1985. Surface Curvature as a Measure of Image Texture. *IEEE Transactions on Pattern Analysis and Machine Intelligence*. Vol. PAMI-7. 6:734–738.

Pratt, W. K. 1991. *Digital Image Processing* (2nd. Edition). New York: John Wiley & Sons.

Russ, J. C. 1990. Surface Characterization: Fractal Dimensions, Hurst Coefficients, and Frequency Transforms. *Journal of Computer Assisted Microscopy*. Vol. 2. 249–257.

Sarkar, N. and B. B. Chaudhuri. 1994. An Efficient Differential Box Counting Approach to Compute Fractal Dimension of Image. *IEEE Transactions on Systems, Man, and Cybernetics*. Vol. 24. 115–120.

Unser, M. 1986. Sum and Difference Histograms for Texture Classification, *IEEE Transactions on Pattern Analysis and Machine Intelligence*, Vol. PAMI-8. 1:118–125.

5

SKELETONIZATION— THE ESSENTIAL LINE

5.1 WHAT IS A SKELETON?

Everyone working in the computer vision field knows what thinning is: it is what you do to produce the *skeleton* of an object, usually a bilevel object. Reasonably enough, one might then ask "What is a skeleton?" We now venture into the realm of opinion because, as with texture, there is no generally agreed-upon definition for what a skeleton is. Worse yet, and unlike with texture, we may not know a skeleton when we see it. This is unfortunate, because the generation of a digital skeleton is often one of the first processing steps taken by a computer vision system when attempting to extract features from an object in an image. A skeleton is presumed to represent the shape of the object in a relatively small number of pixels, all of which are (in some sense) *structural* and therefore necessary. In line images the skeleton conveys all of the information found in the original, wherein lies the value of the skeleton: The position, orientation, and length of the line segments of the skeleton are representative of those of the lines of which the image is composed. This simplifies the task of characterizing the components of the line image.

Thinning, therefore, can be defined as the act of identifying those pixels belonging to an object that are essential for communicating the object's shape: these are the skeletal pixels, and form a set. That no generally agreed-upon definition of a digital skeleton exists has been pointed out by many people (Davies, Haralick) without altering the situation. Of the literally hundreds of papers on the subject of thinning in print, the vast majority are concerned with the implementation of a variation on an existing thinning method, where the novel aspects are related to the performance of the algorithm. Many of the more recent thinning algorithms were designed with an eye on the clock: The speed of the algorithm is improved, while often leaving the basic principles alone. The quality of the skeleton or the means by which it is found are rarely the subject of analysis.

In this chapter a number of approaches to thinning will be examined, and we will always come back to the original issue of the definition without finding a solution. There are, however, three things that can be stated in advance, and these should be kept in mind:

1. Not all objects can or should be thinned. Thinning is useful for objects consisting of lines, whether they are straight or curved, and is not useful for objects having a shape that encloses a significant area. For example, a circle can be thinned since it is represented by a curved line; a disk cannot be meaningfully thinned.

2. What works as a skeleton in one situation may not work in all situations. Thinning is usually one step in preparing an image for further processing. The nature of the subsequent steps often dictates the properties needed of the skeleton.

3. Thinning is the act of identifying the skeleton, and is not defined by the algorithm used. In particular, thinning is not always an iterative process of stripping away the outer layers of pixels.

5.2 THE MEDIAL-AXIS TRANSFORM

Possibly the first definition of a skeleton is that of Blum (1967) in defining the *medial axis function* (MAF). The MAF treats all boundary pixels as point sources of a wave front. Each of these pixels excites its neighbors with a delay time proportional to distance, so that they, too, become part of the wave front. The wave passes through each point only once, and when two waves meet they cancel each other, producing a *corner*. The *medial axis* (MA) is the locus of the corners, and forms the skeleton (Blum says *line of symmetry*) of the object. The MAF uses both time and space information, and can be inverted to give back the original picture. It is possible to implement this directly, but it is difficult: What is needed is to convert the continuous transform to a discrete one. This involves various approximations involving the distance function on a discrete grid. This allows the MAF to be applied to a raster image, for which the medial axis is not defined.

One way to find the medial axis is to use the boundary of the object. For any point P in the object, locate the closest point on the boundary. If there is more than one boundary point at the minimum distance, then P is on the medial axis. The set of all such points is the medial axis of the object. Unfortunately this must be done at a very high resolution, or Euclidean distances will not be equal when they should be, and skeletal pixels will be missed.

An approximation to the medial axis on a sampled grid is more easily obtained in two steps. First, compute the distance from each object pixel to the nearest boundary pixel. This involves computing the distance to all boundary pixels. Next, the Laplacian of the distance image is calculated, and pixels having large values are thought to belong to the medial axis.

The way that distance is measured has an impact on the result, as seen in Figure 5.1. The medial axis was found for a T-shaped object using Euclidean distance, *4-distance*, and *8-distance*. 4-distance between pixels A and B is defined to be the minimum number of horizontal and vertical moves needed to get from A to B. 8-distance is the minimum number of pixel moves, in any of the standard eight directions, needed to get from A to B. There are clear differences in the medial axis depending on which way distance is calculated, but any of them could be used as a skeleton.

The skeleton of the T produced by the medial axis does not have the same shape as the T, nor does it need it. The main concern is whether the skeleton characterizes the basic shape of the object somehow. On the other hand, a simple example

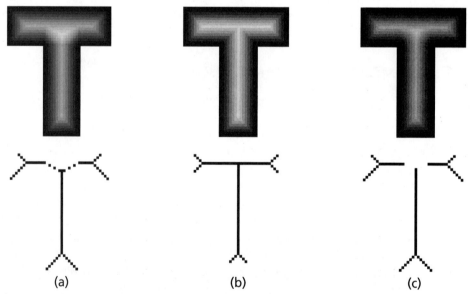

(a)   (b)   (c)

Figure 5.1 The effect of the distance function on the medial axis. (a) Medial axis (above) and skeleton (below) of the T-shaped object, using 4-distance. (b) Medial axis and skeleton computed using 8-distance. (c) Computed using Euclidean distance.

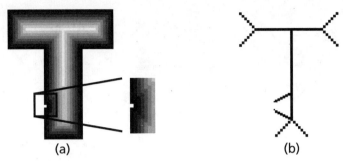

(a)   (b)

Figure 5.2 A single pixel difference between two objects can create a large difference in their skeletons. (a) The T-shaped object, but with one less black pixel. (b) The skeleton of the new object, quite different from those in Figure 5.1.

exposes a fundamental problem with the medial axis as a skeleton. Most people would agree that the skeletons of two objects that are similar to each other should, in turn, be similar. Figure 5.2 shows an object that differs from Figure 5.1a in only a single pixel; the medial axes of these objects, on the other hand, differ substantially.

Most vision researchers would agree that the medial-axis transform often does not yield an ideal skeleton, and takes too long to compute. It does, however, form the basis of a great many thinning methods, and in that regard is a very important concept.

5.3   ITERATIVE MORPHOLOGICAL METHODS

The majority of thinning algorithms are based on a repeated stripping away of layers of pixels until no more layers can be removed. There is a set of rules defining which pixels may be removed, and frequently some sort of template-matching scheme is used to implement these rules. Often, the rules are designed so that it is easy to tell when to stop: when no change occurs after two consecutive passes through the image.

The first such algorithm to be described (Stentiford 1983) is typical of the genre. It uses 3×3 templates, where a match of the template in the image means to delete (set to white) the center pixel. The basic algorithm is:

1. Find a pixel location (i,j) where the pixels in the image I match those in template M1 Figure 5.3a).

2. If the central pixel *is not an endpoint*, and has *connectivity number = 1*, then mark this pixel for later deletion.

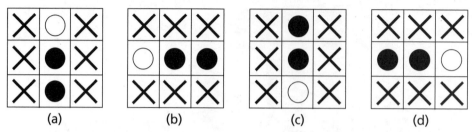

Figure 5.3 Templates for identifying pixels that can be deleted in the Stentiford thinning algorithm. (a) Template M1. (b) Template M2. (c) Template M3. (d) Template M4. The specified black and white pixels in the templates must correspond to pixels of an identical color in the image; the Xs indicate places where we don't care what color the image pixel is.

3. Repeat steps 1 and 2 for all pixel locations matching the template M1.

4. Repeat steps 1–3 for the remaining templates in turn: M2, M3, and M4.

5. If any pixels have been marked for deletion, then delete them by setting them to white.

6. If any pixels were deleted in step 5, then repeat the entire process from step 1; otherwise stop.

The image must be scanned for a template match in a particular order for each template. The purpose of template M_1 is to find removable pixels along the top edge of an object, and we search for a match from left to right, then from top to bottom. M_2 will match a pixel on the left side of an object; this template moves from the bottom to the top of the image, left to right. M_3 will locate pixels along the bottom edge, and moves from right to left, bottom to top. Finally, to find pixels on the right side of an object, match template M_4 in a top-to-bottom, right-to-left fashion. This specific order and direction for applying the templates ensures that the pixels will be removed in a symmetrical way, without any significant directional bias.

There are still two issues to be resolved, both from step 2. A pixel is an endpoint if it is connected to just one other pixel; that is, if a black pixel has only one black neighbor out of the eight possible neighbors. If endpoints were to be deleted, then any straight lines and open curves would be removed completely, rather like opening a zipper.

The concept of a connectivity number is somewhat more challenging. Because we are using only very small parts of an image, the role of that image segment in the overall picture is not clear. Sometimes a single pixel connects two much larger sections of an object, and it is intuitively obvious that such a pixel cannot be removed. To do so would create two objects where there was originally only one.

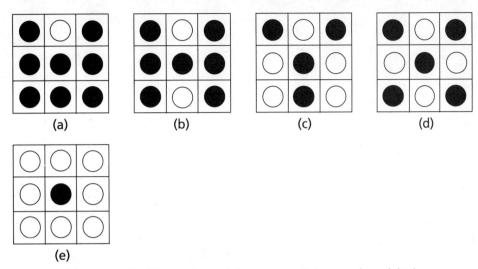

Figure 5.4 An illustration of the connectivity number. (a) The central pixel does not connect any regions, and can be removed. Connectivity number = 1. (b) If the central pixel were to be deleted, then the left and right halves would (might) become disconnected. Connectivity number = 2. (c) Connectivity = 3. (d) Connectivity = 4, the maximum. (e) Connectivity = 0.

A connectivity number is a measure of how many objects a particular pixel *might* connect.

One such connectivity measure, as seen in Figure 5.4, is (Yokoi 1973):

$$C_n = \sum_{k \in S} N_k - (N_k \cdot N_{k+1} \cdot N_{k+2}) \qquad \text{(EQ 5.1)}$$

Where N_k is the color value of one of the eight neighbors of the pixel involved, and $S = \{1,3,5,7\}$. N_1 is the color value of pixel to the right of the central pixel,

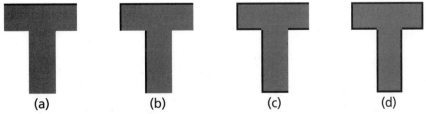

Figure 5.5 The four parts of each iteration of the Stentiford thinning method. (a) After applying template M1. (b) After M2. (c) After M3. (d) After M4. In each case, the black pixels represent those to be deleted in this iteration.

and they are numbered in counterclockwise order around the center. The value of N_k is one if the pixel is white (background) and zero if black (object). The center pixel is N_0, and $N_k = N_{k-8}$ if $k > 8$. Another way that connectivity can be computed is by visiting the neighbors in the order $N_1, N_2 \ldots N_8, N_1$. The number of color changes (black-white) counts the number of regions the central pixel connects.

Figure 5.5 shows one iteration (the first) of this thinning algorithm applied to the T-shaped object of Figure 5.1. One iteration includes one pass for each of the four templates. The black pixels are those marked for deletion, and it is clear from

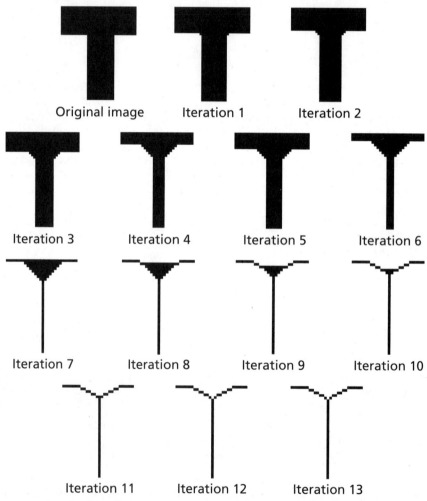

Original image   Iteration 1   Iteration 2

Iteration 3   Iteration 4   Iteration 5   Iteration 6

Iteration 7   Iteration 8   Iteration 9   Iteration 10

Iteration 11   Iteration 12   Iteration 13

Figure 5.6 All iterations of the Stentiford thinning algorithm applied to the T. The last two iterations are the same, since one extra pass is needed to ensure that the skeleton is complete.

the figure exactly what each template accomplishes. Each complete iteration effectively erodes a layer of pixels from the outside of the object, but unlike standard morphological erosion, the deletion of a pixel is contingent upon meeting the endpoint and connectedness constraints.

Complete thinning of this object requires 13 iterations (counting the final iteration, which does nothing except show that we are finished). Figure 5.6 shows the resulting image after each iteration. One iteration makes four passes through the image, which in this case is 60 × 60 pixels, or 3600 pixels. Thus, 187,000 pixels were examined in order to thin this simple image. It gets worse: Each template application looks at three pixels (the maximum is 561,600), and each time a template match occurs, another 18 pixels are looked at (the upper limit is 10,108,800 pixels, but will be a fraction of that in practice). Finally, there will be one extra pass each iteration to delete the marked pixels (10,152,000). This is an expensive way to thin a small image, but is quite typical of template-based mark-and-delete algorithms.

There are a few classic problems with this thinning algorithm that show up as *artifacts* in the skeleton. They are classic because they tend to appear in a great variety of algorithms of this type, and researchers in the area have learned to anticipate them. The first of these is called *necking*, in which a narrow point at the intersection of two lines is stretched into a small line segment (Figure 5.7a).

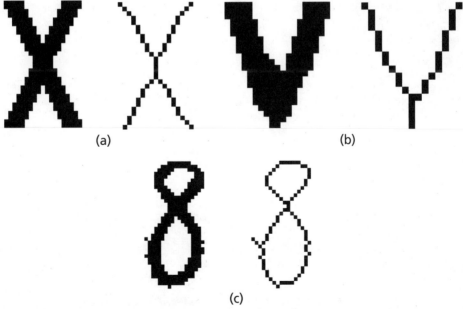

(a)   (b)

(c)

Figure 5.7 Classic thinning artifacts. (a) Necking. (b) Tailing.
(c) Spurious projection (line fuzz).

Tails can be created where none exist because of excess thinning where two lines meet at an acute angle (Figure 5.7b). Finally, and perhaps most common, is the creation of extra line segments joining a real skeletal segment; this has been called a *spurious projection*, *hairs*, or *line fuzz* (5.7c).

Stentiford suggests a preprocessing stage to minimize these thinning artifacts. Since line fuzz is frequently caused by small irregularities in the object outline, a smoothing step is suggested before thinning to remove them. Basically, a pass is made over all pixels, deleting those having two or fewer black neighbors and having a connectivity number less than two.

For dealing with necking, he suggests a procedure called *acute angle emphasis*, in which pixels near the joint between two lines are set to white if they ''plug up'' an acute angle. This is done using the templates seen in Figure 5.8. A match to any template marks the central pixel for deletion, and causes another iteration of less severe acute angle emphasis using only the first three templates of each type. If any pixels were deleted, one last pass using only the first templates of each type is performed.

Smoothing is done first, followed by all passes of acute angle emphasis, followed finally by the thinning steps. Figure 5.9 shows the final skeletons of the characters from Figure 5.7 when the preprocessing steps are included.

As good as these skeletons appear to be, the method is still flawed. The use of three stages of acute angle emphasis will not be sufficient for very thick characters, and the templates do not match all situations that can cause necking and tailing. Also, the smoothing step will not catch all irregularities that can cause line fuzz.

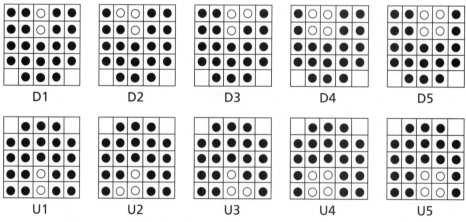

Figure 5.8 Templates used for the acute angle emphasis preprocessing step.

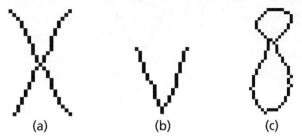

(a)   (b)   (c)

Figure 5.9 Final thinned characters, after both preprocessing steps and thinning.

Still, perfection should not be expected, and the method does pretty well, particularly as a preprocessing step for character recognition.

One thinning algorithm that seems to be in everybody's toolkit is the Zhang-Suen (Zhang 1984) algorithm. It has been used as a basis of comparison for thinning methods for many years, and is fast and simple to implement. It is a *parallel* method, meaning that the new value for any pixel can be computed using only the values known from the previous iteration. Therefore, if a computer having one CPU per pixel were available, it could determine the entire next iteration simultaneously. Since most of us don't have a computer of that size, let's consider only the version of the program that uses one CPU.

The algorithm is broken up into two subiterations instead of, for example, the four subiterations of the Stentiford method. In one subiteration, a pixel $I(i,j)$ is deleted (or marked for deletion) if the following four conditions are all true:

1. Its connectivity number is one (1).
2. It has at least two black neighbors and not more than six.
3. At least one of $I(i,j+1)$, $I(i-1,j)$ and $I(i,j-1)$ are background (white).
4. At least one of $I(i-1,j)$, $I(i+1,j)$ and $I(i,j-1)$ are background.

At the end of this subiteration the marked pixels are deleted. The next subiteration is the same except for steps 3 and 4:

1. At least one of $I(i-1,j)$, $I(i,j+1)$ and $I(i+1,j)$ are background.
2. At least one of $I(i,j+1)$, $I(i+1,j)$ and $I(i,j-1)$ are background.

and again, any marked pixels are deleted. If at the end of either subiteration there are no pixels to be deleted, then the skeleton is complete, and the program stops.

Figure 5.10 shows the skeletons found by the Zhang-Suen algorithm applied to the four example images seen so far: the T, X, V, and 8. The T skeleton is exceptionally good, and the V skeleton does not show any signs of tailing. The X

Figure 5.10 The skeletons produced by the standard Zhang-Suen thinning algorithm when applied to the test images of Figure 5.2 and 5.7.

skeleton does still show necking, and the 8 skeleton still has line fuzz. The pre-processing steps suggested by Stentiford may clear this up.

Before trying this, an improvement of the algorithm was suggested (Holt 1987) that is faster and does not involve subiterations. First, the two subiterations are written as logical expressions which use the 3 × 3 neighborhood about the pixel concerned. The first subiteration above can be written as:

$$v(C) \wedge (\sim\!\text{edge}(C) \vee (v(E) \wedge v(S) \wedge (v(N) \vee v(W)))) \qquad \text{(EQ 5.2)}$$

which is the condition under which the center pixel C survives the first subiteration. The v function gives the value of the pixel (1 = true for an object pixel, 0 = false for background), and the edge function is true if C is on the edge of the object—this corresponds to having between two and six neighbors and connectivity number = 1. The letters E, S, N, and W correspond to pixels in a particular direction from the center pixel C; E means east (as in $I(i,j+1)$) S means south (as in $I(i+1,j)$) and so on.

The second subiteration would be written as:

$$v(C) \wedge (\sim\!\text{edge}(C) \vee (v(W) \wedge v(N) \wedge (v(S) \vee v(E)))) \qquad \text{(EQ 5.3)}$$

Holt and company combined the two expressions for survival (Eqs. 5.2 and 5.3) with a connectedness-preserving condition (needed for parallel execution) and came up with the following single expression for pixel survival:

$$
\begin{aligned}
v(C) \wedge (\sim\!\text{edge}(C) \vee & \\
(\text{edge}(E) \wedge v(N) \wedge v(S)) \vee & \\
(\text{edge}(S) \wedge v(W) \wedge v(E)) \vee & \\
(\text{edge}(E) \wedge \text{edge}(SE) \wedge \text{edge}(S)) &
\end{aligned}
\qquad \text{(EQ 5.4)}
$$

This expression is not a daunting as it appears; the v functions are simply pixel values, and the edge function is just about as complex as the connectivity function used in the Stentiford algorithm. The result from this are good, but not identical to the standard Zhang-Suen. However, there is still more to come.

Sometimes, when thinning is complete, there are still pixels that could be deleted. Principal among these are pixels that form a staircase; clearly half of the pixels in a staircase could be removed without affecting the shape or connectedness of the overall object. Basically, the central pixel in one of the following windows can be deleted:

```
0  1  x      x  1  0      0  x  x      x  x  0
1  1  x      x  1  1      x  1  1      1  1  x
x  x  0      0  x  x      x  1  0      0  1  x
```

To avoid creating a new hole, we simply add a condition that one of the x values be 0. For windows having a northward bias (the first two above) the expression for survival of a pixel in the staircase-removal iteration is:

$$v(C) \wedge \sim(v(N) \wedge$$

$$((v(E) \wedge \sim v(NE) \wedge \sim v(SW) \wedge (\sim v(W) \vee \sim v(S)) \vee \quad \text{(EQ 5.5)}$$

$$(v(W) \wedge \sim v(NW) \wedge \sim v(SE) \wedge (\sim v(E) \vee \sim v(S))))))$$

The pass having a southward bias is the same, but with north and south exchanged. None of the example images seen so far possess any significant amount of staircasing, but the image introduced in Figure 5.11 does. The version thinned using staircase removal seems more smooth and symmetrical than the other skeletons. Figure 5.12 shows the result of applying this method to the four test images

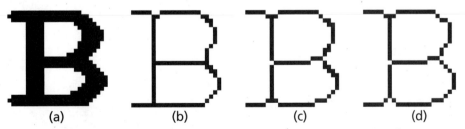

(a)   (b)   (c)   (d)

Figure 5.11 Variations on the Zhang-Suen thinning algorithm.
(a) Original image (b) Thinned using the standard algorithm.
(c) Thinned using Holt's variation. (d) Holt's variation
plus staircase removal.

Figure 5.12 Results from Holt's algorithm with staircase removal applied to the standard test images.

we have been using. The basic problems are still present; in fact, this method does not deal with tails as well as the standard Zhang-Suen method, and the T skeleton is not as good.

If simple speed is what is of importance, then the Holt variation of Zhang-Suen is the better of the methods seen so far. On the other hand, if the quality of the skeleton is of prime importance, it is probable that a merging of the three methods is in order: Stentiford's preprocessing scheme feeding images into Zhang-Suen's basic algorithm, with Holt's staircase removal as a post-processor. The code for this sequence of operations appears in Section 5.8, since it includes all of the techniques of importance that have been discussed to this point. It is available on the accompanying CD as the program thnbest, and does appear to generate the best skeletons of all of the methods seen so far; of course, this is a subjective measure. The best skeletons can be seen in Figure 5.13.

5.4 USE OF CONTOURS

The iterative mark-and-delete methods seen so far have in common that they always delete pixels from the outer layer. These are on the boundary of the object, and form a contour having a distance of zero pixels from the background. A

Figure 5.13 Skeletons obtained from using the Stentiford preprocessing steps combined with the Zhang-Suen thinning algorithm and Holt's staircase-elimination procedure.

contour-based method locates the entire outer contour, or even all contours, and then deletes the pixels on the contour except those needed for connectivity. These methods tend not to use 3 × 3 templates for locating pixels to be removed.

The essential scheme used by a contour-based thinning algorithm is:

1. Locate the contour pixels.
2. Identify pixels on the contour that cannot be removed.
3. Remove all contour pixels but those in step 2.
4. If any pixels were removed in step 3, then repeat from step 1.

The external contour is usually traced in a manner identical to that used when finding the *chain code*. Starting at any black pixel having a horizontal or vertical neighbor in the background (a boundary pixel), the pixels on the contour are visited or traced in a counterclockwise fashion until the starting pixel is seen again. The pixels are saved in a list when visited, giving a fast way to revisit them later. Then the contour pixels are marked somehow and the process is repeated, in order to find internal contours such as would occur around a hole in the object, until no starting pixels remain.

After the contour has been identified, the contour pixels that must not be removed can be located. One way to do this (Pavlidis 1982) uses the concept of a *multiple pixel*. There are three types of multiple pixel, none of which can be safely removed from a contour. The first type (as seen in Figure 5.14a) is one that appears

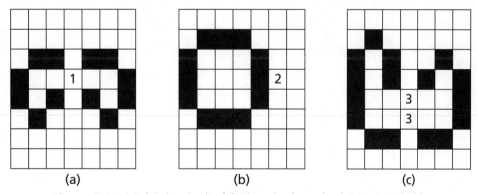

(a)　　　　　　(b)　　　　　　(c)

Figure 5.14 Multiple pixels. (a) The pixel marked 1 is a multiple pixel because it is visited twice in one complete traversal of the contour. (b) The pixel marked 2 is a multiple pixel because it has no neighbors that are not contour pixels (no internal neighbors). (c) The pixels marked 3 are multiple pixels because they are neighbors of each other, but do not occur immediately before or after each other in the list of contour pixels. They belong to different parts of the same contour in this case.

more than once in the list of contour pixels. The reason for this is that there is no way to get from one part of the object to the other without passing through the multiple pixel, and so to delete this pixel would separate the two parts. It is this type of pixel for which the phrase *multiple pixel* was named.

The second type of multiple pixel is one that has no neighbors in the interior of the object; that is, all of its object neighbors belong to the contour (Figure 5.14b). This could only occur if the pixel involved *stuck out* from the boundary; perhaps it is the endpoint of a line, for example. Line endpoints clearly cannot be deleted either.

The third type of multiple pixel is one having a neighbor that is on the contour but that is not its immediate successor or predecessor. This can occur when the contour turns back on itself, or when an internal and an external contour meet and parallel each other. To delete such pixels would create the possibility that two-pixel-wide lines would simply be removed, which is unacceptable.

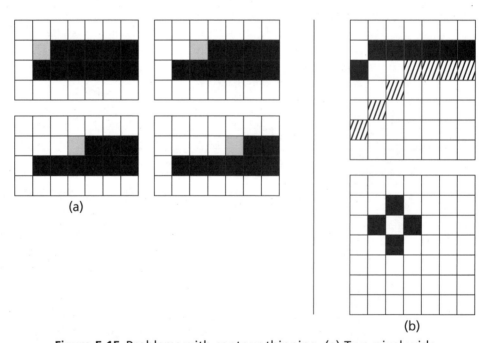

(a)

(b)

Figure 5.15 Problems with contour thinning. (a) Two-pixel-wide lines should be thinned further, in this case by deleting those pixels on the corner of a right angle. (b) Some situations can result in a spurious contour. One cure is to forbid very small contours.

Figure 5.16 Result of using contour-based thinning. Each of the four test images has been thinned by repeatedly stripping away contours, while leaving the multiple pixels behind. Double lines were removed after the fact (Figure 5.15), and staircases were removed. The smoothing pass described by Stentiford was done before thinning was attempted.

The three types of multiple pixel are easy to identify using a pass through the contour, marking the pixels and checking the three conditions. They are marked as nonremovable, then all other contour pixels are set to the background level. Contours are marked, checked, and deleted until no further change takes place.

There are a few problems with the algorithm as presented as far, the most serious of which is that the skeletons obtained are two pixels thick in many places; this is due to multiple pixels of type 3 being neighbors, but not removable. The fix is to add another pass through the thinned image, removing all pixels on a right-angle corner (Zhang 1984) as seen in Figure 5.15a. Since it was useful before, a pass of Holt's staircase removal was added as well.

Another problem is caused by the tracing of the contours. Some tracers (including Pavlidis's) will trace a tiny contour in locations where an external and internal contour pass close to each other. This is illustrated in Figure 5.15b. Rather than mess with the tracer, the program was modified to ignore contours having four or fewer pixels. This may have ramifications if the image is supposed to contain a number of one-pixel holes.

The resulting skeletons suffer from artifacts, especially tailing. The preprocessing methods do not help a great deal, but the smoothing procedure from Stentiford does limit the fuzz, and so was added. The skeletons generated by this system for the four test images can be seen in Figure 5.16. If these do not appear to be better than those of Figure 5.13, remember that the advantage of the contour methods is supposed to be speed. For example, a more recent contour-based algorithm (Kwok 1989) claims execution speeds that are 10–20 times faster than Zhang-Suen.

5.5 USE OF OBJECT OUTLINES—LINE FOLLOWING

Since all thinning activity, such as marking and deleting pixels, takes place at the boundary of the object, it has been suggested that the boundary is all that is really needed to create a skeleton. In addition, the skeletal pixels may be located in a single pass through the image; the point in the object equidistant from the two nearby sides is skeletal. Since the boundaries define the object, why not follow them, selecting the *middle* pixel as being on the skeleton at each step (Baruch 1988). This will be called *thinning by line following*.

Following a thick line is more easily said than done. Baruch's approach uses a small rectangular window that spans the line, moving along it a small number of pixels at a time. Since the window is centered on the line, the skeletal pixel is the one at the center of the window, and a new skeletal pixel is selected each time the window moves.

Using the notation of Baruch, let LP be a pointer to a pixel on the left side of the line, and let RP be a pixel on the right side of the line, as seen in Figure 5.17a.

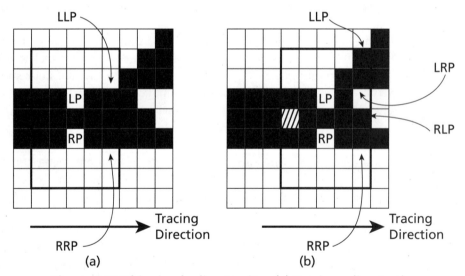

Figure 5.17 Thinning by line tracing. (a) Tracing a line to the left. The pixels are labelled according to the description of the algorithm, and the black rectangle is the window. (b) The next step in the line trace. The window has moved right, the previous window center is marked as skeletal, and new values for LLP and RRP. The line branches in this window, so LRP and RLP exist as well.

The window will always be a fixed distance from LP and RP; in this case the distance $d = 2$. Given values for LP and RP it is a simple matter to determine the coordinates of the corners of the window:

$$W_{ulr} = \min(LP_r, RP_r)$$
$$W_{ulc} = \min(LP_c, RP_c)$$
$$W_{lrr} = \max(LP_r, RP_r)$$
$$W_{lrc} = \max(LP_c, RP_c)$$

(EQ 5.6)

where *ul* mean upper-left, *lr* means lower-right, and the *r* and *c* subscripts refer to row and column indices. The line being traced will intersect the window at some point ahead of (in the direction of tracing) LP and RP unless the line ends within the window. This being true, the set pixels on the left side of the line are traced forward until the window is encountered—this point is labelled LLP. The same is done for the right side of the line, tracing set pixels from RP to RRP. The line ends in this window if, when tracing from LP, the pixel labelled RP is encountered before the window is.

For a normal line, the center pixel would now be marked as skeletal, LP would become LLP, RP would become RRP, and the process repeats. The skeleton will consist of the lines joining the centers of the windows. Figure 5.17b shows the next step in the tracing process; the window moves ahead, leaving behind a skeletal pixel, and a new LLP and LRP is found. The situation becomes much more complex if the line branches within the window, as it must do for any but the most trivial of images, and as it does in the example being followed.

The line branches if, when tracing the pixels along the window's edge from LLP to RRP, any background pixels are encountered. If this is the case (as it is in Figure 5.17b) label the set pixel seen just before the first background pixel seen between LLP and RRP as LRP; label the first set pixel seen after LRP on the window's edge as RLP. Now (recursively) trace the first branch by letting LP = LLP, RP = LRP and tracing as usual. When that branch is complete, return and set LP = RLP, set RP to the old RP, and rebuild the window, relabelling the pixels seen there. If a branch still exists, recursively trace it as before as shown in Figure 5.18; otherwise, simply follow the standard procedure.

The entire process begins by setting LP = RP = the coordinates of the first set pixel in the image. The initial direction is chosen to be right, but this varies as the window moves, depending on the relationship between LP and RP; for example, if LP and RP are on the same row with LP to the left, then the direction is up. If LP and RP are on the same column with LP above RP, the direction is right; and so on. The program ends when the line ends in the window, and no further

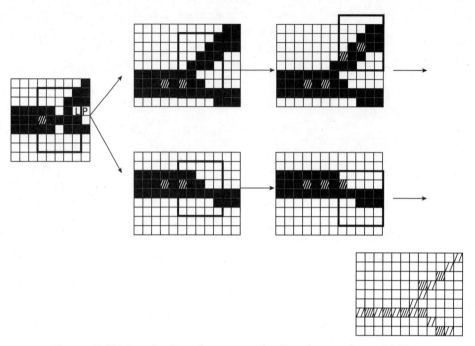

Figure 5.18 Continuing the trace of a line from a branch. The line splits into two parts, each of which can be traced recursively using the same procedure. The skeleton consists of the pixels that were the window centers, plus those that connect them. They can be connected by using a graphics function to draw straight lines between them.

branches exist to continue. To make sure that the program terminates when applied to a closed curve, the pixels in the previous window that are not also in the current window are deleted.

Again, one of the major advantages of this technique is speed; it is between three and ten times as fast as the previous methods. It could be that this method could be refined to the point where it produced better skeletons than the other methods, as well. Since it uses a larger region than other techniques, the skeleton is not a function of a small region of the image, and this could be a great advantage. On the other hand, there appears to be a problem in relinking the skeleton in areas where it branches, especially if the object is very thick at that point. Figure 5.19 shows some of the results from the admittedly experimental procedure thnlf, which implements this technique.

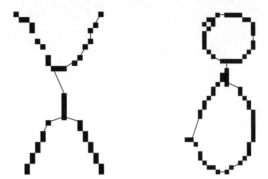

Figure 5.19 Results from line following. The skeletal pixels have been connected here by thinner straight lines so that the connections might easily be seen.

5.6 TREATING THE OBJECT AS A POLYGON

Instead of being treated as a raster object, the boundary of a region can be made into a polygon. The contour-based methods begin this way, since a chain code is really a representation of a polygon, but then fall into old habits and discard successive contours (polygons) until the skeleton remains. An interesting approach (Martinez-Perez 1987) uses geometric properties of the polygon that represents the object boundary to locate the skeleton.

The first step is to obtain the boundary of the object represented as a polygon. This could be done with a chain code, creating many small polygon edges: one edge per pair of pixels. It would be better to convert the boundary into vector form, where each edge in the polygon was stored as its starting and ending pixel coordinates. The resulting polygon should be stored in counterclockwise order so that moving from one vertex to the other is a simple matter. It should be pointed out that vectorizing the boundary is not an easy thing to do.

Figure 5.20 shows a contrived test image as a set of vectors in polygon order. Now the nodes are traversed, and one of two things is done. If the angle made by the node (and its previous and next points) is less than 180 degrees, then the angular bisector is constructed from the node to the point where the bisector meets the opposite face on the polygon; in Figure 5.20, this was done in the case of node 2. Otherwise, the line normal to both the incoming and outgoing edges is drawn to the point where it intersects the polygon; this has been done for nodes numbered 4 and 9, for example.

Now, starting at vertex 1, the path through the midpoints of the line segments constructed in the previous step forms the skeleton. The tracing process is also not easy to implement, but on the face of it the skeleton should be a good one.

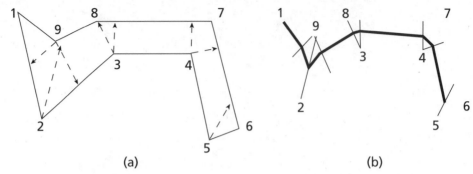

Figure 5.20 Treating the object as a polygon. (a) Some of the projecting lines computed for a hypothetical object. (b) The centers of the lines are points on the skeleton, which has been traced here as the thick black line.

There are some idiosyncracies (such as the possible formation of a loop in a thick corner, and the fact that the first skeletal segment starts in a corner, rather than at the middle of an edge).

This algorithm is intended for thinning objects that are not very thick to begin with. Characters would be included in the set of such objects, as would graphs and many maps. It is included here as an alternative strategy that shows potential, and one that has not been explored to the extent that it should.

5.7 FORCE-BASED THINNING

Up to this point, the elements implicit to definitions of skeleton include:

❏ Skeletal pixels are in some sense as far from the object boundaries as possible.

❏ A skeletal pixel is connected to at least one other, unless the skeleton consists of exactly one pixel.

❏ A line crossing the object boundary as a perpendicular will cross the skeleton exactly once before crossing another boundary, unless it is (a) too close to a point where lines meet, or (b) too close to the end of a line.

As an example, a simple object and its human-computed skeleton is shown in Figure 5.21a, where grey represents a boundary pixel and a black pixel is a skeletal pixel. The skeleton above satisfies all of the discussed properties, and while a six-year-old human could draw it, there are very few (if any) thinning algorithms that could. In most cases, humans perform thinning by computing a medial axis *in a preferred direction*. The center pixel found by slicing the object perpendicular to

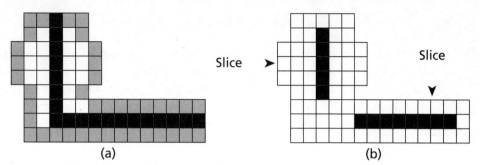

Figure 5.21 (a) A simple figure to be thinned. The human-generated skeleton is composed of the black pixels. (b) Slicing the figure in a direction normal to the boundary gives the bulk of the skeleton.

the stroke is chosen as skeletal wherever possible. This produces Figure 3.21b, which is purely computational.

There is also a perceptual aspect, which involves closing the gaps in the skeleton and extending the lines to the ends. This aspect can perhaps only be approximated on a computer. The direction in which to slice the object is that direction which is perpendicular to the stroke, and this may not be perpendicular to the boundary at all points. Nonlocal information is needed to perform this operation properly. In computer vision applications the skeleton of an object is extracted, and used to locate strokes. What is being proposed here is to reverse this process: Strokes are located and used to generate the skeletons.

Definitions

A *digital band* can be defined as a set of connected pixels with the following properties:

❑ All pixels lie within perpendicular distance d of a discrete curve C, which does not have any loops (i.e. is simple). The minimum distance between C and any boundary pixel is $d/2$.

❑ The value of d is much smaller than the length of the curve C.

❑ The direction associated with each boundary pixel is approximately the same as that of the nearest point on C.

This definition would include most digital lines and curves, either thick or thin, as digital bands. A *digital band segment* is a subset of a digital band obtained by slicing the band at two places in a direction perpendicular to C at those places. This relaxes property two above so that the length of the curve C over the segment must be simply greater than $2d$.

A *stub* is a digital band segment where there are constraints placed on the changes in direction undergone by C. In particular, over the segment: (1) the direction may be constant (linear stub), or (2) the direction may represent either a convex or concave curve (but not both) having an identifiable (if approximate) center and radius of curvature. Finally, the *skeleton of a stub* is the set of pixels obtained by using the center pixel of each slice across the stroke in a direction perpendicular to C. For example, in the case of a linear stroke, these pixels should comprise the principal axis.

Now the approach to skeletonization can be clarified. Given a line image to be thinned, it can be broken down into a set of stubs that have been concatenated so that their boundaries form a continuous digital curve. These each have a clearly defined skeleton, and the first draft of the overall skeleton (the skeletal sketch) is simply the collected skeletons of all of the stubs.

The skeleton may be complete at this point, although it is unlikely. The problem is that it is not possible to accurately determine the stubs comprising the object— some stubs are too short for this given that the image is discrete. It is often possible to fit hundreds of different stub combinations to a given object.

Use of a Force Field

The goal here is to find a method for locating skeletal pixels in a digital band that will also be useful as an approximation for objects consisting of concatenated band segments. Our idea is to have all of the background pixels that are adjacent to the boundary act as if they exerted a $1/r^2$ force on the object pixels. The skeletal pixels will lie in areas having the ridges of this force field, and these areas can be located by finding where the directions of the force vectors change significantly.

The algorithm first locates the background pixels having at least one object pixel as a neighbor and marks them. These will be assumed to exert a repulsive ''force'' on all object pixels: The nearer the object pixel is to the boundary, the greater is the force acting on it. This force field is mapped by subdividing the region into small squares and determining the force acting on the vertices of the squares. The skeleton lies within those squares where the forces acting on the corners act in opposite directions. Those squares containing skeletal areas are further subdivided, and the location of the skeletal area is recursively refined as far as necessary or possible.

The change in the direction of the force is found by computing the dot product of each pair of force vectors on corners of the square regions:

$$d_1 = \hat{f}_1 \cdot \hat{f}_2$$
$$d_2 = \hat{f}_2 \cdot \hat{f}_3 \qquad \text{(EQ 5.7)}$$
$$d_3 = \hat{f}_1 \cdot \hat{f}_4$$

If any one of d_1, d_2, or d_3 is negative, then the region involved contains some skeletal area.

To compute the force vector at each pixel location is time-consuming. For each object pixel, a straight line is drawn to all marked pixels on the object outline. Lines passing through the background are discarded, as illustrated in Figure 5.22, and for each of the remaining lines a vector with length $1/r^2$ and direction from the outline pixel to the object pixel is added to the force vector at that pixel. A graphical illustration of the force calculation is given in Figure 5.23.

This is done for all object pixels; then recursive subdivision can be used to refine the positions of the skeletal areas. From any endpoints of the skeleton found in the previous stage, we consider growing this skeletal line until it hits another skeleton or an edge. If it hits itself, the loop grown thereby is deleted.

The details of the growing process are relatively simple. First, a queue to hold the points to be grown is defined. All of the endpoints of the current stubs are placed into the queue as potential starting points for the growth process. Then points are removed from the queue one at a time and tested to see if growth is possible; if so, it is added to the skeleton and the new skeletal point is added to the queue if it, too, is a potential starting point.

To grow from a point P, the point must satisfy two conditions. P must have

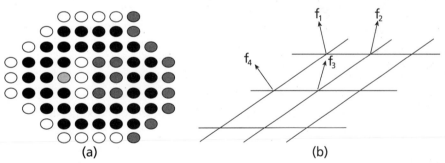

(a)   (b)

○ Pixels exerting a force

⬤ 'Invisible' pixels

● Object pixels

◓ Pixel under consideration

Figure 5.22 (a) When computing the force at a pixel, only the "visible" pixels are considered. The object insulates the others from having an influence. (b) The calculation of the dot product determines whether or not the force becomes zero somewhere in the pixel being tested.

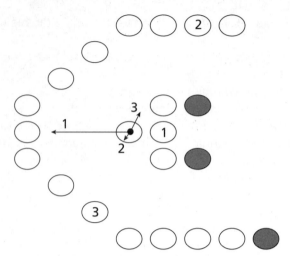

Figure 5.23 The force at a given pixel is the vector sum of the forces to all visible pixels. Only boundary pixels exert a force, and only object pixels have the force computed.

exactly one or two 8-connected neighbors that are skeletal pixels, and if it has two such neighbors, then these must be adjacent to each other. The preferred direction of growth is through these neighbors towards P and beyond to the next pixel. There will be three candidate pixels, and the one of these having the smallest force magnitude is *grown into*: It is added to the skeleton, and placed on the queue for further growth steps. The growing process will stop when the growth front hits an edge or other part of the skeleton.

At a subpixel level, the growth process first attempts to find new skeletal pixels at double the previous resolution. Using the stub endpoints the regions to be refined are identified, and forces are computed for each pixel at the new resolution; the resolution doubles each time. Then the dot products are computed as before, looking for zero crossings. When located, a zero crossing becomes a skeletal pixel at the current resolution and also marks all containing pixels at lower resolutions as skeletal. The refinement can be continued at higher resolutions until no change is seen; then the growth process continues at the original resolution in the original way (minimal force path).

This certainly approximates the set of skeletal pixels S for a digital band. For example, assume an infinitely long, straight band along the x axis, having width $2w$. Then the boundaries of the band are the lines $y = w$ and $y = -w$. Then the force acting on the point (x,y) would be:

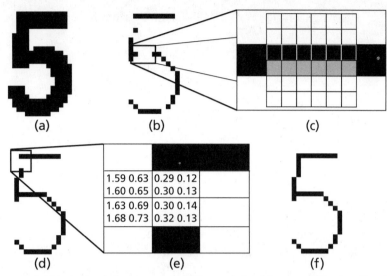

Figure 5.24 Subpixel skeletons. (a) The original image. (b) The first level skeleton, showing zero crossings. (c) A subpixel section of a gap in the level-0 skeleton. (d) The level-1 skeleton. (e) Subpixel force magnitudes in a gap in the level-1 skeleton. (f) The final skeleton with all gaps filled in.

$$F(x,y) = \int_{-\infty}^{\infty} \frac{L_1}{|L_1|^3} \, dl_x + \int_{-\infty}^{\infty} \frac{L_2}{|L_2|^3} \, dl_x \qquad \text{(EQ 5.8)}$$

where $L_1 = (x-l, y-w)$, $L_2 = (x-l, w+y)$, and l is the length along the boundary. This becomes:

$$F(x,y) = \left(0, \frac{4y}{(w+y)(y-w)} \right) \qquad \text{(EQ 5.9)}$$

Now, any of the dot products referred to previously can be written as:

$$d_i = \left(\frac{16y(y+dy)}{(w+y)(y-w)(w+y+dy)(y+dy-w)} \right) \qquad \text{(EQ 5.10)}$$

All that is needed is to know in what circumstances this expression is negative. Since $-w + dy < y < w - dy$ it is known that $y - w$ and $y + dy - w$ are negative and that $w + y$ and $w + y + dy$ are positive, the sign of the dot product is the sign of $y(y + dy)$. Solving this quadratic reveals that it is negative only between 0 and $-dy$. Thus,

$$C(x,y,dx,dy) = \begin{cases} 1 & \text{if } -dy < y < 0 \\ 0 & \text{otherwise} \end{cases}$$

(EQ 5.11)

As dy approaches 0 this becomes:

$$C(x,y) = \begin{cases} 1 & y = 0 \\ 0 & \text{otherwise} \end{cases}$$

(EQ 5.12)

which means that the x axis is the skeleton, as was suspected. This demonstration holds for infinitely long straight lines in any orientation and having any width.

The application of this method to real figures is based on three assumptions. The first is that what is true for infinitely long lines is approximately true for shorter (and curved) ones; the second is that a figure can be considered to be a collection of concatenated digital band segments. And finally, the third assumption is that intersections can be represented by multiple bands, one for each crossing line. From the results so far, these assumptions appear to be at least approximately true.

Subpixel Skeletons

The force-based thinning method has been implemented and tested on a number of images, both artificial and scanned. The results in all cases are either promising or excellent. The subpixel accurate skeletons provide substantially more information about the geometry of the object. There will often be areas in the object where the forces are not actually zero, but are small or known to be changing. By splitting each pixel into four pixels, a more accurate force can be calculated for each such pixel, and the region where the force is zero can be estimated. If this fails, each subpixel can be further split into four, and so on (Figure 5.24).

This is expensive, since for each subpixel the visible pixels must be determined, and then the force accumulated. One way to speed this up is to compute the forces based on the lines formed by the boundary pixel instead of using each boundary pixel individually. Then each line would exert a single force on each pixel, rather than many forces. In addition, the visibility calculation can be simplified by using a simple distance threshold. Line segments further than d units away would not contribute a force.

Figure 5.25 shows the forces computed for a hand-printed 8, and gives the skeleton as determined by the force-based method. For comparison purposes the skeleton found by the Zhang-Suen algorithm is shown also.

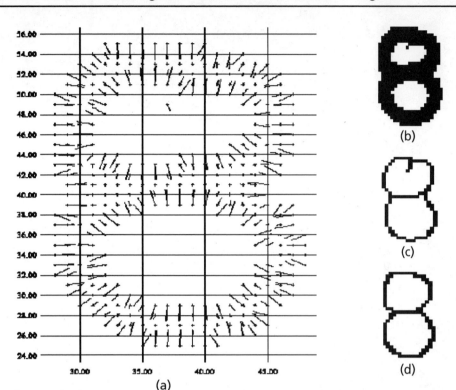

Figure 5.25 Force-based thinning applied to a handprinted 8. (a) The forces at each pixel, where force is proportional to the length of the line drawn from the pixels, and direction is normal to them. (b) The original figure. (c) Thinned using Zhang-Suen. (d) Force-based skeleton.

5.8   SOURCE CODE FOR ZHANG-SUEN/STENTIFORD/HOLT COMBINED ALGORITHM

```
/* Zhang & Suen's thinning algorithm */
#define MAX
#include "lib.h"
#include <math.h>

#define TRUE 1
#define FALSE 0
#define NORTH 1
#define SOUTH 3
#define REMOVE_STAIR 1
```

```
    void thnz (IMAGE im);
    int nays8 (IMAGE im, int r, int c);
    int Connectivity (IMAGE im, int r, int c);
    void Delete (IMAGE im, IMAGE tmp);
    void check (int v1, int v2, int v3);
    int edge (IMAGE im, int r, int c);
    void stair (IMAGE im, IMAGE tmp, int dir);
    int Yokoi (IMAGE im, int r, int c);
    void pre_smooth (IMAGE im);
    void match_du (IMAGE im, int r, int c, int k);
    void aae (IMAGE image);
    int snays (IMAGE im, int r, int c);

    int t00, t01, t11, t01s;

    void main (int argc, char *argv[])
    {
        IMAGE data, im;
        int i,j;

        if (argc < 3)
        {
          printf ("Usage: thnbest <input file> <output file>
                      \n"); exit (0);
        }

        data = Input_PBM (argv[1]);
        if (data == NULL)
        {
            printf ("Bad input file '%s'\n", argv[1]);
            exit(1);
        }
/* Embed input into a slightly larger image */
        im = newimage (data->info->nr+2, data ->info->nc+2);
        for (i=0; i<data->info->nr; i++)
          for (j=0; j<data->info->nc; j++)
            if (data->data[i][j]) im->data[i+1][j+1] = 1;
            else im->data[1+1][j+1] = 0;

        for (i=0; i<im->info->nr; i++)
        {
          im->data[i][0] = 1;
          im->data[i][im->info->nc-1] = 1;
        }
```

```
        for (j=0; j<im->info->nc; j++)
        {
           im->data[0][j] = 1;
           im->data[im->info->nr-1][j] = 1;
        }

/* Pre_process */
        pre_smooth (im);
        aae (im);

/* Thin */
        thnz (im);

        for (i=0; i<data->info->nr; i++)
              for (j=0; j<data->info->nc; j++)
                    data->data[i][j] = im->data[i+1][j+1];

        Output_PBM (data, argv[2]);
}

/*   Zhang-Suen with Holt's staircase removal */
void thnz (IMAGE im)
{
        int i,j,k, again=1;
        IMAGE tmp;
        tmp = newimage (im->info->nr, im->info->nc);

/* BLACK = 1, WHITE = 0. */
        for (i=0; i<im->info->nr; i++);
          for (j=0; j<im->info->nc; j++)
          {
            if (im->data[i][j] > 0) im->data[i][j] = 0;
              else im->data[i][j] = 1;
            tmp->data[i][j] = 0;
          }

/* Mark and delete */
        while (again)
        {
              again = 0;
/* Second sub-iteration */
              for (i=1; i<im->info->nr-1; i++);
                for (j=1; j<im->info->nc-1; j++)
```

```
        {
             if (im->data[i][j] != 1) continue;
             k = nays8(im, i, j);
             if ((k >= 2 && k <= 6) && Connectivity(im,
                     i,j)==1)
             {
              if (im->data[i][j+1]*im->data[i-1][j]
                      *im->data[i][j-1]==0 &&
                  im->data[i-j][j]*im->data[i+1][j]
                  *im->data[i][j-1] == 0)
              {
                  tmp->data[i][j] = 1;
                  again = 1;
              }
             }
        }


        Delete (im, tmp);
        if (again == 0) break;


/* First sub-iteration */
        for (i=1; i<im->info->nr-1; i++)
         for (j=1; j<im->info->nc-1; j++)
         {
             if (im->data[i][j] != 1) continue;
             k = nays8(im, i, j);
             if ((k >= 2 && k <= 6) && Connectivity(im,
                     i,j)==1)
             {
              if (im->data[i-1][j]*im->data[i][j+1]
                      *im->data[i+1][j]==0 &&
                  im->data[i][j+1]*im->data[i+1][j]*im->
                          data[i][j-1] == 0)
              {
                  tmp->data[i][j] = 1;
                  again = 1;
              }
             }
         }
```

```
            Delete (im, tmp);
        }

/* Post_process */
stair (im, tmp, NORTH);
        Delete (im, tmp);
        stair (im, tmp, SOUTH);
        Delete (im, tmp);

/* Restore levels */
    for (i=1; i<im->info->nr-1; i++)
        for (j=1; j<im->info->nc-1; j++)
            if (im->data[i][j] > 0) im->data[i][j] = 0;
            else im->data[i][j] = 255;

    freeimage (tmp);
}

/*   Delete any pixel in IM corresponding to a 1 in TMP*/
void Delete (IMAGE im, IMAGE tmp)
{
    int i,j;

/* Delete pixels that are marked */
    for (i=1; i<im->info->nr-1; i++)
        for (j=1; j<im->info->nc-1; j++)
            if (tmp->data[i][j])
            {
                im->data[i][j] = 0;
                tmp->data[i][j] = 0;
            }
}

/*   Number of neighboring 1 pixels*/
int nays8 (IMAGE im, int r, int c)
{
    int i,j,k=0;

    for (i=r-1; i<=r+1; i++)
        for (j=c-1; j<=c+1; j++)
            if (i!=r || c!=j)
                if (im->data[i][j] >= 1) k++;
    return k;
}
```

```
/*    Number of neighboring 0 pixels*/
int snays (IMAGE im, int r, int c)
{
        int i,j,k=0;
      for (i=r-1; i<=r+1; i++)
        for (j=c-1; j<=c+1; j++)
          if (i!=r || c!=j)
            if (im->data[i][j] == 0) k++;
      return k;
}

/*    Connectivity by counting black-white transitions on the
          boundary*/
          int Connectivity (IMAGE im, int r, int c)
{
      int i, N=0;

      if (im->data[r][c+1]   >= 1 && im->data[r-1][c+1] == 0)
                                    N++;
      if (im->data[r-1][c+1] >= 1 && im->data[r-1][c]   == 0)
                                    N++;
      if (im->data[r-1][c]   >= 1 && im->data[r-1][c-1] == 0)
                                    N++;
      if (im->data[r-1][c-1] >= 1 && im->data[r][c-1]   == 0)
                                    N++;
      if (im->data[r][c-1]   >= 1 && im->data[r+1][c-1] == 0)
                                    N++;
      if (im->data[r+1][c-1] >= 1 && im->data[r+1][c]   == 0)
                                    N++;
      if (im->data[r+1][c]   >= 1 && im->data[r+1][c+1] == 0)
                                    N++;
      if (im->data[r+1][c+1] >= 1 && im->data[r][c+1]   ==0)
                                    N++;

      return N;
}

/*    Stentiford's boundary smoothing method*/
void pre_smooth (IMAGE im)
{
      int, i,j;

      for (i=0; i<im->info->nr; i++)
        for (j=0; j<im->info->nc; j++)
```

```
                if (im—>data[i][j] == 0)
                   if (snays (im, i, j) <= 2 && Yokoi (im, i, j)<2)
                      im—>data[i][j] = 2;

        for (i=0; i<im—>info—>nr; i++)
          for (j=0; j<im—>info—>nc; j++)
            if (im—>data[i][j] == 2) im—>data[i][j] = 1;
}


/*    Stentiford's Acute Angle Emphasis*/
void aae (IMAGE im)
{
     int i,j, again = 0, k;

     again = 0;
     for (k=5; k>= 1; k—=2)
     {
        for (i=2; i<im—>info—>nr—2; i++)
          for (j=2; j<im—>info—>nc—2; j++)
            if (im—>data[i][j] == 0)
                 match_du (im, i, j, k);

        for (i=2; i<im—>info—>nr—2; i++)
          for (j=2; j<im—>info—>nc—2; j++)
            if (im—>data[i][j] == 2)
            {
                 again = 1;
                 im—>data[i][j] = 1;
            }

        if (again == 0) break;
     }
}


/*    Template matches for acute angle emphasis*/
void match_du (IMAGE im, int r, int c, int k)
{

/*D1 */
     if (im—>data[r—2][c—2] == 0 && im—>data[r—2][c—1] == 0
             &&
        im—>data[r—2][c]  == 1 && im—>data[r—2][c+1] == 0
                 &&
        im—>data[r—2][c+2] == 0 &&
```

```
            im->data[r-1][c-2] == 0 && im->data[r-1][c-1] == 0
                   &&
            im->data[r-1][c]   == 1 && im->data[r-1][c+1] == 0
                   &&
            im->data[r-1][c+2] == 0 &&
            im->data[r][c-2] == 0 && im->data[r][c-1] == 0 &&
            im->data[r][c]   == 0 && im->data[r][c+1] == 0 &&
            im->data[r][c+2] == 0 &&
            im->data[r+1][c-2] == 0 && im->data[r+1][c-1] == 0
                   &&
            im->data[r+1][c]   == 0 && im->data[r+1][c+1] == 0
                   &&
            im->data[r+1][c+2] == 0 &&
            im->data[r+2][c-1] == 0 &&
            im->data[r+2][c]   == 0 && im->data[r+2][c+1] == 0 )
      {
          im->data[r][c] = 2;
          return;
      }


/* D2*/
      if (k >= 2)
      if (im->data[r-2][c-2] == 0 && im->data[r-2][c-1] == 1
                &&
            im->data[r-2][c]   == 1 && im->data[r-2][c+1] == 0
                &&
            im->data[r-2][c+2] == 0 &&
            im->data[r-1][c-2] == 0 && im->data[r-1][c-1] == 0
                &&
            im->data[r-1][c]   == 1 && im->data[r-1][c+1] == 0
                &&
            im->data[r-1][c+2] == 0 &&
            im->data[r][c-2] == 0 && im->data[r][c-1] == 0 &&
            im->data[r][c]   == 0 && im->data[r][c+1] == 0 &&
            im->data[r][c+2] == 0 &&
            im->data[r+1][c-2] == 0 && im->data[r+1][c-1] == 0
                &&
            im->data[r+1][c]   == 0 && im->data[r+1][c+1] == 0
                &&
            im->data[r+1][c+2] == 0 &&
            im->data[r+2][c-1] == 0 &&
            im->data[r+2][c]   == 0 && im->data[r+2][c+1] == 0 )
```

```
{
            im->data[r][c] = 2;
            return;
}


/* D3 */
    if (k>=3)
    if (im->data[r-2][c-2] == 0 && im->data[r-2][c-1] == 0
            &&
        im->data[r-2][c]   == 1 && im->data[r-2][c+1] == 1
            &&
        im->data[r-2][c+2] == 0 &&
        im->data[r-1][c-2] == 0 && im->data[r-1][c-1] == 0
            &&
        im->data[r-1][c]   == 1 && im->data[r-1][c+1] == 0
            &&
        im->data[r-1][c+2] == 0 &&
        i->data[r][c-2] == 0 && im->data[r][c-1] == 0 &&
        im->data[r][c]   == 0 && im->data[r][c+1] == 0 &&
        im->data[r][c+2] == 0 &&
        im->data[r+1][c-2] == 0 && im->data[r+1][c-1] == 0
            &&
        im->data[r+1][c]   == 0 && im->data[r+1][c+1] == 0
            &&
        im->data[r+1][c+2] == 0 &&
        im->data[r+2][c-1] == 0 &&
        im->data[r+2][c]   == 0 && im->data[r+2][c+1] == 0
)
{
            im->data[r][c] = 2;
            return;
}


/* D4 */
    if (k>=4)
    if (im->data[r-2][c-2] == 0 && im->data[r-2][c-1] == 1
            &&
        im->data[r-2][c]   == 1 && im->data[r-2][c+1] == 0
            &&
        im->data[r-2][c+2] == 0 &&
        im->data[r-1][c-2] == 0 && im->data[r-1][c-1] == 1
            &&
```

```
        im->data[r-1][c]   == 1 && im->data[r-1][c+1] == 0
                &&
        im->data[r-1][c+2] == 0 &&
        im->data[r][c-2] == 0 && im->data[r][c-1] == 0 &&
        im->data[r][c]   == 0 && im->data[r][c+1] == 0 &&
        im->data[r][c+2] == 0 &&
        im->data[r+1][c-2] == 0 && im->data[r+1][c-1] == 0
                &&
        im->data[r+1][c]   == 0 && im->data[r+1][c+1] == 0
                &&
        im->data[r+1][c+2] == 0 &&
        im->data[r+2][c-1] == 0 &&
        im->data[r+2][c]   == 0 && im->data[r+2][c+1] == 0 )
    {

        im->data[r][c] = 2;
        return;

    }



    /* D5 */
        if (k>=5)
        if (im->data[r-2][c-2] == 0 && im->data[r-2][c-1] == 0
                &&
        im->data[r-2][c]   == 1 && im->data[r-2][c+1] == 1
                &&
        im->data[r-2][c+2] == 0 &&
        im->data[r-1][c-2] == 0 && im->data[r-1][c-1] == 0
                &&
        im->data[r-1][c]   == 1 && im->data[r-1][c+1] == 1
                &&
        im->data[r-1][c+2] == 0 &&
        im->data[r][c-2] == 0 && im->data[r][c-1] == 0 &&
        im->data[r][c]   == 0 && im->data[r][c+1] == 0 &&
        im->data[r][c+2] == 0 &&
        im->data[r+1][c-2] == 0 && im->data[r+1][c-1] == 0
                &&
        im->data[r+1][c]   == 0 && im->data[r+1][c+1] == 0
                &&
        im->data[r+1][c+2] == 0 &&
        im->data[r+2][c-1] == 0 &&
        im->data[r+2][c]   == 0 && im->data[r+2][c+1] == 0 )
```

```
                        {
                            im->data[r][c] = 2;
                            return;
                        }

/* U1 */
            if (im->data[r+2][c-2] == 0 && im->data[r+2][c-1] == 0
                    &&
                im->data[r+2][c]   == 1 && im->data[r+2][c+1] == 0
                        &&
                im->data[r+2][c+2] == 0 &&
                im->data[r+1][c-2] == 0 && im->data[r+1][c-1] == 0
                        &&
                im->data[r+1][c]   == 1 && im->data[r+1][c+1] == 0
                        &&
                im->data[r+1][c+2] == 0 &&
                im->data[r][c-2] == 0 && im->data[r][c-1] == 0 &&
                im->data[r][c]   == 0 && im->data[r][c+1] == 0 &&
                im->data[r][c+2] == 0 &&
                im->data[r-1][c-2] == 0 && im->data[r-1][c-1] == 0
                        &&
                im->data[r-1][c]   == 0 && im->data[r-1][c+1] == 0
                        &&
                im->data[r-1][c+2] == 0 &&
                im->data[r-1][c-1] == 0 &&
                im->data[r-1][c]   == 0 && im->data[r-1][c+1] == 0)
            {
                    im->data[r][c] = 2;
                    return;
            }

/* U2 */
        if (k>=2)
        if (im->data[r+2][c-2] == 0 && im->data[r+2][c-1] == 1
                &&
            im->data[r+2][c]   == 1 && im->data[r+2][c+1] == 0
                &&
            im->data[r+2][c+2] == 0 &&
            im->data[r+1][c-2] == 0 && im->data[r+1][c-1] == 0
                    &&
            im->data[r+1][c]   == 1 && im->data[r+1][c+1] == 0
                &&
            im->data[r+1][c+2] == 0 &&
```

```
            im->data[r][c-2] == 0 && im->data[r][c-1] == 0 &&
            im->data[r][c]   == 0 && im->data[r][c+1] == 0 &&
            im->data[r][c+2] == 0 &&
            im->data[r-1][c-2] == 0 && im->data[r-1][c-1] == 0
                  &&
            im->data[r-1][c]   == 0 && im->data[r-1][c+1] == 0
                &&
            im->data[r-1][c+2] == 0 &&
            im->data[r-2][c-1] == 0 &&
            im->data[r-2][c]   == 0 && im->data[r-2][c+1] == 0)
        {
            im->data[r][c] = 2;
            return;
        }


/* U3 */
        if (k>=3)
        if (im->data[r+2][c-2] == 0 && im->data[r+2][c-1] == 0
                  &&
            im->data[r+2][c]   == 1 && im->data[r+2][c+1] == 1
                  &&
            im->data[r+2][c+2] == 0 &&
            im->data[r+1][c-2] == 0 && im->data[r+1][c-1] == 0
                    &&
            im->data[r+1][c] == 1 && im->data[r+1][c+1] == 0 &&
            im->data[r+1][c+2] == 0 &&
            im->data[r][c-2] == 0 && im->data[r][c-1] == 0 &&
            im->data[r][c] == 0 && im->data[r][c+1] == 0 &&
            im->data[r][c+2] == 0 &&
            im->data[r-1][c-2] == 0 && im->data[r-1][c-1] == 0
                    &&
            im->data[r-1][c] == 0 && im->data[r-1][c+1] == 0 &&
            im->data[r-1][c+2] == 0 &&
            im->data[r-2][c-1] == 0 &&
            im->data[r-2][c] == 0 && im->data[r-2][c+1] == 0 )
        {
            im->data[r][c] = 2;
            return;
        }


/* U4 */
        if (k>=4)
```

```
    if (im->data[r+2][c-2] == 0 && im->data[r+2][c-1] == 1
            &&
        im->data[r+2][c]   == 1 && im->data[r+2][c+1] == 0
            &&
        im->data[r+2][c+2] == 0 &&
        im->data[r+1][c-2] == 0 && im->data[r+1][c-1] == 1
            &&
        im->data[r+1][c]   == 1 && im->data[r+1][c+1] == 0
            &&
        im->data[r+1][c+2] == 0 &&
        im->data[r][c-2] == 0 && im->data[r][c-1] == 0 &&
        im->data[r][c]   == 0 && im->data[r][c+1] == 0 &&
        im->data[r][c+2] == 0 &&
        im->data[r-1][c-2] == 0 && im->data[r-1][c-1] == 0
            &&
        im->data[r-1][c]   == 0 && im->data[r-1][c+1] == 0
            &&
        im->data[r-1][c+2] == 0 &&
        im->data[r-2][c-1] == 0 &&
        im->data[r-2][c]   == 0 && im->data[r-2][c+1] == 0
    {
        im->data[r][c] = 2;
        return;
    }


/* U5 */
    if (k>=5)
    if (im->data[r+2][c-2] == 0 && im->data[r+2][c-1] == 0
            &&
        im->data[r+2][c]   == 1 && im->data[r+2][c+1] == 1
            &&
        im->data[r+2][c+2] == 0 &&
        im+>data[r+1][c-2] == 0 && im->data[r+1][c-1] == 0
            &&
        im->data[r+1][c]   == 1 && im->data[r+1][c+1] == 1
            &&
        im->data[r+1][c+2] == 0 &&
        im->data[r][c-2] == 0 && im->data[r][c-1] == 0 &&
        im->data[r][c]   == 0 && im->data[r][c+1] == 0 &&
        im->data[r][c+2] == 0 &&
        im->data[r-1][c-2] == 0 && im->data[r-1][c-1] == 0
            &&
```

```
                im->data[r-1][c]    == 0 && im->data[r-1][c+1] == 0
                        &&
                im->data[r-1][c+2] == 0 &&
                im->data[r-2][c-1] == 0 &&
                im->data[r-2][c]    == 0 && im->data[r-2][c+1] == 0
        )
        {
            im->data[r][c] = 2;
            return;
        }
    }

/*   Yokoi's connectivity measure*/
int Yokoi (IMAGE im, int r, int c)
{
    int N[9];
    int i,j,k, i1, i2;

    N[0] = im->data[r][c]      != 0;
    N[1] = im->data[r][c+1]    != 0;
    N[2] = im->data[r-1][c+1] != 0;
    N[3] = im->data[r-1][c]    != 0;
    N[4] = im->data[r-1][c-1] != 0;
    N[5] = im->data[r][c-1]    != 0;
    N[6] = im->data[r+1][c-1] != 0;
    N[7] = im->data[r+1][c]    != 0;
    N[8] = im->data[r+1][c+1] != 0;

    k = 0
    for (i=1; i<=7; i+=2)
    {
      i1 = i+1; if (i1 > 8) i1 -= 8;
      i2 = 1+2; if (i2 > 8) i2 -= 8;
      k += (N[i] - N[i]*N[i1]*N[i2]);
    }

    return k;
}

/*   Holt's staircase removal stuff*/
void check (int v1, int v2, int v3)
{
    if (!v2 && (!v1 || (v3)) t00 = TRUE;
    if ( v2 && ( v1 || v3)) t11 = TRUE;
    if ( (!v1 && v2) || (!v2 && v3) )
```

```
        {
              t01s = t01;
              t01 = TRUE;
        }
  }

int edge (IMAGE im, int r, int c)
{
        if (im->data[r][c] == 0) return 0:
        t00 = t01 = t01s = t11 = FALSE;

/* CHECK(vNW, vN, vNE) */
        check (im->data[r-1][c-1], im->data[r-1][c], im
                    ->data[r-1][c+1]);

/* CHECK (vNE, vE, vSE) */
        check (im->data[r-1][c+1], im->data[r][c+1],
                    im->data[r+1][c+1]);

/* CHECK (vSE, vS, vSW) */
check (im->data[r+1][c+1], im->data[r+1][c],
                    im->data[r+1][c-1]);

/* CHECK (vSW, vW, vNW) */
        check (im->data[r+1][c-1], im->data[r][c-1],
                    im->data[r-1][c-1]);

        return t00 && t11 && !t01s;
}

void stair (IMAGE im, IMAGE tmp, int dir)
{
        int i,j;
        int N, S, E, W, NE, NW, SE, SW, C;

        if (dir == NORTH)
        for (i=1; i<im->info->nr-1; i++)
          for (j=1; j<im->info->nc-1; j++)
          {
            NW = im->data[i-1][j-1]; N = im->data[i-1][j]; NE =
                        im->data[i-1][j+1];
            W = im->data[i][j-1]; c = im->data[i][j]; E =
                        im->data[i][j+1];
            SW = im->data[i+1][j-1]; S = im->data[i+1][j]; SE =
                        im->data[i+1][j+1];

            if (dir == NORTH)
```

```
      {
        if (C && !(N &&
              ((E && !NE && !SW && (!W || !S)) ||
               (W && !NW && !SE && (!E || !S)) )) )
          tmp->data[i][j] = 0;/* Survives */
        else
          tmp->data[i][j] = 1;
      } else if (dir == SOUTH)
      {
        if (C && !(S &&
              ((E && !SE && !NW && (!W || !N)) ||
               (W && !SW && !NE && (!E || !N)) )) )
          tmp->data[i][j] = 0;/* Survives */
        else
          tmp->data[i][j] = 1;
      }
    }
}
```

5.9 BIBLIOGRAPHY

Arcelli, C. 1981. Pattern Thinning by Contour Tracing. *Computer Graphics and Image Processing*. Vol 17. 130–144.

Baruch, O. 1988. Line Thinning by Line Following. *Pattern Recognition Letters*. Vol. 8. 271–276.

Blum, H. 1967. A Transformation for Extracting New Descriptors of Shape. *Symposium Models for Speech and Visual Form*. Weiant Whaten-Dunn (Ed). Cambridge, MA: MIT Press.

Bookstein, F. L. 1979. The Line Skeleton. *Computer Graphics and Image Processing*. Vol. 11. 123–137.

Chen, Y. and W. Hsu. 1988. A Modified Fast Parallel Algorithm for Thinning Digital Patterns. *Pattern Recognition Letters*. Vol. 7. 99–106.

Chen, Y. and W. Hsu. 1988. An Interpretive Model of Line Continuation in Human Visual Perception. *Pattern Recognition*. Vol. 22. 5:619–639.

Davis, E. R. and A. P. N. Plummer. 1981. Thinning Algorithms: A Critique and a New Methodology. *Pattern Recognition*. 14:53–63.

Guo, Z. and R. W. Hall. Parallel Thinning with Two-Subiteration Algorithms. *Communications of the ACM*. Vol. 32. 3:359–373.

Haralick, R. M. 1991. Performance Characterization in Image Analysis: Thinning, a Case in Point. *ICDAR 91, First International Conference on Document Analysis and Recognition*. Saint-Malo, France. September 30–October 2, 1991.

Hilditch, C. J. 1969. Linear Skeletons from Square Cupboards. *Machine Intelligence IV.* 1969. (B. Meltzer and D. Mitchie, Eds). Edinburgh: University Press.

Holt, C. M., Stewart, A., Clint, M. and R. H. Perrott. 1987. An Improved Parallel Thinning Algorithm. *Communications of the ACM.* Vol. 30. 2:156–160.

Jang, B. K. and R. T. Chin. 1990. Analysis of Thinning Algorithms Using Mathematical Morphology. *IEEE Transactions on Pattern Analysis and Machine Intelligence.* Vol. PAMI-12. 541–551.

Kwok, P. C. K. 1988. A Thinning Algorithm by Contour Generation. *Communications of the ACM.* Vol. 31. 1314–1324.

Montanari, U. 1968. A Method For Obtaining Skeletons Using a Quasi-Euclidian Distance. *Journal of the ACM.* Vol. 15. 600–624.

Montanari, U. 1969. Continuous Skeletons from Digitized Images. *Journal of the ACM.* Vol. 16. 4:534:549.

Pal, S. K. 1989. Fuzzy Skeletonization of an Image. *Pattern Recognition Letters.* 10:17–23.

Parker, J. R. and C. Jennings. 1992. Defining the Digital Skeleton. *SPIE Conference on Vision Geometry.* Boston.

Piper, J. 1985. Efficient Implementation of Skeletonization Using Interval Coding. *Pattern Recognition Letters.* 3:389–397.

Sinha, R. M. K. 1987. A Width-Independent Algorithm for Character Skeleton Estimation. *Computer Vision, Graphics, and Image Processing.* Vol 40:388–397.

Sossa, J. H. 1989. An Improved Parallel Algorithm for Thinning Digital Patterns. *Pattern Recognition Letters.* 10:77–80.

Stefanelli, R. 1986. A Comment on an Investigation into the Skeletonization Approach of Hilditch. *Pattern Recognition.* Vol 19. 1:13–14.

Stentiford, F. W. M. and R. G. Mortimer. 1983. Some New Heuristics for Thinning Binary Handprinted Characters for OCR. *IEEE Transactions on Systems, Man, and Cybernetics.* Vol. SMC-13, No. 1, January/February. Pp. 81–84.

Suzuki, S. and K. Abe. 1986. Sequential Thinning of Binary Pictures Using Distance Transformation. *Eighth International Conference on Pattern Recognition.* 289–292.

Suzuki, S. 1987. Binary Picture Thinning by an Iterative Parallel Two-Subcycle Operation. *Pattern Recognition.* Vol. 20. 3:297–307.

Xia, Y. 1989. Skeletonization VIA the Realization of the Fire Front's Propagation and Extinction in Digital Binary Shapes. *IEEE Transactions on Pattern Analysis and Machine Intelligence.* Vol PAMI-11. 1076–1086.

Yokoi, S., Toriwaki, J. and T. Fukumura. 1973. Topological Properties in Digitized Binary Pictures. *Systems Computer Controls.* Vol. 4. 32–39.

Zhang, S. and K. S. Fu. 1984. A Thinning Algorithm for Discrete Binary Images. *Proceedings of the International Conference on Computers and Applications.* Beijing, China. 879–886.

6

IMAGE RESTORATION

6.1 IMAGE DEGRADATIONS—THE REAL WORLD

Anyone who has ever taken a photograph will understand that capturing an image exactly as it appears in the real world is very difficult, if not impossible. There is noise to contend with, which in the case of photography is caused by the graininess of the emulsion, motion blur, focus problems, depth-of-field issues, and the imperfect nature of even the best lens system. The result of all of these *degradations* is that the image (photograph) is an approximation of the scene.

Very often the image is good enough for the purpose for which it was produced. On the other hand, there are some instances where the correction of an image by computer is the only way to obtain a usable picture. The recent problems with the Hubble Space Telescope are a case in point; the optics produced images that did not approach the potential of the telescope, and a repair mission was not immediately possible. Computers were used to repair some of the distortion caused by the optics and give images that were of high quality.

Image restoration is the art and science of improving the quality of an image based on some absolute measure. It usually involves some means of undoing a distortion that has been imposed, such as motion blur or film graininess. This can't be done in any perfect way, but vast improvements are possible in some circumstances.

The techniques of image restoration are very mathematical in nature, and this may distress some people who are interested in the subject. The purpose of this section is to enlighten, rather than frighten, and so a very practical approach is taken. The mathematics will be skimmed over, and those interested in the details will find references at the end of this chapter to explore further. However, not all of the math can be eliminated.

The example of the Hubble Space Telescope is an opportune one, since it is an ideal way to introduce a technique for characterizing the distortion inherent in an image. A star, when viewed through a telescope, should be seen as a perfect point of light. Ideally, all of the light energy of the star would be focused on a single pixel. In practice this is not so; the distortions of the atmosphere and the telescope optics will yield a slightly blurred image in which the central pixel is brightest, and a small region around it is also brighter than the background. The distortions that have been inflicted on the point image of the star are reflected in the shape and intensity distribution of the star's image. All stars (for a reasonable optical system) will have the same distortions imposed upon them; indeed, all points on the image have been replaced by these small blobs, and the sum of all of the blobs is the sampled image.

The effect that an image acquisition system has on a perfect point source is called the *point spread function* (PSF). The sample image has been produced by convolving the PSF with the perfect image, so that the same blur exists at all points. Figure 6.1 shows a diagrammatic view of how distortion and noise have been applied to the original image to give the sampled, observed image. To obtain the perfect image given the sampled one is the goal of restoration, and it is not generally possible. We therefore wish to improve the image as much as possible, and the PSF tells us what has been done to the image. The ideal solution is to *deconvolve* the image and the PSF, but this can only be done approximately and at some significant expense.

This discussion assumes that the PSF is the same at all points of the image, in

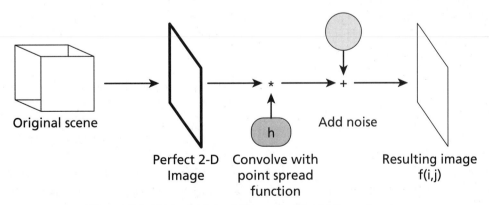

Original scene   Perfect 2-D   Convolve with   Add noise   Resulting image
                    Image   point spread   f(i,j)
                                   function

Figure 6.1 One model of how a perfect image becomes distorted by imperfect (real) acquisition systems.

which case the system is said to be spatially invariant. This is the situation generally assumed in the literature, but the Space Telescope was not spatially invariant. In cases like this the solution is to assume that the PSF is almost constant over a small region of the image, and to restore the image in pieces using very similar techniques to those that will be discussed.

The first thing to do is to see if a blurred image can be created artificially, by convolving a known point spread function with a created image. Then methods of reducing the blur can be applied to these known images, and the results can be assessed objectively. Since it is important to know the PSF, methods of estimating it from a distorted image must also be discussed, as will certain special cases (such as motion blur) for which specific restoration schemes have been devised.

6.2 THE FREQUENCY DOMAIN

A convolution can be carried out directly on an image by moving the convolution matrix (image) so that it is centered on each pixel of the image in turn, then multiplying the corresponding elements and summing the products. This was described in Equation 1.13, for example. This is a time-consuming process for large images, and one that can be speeded up by using the *Fourier transform*.

A *transform* is simply a mapping from one set of coordinates to another. For example, a *rotation* is a transform; the rotated coordinate system is different from the original, but each coordinate in the original image has a corresponding coordinate in the rotated image. The *Hough transform* is another example, in which pixel coordinates (i,j) are converted into coordinates (m,b) representing the slope and intercept of the straight lines that pass through the pixel.

The Fourier transform converts spatial coordinates into frequencies. Any curve or surface can be expressed as the sum of some number (perhaps infinitely many) of sine and cosine curves. In the *Fourier domain* (called the *frequency domain* as well) the image is represented as the parameters of these sine and cosine functions. The Fourier transform is the mathematical mechanism for moving into and out of the frequency domain.

The frequency domain is so named because the two parameters of a sine curve are the amplitude and the frequency. The fact that an image can be converted into a frequency domain representation implies that the image can contain high-frequency or low-frequency information; this is true. If the grey level of some portion of the image changes slowly across the columns, then it would be represented in the frequency domain as a sine or cosine function having a low frequency. Something that changes quickly, such as an edge, will have high-frequency components.

It is therefore possible to build filters that will remove or enhance certain frequencies in the image, and this will sometimes have a restorative effect. Indeed, noise consists of mainly high-frequency information, and so filtering out of the very high frequencies should have a noise reduction effect. It unfortunately also has an edge-reduction effect.

The Fourier Transform

The Fourier transform breaks up an image (or, in one dimension, a signal) into a set of sine and cosine components. It is important to keep these components separate, and so a vector of the form (*cosine,sine*) is used at each point in the frequency domain image; that is, the values of the pixels in the frequency domain image are two component vectors. A convenient way to represent these is as *complex* numbers.

Each complex number consists of a real part and an imaginary part, which can be thought of as a vector. A typical complex number could be written as:

$$z = (x, jy) = x + jy \qquad \text{(EQ 6.1)}$$

where j is the imaginary number $\sqrt{-1}$. The exponential of an imaginary number can be shown to be the sum of a sine and cosine, which is exactly what we want:

$$e^{j\theta} = \cos\theta + j\sin\theta \qquad \text{(EQ 6.2)}$$

This polar form is what will be used from here on, but it is important to remember that is it really a shorthand for the sum of the sine and cosine parts.

In one dimension, the Fourier transform of a continuous function f(x) is:

$$F(w) = \int_{t=0}^{\infty} f(t)e^{-jwt}dt \qquad \text{(EQ 6.3)}$$

If the function has been sampled so that it is now discrete, the integral becomes a sum over all of the sampled points:

$$F(w) = \sum_{k=0}^{N-1} f(k)e^{-\frac{2\pi jwk}{N}} \qquad \text{(EQ 6.4)}$$

If the function f(k) is a sample sine curve, then the Fourier transform F(w) should yield a single point showing the parameters of the curve. Figure 6.2a shows just such a sampled sine curve, which has the form

$$f(k) = 2\sin\left(\frac{2\pi k}{128}\right) \qquad \text{(EQ 6.5)}$$

Figure 6.2b shows the Fourier transform of the curve. Note that it has a single peak at the point $w=8$, which happens to correspond to the frequency of the original sine curve: eight cycles per 1024 pixels, or one cycle in 128 pixels. Figure

6.2c and d show a pair of sine curves and their Fourier transform, which has two peaks (one per sine curve).

The Fourier transforms shown in Figure 6.2 were computed by the C procedure slow.c, which uses Equation 6.4 to do the calculation. This does work fine, but is very slow, and it would not likely be used in any real system. Because of the very useful nature of the Fourier transform, an enormous effort has been extended to make it computationally fast. The essential C code from slow.c is shown in Figure 6.3, this can be compared with the code for the Fast Fourier Transform (FFT), which will be discussed in the next section. The complex numbers are implemented as structures, each having a real and imaginary component.

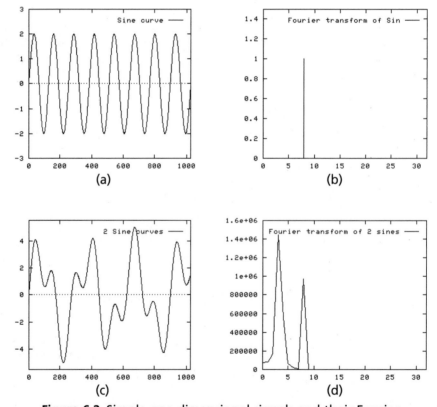

Figure 6.2 Simple one-dimensional signals and their Fourier transforms. (a) Sine function with a period of 128 pixels. (b) Fourier transform, showing a peak at 8 for a signal of duration 1024, giving eight periods/duration. (c) Sum of two sine curves: period=128 + period =300. (d) Fourier transform, showing two peaks, one per sine function.

```
void slowft (float *x, COMPLEX *y, int        void cexp(COMPLEX z1,
                                                       COMPLEX *res)
n)
{                                             {
    COMPLEX tmp, z1, z2, z3, z4;                  COMPLEX x, y;
    int m, k;
                                                  x.real =
                                                  exp((double)z1.real);
                                                  x.image = 0.0;
    cmplx(0.0,atan(1.0)/n* −8.0,&tmp);        y.real=(float)cos
                                                  ((double)z1.imag);
    for (m = 0; m<=n/2; m++)                   y.imag=(float)
                                                  sin((double)z1.imag);
                                                      cmult (x, y, res);
    {                                             }
      y[m].real=x[0]; y[m].imag=0.0;
      for (k=1;k<=n−1; k++)
      {
                                              void cmult (COMPLEX z1,
                                              COMPLEX z2,
/*Exp (tmp*k*m) */                                      COMPLEX *res)
          cmplx ((float)k, 0.0, &z2);        {
          cmult (tmp, z2, &z3);                  res−>real =
                                                  z1.real*z2.real−
          cmplx ((float)m, 0.0 &z2);                  z1.imag*z2.image;
          cmult (z2, z3, &z4);              res−>image=z1.real*
                                                  z2.image +
          cexp (z4, &z2);                   z1.imag*z2.real;
/* *x[k] */                                 }
          cmplx (x[k], 0.0, &z3);
          cmult (z2, z3, &z4);              void csum (COMPLEX z1,
                                              COMPLEX r2,
/* + y[m] */                                  COMPLEX *res)
          csum (y[m], z4, &z2);            {
          y[m].real = z.real;                     res−>real = z1.real
                                                  + z2.real;
          y[m].imag = z2.imag;                    res−>imag = z1.imag
                                                  + z2.imag;
      }                                       }
    }
}

                                              float cnorm (COMPLEX z)
```

Figure 6.3 Source code for the obvious implementation of the
Fourier transform.

```
void cmplx(float rp, float ip, COMPLEX {
*z)                                      return z.real*z.real
                                         +z.imag*z.imag;
{                                        }
    z->real = rp;
    z=>imag = ip;
}
```

Figure 6.3 (continued)

The Fast Fourier Transform

Make no mistake, the FFT is simply a faster way to compute the Fourier transform, and is not a new or different transform in its own right (Cooley 1965). The optimizations needed to speed up the calculation are partly standard programming tricks (such as computing some of the values in advance outside of the loop) and partly mathematical techniques. There are a number of very good references on the FFT (Bracewell 1965; Brigham 1974), but these deal rather rigorously with the subject. Here, the code in Figure 6.3 will be successively improved until it implements the basic FFT method.

The first optimization involves moving the exponential calculation (cexp) to a position outside of the inner loop. This is done by precomputing all of the N possible products:

$$F(w) = \sum_{k=0}^{n-1} f(k)e^{(-2\pi j/n)(wk)} \quad f(k) = \sum_{k=0}^{n-1} pre[wk \bmod n]f(k) \quad \text{(EQ 6.6)}$$

This reduces the strength of the operation within the loop from a complex exponentiation to a complex product. For the transform computed in Figure 6.2a–b, as an example, the program (Figure 6.3) requires 7.4 seconds to execute on a Pentium 90 PC. The program slow2.c (Figure 6.4), which uses precomputed exponentials, requires only 1.6 seconds.

The next step involves the mathematical observation that the even-numbered elements can be computed separately from the odd ones. In cases where n is even, this will reduce the number of multiplications by half. The even coefficients are found using:

$$F(2a) = \sum_{k=0}^{n/2-1} e^{(-2\pi j/n)(ak)} Sum[k]$$

$$Sum[k] = \frac{(f(k) + f(k + m))}{2}$$

$$\text{(EQ 6.7)}$$

```
void slowft(float *x, COMPLEX *y, int n)    /* Compute all Y values
                                            */
{
  COMPLEX tmp,z1, z2, z3, z4, pre[1024];    for (m = 0; m<=n; m++)
      int m, k, i, p;                         {
                                              cmplx (x[0], 0.0,
                                              &(y[m]));
/* Constant factor −2 pi */                   for (k=1; k<=−1;
                                              k++)
  cmplx (0.0, atan(1.0)/n * −8.0, &z1);       {
  cexp (z1, &tmp);                              p = (k*m % n);
                                              cmplx (x[k], 0.0,
                                              &z3);
/* Precompute most of the exponential */        cmult (z3,
                                                pre[p], &z4);
  cmplx (1.0, 0.0, &z1);/*Z1=1.0; */            csum (y[m], z4,
                                                &z2);
  for (i=0; i<n; i++)                             y[m].real =
                                                z2.real;
  {                                             y[m].imag =
                                                z2.imag;
    cmplx(z1.real, z1.imag, &(pre[i]));        }
    cmult (z1, tmp, &z3);                     }
    cmplx (z3.real, z3.imag, &z1);          }
  }
```

Figure 6.4 The program slow2, obtained from slow by precomputing the complex exponential entries.

where *a* runs from 0 to $n/2-1$. Similarly, the odd elements are found by:

$$F(2a + 1) = \sum_{k=0}^{n/2-1} e^{(-2\pi j/n)(ak)} \, Diff[k]$$

$$Diff[k] = \frac{(f(k) - f(k + m))e^{(-2\pi j/n)k}}{2}$$

(EQ 6.8)

The Sum and Diff arrays can be calculated in advance. The odd and even parts of the Fourier transform are computed separately, and then merged into a common matrix F. The Fourier transform of Figure 6.2 requires 0.81 seconds using this enhancement (program slow3.c, Figure 6.5). In the code shown in the figure, the

```
void evenodd (float *x, COMPLEX *y, int n)      cmplx (xs, 0.0,
                                                    &(Sum[i]));
{                                               cmplx (ys, 0.0, &z2);
    int m, i;                                   cmult (z1, z2,
                                                    &(Diff[i]));
    COMPLEX Sum[1024],Diff[1024], z1, z2;       cmult (z1, tmp, &z2);
    COMPLEX Even[512], Odd[512], tmp;           cmplx(z2.real,z2.imag,
                                                    &z1);
    float xs, ys;                               }
    m = n/2;                                    slowft (x, Even, m);
    cmplx (0.0, atan (1.0)/n * -8.0,            slowft (x, Odd, m);
    &z1);
    cexp (z1, &tmp);
    cmplx (1.0, 0.0, &z1);                      for (i=0; i<m; i++)
                                                {
    for (i=0; i<m; i++)                             y[i<<1] = Even[i];
    {                                               y[i<<1 + 1] = Odd[i];
      xs = (x[i] + x[i+m])/2.0;                 }
      ys = (x[i] - x[i+m])/2.0;         }
```

Figure 6.5 The program slow3, in which the odd and even transform elements are computed separately.

function evenodd finds the Sum and Diff arrays, and the previous version of the FTT (slow2.c) is called to compute the actual transform.

Now comes an obvious step, but one that restricts the input data set even further. It seems obvious that if the number of elements is a *power of two* rather than simply being even, then the number of even elements is still even and can profit from a repeated application of Equation 6.7. Ditto, of course, for the odd elements, down to the point where there is only one element, which is a very simple case. This means that the calculation now reduces to the calculations of Eqs. 6.7 and 6.8, followed by a recursive transform calculation of the odd and even halves, and then the merging of the two halves.

With this step, the basic FTT algorithm is in place. There are more optimizations that are often associated with a good FFT procedure, but the essentials are present in the program slow4.c (Figure 6.6); this program requires only 0.07 seconds to complete the Fourier transform we have been using as an example.

The accompanying CD contains a Fourier transform library named fftlib.c that will be used in the remainder of this chapter. The basic FFT procedure in this library is called, simply, fft. The initialization procedure fftinit must be called first,

```
void slowft(float *x,COMPLEX *y,int n)          Even = (COMPLEX *)
{                                                   malloc (sizeof (struct
                                                    cpx) * m);
    COMPLEX xx[1024];                           Odd = (COMPLEX *)
    int i;                                          malloc (sizeof (struct
                                                    cpx) * m);
                                                if (Sum==0 || Diff==0 ||
    for (i=0; i<n; i++)                             Even==0 || Odd==0)
      cmplx (x[i], 0.0, &(xx[i]));               {
    evenodd (xx, y, n);                             printf ("Panic-
                                                    memory.\n");
}                                                   exit(1);
                                                    }
void evenodd (COMPLEX *x,
              COMPLEX *y,int n)  for (i=0; i<m; i++)
{                                               {
  int m, i;                                       csum (x[i], x[i+m], &z3);
  COMPLEX *Sum, *Diff;                            cdiv (z3, two,
                                                    &(Sum[i]));

  COMPLEX *Even, *Odd;
  COMPLEX z1, z2, z3, z4, tmp, two;               cdif (x[i], x[i+m], &z3);
  float xs, ys;                                   cmult (z3, z1, &z4);
                                                  cdiv (z4, two,
                                                    &(Diff[i]));

  if (n<1) printf ("What???? \n");                cmult (z1, tmp, &z2);
                                                  cmplx (z2.real, z2.imag,
/* The simple case, where N=1 */                    &z1);

  cmplx (2.0, 0.0, &two);                       }
  if (n == 1)
  {                                             evenodd (Sum, Even, m);
    cmplx(x[0].real,x[0].imag,&(y[0]))  evenodd (Diff, Odd, m);
    return;
  }                                             for (i=0; i<m; i++)
  /* Otherwise, N is even */                    {
  m = n/2;                                          y[i*2.real =
                                                    Even[i].real;
  cmplx (0.0,atan (1.0)/n* -8.0, &z1);              y[i*2.imag =
                                                    Even[i].imag;
```

Figure 6.6 The program slow4, which is the essential code for
the Fast Fourier Transform.

```
cexp (z1, &tmp);                          y[i*2 + 1].real =
                                            Odd[i].real;
cmplx (1.0, 0.0, &z1);                    y[i*2 + 1].imag =
                                            Odd[i].imag;
/* Allocate temporary space */            }
  Sum = (COMPLEX *)
     malloc(sizeof (struct cpx)*m);       free(Sum); free(Diff);
  Diff = (COMPLEX *)                       free (Even); free(Odd);
     malloc (sizeof (struct cpx) * m);    }
```

Figure 6.6 (continued)

passing the size of the data array to be transformed. There are many useful functions in this library that will be described as the need arises.

The Inverse Fourier Transform

The inverse Fourier transform will undo the transformation; when given the Fourier transform of a set of data, the inverse transform will reconstruct the original data. The log function and the exp function have a similar relationship, where one undoes the other.

The formula for the discrete inverse Fourier transform is:

$$f(k) = \frac{1}{N} \sum_{w=0}^{N-1} F(w)e^{2\pi jwk/N} \qquad \text{(EQ 6.9)}$$

which differs from the forward transform in the sign of the exponent. Now might be the time to point out that the constant factor $1/n$ is somewhat flexible. Some people apply it to the forward transform, some split it between the forward and inverse transforms, and some apply it only to the inverse transform. In fact, the programs slow1.c–slow4.c produce somewhat different numerical results because the multiplicative constant was ignored utterly.

Of course, the fast algorithm can be applied to the inverse transform, so that a set of data can be transformed just as easily in either direction. In the fftlib.c routines, the inverse 1D FFT function is the same as the forward FFT function; there is a parameter that specifies a forward or inverse direction.

Two-Dimensional Fourier Transforms

So far, the application of the Fourier transform to images has been vague, since the transforms seen so far apply to one-dimensional data only. The extension to two dimensions is simple; mathematically, we have:

$$F(u,v) = \frac{1}{\sqrt{nm}} \sum_{i=0}^{n-1} \sum_{k=0}^{m-1} e^{-2\pi j(ui+vk)/nm} f(i,k) \qquad \text{(EQ 6.10)}$$

The inverse transform is the same, but with the sign reversed. Note that the constant multiplier is split between the forward and inverse transforms, which is not always done.

The Fourier transform of an image f is calculated by first computing the Fourier transform of each row, giving an image f'. Then the Fourier transform of each column of f' is computed, giving F, the transform of the image. This allows us to use the one-dimensional FFT methods already discussed to compute the two-dimensional transform. Figure 6.7 gives a sample 2D FFT routine based on this, which was in fact taken from fftlib.c.

Equation 6.10 describes the general case. For the purposes of image restoration, it will be assumed that the images are square $N \times N$ arrays, where N is a power of two. If this is not initially true, then the images can be enlarged by adding rows and columns containing all zero pixels until it is true.

In addition to the use of the Fourier transform to allow the filtering of certain frequencies, there are other useful properties that become quite important when discussing two-dimensional data. Most important from the point of view of image processing is that a convolution is much easier to do in the frequency domain than in the spatial domain. In fact, a convolution is simply an element-by-element product of the Fourier transforms of the two images being convolved. Specifically, the frequency domain convolution of image a with image b is performed as follows:

1. Check the image sizes to ensure that they are the same. If not, add zeros to the smaller image until it is the same size as the larger one.
2. Compute A, the Fourier transform of the image a; also compute B, the Fourier transform of the image b.
3. Compute the new image C as the product of the corresponding pixels in A and B; that is, $C(i,j)=A(i,j)\times B(i,j)$.
4. Compute the image c, the inverse Fourier transform of C. This is the result of the convolution.

In spite of the complexity of the Fourier transform computation, this process is actually faster than the straightforward method of Equation 1.13 when the smaller of the two images is larger than about 16×16 pixels.

Creating Artificial Blur

Since a convolution can be performed in the frequency domain, and an image can be blurred by convolving it with a point spread function, it should be a simple

```
void fft2d ( COMPLEX_IMAGE image,
            float direction )
{
    float temp[1024]; /* For columns */
    int i, j; /* Iteration counters */
    int d, nu;

    nu = vlog2(FFTN);
    if (direction == FORWARD)
     d = 0;
    else d = 1;
/* Transform Rows */
    for ( i = 0; i < FFTN; i++ )
        fft (image[i], direction);

/* Transform Columns */
    for ( i = 0; i < FFTN; i++ )
    {
            for ( j = 0; j < FFTN; j++)
            {
             temp[j] = image[j][i];
             temp[j+FFTN] =image [j][i+FFTN];
            }
            fft (temp, direction);
            for ( j = 0; j < FFTN; j++ )
            {
             image[j][i] = temp[j];
             image[j][i+FFTN] = temp[j+FFTN];
            }
    }
}
```

Figure 6.7 The basic two-dimensional FFT. The row transformation is performed in place but the columns must be copied into consecutive locations in a temporary array. The direction parameter controls whether a forward or inverse transform is done.

matter to introduce blur into some perfect images to obtain blurred versions that can be used for experimentation. Restoration methods can be tested on these known images, and the quality of the result can be determined by simply comparing the original against the restored image.

Figure 6.8 shows a simple image that can be used for experimentation—it is a 128×128 image that simply contains the words *The Fourier Transform*. The point spread function to be used is also shown. This particular PSF should blur the image equally in all directions, and is circular with a diameter of five pixels. The blurred version of the image (Figure 6.8c) is unreadable.

It is important to note that the pixel values in the PSF image are all less than or equal to 1.0, since a PSF should not add energy (light, pixel levels) to the image; a PSF only spreads out the existing energy. If the pixel values in the PSF image were in the usual range of 0–255, the distortions introduced may be beyond the scope of image restoration to fix.

The blurred image was created using software that is provided on the CD. While discussing the various aspects of image restoration, we will be building a software system that actually performs the operations described. This will be unlike the MAX system of Chapter 2 in that the restoration system (to be called Eagle so as to avoid always referring to it as *the system*) consists of a collection of stand-alone programs and their accompanying libraries. Each program will perform a specific task related to image restoration.

The first module in the Eagle system is align.c; its purpose is to embed an arbitrary PBM format image file into a background of zeros, so that the result is a square $N \times N$ image, where N is a power of 2. If no size is given on the command

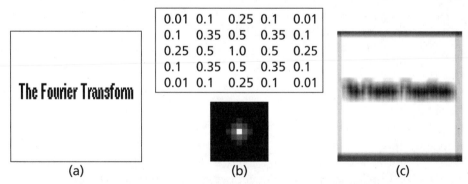

(a) (b) (c)

Figure 6.8 Blurring an image using a frequency domain convolution. (a) The original image. It was obtained using a screen capture, and is without noise. (b) The point spread function used to generate the blur. (c) The result of convolving the image with the point spread function.

line, the image specified by the first parameter will be scaled up to the next larger power of two in size. Also, the image will be centered, which is sometimes very convenient. The align.c module makes it much easier to experiment with more-or-less arbitrary images.

It may be a little confusing that align.c is referred to in the code and documentation as module *two*, rather than module *one*. This is because there is a missing module: convert. Not everyone uses the PBM format for their images, where Eagle insists on it. The convert module must be written by the user who wants to use some other format for their data. It will convert their format into a PBM/PGM/PPM file, at which point Eagle can deal with it. There are far too many image formats available to deal with them all, so it was decided to omit this step altogether.

The next module (3) is blur, the program used to create Figure 6.8c. It accepts an image file and a PSF file, and does the frequency domain convolution, saving the result in a specified file. The program is invoked:

```
blur input.pgm psf.pgm output.pgm
```

It assumes that the images are square, and refuses to proceed if not. It, of course, uses the fftlib.c procedures to perform the Fourier transforms (fftlib.c could be considered to be module *zero*). The blur program also scales the values of the PSF to between 0 and 1 so that the resulting intensities stay within the bounds of our usual implementation.

6.3 THE INVERSE FILTER

It was a useful exercise to show in detail how an image can be blurred, since the reverse is about to be attempted. The blurring was accomplished by convolving the image with the point spread function. Although no noise was added, in the real case it would be (Figure 6.1), giving the following process:

$$F = I \times H + \eta \qquad \text{(EQ 6.11)}$$

where F is the Fourier transform of the blurred image, I is the Fourier transform of the perfect image, and H is the Fourier transform of the PSF. The η term is the noise, which can be characterized statistically but never known perfectly. The multiplication in the frequency domain corresponds to a convolution of the two images i and h.

The goal of image restoration is to reproduce the original image i as well as possible, given f and h. Algebraically, it seems to make sense to divide by H and ignore η in equation 6.11, giving:

$$\frac{F}{H} = I \qquad\qquad \text{(EQ 6.12)}$$

The mathematics is really vastly more involved than this, but the end result is the same: This is the inverse filter, which is the least-squares restoration of f.

In detail: given an input image f and a point spread function in the form of an image h:

1. Compute the 2D FFT of the image f; call this F.
2. Compute the 2D FFT of the PSF image h; call this H.
3. Compute the new image $G(i,j) = F(i,j)/H(i,j)$
4. Compute the inverse FFT of G, giving the restored image g.

This can't be done naively or serious problems will result. The image H is certain to contain regions where the values are zero, and dividing by zero usually has disastrous results. In fact, even if H becomes too small, the result is that noise will dominate the restored image.

One solution is to check the norm of H at each pixel, and if it is below a specified threshold value, the division is not performed. Instead, the values from F can be left undisturbed, the pixel could be set to zero, or a default value can be used.

The Eagle module that implements the inverse filter is inverse.c. It is invoked by:

```
inverse blurredimage.pgm psf.pgm result.pgm
```

For example, Figure 6.9 shows the result of applying the inverse filter to the artificial image of Figure 6.8c. The inverse module will ask for a threshold value for discarding H pixel values that are too small; the value used in Figure 6.9 was 0.0001.

The implementation of the inverse filter uses a new twist on the Fourier transform: the *origin-centered* Fourier transform. When the Fourier transform of an image is calculated, it is done in such a way that the origin (and the brightest spot) is the pixel (0,0). This point is at the geometric center of an origin-centered transform, making the image symmetrical about its own center. It is a very easy thing to do—simply multiply every pixel (i,j) in the image by $(-1)^{i+j}$ before computing the FFT. This may be more a matter of personal preference than of necessity, but all of the restoration modules use origin-centered transforms.

The inverse filter is very susceptible to noise, to the point where the inverse restoration of a very noisy image could be subjectively worse than the original. Adjustments to the threshold could be somewhat useful in these cases, and noise filtering might be useful, but a more sophisticated method is probably a better idea.

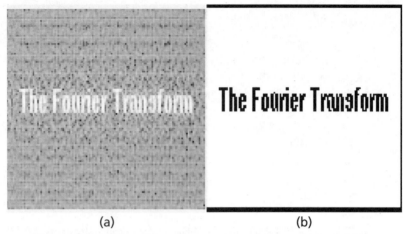

(a)   (b)

Figure 6.9 Inverse filter restoration of Figure 6.8c. (a) The image as it appears after the restoration. (b) The same image after thresholding to remove the worst of the clutter. Note that the dot above the i is visible.

6.4   THE WIENER FILTER

The Wiener filter (Helstrom 1967) and its variants are designed to work in cases where the noise has become significant. This filter in its complete form requires that we know a good deal about the signal and the properties of the noise that infects it. Without going into great detail, an approximation of this filter can be expressed as

$$I \approx \left[\frac{1}{H} \frac{\|H\|^2}{\|H\|^2 + K} \right] F \qquad \text{(EQ 6.13)}$$

where $\|H\|^2$ is the norm of the complex number H, and K is a constant. One suggestion (Gonzalez 1992) for a value of K is $2\sigma^2$, where σ^2 is the variance of the noise.

Figure 6.10 shows the Wiener filter restoration of the test image of Figure 6.8c. Because this image has no noise associated with it, any advantage of the Wiener filter is not clearly shown; indeed, in the absence of noise the Wiener filter reduces to the inverse filter. Thus, the face image first seen in Chapter 3 (Figure 3.4) was blurred and then restored using both the inverse and Wiener filters. These results also appear in Figure 6.10. The image restored using the inverse filter shows a grid pattern, which is absent in the Wiener restored image.

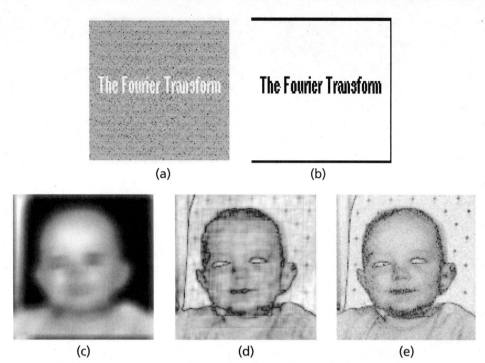

(a)   (b)

(c)   (d)   (e)

Figure 6.10 Wiener file restoration. (a) Restored test image.
(b) The same image thresholded. (c) Blurred version of the face
image. (d) Inverse filter restoration. (e) Wiener filter
restoration. Note that the pattern in the background can be
seen clearly.

6.5   STRUCTURED NOISE

In some cases the distortion imposed on an image has a regular pattern associated with it. For example, when an electric motor is operated close to a television or other video device, it is common to see a pattern of lines on the screen. This is caused by the fact that the motor generates a signal that interferes with the television, and the interference has a frequency associated with it that is related to the speed of the motor.

There is a wide variety of causes for structured noise, and it can be quite a problem. However, because the noise is periodic, the Fourier transform can be used to determine where the peak frequencies are. The noise will correspond to one of these, and it can be virtually eliminated by clearing those regions in the frequency domain image that correspond to the noise frequencies, and then back-transforming it into a regular image.

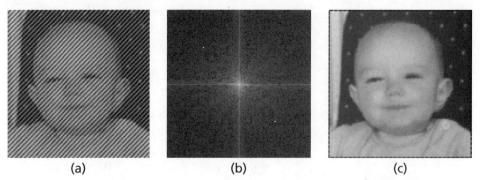

Figure 6.11 Example of structured noise removal. (a) Face image with an imposed sinusoidal pattern. (b) Fourier transform of the noisy image, showing the two spikes responsible for the pattern (Circled in white in the above image). (c) Restored image; the spikes were set to zero and then the inverse Fourier transform was computed (has been contrast enhanced).

As a simple example, Figure 6.11a shows the face image with high-frequency sinusoidal interference imposed on it. The Fourier transform of this image (Figure 6.11b) shows a number of bright spots (*spikes*). A matching pair of spikes appear in the upper left and lower right quarters of the image, and these correspond to the periodic signal causing the pattern of diagonal lines. To correct this, edit the Fourier domain image and set the two spikes to zero; then apply an inverse FFT to obtain the space domain image. The result, after some contrast improvement, appears in Figure 6.11c.

There are a number of questions still to be addressed. First among these concerns exactly which spikes to remove, and unfortunately there is no good answer. Experience with the appearance of Fourier domain images will help, and for this purpose the fftlib.c procedures will be very useful. In particular, it will be quickly learned that the peak in the center of the image contains much of the interesting information in the image, and must not be removed. Periodic signals cause symmetrical spikes on each side of the central peak, and though there can be many of these, they can be removed in pairs to see what happens. When the correct spikes are found, the image will be improved by their removal. Depending on the type of noise there could be more than one pair of spikes to be removed.

The restoration in this figure was performed by the program snr.c (Structured Noise Removal). This program computes the Fourier transform of the input image, and then interactively asks for the coordinates of small regions to be set to zero. After clearing the specified regions the image is back-transformed and saved. The restored image in Figure 6.11c was created by the following interactive session:

```
snr fsn restored
Enter UL corner of area to be cleared: 32 32
Enter LR corner of area to be cleared: 32 32
Setting to 0 elements in that region.
Another region? (1 for yes, 0 for no): 1
Enter UL corner of area to be cleared: 96 96
Enter LR corner of area to be cleared: 96 96
Another region? (1 for yes, 0 for no): 0
```

This results in the pixel at (32,32) and the one at (96,96) in the Fourier transform of the corrupt face image being set to zero.

Just as one person's weed is another's flower, just what constitutes noise is in the eye of the beholder. One fairly common issue in document analysis is the existence of grid lines in the data. As a specific example, many types of pen recorder plot lines in ink on a sheet of graph paper. The grid lines interfere with the extraction of the plotted data lines, making them difficult to extract properly.

In this instance, knowledge of the behavior of the Fourier transform helps a lot. The transform of a horizontal line appears like a vertical line in the frequency domain image, and a vertical line transform as a horizontal one. Therefore, it seems like a variation of the snr.c procedure would have a chance of removing the grid lines. After creating the Fourier transform, remove those pixels in the center rows and columns of the frequency domain image, taking care not to remove pixels too close to the center peak. This is called a *notch filter*, and is implemented by the program notch.c.

Figure 6.12a contains an image that was obtained by scanning the original paper document. It is simply a handwritten note on graph paper. The goal is to remove the grid lines as completely as possible. The Fourier transform of the image (Figure 6.12b) is obtained, and the pixels within the specified notch regions are set to zero (Figure 6.12c) before performing the inverse Fourier transform. The result (Figure 6.12d) shows an astonishing lack of grid lines. Using this method it would be possible to remove patterns in either direction.

The interactive sessions that accomplished the grid line removal is:

```
notch grid.pgm z
Image Restoration System module 9 - notch filter
Select notch: Enter the horizontal center: 256
Enter the vertical center: 256
Enter width/2 (in pixels). i.e. Pixels to the left of center:
2
Enter the distance of the notch from the center: 15
Setting to 0 elements in that region.
```

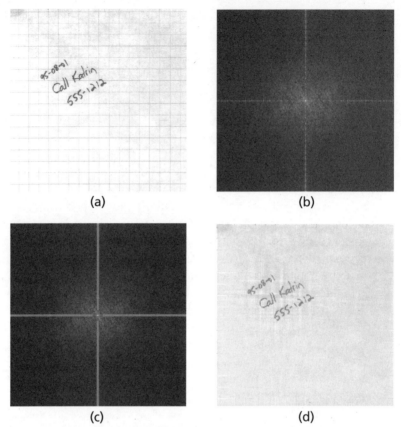

Figure 6.12 Removal of grid lines using a notch filter.
(a) Original scanned image. (b) Fourier transform of scanned
image. (c) Notches along the center lines, removing both the
vertical and horizontal lines. (d) The restored image.

6.6 MOTION BLUR—A SPECIAL CASE

If an image has been blurred due to the motion of either the camera or the object, the point spread function will be an extended blob with the long axis indicating the direction of motion. While it is possible to use an inverse or Wiener filter restoration in these cases, there is a special solution that should not be as susceptible to noise.

If the motion can be assumed to be uniform and in the x (horizontal) direction, a very nice expression (Gonzalez 1992; Sondhi 1972) can be used to remove most of the blur without resorting to a Fourier transform:

$$I(y,x) \approx \overline{f} - \frac{1}{K} \sum_{k=0}^{K-1} \sum_{j=0}^{k} f'(y,x - ma + (k - j)a)$$

$$+ \sum_{j=0}^{m} f'(y,x - ja)$$

(EQ 6.14)

where

$\overline{f}$ is the mean value of the blurred image f.

a is the distance of the blur.

K is the number of times that the distance a occurs in the image; that is, the number of columns $= Ka$. K is approximated as an integer, where necessary.

m is the integer part of x/a, for any specified horizontal position x.

$f'(i,j)$ is the derivative of f at the point (i,j). This can be approximated by a difference, as was done in Chapter 1.

As an example, Figure 6.13 shows this method applied to a blurred version of the sky image (Figure 3.2). This image is blurred by about 20 pixels in the horizontal direction. The restored version suffers from some artifacts, but is a noticeable improvement over the blurred image. The program motion.c (Eagle module 11) performed the restoration, when called as:

motion skymb.pgm 20 restored

where the value 20 indicates the amount of blur. This can be estimated from the image, or arrived at by trial and error. To estimate the amount of blur, look for an edge that is as close to perpendicular to the direction of motion as possible. If the amount of motion is significant, it should be possible to determine the original and final position of the edge; that is, the location of the edge when the motion started (or the shutter opened) and its position when it stopped (the shutter closed). This is illustrated in Figure 6.13d. From the expanded view of the edge, we can see that motion appears to encompass about 19 pixels. The result of a motion correction of 19 pixels (Figure 6.13e), 20 pixels (6.13c), and 21 pixels (6.13f) shows that the best result was achieved with a value of 20.

6.7 THE HOMOMORPHIC FILTER—ILLUMINATION

Homomorphic filtering is a technique in which an image is transformed to a new space or coordinate system in which the desired operation is simpler to perform. Specifically, the problem to be addressed is one of improving the quality of an image that has been acquired under conditions of poor illumination. As was seen in Chapter 3, illumination can have a very important influence on the appearance of the image, and on what it can be used for. The ideal situation would be to generate the original set of objects in an image without regard to the impinging

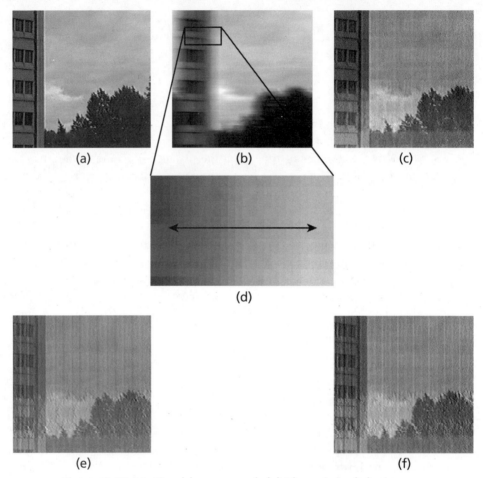

Figure 6.13 Motion blur removal. (a) The original sky image. (b) The same image blurred by about 20 pixels horizontally. (c) Restored, using the motion program. (d) Estimation of the amount of motion by examining the vertical edge. The approximate start and end of the edge can be seen in the blurred image. (e) The blurred image restored, assuming a motion of 19 pixels. (f) Result of the restoration assuming 21 pixels.

illumination. This can't be done exactly or in all cases, but some steps can be made to improve the situation.

An image is an array of measured light intensities, and is a function of the amount of light reflected off the objects in the scene. The intensity is the product of the reflectance of the object R and the intensity of the illumination I:

$$f(i,j) = I(i,j)R(i,j) \qquad \text{(EQ 6.15)}$$

The methods used so far for restoration involve using the Fourier transform, which will not separate I from R; it would if they were summed, of course. Fortunately, a sum can be created: Simply take the log of both sides:

$$\log f(i,j) = \log I(i,j) + \log R(i,j) \qquad \text{(EQ 6.16)}$$

Now all that is needed is a way to separate these two components. A simple observation will help: Illumination tends to vary slowly, or relatively so, across an image. The reflectance, on the other hand, is characterized by sharp changes, especially at boundaries (edges). This means that if the low-frequency components (illumination) could be decreased, while increasing the high-frequency (reflectance) components, the problem would be solved. The Fourier transform is exactly what is needed to do this.

Frequency Filters in General

The use of the Fourier transform as a filter to pass or block certain *spatial frequencies* will be illustrated by example. Consider the example image first seen in Figure 6.8a, consisting of the words *The Fourier Transform*. The origin-centered Fourier transform of this image will have a peak at the center—let's see what happens when pixels near the center of the transform are set to zero.

Figure 6.14 a–d show the results of clearing pixels near the center peak of the transform before back-transforming; pixels within a radius of 2, 8, 16, and 32 pixels of the center (respectively) were affected. The effect on the image is curious: The more of the center region that is cleared, the more the image seems to consist of isolated lines and spots. The reason is that the outlying regions of the Fourier transformed image corresponds to high-frequency information, and removing high-frequency information affects details. On the other hand, passing only the

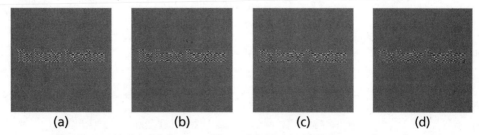

(a)   (b)   (c)   (d)

Figure 6.14 The high-pass filter. (a) Pixels within a radius of 2 of the center of the Fourier transform were set to zero before back-transforming. (b) Radius = 8. (c) Radius = 16. (d) Radius = 32.

central region and setting to zero the remainder of the Fourier transform allows the low-frequency information to be retained, while removing the high frequencies. This is seen in Figure 6.15. Only the basic outline or position of the objects remain, and details are progressively lost. This is called a *low-pass* filter, with the former filter being a *high-pass* filter.

A particular spatial frequency will correspond to points in the Fourier transform that are a fixed distance from the center; this is true for origin-centered transforms only. The center itself is the lowest frequency, with the higher ones towards the outside. A *frequency domain filter* is an image having values that correspond to the desired frequencies in the output. For example, the frequency domain filter that was used to give Figure 6.14d has zeros in a disk of radius 32 at the center of the image, and ones everywhere else. Values less than one will suppress the corresponding frequency in the output, and values greater than one will enhance that frequency.

A band, containing any particular set of spatial frequencies, can be either allowed to remain (*band-pass* filter) or be blocked (*band-stop* filter) to varying degrees. This would correspond to a ring of one or zero pixels in the frequency domain filter. In addition, a set of frequencies can be enhanced by increasing their relative values in the Fourier transform image, instead of simply passing or blocking them. This can be done at the same time as other frequencies are reduced or blocked altogether.

This happens to be what we want to do for the homomorphic filter. The high frequencies should be emphasized, so they will be increased. The low frequencies correspond to illumination, and so will be decreased. This will be called a *high-emphasis* filter, and its shape is shown in Figure 6.16a. Other such filters could be used, and the shape of the filter can be changed to meet specific needs (Stearns 1988).

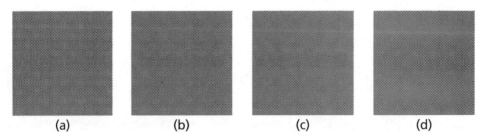

(a)   (b)   (c)   (d)

Figure 6.15 The low-pass filter. (a) Pixels outside of a circle of radius 32 of the center of the Fourier transform were set to zero, allowing only the center pixels to be used in the inverse transform. (b) Radius = 16. (c) Radius = 8. (d) Radius = 2.

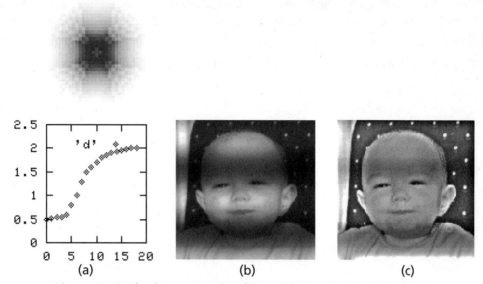

Figure 6.16 The homomorphic filter. (a) The shape of the high-emphasis filter, which is multiplied element-by-element with the Fourier transform of the log or the original image. The graph shows a cross-section through the center of the filter. (b) Test image—this is the face image with sinusoidal illumination. (c) Result of homomorphic filtering. Detail is much clearer, particularly in the areas that were dark.

Isolating Illumination Effects

Now the homomorphic filter can be completed. The stages in processing are:

1. Take the log of all pixels in the image.
2. Compute the Fourier transform of the image obtained in 1.
3. Apply the high-emphasis filter by multiplying the elements in the filter mask by those in the Fourier transform image.
4. Compute the inverse Fourier transform.
5. Compute the exponential of all pixels; this reverses the logarithm of step 1. Stretch the contrast, if needed.

Figure 6.16 shows an application of the homomorphic filter to the face image having an imposed sinusoidal illumination gradient (originally seen in Figure 3.4).

The result is much clearer in the formerly dark areas, and the overall contrast is better. The suppression of the bands is not complete, but appears to be sufficient.

6.8 THE EAGLE RESTORATION SYSTEM—A SUMMARY

The system consists of 16 modules, some of which exist for the purposes of experimentation.

Module 1:   Convert: This must be written by the user if a format other than PBM is to be used. It simply converts the host format into the appropriate PBM/PGM/PPM form.

Module 2:   Align: Embed the target image into another that is a power of two in size in each dimension. The target image will be centered within the new one, and surrounded by zero-valued pixels.

```
align filename {size}
```

Output file name is the same as input name with adj appended.

Module 3:   Blur: Introduce a blur into an image. Accepts a PSF image, which is then convolved with the target image to produce a blurred version. (for experimentation; it creates a blurry image)

```
blur imagefile PSFfile output
```

Module 4:   Inverse: Accepts a PSF, which is an estimate of the degradation found in the target image. An inverse filter is performed in an attempt to restore the image.

```
inverse imagefile PSFfile output
```

Module 5:   Wiener filter: Accepts a PSF, and performs a Wiener filter restoration (an approximation, really) on the target image.

```
wiener imagefile PSFfile output
```

Module 6:   Structured noise: Introduce structured noise into an image. (for experimentation; it creates a noisy image)

```
snoise imagefile output
```

Module 7:   Shuffle: Rearrange the quadrants of an image that has been shuffled by a Fourier transform.

```
shuff imagefile
```

Creates a new image in a file of the same name with .shf appended

Module 8: SNR: Structured noise removal. The program interactively determines portions of the Fourier transform image to be cleared, and then does so. Produces a restored image.

```
snr imagefile output
```

Module 9: Notch: Asks for the parameters of a notch filter and then imposes it on the target image.

```
notch imagefile output
```

Module 10: mblur: Introduce motion blur into an image. The amount of blur is a command-line argument. (for experimentation)

```
mblur imagefile blur_amount output
```

The value of blur_amount is integer, and is the number of pixels of blur.

Module 11: motion: Remove motion blur by an amount specified on the command line.

```
motion imagefile blur_amount output
```

Module 12: Transform: Compute the 2D FFT of the target image and save it as a PGM file. Included so that users can view frequency domain images. FFT is origin-centered.

```
transform imagefile output
```

Module 13: hipass: High-frequency pass filter. Radius is specified on the command line.

```
hipass imagefile radius output
```

Module 14: lopass: Low-frequency pass filter. Radius is specified on the command line.

```
lopass imagefile radius output
```

Module 15: hiemph: High-emphasis filter, of the type used in the homomorphic filter.

```
hiemph imagefile output
```

Module 16: homo: Homomorphic filter.

```
homo imagefile output
```

6.9 BIBLIOGRAPHY

Andrews, H. C. and B. R. Hunt. 1977. *Digital Image Restoration*. Englewood Cliffs, NJ: Prentice-Hall.

Andrews, H. C. 1974. Digital Image Restoration: A Survey. *Computer*. Vol. 7. 5:36–45.

Bracewell, R. 1965. *The Fourier Transform and Its Applications*. New York: McGraw-Hill.

Brigham, E. O. 1974. *The Fast Fourier Transform*. Englewood Cliffs, NJ: Prentice-Hall.

Cooley, J. W. and J. W. Tukey. 1965. An Algorithm for the Machine Calculation of Complex Fourier Series. *Mathematical Computation*. Vol 19. 297–301.

Geman, S. and D. Geman. 1984. Stochastic Relaxation, Gibbs Distributions, and Bayesian Restoration of Images. *IEEE Transactions on Pattern Analysis and Machine Intelligence*. Vol. PAMI-6. 6:721–741.

Gonzalez, R. C., and R. E. Woods. 1992. *Digital Image Processing*. Reading, MA: Addison-Wesley.

Gull, S. F. and G. J. Daniell. 1978. Image Reconstruction from Incomplete and Noisy Data. *Nature*. Vol. 292. 686–690.

Hall, E. L. 1979. Computer Image Processing and Recognition. New York: Academic Press.

Helstrom, C. W. 1967. Image Restoration by the Method of Least Squares. *Journal of the Optical Society of America*. Vol. 57. 3:297–303.

Hunt, B. R. 1973. The Application of Constrained Least Squares Estimation to Image Restoration by Digital Computer. *IEEE Transactions on Computers*. Vol. C-22. 9:805–812.

Lee, H. C. 1990. Review of Image-Blur Models in a Photographic System Using the Principles of Optics. *Optical Engineering*. Vol. 29.

Macnaghten, A. M. and C.A.R. Hoare. 1975. Fast Fourier Transform Free from Tears. *The Computer Journal*. Vol. 20. 1:78–83.

MacAdam, D. P. 1970. Digital Image Restoration by Constrained Deconvolution. *Journal of the Optical Society of America*. Vol. 20. 12:1617–1627.

Pavlidis, T. 1982. *Algorithms for Graphics and Image Processing*. Rockville, MD: Computer Science Press.

Pratt, W. K. and F. Davarian. 1977. Fast Computational Techniques for Pseudoinverse and Wiener Restoration. *IEEE Transactions on Computers*. Vol. C-26. 6:571–580.

Pratt, W. K. 1972. Generalized Wiener Filter Computation Techniques. *IEEE Transactions on Computers*. Vol. C-21. 7:636–641.

Sezan, M. I. and A. M. Tekalp. 1990. Survey of Recent Developments in Digital Image Restoration. *Optical Engineering*. Vol. 29. 5:393–404.

Singleton, R. C. 1967. On Computing the Fast Fourier Transform. *Communications of the ACM*. Vol. 10. 10:647–654.

Slepian, D. 1967. Restoration of Photographs Blurred by Image Motion. *Bell System Technical Journal*. 2353–2362.

Stearns, S. D. and R. A. David. 1988. *Signal Processing Algorithms*. Englewood Cliffs, NJ: Prentice-Hall.

Stockham, T. G. 1972. Image Processing in the Context of a Visual Model. *Proceedings of the IEEE*. Vol. 60. 828–841.

7

WAVELETS

7.1 ESSENTIALS OF WAVELET DECOMPOSITION

In Chapter 6, the Fourier transform was found to be an essential tool for image restoration. The idea that an image can be decomposed into the sum of weighted sine and cosine components is, initially, curious enough; that the decomposition is a useful one is interesting, and leads inevitably to a study of what other functions might be used in a similar decomposition.

There are many (infinitely many) such functions, in fact. A function used in such a decomposition is usually called a *basis function*, and only some basis functions will produce a decomposition that has interesting properties. The Fourier transform is merely one of a large class of transforms that has the following form:

$$Trans(u,v) = \sum_{x=0}^{N} \sum_{y=0}^{N} f(x,y)g(x,y,u,v) \qquad \text{(EQ 7.1)}$$

where f is the two-dimensional function being transformed, and g is called the *kernel* of the transformation, wherein reside the basis functions. For the Fourier transform, the kernel is:

$$g(x,y,u,v) = \frac{e^{-2\pi j\ (ux+vy)/N}}{N} \qquad \text{(EQ 7.2)}$$

which is, as we have seen, the sum of sine and cosine terms. So, the idea of an image transform is really quite a general one, and the Fourier transform is a special case, rather than being unique.

Possibly the simplest example of an image transform is the *Walsh transform*, which uses the values 1 and -1 as the basis of the series expansion. The transformation kernel for the two-dimensional case is:

$$g(x,y,u,v) = \frac{1}{N} \prod_{i=0}^{nbits-1} - 1^{bit(i,x)bit(n-i-1,u)+bit(i,y)bit(n-i-1,v)} \qquad \text{(EQ 7.3)}$$

where the function $bit(i,x)$ returns the value of bit number i of the number x. The resulting transform is not of enormous utility, but it can be used as a primitive compression tool. The program walsh2d.c will compute the Walsh transform of an image, and stores a specified subimage to a file named walsht.dat. For example,

```
walsh2d face128.pgm 64
```

finds the Walsh transform of the 128 × 128 image face128.pgm, and saves the upper left 64 × 64 pixels in the file walsht.dat. The inverse transform

```
unwalsh walsht
```

will reconstruct the image from the subimage at its disposal, in this case one that is ¼ as big as the original.[1] Figure 7.1 shows how the image looks after being reconstructed using all of the pixels, a 64 × 64 image, a 32 × 32 image, and a 16 × 16 image. The quality goes down as the number of pixels used in the reconstruction goes down. The Fourier transform can be used in this way too; in that case, the *largest* components in the frequency domain would be used in the reconstruction.

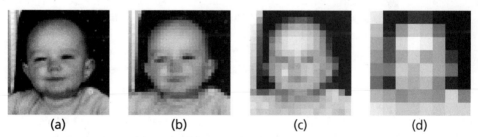

(a)   (b)   (c)   (d)

Figure 7.1 Walsh transform applied to the face image. (a) All of the transform is used to reconstruct. (b) Only the first 64 × 64 pixels of the transform are used to reconstruct. (c) 32 × 32 pixels used to reconstruct. (d) 16 × 16 pixels used in the reconstruction.

1. A harmless fib—it has ¼ as many pixels, but they are floating point numbers, which are bigger. A reasonable compression ratio can be achieved by scaling and using symmetry.

Most of this is beside the main point, which is that even a 'function' as simple as a simple numeric constant can be used as a basis for a transformation of this type. The idea of using *wavelets* as a basis is not really new, although there has been a lot of interest recently in using them as applied to images, especially for compression. A wavelet is simply a function that, unlike the Fourier transform, not only has a *frequency* associated with it, but also a *scale*.

An Intuitive Approach

The word *wavelet* should literally mean *small wave*, so for a function to be a wavelet it must be small, and it must be a wave. It seems to be clear what is meant by a wave—a function that has some periodicity (like the sine function) represents a wave. What is meant by small in this case is the amplitude of the function—a wavelet decreases in amplitude (decays) as a function of the distance from its center. A wavelet must have *both* properties, as seen in Figure 7.2 and this gives the wavelet transform a unique characteristic: It is *local*. That is, it only has a significant value in a small region of space. It also has the frequency characteristics of a Fourier transform, on the other hand.

Let's look at a more detailed example, using a specific function g for expository purposes only.[1] Consider the function:

$$g(x) = \sin (4x)e^{-x^2} \qquad\qquad (EQ\ 7.4)$$

This is a sine function, damped by a Gaussian so that it quickly decays. If this function is used as the mother wavelet, then a function to be decomposed is expressed as a *linear combination of different scalings and translations* of this wavelet. This wavelet can be *translated* by subtracting a value t from its argument; that is g(x−t) is just g(x) translated by t units. For a one-dimensional function (signal) a translation simply shifts the wavelet along the axis. *Scaling* is performed by dividing the argument by a scaling factor. The wavelet g(x/s) is simply g(x) scaled by a factor of s. This stretches or compresses the wavelet, depending on whether s is greater than one or less than one, respectively.

Figure 7.2 shows the wavelet of Equation 7.4 scaled and translated by various values. A positive t value moves the wavelet along the positive x axis, but otherwise leaves the shape alone (Figure 7.2c). A values of s that is greater than one (Figure 7.2d) stretches the wavelet so that it occupies more of the x axis, while 0<s<1 compresses it (Figure 7.2b) so that it occupies less horizontal space. The default wavelet uses s = 1.0 and t = 0.0.

---

1. That is, this function might or might not be useful as a wavelet, but is a function with which we can work.

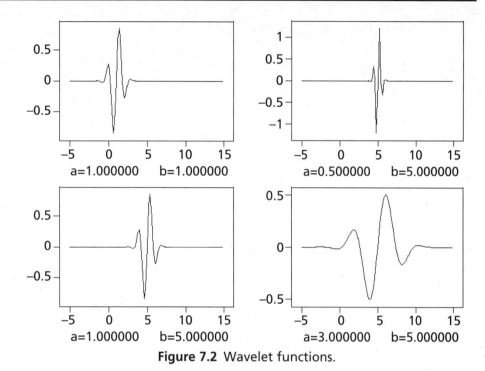

Figure 7.2 Wavelet functions.

Thus, the scaled and translated wavelet can be written as:

$$w_{s,t}(x) = g\!\left(\frac{(x - t)}{s}\right) \qquad \text{(EQ 7.5)}$$

where s and t refer to a scaling and translation of the wavelet g. Now for a given function of set of sampled data f(x), the wavelet decomposition can be written:

$$f(x) = \sum_{i=0}^{S} \sum_{j=0}^{T} c_{i,j} w_{i,j}(x) \qquad \text{(EQ 7.6)}$$

which is a linear combination of the $w_{i,j}$ functions. The c_{ij} are wavelet coefficients, and their values represent the relative contribution of that specific wavelet in the decomposition. What this means is that the wavelet decomposition of f can be thought of as a two-dimensional function of s and t.

The wavelet transform could be computed by using the basic definition of a transform (Equation 7.1). This is educational from a number of perspectives, but takes far too long in practice. However, it does raise a few issues that are important, such as the need to determine which scales and translations to use.

The basic one-dimensional wavelet transform is

$$W_{f(x)}(s,t) = \frac{1}{\sqrt{s}} \int f(x) w_{s,t}(x) dx \qquad \text{(EQ 7.7)}$$

for a continuous function f. This would become a sum for a discrete transform. This gives the wavelet coefficient at $W(s,t)$, so the calculation would be repeated for each value of s and t that we want. The result is a two-dimensional function, or a set of two-dimensional data points in the discrete case, which can be plotted for any particular f.

One of the simplest examples occurs when f is simply an *impulse*: a data set having one peak at some value of x, and which is zero elsewhere. Figure 7.3 shows the wavelet transform of this as a surface, one axis being s and the other t. It is not completely plain from this graph, but a slice of the surface at any point along the t axis yields a version of the wavelet.

Another simple example occurs when the impulse is given width, so that it becomes a rectangle. The transform of this signal (Figure 7.4) appears to split into two distinct parts. Still, the basic shape of each slice along t is that of the original wavelet.

In order to compute the transform the s and t axes had to be sampled. Starting at some initial values, each consecutive row uses a slightly different value of t, and each column uses a slightly different s. The rate at which s and t change is important, and is a function of the mother wavelet used and of the nature of f (Young 1993). The sampling used to produce Figures 7.3 and 7.4 was determined

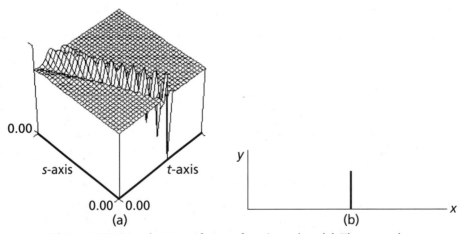

Figure 7.3 Wavelet transform of an impulse. (a) The wavelet domain surface. (b) The impulse; simply one peak at x = 64.

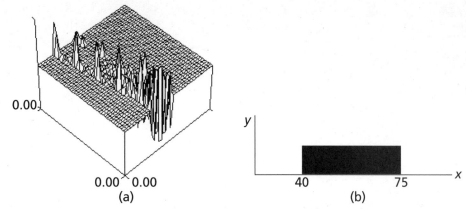

Figure 7.4 Wavelet transform of a rectangular signal.
(a) Wavelet domain representation. (b) The one-dimensional
signal being transformed.

in an ad hoc fashion, and the program for Figure 7.3 appears in Figure 7.5. This
program is simple and obvious, but could take hours on a PC to produce a simple
one-dimensional transform.

The inverse wavelet transform is used to reconstruct the function from its wavelet representation. This is essentially Equation 7.6, but in the general case:

$$f(x) = C_0 \int \frac{1}{i^2} \int c_{i,j} \frac{w_{i,j}(x)}{\sqrt{i}} \, dj \, di \qquad \text{(EQ 7.8)}$$

This is calculated as a sum in the program shown in Figure 7.5. In the two
examples shown so far the reconstruction is not very good; the wavelet functions
used and the domain over which the transform is constructed are important things
to consider when attempting an analysis of this sort. In this case, no effort was
made to do a good job of the decomposition, but merely to perform one.

A More Realistic View—The Haar Wavelet

The Haar wavelet is probably the simplest of all wavelets, and is also the oldest.
It has been used in image analysis for many years as the Haar transform (Pratt
1991). It also strongly resembles the Walsh basis, because the Haar wavelet is a
step function taking the values $+1$ and -1. Specifically:

$$\psi_H(t) = \begin{cases} 1 & 0 < t < 1/2 \\ -1 & 1/2 \le t < 1 \\ 0 & \text{Otherwise} \end{cases} \qquad \text{(EQ 7.9)}$$

```
/* Obvious forward wavelet transform */
void dwt_1d (float *data,
     float wt[256][256], int n)
{

     int i,j,k;
     float s, x, t, sum, sqa;


     wt[0][0] = 0.0;

     s = a0;
     for (i=0; i<n; i++)
     {

       sqa = sqrt((double)s);

       t = s*.99;
       for (j=0; j<n; j++)
       {
         sum = 0.0;
         for (k=0; k<n; k++)
         sum += data[k] *
           mother(s,t,(float)k);
         wt[i][j] = sum/sqa;
         t *= 1.03;
       }
       s *= 1.01;
     }
}



/* Obvious inverse wavelet transform */

 void dwti_1d (float *data,
     float wt[256][256], int n)
{
```

```
  for (k=0; k<n; k++)
  {
    sum = 0.0; s = a0;
    for (i=0; i<n; i++)
    {
      sqa =
        sqrt((double)s);
      t = s*0.99;
      for (j=0; j<n;
        j++)
      {
        sum +=
          mother(s,t,
          (float)k)
            * wt[i]
            [j]/sqa;
        t *= 1.03;
      }
    s *= 1.01;
    }
    data[k] = sum;
  }
}

float mother (float a,
        float b, float t)
{

  float y, z;

  z = (float)sqrt
  ((double)a);
  if (z != 0.0) z =
  1.0/z;
  else z = 0.0;
  return z*g((t+b)/a);
}
```

Figure 7.5 Simple and slow code for a forward and inverse
wavelet transform, using the sample wavelet function
g as a basis.

```
int i,j,k;
float, sqa, sum, s, t;              float g(float x)
                                    {
                                        return (float)
                                        (sin((double) (4*x))
                                                *exp((double)
                                                (-(x*x)))));
                                    }
```

Figure 7.5 (continued)

A convenient (but not the only) way to scale these wavelets is by powers of two. For example, the functions $\psi_j(t) = \psi_H(2^j t)$ are scaled versions of $\psi_H(t)$. This is really the same way that scaling was defined originally, but with $s = 1/2^j$. Translation is done by shifting the function along the axis, as before. A scaled and translated Haar wavelet could be described as

$$\psi_{jk}(t) = \psi_H(2^j t - k) \qquad \text{(EQ 7.10)}$$

A sample collection of these wavelets can be seen as graphs in Figure 7.6. They have the appearance of square waves, scaled and translated over a small range. It is common knowledge in mathematical circles that a continuous function can be approximated by these Haar functions, in a way similar to the use of sine and

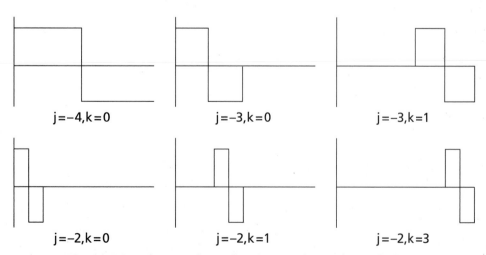

j=−4,k=0   j=−3,k=0   j=−3,k=1

j=−2,k=0   j=−2,k=1   j=−2,k=3

Figure 7.6 Haar wavelets of various scales and translations.

cosine functions in the Fourier series approximations. A linear combination of Haar functions is constructed, whose sum approximates the required function:

$$f(t) = \sum_{j=-\infty}^{\infty} A_j \sum_{k=-\infty}^{\infty} B_{jk}\psi_H(2^j t - k) \qquad \text{(EQ 7.11)}$$

which has the same appearance as Equation 7.6, but with $c_{jk} = A_j B_{jk}$. For any problem that is to be solved using a computer, the bounds of the sums will be finite, which is okay for an approximation as long as the result has a small specified error bound. Indeed, for image processing and vision purposes, the function f will actually consist of regularly sampled values, the grid being imposed by the digitization process.

What is called a wavelet transform with respect to the Haar basis is really the calculation of the values for c_{jk}. According to Equation 7.7, with modifications to allow for what we have done since then, these can be found by:

$$c_{jk} = 2_j \int_{2^{-jk}}^{2^{-j(k+1)}} f(t)\psi_{jk}(t)dt \qquad \text{(EQ 7.12)}$$

Computing a Wavelet Transform

An attempt will be made in the discussion that follows to walk a fine line between mathematical rigor and intuition. Where the two conflict, rigor will yield to intuition. For a truly excellent introduction, the discussion in Lancaster (1996) is highly recommended.

The series in Equation 7.11 can be rewritten as:

$$f(t) = \sum_{j=-\infty}^{-1} \sum_{k=-\infty}^{\infty} c_{jk}\psi_{jk}(t) \qquad \text{(EQ 7.13)}$$

by assuming (correctly, in this case) that the highest frequency present is 2^{-1}, which corresponds to a scale of 2. A first step in the determination of the coefficients c_{jk} is to factor out the highest frequencies; that is, those at the $j = -1$ level. The sum becomes:

$$f(t) = \sum_{k=-\infty}^{\infty} c_{-1,k}\psi_{-1,k}(t) + \sum_{j=-\infty}^{-2} \sum_{k=-\infty}^{\infty} c_{jk}\psi_{jk}(t)$$
$$= W_{-1}(t) + f_{-1}(t) \qquad \text{(EQ 7.14)}$$

where the sum represented by $W_{-1}(t)$ corresponds to the highest frequency level, and $f_{-1}(t)$ is the remainder. The coefficients of the highest frequency layer all have $j = -1$; solving Equation 7.12 using the Haar wavelets gives:

$$c_{-1,k} = \frac{1}{2} \int_{2k}^{2(k+1)} f(t)\psi_{-1,k}(t)dt = \frac{(f(2k) - f(2k+1))}{2} \qquad \text{(EQ 7.15)}$$

The integral can be evaluated either by hand, or by using a symbolic mathematics package such as Maple. The result is twofold: the actual values for all of the coefficients at $j=-1$ can be calculated directly given the sampled data in f, and we now have a process for computing the next level of coefficients. The next highest frequency layer, $W_{-2}(t)$, can be extracted from $f_{-1}(t)$ in the same way that $W-1(t)$ was obtained from f.

$$W_{-2}(t) = \sum_{k=-\infty}^{\infty} c_{-2,k} \psi_{-2,k}(t) \qquad \text{(EQ 7.16)}$$

$$f_{-2}(t) = \sum_{j=-\infty}^{-3} \sum_{k=-\infty}^{\infty} c_{jk} \psi_{jk}(t)$$

Again, using Equation 7.12 and evaluating the integral, the next layer of coefficients is found to be:

$$c_{-2,k} = \frac{1}{4} (f(4k) + f(4k + 1) - f(4k + 2) - f(4k + 3)) \qquad \text{(EQ 7.17)}$$

Each layer can be computed in this way, one at a time. Because every layer doubles the number of terms, it is more convenient to calculate these as a recurrence relation, in which an arbitrary layer is expressed in terms of the previous one. In this instance, the relation is:

$$c_{j,k} = \frac{1}{2} (a_{j+1,2k} - a_{j+1,2k+1}) \qquad \text{(EQ 7.18)}$$

$$a_{j,k} = \frac{1}{2} (a_{j+1,2k} + a_{j+1,2k+1})$$

Now, because the function f is really a set of data samples, and because the assumption is that the function is a constant over the sample width (*piecewise constant*), the values of $a_{0,k}$ are simply the data values f(k), and all of the $c_{j,k}$ values can be calculated. As a real example, let's assume that f contains 16 data points, the values of which are:

0 1 2 2 4 4 2 2 0 0 2 2 0 0 0 0

These are also the values of $a_{0,k}$. According to Equation 7.18, the first set of coefficients ($c_{-1,k}$) are:

−0.5 0.0 0.0 0.0 0.0 0.0 0.0 0.0 0.0 0.0 0.0 0.0 0.0 0.0 0.0 0.0

and the $a_{-1,k}$ are:

0.5 2.0 4.0 2.0 0.0 2.0 0.0 0.0 0.0 0.0 0.0 0.0 0.0 0.0 0.0 0.0

The rest of the layers can now be computed in terms of these. Each successive set of coefficients has half the number of the previous set, so there are only four layers altogether. They are summarized in Table 7.1.

To confirm that the $c_{j,k}$ coefficients are indeed those of the Haar wavelet decomposition of f, simply use them to reconstruct the original data. Because all of the coefficients are available, the reconstruction should be exact. Let's reconstruct the sample data starting at the lowest frequencies, and working up to the highest. In this way, the overall shape of the data should appear initially, and detail will be added with each set of frequencies that are added.

The lowest frequencies appear to be those associated with $c_{-4,k}$. The portion of the reconstruction at this level is:

$$f_4(t) = \sum_{k=0}^{0} c_{-4,k}\psi_{-4,k}(t) = c_{-4,0}\psi_{-4,0}(t) \qquad \text{(EQ 7.19)}$$

which is shown in Figure 7.7b, for the 16 data points in our sample. The next frequency level contains two translations, 0 and 1:

$$f_3(t) = c_{-3,0}\psi_{-3,0}(t) + c_{-3,1}\psi_{-3,1}(t) \qquad \text{(EQ 7.20)}$$

This level, as seen in Figure 7.7c, contains more detail; Figure 7.7d shows the sum of these two levels, which is becoming closer to the original data. The figure continues to show higher levels and the accumulated sum, until all four have been accounted for. At this point the shape is correct (Figure 7.7h) but the values are all off by a constant value of 1.312, which happens to be the value of $a_{-4,0}$ (= $c_{-5,0}$). This corresponds to the actual lowest frequency, which is really just a constant for the entire array of data.

The decomposition can be seen to be a hierarchy of components, the lowest level being a constant on all 16 elements, the next lowest being constant on each

Table 7.1 Four Layers of Wavelet Transform Data

	k=0	k=1	k=2	k=3	k=4	k=5	k=6	k=7
c_{-1}	−0.5	0.0	0.0	0.0	0.0	0.0	0.0	0.0
a_{-1}	0.5	2.0	4.0	2.0	0.0	2.0	0.0	0.0
c_{-2}	−0.75	1.0	−1.0	0.0				
a_{-2}	1.25	3.0	1.0	0.0				
c_{-3}	−.875	.5						
a_{-3}	2.125	.5						
c_{-4}	0.812							
a_{-4}	1.312							

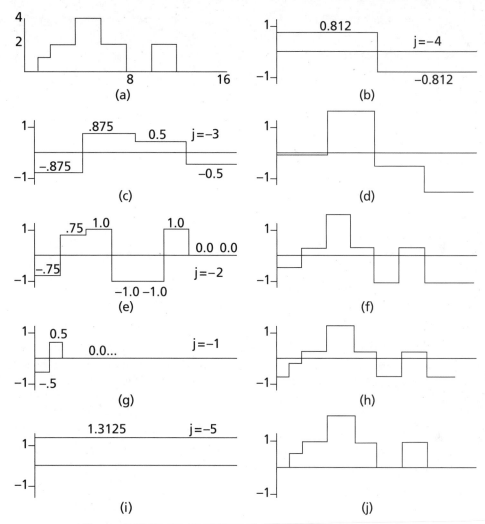

Figure 7.7 Reconstruction of a signal from the wavelet coefficients. (a) The original signal. (b) Level −4 coefficients give a two step signal. (c) Level −3 coefficients give a four step signal. (d) Sum of levels −4 and −3 give a partial reconstruction. (e) Level −2 coefficients (8 steps). (f) Sum of the three levels. (g) Level −1 coefficients (16 steps). (h) Sum of the four levels. (i) The constant j=−5 level. (j) Reconstructed signal, which is the sum of all five levels.

```
float recur (int level, float *data, int k)
{
        if (level==0)
          return data[k];
        else
          return ( recur(level+1, data, 2*k)
               + recur(level+1, data, 2*k+1) )/2.0;
}

float coef (int level, float *data, int k)
{
        return ( recur(level+1, data, 2*k)
             - recur(level+1, data, 2*k+1) )/2.0;
}
```

Figure 7.8 Recursive functions to compute a_{jk} (recur) and c_{jk} (coef), using Equation 7.18.

half, the next level being constant on each quarter, and so on. Like the Walsh transform, the reconstruction could be halted prematurely at any level, and an approximate reconstruction would be available. Because the values of a and c are defined by a recurrence relation, we can write a recursive function to calculate them. Figure 7.8 gives such a function for the current example.

The reconstruction of the data from the coefficients is a linear combination of the $\psi_{j,k}$ functions with the c_{jk} multipliers. Thus, the reconstructions of a 16-point data set can be written as a set of 16 equations:

$$f(0) = c_{-5,0} + \psi_{-4,0}(0)c_{-4,0} + \psi_{-3,0}(0)c_{-3,0} + \psi_{-3,1}(0)c_{-3,1}$$
$$+ \ldots + \psi_{-1,7}(0)c_{-1,7} \quad \text{(EQ 7.21)}$$

$$f(1) = c_{-5,0} + \psi_{-4,0}(1)c_{-4,0} + \psi_{-3,0}(1)c_{-3,0}$$
$$+ \psi_{-3,1}(1)c_{-3,1} + \ldots \psi_{-1,7}(1)c_{-1,7}$$

$$\ldots$$

$$f(15) = c_{-5,0} + \psi_{-4,0}(15)c_{-4,0} + \psi_{-3,0}(15)c_{-3,0}$$
$$+ \psi_{-3,1}(15)c_{-3,1} + \ldots + \psi_{-1,7}(15)c_{-1,7}$$

This can be written as a matrix equation, but one that is specific for the number of data points N and the basis functions that are used. For 16 points using the Haar basis, the equation is:

$$\hat{f} = \psi\hat{c} \qquad \text{(EQ 7.22)}$$

where $\hat{f}$ is the vector of data values $f(0) \ldots f(15)$, $\hat{c}$ is the vector of coefficients, and ψ is the matrix of values of the function ψ_{jk}. For this case, the matrix is:

$$\psi = \begin{bmatrix}
1 & 1 & 1 & 0 & 1 & 0 & 0 & 0 & 1 & 0 & 0 & 0 & 0 & 0 & 0 & 0 \\
1 & 1 & 1 & 0 & 1 & 0 & 0 & 0 & -1 & 0 & 0 & 0 & 0 & 0 & 0 & 0 \\
1 & 1 & 1 & 0 & -1 & 0 & 0 & 0 & 0 & 1 & 0 & 0 & 0 & 0 & 0 & 0 \\
1 & 1 & 1 & 0 & -1 & 0 & 0 & 0 & 0 & -1 & 0 & 0 & 0 & 0 & 0 & 0 \\
1 & 1 & -1 & 0 & 0 & 1 & 0 & 0 & 0 & 0 & 1 & 0 & 0 & 0 & 0 & 0 \\
1 & 1 & -1 & 0 & 0 & 1 & 0 & 0 & 0 & 0 & -1 & 0 & 0 & 0 & 0 & 0 \\
1 & 1 & -1 & 0 & 0 & -1 & 0 & 0 & 0 & 0 & 0 & 1 & 0 & 0 & 0 & 0 \\
1 & 1 & -1 & 0 & 0 & -1 & 0 & 0 & 0 & 0 & 0 & -1 & 0 & 0 & 0 & 0 \\
1 & -1 & 0 & 1 & 0 & 0 & 1 & 0 & 0 & 0 & 0 & 0 & 1 & 0 & 0 & 0 \\
1 & -1 & 0 & 1 & 0 & 0 & 1 & 0 & 0 & 0 & 0 & 0 & -1 & 0 & 0 & 0 \\
1 & -1 & 0 & 1 & 0 & 0 & -1 & 0 & 0 & 0 & 0 & 0 & 0 & 1 & 0 & 0 \\
1 & -1 & 0 & 1 & 0 & 0 & -1 & 0 & 0 & 0 & 0 & 0 & 0 & -1 & 0 & 0 \\
1 & -1 & 0 & -1 & 0 & 0 & 0 & 1 & 0 & 0 & 0 & 0 & 0 & 0 & 1 & 0 \\
1 & -1 & 0 & -1 & 0 & 0 & 0 & 1 & 0 & 0 & 0 & 0 & 0 & 0 & -1 & 0 \\
1 & -1 & 0 & -1 & 0 & 0 & 0 & -1 & 0 & 0 & 0 & 0 & 0 & 0 & 0 & 1 \\
1 & -1 & 0 & -1 & 0 & 0 & 0 & -1 & 0 & 0 & 0 & 0 & 0 & 0 & 0 & -1
\end{bmatrix}$$

$$\text{(EQ 7.23)}$$

So this matrix, when multiplied by the vector of coefficients, gives the original data set. Better yet, the matrix inverse of ψ, which is referred to as ψ^{-1}, can be used to find the coefficients for a particular data vector f:

$$\psi^{-1}\hat{f} = \psi^{-1}\psi\hat{c} = \hat{c} \qquad \text{(EQ 7.24)}$$

This means that the coefficients can be found for any 16-point set of data by doing a matrix multiplication.

The Two-Scale Relation

Wavelet functions themselves can be thought to be composed of even simpler functions. Continuing the example of the Haar wavelets, consider the simple rectangular pulse:

$$\varphi(t) = \begin{cases} 1 & 0 \le t \le 1 \\ 0 & \text{Otherwise} \end{cases} \qquad \text{(EQ 7.25)}$$

This function can be scaled and translated too. It is plain that $\varphi(2t)$ has the value one between 0 and ½; similarly, $\varphi(2t - 1)$ has the value one between ½ and 1 (Figure 7.8). It is therefore possible to construct a Haar wavelet by:

$$\psi(t) = \varphi(2t) - \varphi(2t - 1) \tag{EQ 7.26}$$

The function $\varphi(t)$ is called a *scaling function*,[1] because it shows clearly how the functions behave as they are rescaled. These functions also satisfy:

$$\varphi\left(\frac{t}{2}\right) = \varphi(t) + \varphi(t - 1) \tag{EQ 7.27}$$

which is the so-called *two-scale relation*, which shows how the function behaves at different resolutions. This specific two-scale relation holds for the Haar wavelets, but in general it is a linear combination of scaling functions:

$$\varphi\left(\frac{t}{2}\right) = \ldots + h_{-1}\varphi(t + 1) + h_0\varphi(t) + h_1\varphi(t - 1) \tag{EQ 7.28}$$

$$+ h_2\varphi(t - 2) + \ldots$$

$$= \sum_{k=-\infty}^{\infty} h_k\varphi(t - k)$$

where, for the Haar wavelet, $h_0 = h_1 = 1$, all others being 0. Equation 7.27 can be scaled so that it has the appearance of Equation 7.26:

$$\varphi(t) = \varphi(2t) + \varphi(2t - 1) \tag{EQ 7.29}$$

and Equations 7.26 and 7.29 define the *dilation equations* for the Haar wavelet.

The values of h_i define the wavelet, and in combination with the two-scale relation can be used to compute the wavelet transform recursively, similar to the way that the Fourier transform was calculated. It is very common in practice to specify the wavelet as an array of floating point h_i values and nothing else. Of course, not all values will work as filter coefficients, and a great deal of effort can be expended to determine therm. One well-known wavelet basis is the set found by Daubechies (Daubechies 1988), the simplest of which has four coefficients:

$$h_0 = \frac{1 + \sqrt{3}}{4} \quad h_1 = \frac{3 + \sqrt{3}}{4}$$
$$\tag{EQ 7.30}$$
$$h_2 = \frac{3 - \sqrt{3}}{4} \quad h_3 = \frac{1 - \sqrt{3}}{4}$$

These can be substituted into Equation 7.28 to get a four-term, two-scale relation, and into Equation 7.26 to find the form of the mother wavelet:

---

1. Also called a *father wavelet* (Lancaster 1995).

$$\psi\left(\frac{t}{2}\right) = -h_3\varphi(t + 2) + h_2\varphi(t + 1) - h_1\varphi(t) + h_0(t - 1) \quad \text{(EQ 7.31)}$$

There is no representation of φ as a function; it can be calculated only through the use of a recurrence relation, which can be implemented as a recursive C function.

The Fast Wavelet Transform

In order to describe the fast wavelet transform, return for a moment to the Haar wavelet and the recursive implementation of Figure 7.7. Two items are important here: First, that the recursive implementation could be coded iteratively, and each layer (value of j) could be computed before proceeding with the next. This would save recalculation of the a_{jk} values. The second item is the fact that, while the result of the transform is two-dimensional in j and k, there are the same number of coefficients in total as there were data points originally, because each layer has half the number of components as does the layer before.

Considering the Haar wavelet, the following implementation comes to mind: calculate the $j=-1$ layer from the data points using Equation 7.18, storing the a_{jk} values over top of the original data in the first ($n/2(=8)$) positions, and the c_{jk} in the final $n/2$ positions. Now compute the $j=-2$ layer, again using the first $n/4(=4)$ positions for the $a_{2,k}$ values and the next $n/4$ places for the $c_{-2,k}$ values. This continues until all of the coefficients are found and have replaced the original data. This can be done because each layer has half the number of coefficients of the previous layer, and because the a_{jk} values are only needed to calculate the $a_{j-1,k}$ coefficients.

Consider the data used in the original example. The values of a_{jk} and c_{jk} for $j=-1$ have been calculated, and occupy the first two rows in Table 7.1. Thus, after the first stage of the computation described above, the data array would appear as:

0.5 2.0 4.0 2.0 0.0 2.0 0.0 0.0   −.5 0.0 0.0 0.0 0.0 0.0 0.0 0.0
        $a_{1,k}$ values $c_{1,k}$ values

After the next step (the $j=-2$ layer) the last 12 elements of the array are c_{jk} values, and the first eight elements are the same as the second pair of rows in Table 7.1:

1.25 3.0 1.0 0.0   −.75 1.0 −1.0 0.0   −.5 0.0 0.0 0.0 0.0 0.0 0.0 0.0
    $a_{2,k}$ values $c_{-2,k}$ values $c_{-1,k}$ values

Finally, after two more steps, the resulting transform is

1.3125 .8125 −.875 0.5 −.75 1.0 −1.0 0.0 −.5 0.0 0.0 0.0 0.0 0.0 0.0 0.0

Note that the lowest-frequency information comes first, followed by successively higher ones. This makes filtering by frequency a rather simple task.

The inverse transform is done in the reverse order. First, the constant $c_{-5,0}$ is added to the one step $c_{4,0}$; that is, for the first eight elements the reconstruction is $c_{-5,0}+c_{-4,0}$, and the last eight are $c_{-5,0}-c_{-4,0}$. However, eight locations are not needed because the value of j indicates how many locations in the result will be occupied by the result, so these new values are written over the original data array in the first two positions. For the transform that was just performed, the resulting data array after the first step in the reconstruction is:

2.125 0.5   −.875 0.5 −.75 1.0 −1.0 0.0 −.5 0.0 0.0 0.0 0.0 0.0 0.0 0.0
   Level 1   Original wavelet coefficients
reconstruction

The next level creates a four-valued signal from the level one reconstruction and the next set of two coefficients. The four values are:

$c_{-5,0}+c_{-4,0}+c_{3,0}$	$c_{5,0}+c_{-4,0}-c_{3,0}$	$c_{-5,0}-c_{4,0}+c_{-3,1}$	$c_{-5,0}-c_{-4,0}-c_{-3,1}$
2.145+(−.875)	2.145−(−.875)	0.5+0.5	0.5−0.5
1.25	3.00	1.00	0.0

These are stored in the first four locations of the data array, which now looks like:

1.25 3.0 1.0 0.0   −.75 1.0 −1.0 0.0 −.5 0.0 0.0 0.0 0.0 0.0 0.0 0.0
   Level 2   Original wavelet coefficients
reconstruction

This process continues until none of the original wavelet coefficients remain, at which point the data array contains the original data.

Figure 7.9 shows the C program that implements this fast wavelet transform. The inverse transform and the forward transform are both computed by the function fwt1d.c, depending on the value of the parameter direction. This code was designed specifically to perform a discrete wavelet transform using the Haar basis on a data array containing 16 points, but can easily be changed to accommodate larger data sets.

On the CD can be found one other one-dimensional wavelet program. The procedure daub in the program daub2d.c implements a four-coefficient Daubechies wavelet transform, using the filter coefficients in Equation 7.30. These programs have been provided for experimentation purposes; they permit easy access to a wavelet transform of a few different types, so that intuition can be acquired concerning exactly how the transform will affect the data.

```
#include <math.h>
#define FORWARD 1
#define INVERSE -1

float rec[16] = {0,0,0,0,0,0,0,0,0,0,0,0,0,0,0,0};
float data[16] = { 0,1,2,2,4,4,2,2,0,0,2,2,0,0,0,0};
void fwt_1d (float *data, int N, int direction);
void wavelet (float *data, int N, int direction);
void Haar_2 (float *data, int N, int direction);

main()
{
    int i;

    printf ("Computing a wavelet transform on a Haar
basis:\n");
    fwt_1d (data, 16, FORWARD);
    printf ("Reconstructing the data from the
wavelets:\n");
    for (i=0; i<16; i++)
      rec[i] = data[i];
    fwt_1d (rec, 16, INVERSE);

    printf ("I WT Data\n");
    for (i=0; i<16; i++)
      printf ("%d: %7.4f %7.4f\n", i, data[i], rec[i]);
}

void fwt_1d (float *data, int N, int direction)
{
    int thisn;

    if (N > 2)
    {
      if (direction >= 0)
      {
        thisn = N;
        while (thisn >= 2)
        {
```

Figure 7.9 Source code for a fast wavelet transform. This code transforms 16 data points using a Haar basis.

```
              wavelet (data, thisn, direction);
              thisn /= 2;
          }
       } else if (direction == INVERSE)
       {
          thisn = 2;
          while (thisn <= N)
          {
              wavelet (data, thisn, direction);
              thisn *=2;
          }
       }
     }
}

void wavelet (float *data, int N, int direction)
{
     Haar_2 (data, N, direction);
}

void Haar_2 (float *data, int N, int direction)
{
     int i,j,nover2;
     float h0, h1, *tmp;
/*   h0 = 1.0/sqrt(2.0); h1 = 1.0/sqrt(2.0);*/
     h0 = h1 = 0.5;
     tmp = float *)malloc (sizeof(float)*N);

     nover2 = N/2;
     if (direction == FORWARD)
     {
       i=0;
       for (j=0; j<N−1; j+=2)
       {
          tmp[i]        = h0*data[j] + h1*data[j+1];
          tmp[i+nover2] = h0*data[j] − h1*data[j+1];
          i++;
       }
     } else if (direction == INVERSE)
     {
```

Figure 7.9 (continued)

```
/* Comment the next line out for symmetric scaling */
     h1 = h0 = 1.0;
     i = j = 0;
     do
     {
        tmp[j]   = h0*data[i] + h1*data[i+nover2];
        tmp[j+1] = h0*data[i] − h1data[i+nover2];
        j += 2; i++;
     } while (i <= nover 2);
   }

   for (i=0; i<N; i++)
     data[i] = tmp[i];
   free(tmp);
}
```

Figure 7.9 (continued)

7.2   OBJECTS AND 2D WAVELETS

Like the Fourier transform, the wavelet transform is *separable*. This means that the two-dimensional version of a wavelet transform can be expressed in terms of a number of one-dimensional transforms. For example, each of the rows can be transformed by fwt1d.c followed by each of the columns. This is exactly what is done by the program fwt2d.c and its companion fwti2d.c, which performed the inverse 2D transform. These two procedures can therefore be used to perform wavelet transforms on images.

Figure 7.10 shows a sample image, a pile of keys on a textured background, and its wavelet transform; since fwt1d was used by fwt2d.c, the basis is that of Haar. One of the simplest experiments to perform, and one that is possible using fwt2d.c, is to reconstruct the transformed image using only the first N rows and columns (N is requested by the program). As the number of coefficients used in the reconstruction decreases, the quality of the reconstruction also decreases.

Another way to select wavelet coefficients to keep or remove is by thresholding. For a particular threshold T, all coefficients greater than T will be left alone, and those less than T will be set to zero. This is done by the program wthresh.c, which prompts the user for a threshold. Again, it is to be expected that lower thresholds will result in better reconstructions. This suspicion is true, as shown in Figure 7.11. Here, thresholds between -20 and $+20$ are used in the reconstruction of the image, with an increasing degradation being apparent.

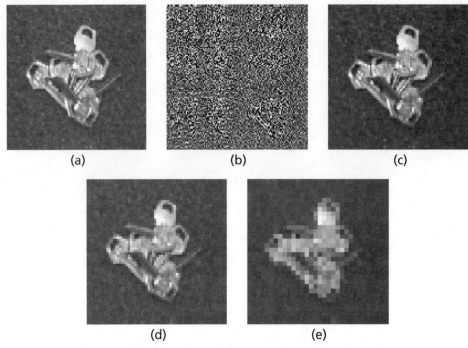

(a)   (b)   (c)

(d)   (e)

Figure 7.10 Examples of the two-dimensional wavelet transform. (a) Example image of keys. (b) Wavelet domain version. (c) Reconstructed using the upper left 100×100 coefficients. (d) Reconstructed using a 60×60 subimage. (e) Reconstructed using the upper left 30×30 coefficients.

From the examples seen so far, the practical use of the wavelet transform when applied to images is not clear. The transformed and restored images do not appear to be especially useful; no features have been extracted, no enhancement is obvious, and as a compression tool it appears to be much less useful than others in existence. The reason for this is that all images so far have been transformed using the Haar basis, which was chosen for its simplicity. Other basis functions will yield different images and have different applications; some for filtering, some for compression.

Figure 7.12 shows the keys image transformed using another basis, the Daubechies wavelets (Equation 7.30). From the results of the reconstructions, using the same amount of data as in Figure 7.10, this would be a far better choice for image compression, although there are better yet. The reconstruction using the first 900 coefficients is still rather good.

The program daub2d.c performs a two-dimensional transform on this basis, asking, as before, for a reconstruction based on a subimage. The dthresh.c pro-

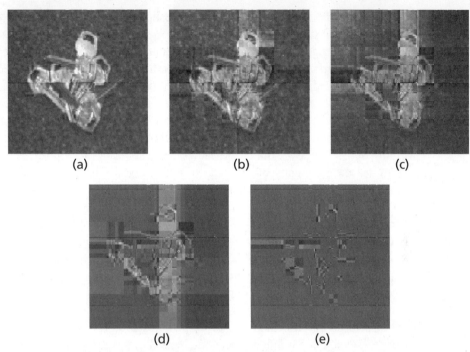

(a)   (b)   (c)

(d)   (e)

Figure 7.11 The effect of thresholding the wavelet domain image before reconstruction. (a) Values less than −20 were set to zero (deleted 49 points). (b) Values less than −10 were removed (deleted 328 values). (c) Values less than zero were removed (deleted 8001 values). (d) Threshold was 10 (deleted 16043 values). (e) Threshold was 20 (deleted 16318 values). The image has 16384 pixels in total.

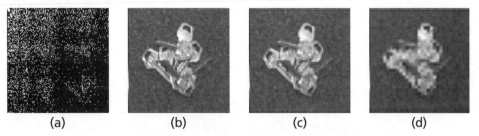

(a)   (b)   (c)   (d)

Figure 7.12 Two-dimensional wavelet transform based on the four coefficient Daubechies wavelet. (a) Wavelet domain image. (b) Reconstructed using upper left 100×100. (c) Reconstructed using 60×60. (d) Reconstructed using 30×30.

gram performs a reconstruction on the thresholded image, like wthresh.c. A PGM image showing the wavelet domain image can be created using showdaub.c. The showdaub.c program asks for which *level* and *quad* to display, and then does so. The level refers to the scaling, and is specified as an exponent of 2. Remember that in the one-dimensional transform, the top (right, largest indices) half of the coefficients all represent the highest frequency in the transformed data, the next $N/4$ are stored in the next locations, and so on. In two dimensions this becomes a clear distribution of power-of-two-sized subimages for each frequency, as seen in Figure 7.13. The level that showdaub.c requests refers to the power of two that identifies the frequency of the data to be displayed. The quad refers to which of the four subimages is to be displayed.

Figure 7.14 also shows the four-coefficient Daubechies wavelet transform of a very simple image, in this case a square. The structure of the transformed image is clearly seen in this case, with the subimages decreasing in size by half as we look from the lower right to the upper left (Figure 7.13c). The quads numbered 1 at each level contain information related to the decomposition in the vertical direction. Those numbered 2 contain horizontal information, and the quads numbered 3 can be thought of as a 45-degree orientation. Since the wavelet transform has structured the information into frequencies and orientations, it should be possible to reconstruct an image that contains only those frequencies and orientations that are of interest. While it may not be a simple matter in general to determine

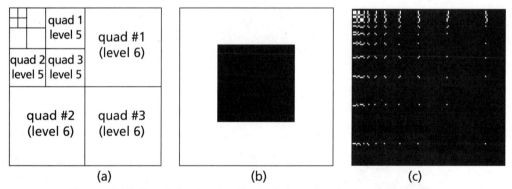

(a)   (b)   (c)

Figure 7.13 Spatial organization of the wavelet transformed image. (a) Breakdown of the information content by frequency (level) and orientation (quad). The larger quads hold the high frequencies. (b) An image of a square, to be used as an example. It is 128×128 pixels. (c) The four coefficient Daubechies wavelet transform, showing that the vertically oriented information seems to be concentrated in quad 1, horizontal in quad 2, and diagonal in quad 3. Quad 0 always contains the next lower frequencies.

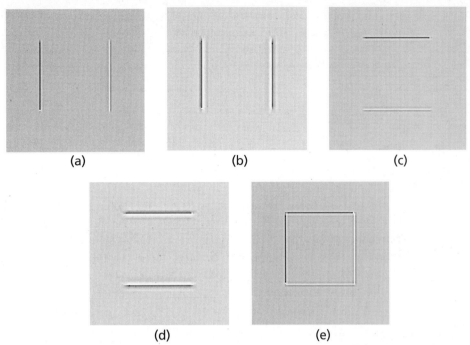

Figure 7.14 Extracting specific frequencies and orientations from the wavelet domain image. (a) The result of keeping only the highest frequency in quad 1, setting all other quads and frequencies to zero. (b) The result of keeping the highest two frequencies in quad 1. (c) Keeping the highest frequency in quad 2. (d) Keeping the highest two frequencies in quad 2. (e) Result of keeping the highest two frequencies in quads 1 and 2.

exactly which frequencies and orientations are interesting, for the image of the square it should be possible.

Consider again the problem of finding edges. In Chapter 1 it was made clear that edges correspond to high-frequency information in the image, so when finding edges using the wavelet transform the high-frequency information should be retained, while discarding the lower frequencies. If vertical edges are of interest, then the quads numbered 2 are of interest, and the others should be discarded. The only real problem that remains is determining exactly which of the high frequencies should be kept and which are not; this can be done by experiment, in this case.

The program dfilter.c allows a user to specify which quads and which frequencies are to be discarded, or set to zero in the wavelet domain. This is done interactively. For example, the following session shows how to set all of the quads numbered 3 (diagonal) to zero before reconstruction:

```
%dfilter sq128.pgm
Delete which quads? 3
Start filter at level: 6
End filter at level: 0
Delete which quads? −1
Xmax is  0.00000 Xmin is  −2.874057
```

Entering the final value (-1) indicates to the program that data entry is complete, and to now reconstruct using whatever wavelet coefficients remain.

Figure 7.14 shows that, by setting to zero unwanted frequencies and scales, the wavelet transform can be used to enhance certain features such as edges. The source image was the square (Figure 7.13b). Using different bases, one can design filters that will isolate specific kinds of feature within an image. This has the potential of improving the capability of vision systems, but at this point the field is relatively immature.

7.3   BIBLIOGRAPHY

Chui, C. K. 1992. *An Introduction to Wavelets*. San Diego: Academic Press.

Chui, C. K. (Ed.). 1992. *Wavelets: A Tutorial in Theory and Applications*. San Diego: Academic Press.

Coombes, J. M., Grossman, A., and P. Tchamitchian. (Eds.). 1990. *Wavelets: Time-Frequency Methods and Phase Space*. Berlin: Springer-Verlag.

Holschneider, M. 1995. *Wavelets—An Analysis Tool*. Oxford: Oxford University Press.

Lancaster, P. and K. Salkauskas. 1996. *Transform Methods In Applied Mathematics: An Introduction*. New York: John Wiley & Sons.

Pratt, W. K. 1991. *Digital Image Processing*. New York: Wiley-Interscience.

Young, R. K. 1993. *Wavelet Theory and Its Applications*. Boston: Kluwer Academic.

8

OPTICAL CHARACTER RECOGNITION

8.1 THE PROBLEM

Reading is such a fundamental part of daily life that few of us give much thought to how it is accomplished, unless we are actively involved in either learning to read or teaching someone else how to read. The first step in teaching reading is often the teaching of the alphabet. The ability to recognize letters and digits (*characters*) is fundamental to intepreting printed language; however, for a computer, a character on a page is merely another image or object to be recognized. Much of the power of the techniques that have been discussed to this point needs to be brought to bear on the apparently simple problem of recognizing the letter *a*.

It is not known how humans recognize visual objects with so little effort. Even if it were, there is no compelling reason to think that the same method could be used on a computer; the human brain and a computer are not all that similar at a detailed level. The problem of *optical character recognition* (OCR), which is the problem of the automatic recognition of raster images as being letters, digits, or some other symbol, must be approached like any other problem in computer vision.

The problem is useful and interesting because of how much information is stored in printed form. A visit to the local library is enough to convince anyone of the utility of a computer system that can visually process the printed word. In addition, characters appears in almost any real-world scene, printed on billboards, license plates, menus, signs, and even tattooed on flesh. Maps and charts (even in digital form) frequently contain raster versions of place names and directions. Even the ubiquitous fax machine transmits its data as an image; most computers that can receive a fax cannot convert it into an ASCII text file, but instead store it as a (much larger) binary image.

An optical character recognition system must do a number of things, and do them with a high degree of precision. Let's assume that the input to the system is an image of a page of text. The first thing to do is to confirm the orientation of the text on the page; sometimes a page is not quite square to the scanning device. The image must then be segmented, first into black and white pixels, then into lines of text, and finally into individual *glyphs*, which are images of individual symbols. A recognition strategy is then applied to each glyph. If the symbol is one that the system has been trained to recognize, then there is a measured probability of a correct recognition, and usually a nonzero probability of a wrong answer. The recognized characters are collected into words and sentences, and must be output in the correct order.

A good spelling checker is useful here. Most people read words rather than individual letters, and the additional information provided by context can be useful. For a simple example, consider the word *Because*. The uppercase letter *B* is often confused with the digit *8* by character recognition systems, and for an obvious reason. If this occurred, the result would be *8ecause*, and a spelling checker would immediately discard this as a possibility—a good one would even fix it! Otherwise, the letters would be replaced, one after the other and starting with the most likely error, with the most probable mistakes. Sooner or later the *8* would be replaced by a *B*, and the word would be complete.

There are other problems to be solved, especially in mixed documents containing both graphics and text. What parts of the page correspond to graphics? Should the graphics areas be examined to see if they contain text, also? What about different sizes and styles of text (italics, bold, various fonts)? And, in particular, handprinted characters are a nightmare—no two of them are exactly alike, even when printed carefully by the same writer.

These problems will be dealt with one at a time, and in isolation from one another. The goal is to produce a working OCR system that can be used to extract the text from a fax received by a PC, but other issues such as handprinted characters will be examined as well.

8.2   OCR ON SIMPLE PERFECT IMAGES

The basic recognition problem will be addressed first, followed by a discussion of the outlying problems. Consider that a bilevel image of a page of text exists: The problem is to recognize the characters (and therefore the words) on the page, and create a text file from them. Except in special circumstances (such as pages containing mathematics or multiple languages) there would be no more than 128 different characters that need to be identified. Since a computer is a rather fast machine, it is possible to check an incoming glyph against all possible characters, and *classify* the input as the best match.

In order to do this the program must be trained to recognize all of the possible characters. This may be a simple matter of providing templates for each one, or a complex issue involving the processing of thousands of known documents, depending on the method used. A standard text image is useful at this stage, one that contains all of the characters to be recognized in a known order. In this way the program can train itself—the first character on the text image is known, and the example on the page is measured by the program and used as an example of its class.

Figure 8.1 shows the training image that will be used by the system being devised. All of the typical characters found on a North American keyboard are present twice. The use of variations in spacing is intended to at least partially account for variations in sampling. A letter that occurs one centimeter from the left margin may have a different appearance as a raster glyph from the same letter that occurs 1.5 centimeters from the margin, depending on the actual size of a pixel.

Since the orientation is perfectly horizontal, the first step is to determine the position and extent of the lines of text in the image. This can be done by constructing a horizontal *projection* and searching it for minima. The projection is simply the sum of the pixel values in a specified direction, so a horizontal projection is the sum of the pixels in each row. The row of pixels that begins a new line will be one in which some of the pixels are black, and the last row belonging to that line will be the last one having any black pixels. The start and end columns

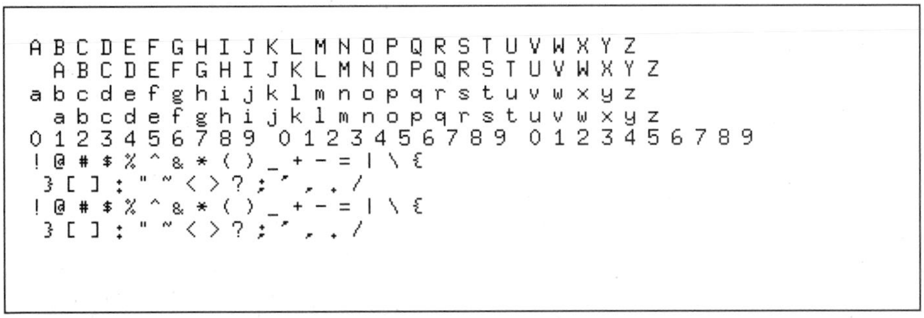

Figure 8.1 Example text image, used to teach the OCR system the basic character set. All of the usual characters on a North American keyboard are present in various positions.

for the line are found by searching the rows that belong to that line, from column zero through to the first column having a set pixel. The same is done, but in the reverse direction, to find the last set pixel in a line.

When this has been done, the bounding box for the text lines is known. Individual characters can be found beginning at the leftmost column belonging to the uppermost line. Starting at the first column containing a black pixel, copy pixels from the image into a temporary glyph image until a column having no black pixels is seen; the range for the rows is the row range for the entire line, as found previously (the row extents of the bounding box). Now, the eight lines of text are known initially, since the program will be run using the test image as input data. This means that each character read from the image has a known classification. The width, height, and spacing of these characters can be measured and saved in a database for this particular font, along with the sample of the glyph that was extracted from the image.

The database thus obtained has a very simple structure, as seen in Figure 8.2. The entire collection of information is stored as an array having 256 elements, and which is indexed by the ASCII code for the character involved. Each entry in this array is a list of templates in which the actual size of the glyph (as well as the pixels themselves) can be found. The list contains multiple entries that can be used to store variations on the extracted glyphs, including different sizes and styles of the same character, if needed. The database can be saved in a file and used

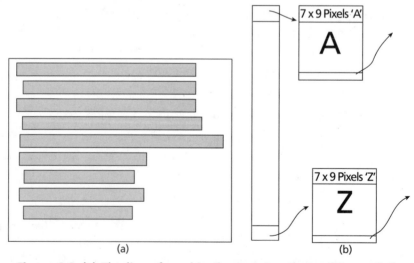

(a)   (b)

Figure 8.2 (a) The lines found in the training image (Figure 8.1). (b) The structure of the database in which the glyph information is stored. Everything needed for template matching is available in the initial version seen here.

when needed. New fonts and styles can be learned and added to the database; as it grows, the recognition system that uses it becomes able to recognize a wider variety of characters.

The program named learn.c will examine a sample image and create a new database. The sample image must be that of Figure 8.1, and the database file created is specified as an argument. For example,

```
learn testimage.pbm helv.db
```

was used to create the small database for the Helvetica-like font; this database can be found on the CD. The image testimage.pbm was obtained from a screen capture.

In this form, the database can be used for the simplest form of character recognition: *template matching*. In this case, template matching amounts to performing a pixel-by-pixel comparison between the saved glyphs and the input glyphs. The saved ones are classified, so a perfect match implies that the class of the input glyph is the same as that of the saved one.

Consider the input image seen in Figure 8.3. The database contains saved templates for each character, and each of these is compared against the input glyph.

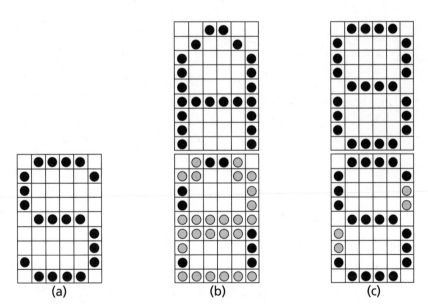

Figure 8.3 Template matching. (a) Third input glyph, extracted from an image containing text. The question is: "What character is this?" (b) The letter A as it appears in the database. The pixels in common with the input character appear below, in black. Pixels that do not match are grey. There are eight pixels in the match. (c) The digit 8 as it appears in the database, and the match with the input. The match is better in this case.

Figure 8.3b, for example, is a comparison of the input against the character *A*. Note that the black pixels that the two glyphs have in common are counted in favor of the match, and differences count against. White pixels do not count; if they did, it would introduce a bias in favor of large characters having few black pixels.

The simplest possible OCR system uses this scheme to recognize characters. The program ocr1 assumes that the image is bilevel, aligned properly, and that the database created by learn exists and is correct. It determines the positions of the lines by using projections, extracts characters from each line one at a time, and performs a template match against all of the characters in the database. The best match corresponds to the correct classification.

The existence of spaces (blanks) is inferred from the character spacing. Any character having a distance greater than the mean plus the width of a space as measured from the training image is assumed to be followed by a space; multiple spaces are found in the same way. The learn program determined the size of a space by examining the differences in where the various lines began. For example, the second line is indented an extra space relative to the first line; this difference is measured as pixel widths, and averaged over the four instances of indented lines.

When the ocr1.c program is run there are a few problems, none terribly serious. The actual position of the glyphs relative to one another is not saved in the database, which means that commas are recognized as single quotes—they are identical except for position. This could easily be repaired by simply noting that comma must appear at the bottom of the line, while quotes are at the top. Another problem occurs with double quotes, which are the only character having two horizontally separated black regions. They would be extracted as a pair of single quotes, which could be converted into a double quote with a post-processing stage.

When run using a text image that was captured from the screen of a small workstation sample.pbm, the ocr1.c program successfully recognized all characters in the sample except for the commas. The font was, of course, the same one on which it was trained.

8.3 OCR ON SCANNED IMAGES—SEGMENTATION

When using a scanner as a text input device, the problem becomes much more difficult. Most scanners will produce a grey-level image, so thresholding becomes an issue. The resolution of the scanner is finite, so the position of the document when scanned will affect the pixel values over the entire image. This means that a letter will have slightly different pixel values depending on its horizontal and vertical position on the page, and so will have a number of possible templates after thresholding.

The orientation of the image is no longer assured, either. Although it should be close, the page need not be aligned exactly to the horizontal; the ocr1.c program assumed a perfect alignment. Finally, and most difficult of all, the characters in the text image may touch each other after thresholding. Two or three characters that are connected by black pixels, such as those in Figure 8.4, will be extracted as a single glyph. The problem is serious, because not only is it not known where to split this glyph to get the three characters, but it may not even by clear that the glyph contains more than one character. Because of the use of the proportional fonts in many documents, in which the spacing between characters is a function of the character, the width of a multiple glyph does not always exceed that of a single one. For example, the characters *ij* occupy less horizontal space than does the single character *M*.

Finally, the use of a scanner introduces noise to the image. When thresholded, grey-level noise becomes random black pixels, or small black regions. All of these issues combine to greatly increase the complexity of the situation.

Let's deal with these problems one at a time. The thresholding issue was dealt with in Chapter 3, and almost any of the methods described there should work reasonably well on a text image. The adaptive algorithm found in the program thrdd.c is, in addition to being acceptable, fairly quick, and will be used in the examples that follow. Therefore, the first problem to be dealt with should be that of noise reduction.

Noise

If noise is a problem, there are a few ways in which it might be dealt with if it is to be done before thresholding. The first step is to acquire multiple images of the same page. Averaging the grey levels of each pixel across all of the samples will give a much better image as far as noise is concerned. Averaging four samples, for example, cuts the noise in half. Of course this takes longer, and care must be taken not to move the document at all between scans. Another possibility is to acquire multiple samples of the page, threshold them, and use only those pixels that are black in all samples (or a majority vote). This takes even longer.

Figure 8.4 Glyphs extracted from text that uses proportional spacing, and where the characters are too close together to be easily separated. The fact that the characters are connected by black pixels leads to the problem of selecting a location at which to split them.

If it is not possible to acquire multiple samples, then a *median filter* will reduce the noise level. It will, unfortunately, also reduce the contrast of the edges, and might result in the closing of small gaps. A median filter is a pass through all pixels in the image, looking at an $N \times M$ region centered at each pixel. The pixel in the center is replaced by the median value of all of the pixels in the region. Not all of the pixels must be considered when computing the median; for example, if only a horizontal row of pixels is used, then vertical edges are preserved.

The median filter is slow, requiring not only a pass through the image of the window, but also needing a sort of the pixels values in that window to find the median; in a sorted array of 100 elements, the median is found at array element 50. While the mean is easier to calculate, the blurring introduced by replacing a pixel with the mean of its neighbors is generally more than can be tolerated (Huang 1979).

If the noise is to be removed after thresholding, then the problem becomes one of filling small holes in the characters and removing small isolated black regions. Specific noise reduction filters have been designed for use in OCR systems that take advantage of existing knowledge about the characteristics of text images. Some of these are small (3×3) templates that are passed over the image, deleting or setting a pixel whenever a match is encountered.

For larger regions morphology has been used, but a relatively recent method called the kFill filter (O'Gorman 1992) is very interesting. This method uses a square $k \times k$ pixel window passed over the image multiple times. The outer two rows and columns of the window are called the *neighborhood*, with the center portion called the *core*. The first pass of the window will set all of the core pixels to white (the background level) if certain parameters computed from the neighborhood allow this; the second pass will set the core pixels to black, again depending on the neighborhood.

For the sake of explanation, assume that $k = 5$. Since the neighborhood consists of the outside two rows and columns, this means that the core is just the single pixel in the middle of the window. On the first of the two passes of the 5×5 window over the image, we are looking for locations where the core is black. At any such locations, the following values are measured:

1. The total number of white (background) pixels in the neighborhood. This value is n.
2. The number of white corner pixels. This value is r.
3. The number of distinct connected white regions encountered in the neighborhood. This value is c.

If c has any value except 1, this window is left alone and the next one is processed. The reason is that the core pixels may connect two regions, and deleting the core pixels will create two objects where one existed before.

Assuming that $c=1$, the core pixels are set to white if:

$$\left(n > 3k - \frac{k}{3}\right) \vee \left(\left(n = 3k - \frac{k}{3}\right) \wedge (r = 2)\right) \qquad \text{(EQ 8.1)}$$

Figure 8.5a shows a glyph containing salt-and-pepper noise resulting from thresholding a noisy image. After the first pass, the isolated black pixels are gone (Figure 8.5b), as are some of the boundary pixels. After the next pass the isolated white pixels are gone, too (Figure 8.5c), and processing could stop here. However, the algorithm continues until no changes occur in two consecutive passes, and there remain a few boundary pixels that satisfy the removal criterion. The final glyph appears in Figure 8.5d.

The program kfill.c provides a sample implementation of this technique.

Isolating Individual Glyphs

The connected glyphs in Figure 8.4 illustrate a part of the problem that occurs when multiple glyphs connect to each other, due to noise or undersampling. The problem is quite serious, because a template match will give very poor results in these cases, and a statistical approach (Section 8.2.4) requires isolated glyphs from which to measure features. Ultimately, separating these connected glyphs is essential if a reasonable recognition rate is to be achieved, but there are many ways in which the connections can be formed, and some valid glyphs can appear to be two connected ones. An example of the latter case is the letter m, which can be split into two good matches of r and n. It might well be that a good separation cannot be done as an isolated case, and that contextual information will be nec-

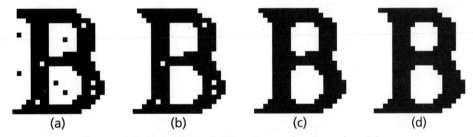

(a)   (b)   (c)   (d)

Figure 8.5 Use of the kFill noise-reduction algorithm.
(a) Original noisy glyph. (b) After the first pass with k=5; the isolated black pixels are removed. (c) After the second pass, which removes isolated white regions. (d) Processing continues until no further changes are seen in two consecutive passes.

essary for a proper segmentation. Continuing the example, if the letter *m* appears at the end of the word *farm*, then the separation into *rn* would yield the word *farrn*, which would not make sense.

It would be only fair to point out that this is an unsolved problem. There is no algorithm that works in all of the cases that might be encountered while scanning any document of a reasonably large size. Still, something must be done, and the most commonly encountered methods use some variation of a vertical projection. Most simple of all is to locate the minima in the vertical projection and segment the image at those places, but this has some unfortunate problems.

Consider the small text image in Figure 8.6. Many of these characters have clear separations, and would be isolated by the process of identifying connected components. The vertical profile (projection) appears below as a line graph, and solid vertical lines spanning the two show the positions where the characters should be split. The dashed vertical lines show places where a projection-based method would split a character into two parts, creating an error. These locations occur in places where the projection is a local minimum having a smaller value than the minimum between the *t* and *h* in the word *the*. Thus, any reasonable

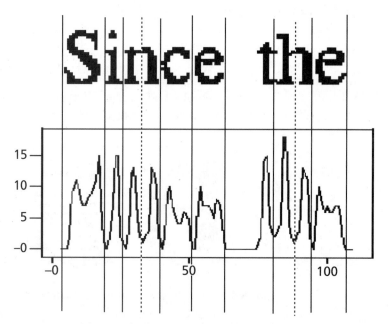

Figure 8.6 Use of simple projections to locate isolated characters. Using minima in the profile results in splitting some legitimate glyphs into two parts. Splitting the *n*, for example, could result in seeing *ri* instead.

threshold value used to identify minima would either fail to split the *th* in *the*, or would also split the *n* and the *h* into two parts.

A related technique computes a *break cost* (Tsujimoto 1991), which uses two adjacent columns. This value is defined as the number of black pixels in a column that also have a black neighbor in the same row of the previous columns, as shown in Figure 8.7. Columns in which the break cost is small are candidates for locations at which to split the glyph. The break cost is plotted in Figure 8.7 below the text image and, as before, solid lines are drawn where the segmentation into glyphs would occur—in this case, places where the break cost is zero.

While the segmentation of the image in the figure is perfect, this is not always the case. The addition or removal of one strategic pixel could alter the situation; for instance, if the *t* in *the* were connected at the bottom by one more pixel, then the *t* and the *h* would not be split.

Applied alone, none of the glyph segmentation methods will successfully isolate a large fraction of the connected glyphs. The problem might be fundamentally ambiguous, and so the solution is to use other information. The use of context is possible, as is the optimization of the recognition probabilities for the entire collection of connected components. This latter idea can be implemented at a relatively low level, and so is generally tried first. The use of context generally means

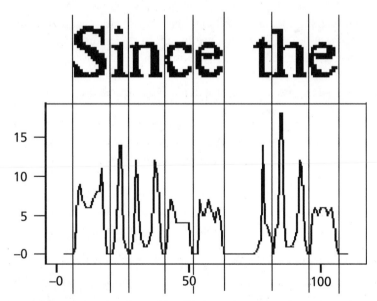

Figure 8.7 The use of break cost for locating isolated characters. The vertical lines are drawn where the break cost is zero. This happens to segment the image perfectly, which is not true in general.

checking words to make sure they exist in a dictionary, and correcting the spelling accordingly. This can only be done after all of the component glyphs have been extracted and recognized.

A typical approach would work as follows: The connected glyph image would have cut locations identified by one of the previously discussed methods. The pixels between each two cut positions would then be considered to be a glyph, and recognition would be attempted. The set of cut positions for which all glyphs were recognized (and having the highest probability of being correct) would be chosen as the correct segmentation.

Consider the image in Figure 8.8. This consists of five character glyphs, all of which are connected as a single connected region. The cut positions as determined by break costs are shown in the figure as arrows pointing to the position at which to cut; there are six of them, any of which (or any consecutive combination of which) might be an actual character. A possible next step in the segmentation process is to create a *decision tree* containing the possible groupings of the regions in the image. Each contiguous region corresponds to a node in the tree, as seen in Figure 8.8b. Also associated with each node is a character (which is the classification of the region) and a measure of likelihood. The most likely path through the tree will be selected as the correct segmentation, and the classifications will therefore be immediately available.

When a node (a set of contiguous regions) is able to be accepted (classified with a significant likelihood) the classification and likelihood are stored in the relevant node. Only then are the child nodes processed; the children are the possible combinations of the remaining nodes (regions). Nodes that give a very poor classification are not evaluated further, at least initially. If it happens that none of the paths through the tree result in a good classification, then the less likely branches can be evaluated.

The tree can be constructed as described, or a recursive decomposition can be devised. The set of all possible recursive calls forms a tree, and the best segmentation will be the only one retained, the others being discarded as soon as a better one is found.

This approach depends for its accuracy on the character recognition method that is applied to the cut regions, but is independent of that algorithm in the sense that any recognition method will result in a segmentation.

Matching Templates

In general, template matching does not work as well on scanned glyphs as it did on the perfect images of the previous section. Noise and the resulting errors caused by thresholding creep into the picture, causing deviations to be registered when matching characters against even correct templates. Taking noise reduction seriously does help, and using a good thresholding algorithms helps, too. Possibly

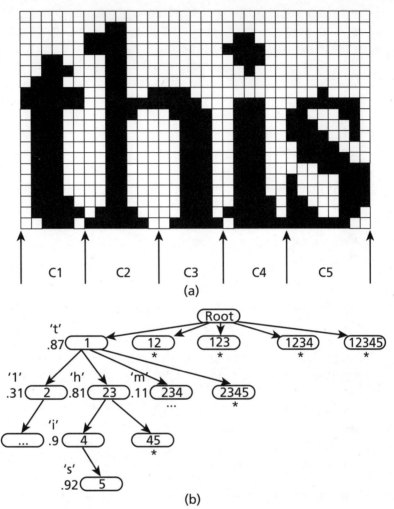

Figure 8.8 A connected glyph and its decision tree. (a) Each of the five regions may themselves be a glyph, or any set of adjacent regions may combine to form a glyph. (b) The decision tree. At the first stage, the first region is determined to be a *t*. The second character could be any of *l*, *h*, or *m*, with only the path corresponding to this giving a reasonable classification.

more important is to use a wide selection of templates, though. The standard image used for teaching a font (Figure 8.1) has only two instances of each character, when in fact a dozen may not be too many. Variations can be obtained by scanning the template image many times, saving each set of templates in the same database. More templates can be had by using variations on the thresholds, again saving all of the variants.

There are also variations possible in the template-matching procedure. When dealing with perfect glyphs, the number of mismatches was subtracted from the number of matches. It is better to normalize the match measure to account for the number of pixels involved. For example, a normalized match index (NMI) can be found by counting the number of pixels that match (M^+) and those that do not (M^-). The normalized match index is then:

$$NMI = \frac{M^+ - M^-}{M^+ + M^-}$$ (EQ 8.2)

This value has a minimum of -1 and a maximum of 1, which is convenient for many reasons.

Small variations in the glyphs will produce glyphs of slightly varying sizes. This has the effect of causing a misalignment of the template and the glyph, which can produce a poor match. Therefore it is necessary to find a number of possible matches, each corresponding to a different position of the template over the glyph. A few pixels (perhaps five or six in each dimension) are all that is needed, but this means between 25 and 36 matching attempts. This slows down the template-matching process dramatically.

Another issue is that of holes. The background pixels that match are not counted, as a general rule, since that would give a strong bias towards matching a large, empty glyph. However, a hole can be considered to be structural. The large set of background pixels in the center of, for instance, a letter O, can be used to match the character.

To do this, the holes are marked with a pixel value other than those used for background and object pixels. Then an extra case is inserted into the function that computes the match: A hole pixel in the template should match a hole pixel in a glyph, and (if so) record a match; else record a mismatch. In essence, hole pixels are treated in the same way as object pixels, but are a distinct class and don't match an object pixel.

Given an isolated glyph, the holes can be found in the following way: Any background pixel connected to the bounding box of the glyph is marked with, for example, the value 3. Then any background pixel connected to a 3-valued pixel is also marked with a 3, recursively. When no further pixels are marked or markable, any remaining background pixels within the bounding box belong to a hole. These are then marked, while the 3-valued pixels revert to the background level.

The use of 4-connected pixels in the marking process ensures that a thin line will not be ''jumped over,'' resulting in a hole being missed.

This is the template-matching process used by the program ocr2.c and the corresponding learning module learn2.c. The learn2.c module reads the standard test image and creates a database of templates. ocr2.c reads the database, and then attempts to recognize the characters in an input image by using a template match. The input images correspond to scanned documents. For example, the image file paged.pbm is an image of printed 10-point text, scanned at 300 DPI (dots per inch). Of course, the test image must also be 10-point text in the same font, and must have been scanned at the same rate; the corresponding test image is pagec.pbm. These images have already been thresholded.

A sample result from ocr2.c appears in Figure 8.9. The data used was scanned from a page in this book, and appears in the figure above the text that was extracted, the spaces having been edited. Most of the errors occurred because of a failure to separated joined glyphs, and because the letter *l* was repeatedly mistaken for the special character |.

The errors in the first two lines of output and their causes are as follows:

1. *m* should have been *ta*. Caused by the *t* being joined to the *a*.
2. | should have been *l*. Template matching error.
3. *m* should have been *ta*. Joined glyphs, again.
4. | should have been *l*.
5. *h* should have been *fi*. Joined glyphs.
6. Missing *o*. Joined glyphs
7. *!* should have been *th*. Joined glyphs.
8. | should have been *l*.

There is a pattern in the repetition of errors. The mismatch of | for *l* is pathological, and occurs 14 times in this small image (counted as 14 distinct errors). Certain combinations of letters are repeatedly misclassified; *m* is seen for *ta*, *h* for *fi*, and *!* for *th*. This latter error, for example, happens four times in this passage alone. One serious set of errors occurs in the second line of the original text, where the word *projection* appears in italics. Since there are no templates for the italic font, it is not too surprising that the recognizer fails miserably at this point. For this example, the overall success rate (percentage of correct characters) is 86.3%.

Adding code that will attempt to split a glyph if it classifies with a low probability does improve the situation. Deleting the template for | is also a good idea, at least in this case; it causes more errors than its removal would cause, by a large factor. The addition of glyph splitting and deletion of the | improves the recognition, giving a success rate of 88.9% for the test data of Figure 8.9.

Template matching is an intrinsically slow process. One way to speed it up is

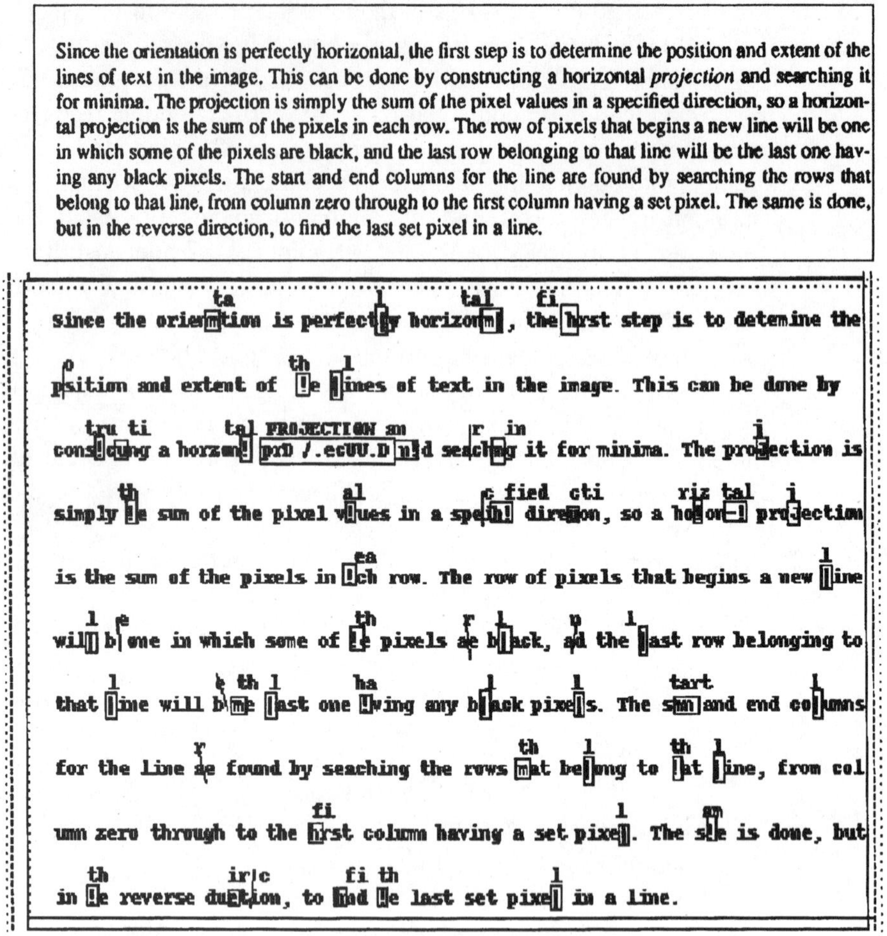

Since the orientation is perfectly horizontal, the first step is to determine the position and extent of the lines of text in the image. This can be done by constructing a horizontal *projection* and searching it for minima. The projection is simply the sum of the pixel values in a specified direction, so a horizontal projection is the sum of the pixels in each row. The row of pixels that begins a new line will be one in which some of the pixels are black, and the last row belonging to that line will be the last one having any black pixels. The start and end columns for the line are found by searching the rows that belong to that line, from column zero through to the first column having a set pixel. The same is done, but in the reverse direction, to find the last set pixel in a line.

Figure 8.9 A text image (above) and the text extracted by template matching (below).

to initially match only a sample of the pixels; say, one in every four. This can be thought of as a resampling. If the match to the subset of pixels is sufficiently good, then the remainder can be tried, to get the actual match index. If the match is very poor, then there would appear to be no point in pursuing the template involved, and so the match would be aborted. Figure 8.10 shows how this would work if the template were split into four parts. A serious failure at any of the four parts will abort the match. This method works quite well in some cases, and is used in the printed music recognition system (Section 9.3). In this case a speedup of about three times is achieved over the basic template software.

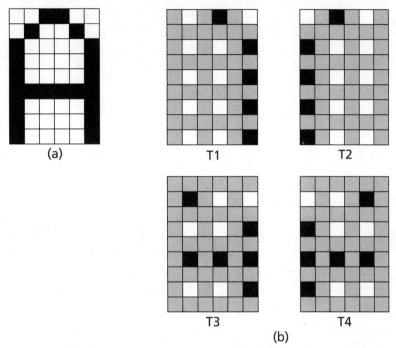

Figure 8.10 Hierarchical template matching. (a) The original template. (b) The four parts of the template used in a match. Each of these has one quarter of the pixels of the template, so early match failures can speed things up by a factor of four. Actually, a factor of about three is attained.

Statistical Recognition

There are two ways to use features to classify objects. In *statistical* approaches many features are combined into a large feature vector. A feature is a measurement made on a glyph, and combining them into a vector is a simple way of collating multiple measurements. Because of this, the same object can correspond to a wide variety of feature vectors just through the errors in the measurements. However, these measurements will be clustered in some region of N-space, where N is the dimension of the feature vector. Hence, a statistical recognizer will construct a feature vector from a data object and classify it based on how far (Euclidean distance) it is in N-space from the feature vectors for known objects.

As a contrast, the basic idea behind *structural* pattern recognition is that objects are constructed from smaller components using a set of rules. Characterizing an object in an image is a matter of locating the components, which at the lowest level are features, and constructing some representation for storing the relationships between them. This representation is then checked against known patterns to see if a match can be identified. Structural pattern recognition is, in fact, a sophisticated variation on template matching, one that must match relationships between objects as well as the objects themselves. The problems involved in structural pattern recognition are two: locating the components, and finding a good representation for storing the relationships between the components. Some structural approaches will be discussed in Section 8.4.

A successful statistical classifier depends on an astute selection of the features (measurements, or properties) and their accurate measurement. Of course, very large vectors can be used, but the execution time grows as the size of the vector grows, and at some point the problem becomes intractable. Still, sizes of many hundreds of elements have been used in real systems.

The features themselves should be easy to measure or, again, the execution time of the classifier will become an issue. Fortunately there are many such features. For instance, the ratio of the area of a glyph to its perimeter can characterize shape, although crudely. For a circle, the area is computed by $a = \pi r^2$, and the perimeter by $p = 2\pi r$. The ratio of p^2/a is $4\pi^2 r^2/\pi r^2 = 4\pi$. Hence, the expression:

$$C = \frac{p^2}{4\pi a} \qquad \text{(EQ 8.3)}$$

will be unity, or nearly so, for a circular object, and will increase in value as the shape of the region deviates from a circle (a disk, really). This measure, called *circularity*, can be used as one of the features.

Since the area has already been calculated, another feature that is simple to compute is *rectangularity*, denoted by R. This is simply the ratio of the area of the region to that of its bounding box; as the shape of the region varies from perfectly rectangular, the value of R decreases.

The aspect ratio can be defined as the ratio of the object's height H to its width W. If rectangularity has been calculated, then the bounding box is available, and the aspect ratio A can be found from that.

Other features that can be used include: the number, size, and location of any *holes* (enclosed background regions) in the object; the *convexity*, which is the relative amount that the object differs from a convex object; *moments*, of any order; *shape numbers* (Gonzalez 1992); *Euler* number; and a host of others (Parker 1994).

Some "features" consist of a collection of values, and are themselves vectors. For example, a glyph can be resampled to a small, constant size. For example, to resample a 12×12 glyph to size of 3×3, simply group the pixels into three groups of four in each direction (Figure 8.11). The value of each of the new pixels is the average of the pixels in each of the nine regions, scaled to a known range

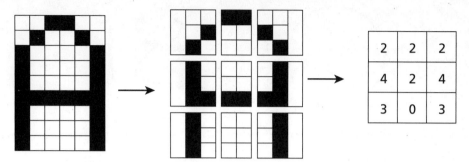

Figure 8.11 Resampling of a glyph to provide a multiple feature. The original is split into three parts, both horizontally and vertically. The number or fraction of black pixels in each of the nine resulting regions contributes to the feature vector.

so that they can be compared fairly. The nine pixels in the resulting 3×3 image can be stored in consecutive locations in the feature vector. This will be called a *multiple* feature.

Other examples of a multiple feature include the *slope histogram*, *profiles* in any direction, and *signatures*. A slope histogram (for example, as in Wilkinson (1990)) is the histogram of directions of the lines comprising the boundary of the object. The size of the histogram depends on the bin size; for machine printed characters, it is unlikely that more than 16 directions will be useful, and eight would be sufficient when used with other features. A profile, as has already been discussed, is the sum of the pixel values in some specified direction. Multiple directions can be used, which is rather like taking a CAT scan of the glyph.

A signature is an interesting concept, and it can be defined in a few different ways. While some define a signature as being the same as a projection, it can also be defined as a one-dimensional representation of the boundary. This is found by computing the distance from the centroid (center of ''mass'') of the object to the boundary as a function of angles, from zero degrees to 360 in any chosen increment. The resulting set of distances, when properly scaled, can be included in the feature vector. Figure 8.12 illustrates this process. In this example the signature values are distances indexed by the angle to the boundary pixel. If a distance already exists at a particular angle the longer of the two is used, yielding an outer boundary signature.

The signature computed in this latter manner is dependent on rotation and scaling. This means that a signature found for a 12-point character can't be used as a template for matching a 10-point character. Attempts have been made to normalize the signature to make it scale-independent. This is not as simple as it may seem, although dividing all bins by the variance has been used with some

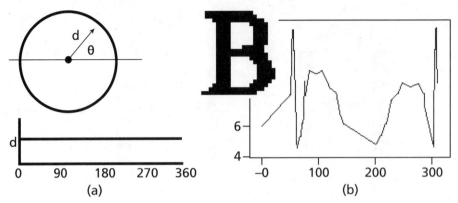

Figure 8.12 One way to compute a signature. (a) For a perfect, real circle. (b) For a sampled glyph.

degree of success (Gonzalez 1992). The program sig is one implementation of the procedure.

8.4 OCR ON FAX IMAGES—PRINTED CHARACTERS

The use of fax images introduces further complications. While it is easily possible to place a document on a scanner and collect an image that is within three degrees of the true orientation, fax machines generally have page feeders, and the intrinsic error is greater. Noise is also a greater problem; often the image has been sent thousands of miles over somewhat grubby phone wires, and fax image standards can use lossy compression methods. A better choice of features may be of some help in decreasing the impact of the intrinsic distortions.

Orientation—Skew Detection

When using a scanner, a careful user can place a document so that the lines of text are within about three degrees of the true horizontal. When using a fax or other such device, there is no guarantee of this. The device itself often feeds the paper across a recording device, and the text on the page may or may not be properly aligned in the first place. Thus, one of the first steps in attempting to read a fax image is to estimate the orientation angle of the lines of text; this is called the *skew angle*, and the measurement is called *skew detection*.

Skew detection can be performed in many ways, and the methods described here form only a summary of the possibilities. In the case where an approximate skew angle is known, a horizontal projection can be used. Recall that these were used to identify the line positions of the text in Sections 8.1–8.3. In cases where the skew angle is large, there will be no parts of the projection that correspond to a completely white band between lines. However, if the approximate angle is known, the image can be rotated by that amount; then projections are computed for small angles until a maximum line height and maximum white space between lines is found. The resulting angle is the skew angle, assuming a reasonable noise level.

For any character not having a descender (characters other than *g, j, p, q,* and *y*) the bottom of the characters in each line are colinear. Therefore, if the bounding box of each glyph is found, the center point of the bottom edge of the boxes should be colinear for each line of text.

This suggests the following algorithm (Baird 1987):

1. Identify all of the connected regions; presume that each represents a character, unless it exceeds some size threshold.
2. Find the bounding box of each region, and locate the center of the bottom edge of the bounding box.
3. For a given angle θ compute the projection of the points obtained in step 2, yielding a one-dimensional projection array P(θ). Baird uses a bin size corresponding to $\frac{1}{3}$ of the size of a 6-point character at the sampled resolution. $P_i(q)$ is the value of the *i*th bin found for angle θ.
4. Maximize the function:

$$A(\theta) = \sum_{i=1}^{n} P_i^2(\theta) \qquad \text{(EQ 8.4)}$$

where *n* is the number of bins. The angle that gives the maximum is the correct skew angle.

Once again an estimate of the skew angle is useful, since it will reduce the amount of searching needed to find a maximum. If no estimate is available, an exhaustive search can be used, but this is time-consuming. However, once in the correct neighborhood, a coarse-to-fine search can be used. A nonlinear least-squares method has also been suggested. The reported accuracy of this algorithm can approach $\frac{1}{30}$ of a degree, with $\frac{1}{2}$ of a degree being typical.

Figure 8.13 provides an example of this method applied to a rotated image—this was done so that the skew angle would be known, and could be compared against the value found by the algorithm. Figure 8.13a is a portion of a text image that has been rotated by 10 degrees; Figure 8.13b shows a 15-degree rotation. After thresholding (Figures 8.13c–d) the first two steps of the Baird algorithm were applied, and the points at the center of the bounding boxes were drawn as black pixels (Figure 8.13e–f). The best-fit straight lines through the black pixels should be at the skew angle of the text.

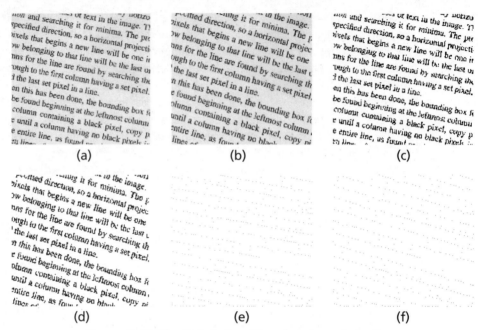

Figure 8.13 The Baird algorithm for skew detection.
(a) Document rotated 10 degrees. (b) Document rotated 15 degrees. (c) Thresholded version of (a). (d) Thresholded version of (b). (e–f) Black pixels represent the bottom center of the bounding boxes of the connected regions; these should be characters, or parts of characters. Connecting the dots in the best way should give lines at 10 and 15 degrees.

However, instead of completing the algorithm and determining the best angle by using projections, histograms, and least-squares computations, a different method for estimating the angle was tried. After all, the least-squares criteria have been used many times already, and we won't learn anything new. Let's try a *Hough transform* for finding the lines.

The Hough transform (Hough 1962) is a method for detecting straight lines in a raster image. Any black pixel in an image has infinitely many straight lines that *could* pass through it, one for every possible angle. Each of these lines can be characterized by the slope-intercept form of the equation for a line:

$$Y = mX + b \qquad \text{(EQ 8.5)}$$

where the coordinates of the pixel involved are (X,Y), the slope of the line is m, and the intersection of the line with the Y axis occurs at $Y = b$. Now, if this equation is interpreted differently, so that X and Y are constants and m and b are the coordinates, the equation can be reorganized as:

$$b = -Xm + Y \qquad\qquad \text{(EQ 8.6)}$$

which is the equation of a line in (m,b) space. Thus, a single point in two-dimensional image space (X,Y) corresponds to a straight line in (m,b) coordinates (Figure 8.14b).

Each pixel in an image corresponds to such a family of lines, expressed in (m,b) space as a straight line itself. What is more, places in (m,b) space, which will now be called *Hough space*, where two lines intersect correspond to colinear points in image space. This is no big deal, because *any* two points are colinear, but the same is true for multiple intersections. This leads to the following observation:

If the N straight lines in Hough space that correspond to N given pixels in image space intersect at a point, then those N pixels reside on the same straight line in image coordinates. The parameters of that line correspond to the Hough coordinates (m,b) of the point of intersection.

This is the basis for the Hough transform; all pixels are converted into lines in (m,b) space, and the points of intersection of many lines are noted, and collected into line segments. Because there are in reality infinitely many lines, and infinitely many points on each, the implementation is actually very much like a histogram. A degree of quantization in (m,b) coordinates is decided upon in advance, and a

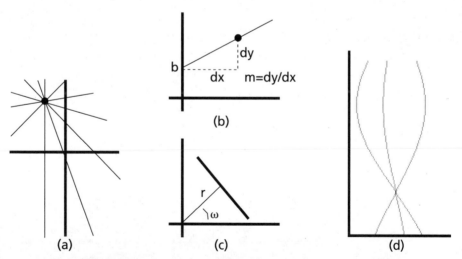

Figure 8.14 The Hough transform. (a) Family of lines through an image pixel. (b) Slope-intercept form of a straight line; one form of Hough space. (c) Normal form, which can represent lines of any angle. (d) (r,w) Hough representation of three colinear points; (2,2), (22,22) and (55,55). Angle should be 45 degrees; the estimate is 44 degrees.

Hough image is created. For each pixel in the original image, the line in Hough space is computed, and each pixel on that line in the Hough image is incremented. After all pixels have been processed, the pixels in the Hough image that have the largest values correspond to the largest number of colinear pixels in the original image.

The slope-intercept line equation has the unfortunate property of being unable to deal with vertical lines: The slope becomes infinite. There are other forms of the equation of a line that do not have this pitfall, including the *normal form*:

$$r = x \cos \omega + y \sin \omega \qquad \text{(EQ 8.7)}$$

where r is the perpendicular distance from the origin to the line, and ω is the angle of that perpendicular line to the x axis. Using this equation, the Hough space coordinates are (r, ω) as seen in Figure 8.14c–d.

The relationship between the Hough transform and skew detection should be clear. The first steps of Baird's skew-detection algorithm give an image with a large collection of sets of colinear pixels. The Hough image of this should have a primary peak at an angle corresponding to the skew angle. Taking the Hough transform of the two examples seen in Figure 8.13 yields skew angles of 10 and 15 degrees respectively, both of which are exactly correct. The Hough images for these examples can be seen in Figure 8.15; the source code for a Hough transform implementation is also shown.[1]

Another skew-detection method, and one that also requires that the connected regions be identified first, is based on the observation that the spacing between characters on a line is smaller than the spacing between lines (Hashizume 1986). This being the case, a line drawn between the centroids of pairs of nearest neigh-

---

1. This is included here partly because there was a bug in the program given in my previous book. Sorry folks; this one works fine.

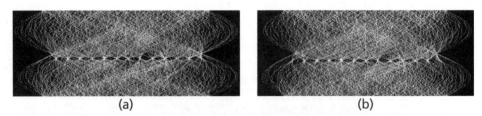

(a)   (b)

Figure 8.15 The Hough transform. (a) Hough transform of the image seen in Figure 8.13e. (b) The Hough transform of the image seen in Figure 8.15f. (c) Source code for implementing a Hough transform.

```
void hough (IMAGE x, float *theta)
{
    float **z;
    int center_x, center_y, r, omega, i, j, rmax, tmax;
    double conv;
    double sin(), cos(), sqrt();
    float tmval;

conv = 3.1415926535/180.0;
    center_x = x->info->nc/2;center_y = x->info->nr/2;
    rmax =
     (int)(sqrt((double)(x->info->nc*x->info->nc +
                         x->info->nr*x->info->nr)) /2.0);

/* Create an image for the Hough space - choose your own
           sampling */
    z = (f2d (180, 2*rmax+1);
    for (r = 0; r < 2 * rmax+1; r++)
       for (omega = 0; omega < 180; omega++)
          z[omega][r] = 0;

    tmax = 0; tmval = 0;
    for (i = 0; i < x->info->nr; i++)
      for (j = 0; j < x->info->nc; j++)
          if (x->data[i][j])
             for (omega = 0; omega < 180; ++omega)
             {
                 r = (i - center_y) *
                 sin((double)(omega*conv))
                    + (j - center_x) *
                    cos((double)(omega*conv));
                 z[omega][rmax+r] += 1;
             }

    for (i=0; i<180; i++)
      for (j=0; j<2*rmax+; j++)
        if (z[i][j] > tmval)
        {
           tmval = z[i][j];
           tmax = i;
        }
    *theta = tmax;
    free (z[0]); free (z);
}
```

Figure 8.15c (continued)

bors should join adjacent characters, and the angle of the line will be near to the skew angle. The histogram of the angles should have a peak at the best estimate of the skew angle.

The Use of Edges

A glyph has, until now, been treated as a connected black region; it is fundamentally a raster entity. On the other hand, it is clear that the character can be recognized using only the edge information. The basic shape and topological properties of the character are present in an edge representation, and there are fewer pixels to be considered, so processing times may be shorter. The problem of locating the edges was discussed in Chapter 1, leaving the problem of *edge linking* and *classification* using edges to be dealt with here.

Edge linking is the process of collecting the pixels into line segments. This has also been called *vectorization*, when used in the context of creating a line drawing from a raster image of an engineering diagram or a map. We begin with either a set of edge pixels, found by applying an edge detector to a grey level image, or the object boundary, obtained from the bilevel glyph. Each pixel is presumed to belong to a straight line segment, and so adjacent pixels are added to a set until some linearity constraint is violated. When a set is complete, the line segment is saved as its endpoints, and the pixels in the set are removed from the image; the next line is extracted in the same way, and so on until no pixels remain.

The program vect.c is a simple yet quite effective boundary vectorizer that can be used on characters. It works in the following way:

1. The object boundary is identified, and all nonboundary object pixels are set to the background level.
2. Starting at any pixel on the outside boundary, the *chain code* (Freeman 1961; Parker 1993) of the outline is found; then a list of pixels comprising the outline is created.
3. Starting at the first pixel in the list created in 2 above, add the next pixel in the list to a set that will be the set of pixels belonging to the next line in the boundary.
4. Check the distance between all pixels in the set created in 3 above and the real straight line between the first and last pixels in the set.
5. If the distance found is less than some threshold D, then continue from step 3, using the next pixel in the list.
6. If the distance is greater than D, then stop adding pixels to the current line. Omit the first and last pixel in the set as the segment endpoints, and let the next pixel in the list be the new starting point. Resume the process from step 3.

This is a classical vectorization strategy, and succeeds for smaller images like glyphs but may be less than useful for large images, such as maps and line drawings.

An alternative to this process involves finding the longest straight line that can be found that passes through black pixels only. This line is saved, the component pixels are removed, and the process is repeated. One problem with this latter method is that the lines found need not form a connected sequence, and some post-processing work is required to reconnect the segments into a sensible representation of the glyph.

Figure 8.16 shows the vectorized version of a glyph, in this case a *B* (first seen in Figure 8.5), and shows the effect of varying the distance threshold. The advantages of a vectorized outline are many, including that the length and the orientation of the line segments are now easily and accurately found, and a rotation can be done precisely, so that the glyph orientation can be repaired.

Once the boundary of an input glyph is available in vector form, there are a few ways that it might be used in classification. Edge matching is a tricky technique that attempts to identify edges in the input image that correspond to edges in each of a set of model images. The models are classified, so the best match will provide a classification. The vectorized edges are converted into the form (X_c, Y_c, L, θ), where (X_c, Y_c) is the center of the line, L is its length, and θ is the angle the line segment makes with the *x* axis. If properly scaled, a distance measure can be used to match the lines in the image with the lines in the model. However, inaccuracies creep in since small errors in the outline can be reflected in the vectors extracted, and the coordinate system is usually based on a bounding box (which can also vary slightly).

The *slope histogram*, as mentioned previously, can also be useful, and is more accurately generated from a vector image than from a raster one. We start by

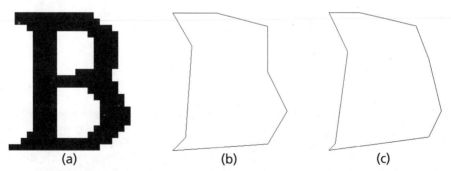

(a)   (b)   (c)

Figure 8.16 Vectorizing a glyph boundary. (a) Original glyph.
(b) Vectorization of outer boundary with an error threshold of
1.0. (c) The same vectorization, but with a threshold of 2.0.

quantizing the possible angles of line segments in the image; then we simply create a frequency histogram of the angles that actually appear in a specific glyph; this defines the slope histogram. The frequency with which an angle occurs will be the sum of the lengths of the line segments having that angle.

The degree of quantization will dictate the number of bins needed in the histogram, and will also be reflected in the accuracy with which a match can be made. It seems likely that no more than between eight and 16 different angles are required in the case of character recognition.

The example in Figure 8.17 uses eight different angles, in 22.5 degree increments from 0 to 180 degrees. The histograms computed for the samples in the figure are:

B: (0.3815, 0.0, 0.1439, 0.0, 0.3307, 0.0, 0.1439, 0.0)
C: (0.2733, 0.0, 0.26, 0.0, 0.2050, 0.0, 0.2609, 0.0)
D1: (0.3409, 0.0, 0.1875, 0.0, 0.2841, 0.0, 0.1875, 0.0)
D2: (0.3118, 0.0, 0.2004, 0.0, 0.2740, 0.0, 0.2138, 0.0)
D3: (0.3714, 0.0, 0.1751, 0.0, 0.2785, 0.0, 0.1751, 0.0)

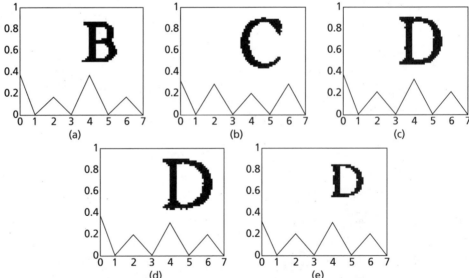

Figure 8.17 Slope histograms for a set of sample glyphs. (a) The B glyph, seen previously (Figure 8.16a, for example). (b) A C glyph. (c) The D1 glyph. (d) D2, a D the same size as D1. (e) D3, a D smaller than D1 and D2. All of the D histograms are closer to each other (Euclidean distance) than they are to the other glyphs.

Written as they are above, these histograms are feature vectors, or components of a larger feature vector. This set of characters was selected because, on the face of it, they appear to contain similar sets of directions (although in different places). The C was selected for contrast. When the histograms, which have been normalized by dividing by the total length of all of the vectors, are treated as vectors, the smallest distance between any of the D histograms is smaller than the distance between a D glyph and either of the others. There is one case (D3) where the B is closer to D3 than is D2, but the glyph would still be classified correctly. Program slhist.c provides a sample implementation.

The matrix of distances for this small case is:

BCD1D2D3

	B	C	D1	D2	D3
B	0.00000	0.23383	0.08730	0.12709	0.06909
C	0.23383	0.00000	0.14653	0.10961	0.17203
D1	0.08730	0.14653	0.00000	0.04251	0.03562
D2	0.12709	0.10961	0.04251	0.00000	0.07557
D3	0.06909	0.17203	0.03562	0.07557	0.00000

One last suggestion is a *vector template* style of match—this involves reducing the shortest vector to one pixel in length, and then scaling the rest of the vectors by the same factor. The result is replotted in a small raster, and a standard template match is performed against templates found in the same way from training data. If the match value is worse than some value X, we rescale again using the next shortest line, and so on.

The program learn3.c will read the standard test image and create a database of feature vectors. It can be modified to calculate any set of features desired, and store these in a file. ocr3.c will read this database, then read a text image and attempt to match the feature vectors from the image against those in the database, performing a minimum distance classification.

8.5 BIBLIOGRAPHY

Baird, H. S. 1987. The Skew Angle of Printed Documents. *Proceedings of the Conference of the Society of Photographic Scientists and Engineers.* SPIE. Bellingham, WA: 14–21.

Ballard, D. H. 1981. Generalizing the Hough Transform to Detect Arbitrary Shapes. *Pattern Recognition.* Vol. 13. 2:111–122.

Bayer, T. A. and U. Kressel. 1993. Cut Classification for Segmentation. *Second International Conference on Document Analysis and Recognition (ICDAR).* Tsukuba, Japan. 565–568.

Duda, R. O. and P. E. Hart. 1972. Use of the Hough Transform to Detect Lines and Curves in Pictures. *Communications of the ACM*. Vol. 15. 1:11–15.

Freeman, H. and R. Shapira. 1961. On the Encoding of Arbitrary Geometric Configurations. *IEEE Transactions on Electronic Computers*. Vol. EC-10. 260–268.

Gonzalez, R. C. and R. E. Woods. 1992. *Digital Image Processing*. Reading, MA: Addison-Wesley.

Hashizume, A., Yeh, P. S., and A. Rosenfeld. 1986. A Method of Detecting the Orientation of Aligned Components. *Pattern Recognition Letters*. 4:125–132.

Hinds, S. C., Fischer, J. L., and D. P. D'Amato. 1990. A Document Skew Detection Method Using Run Length Encoding and the Hough Transform. *Proc. 10th International Conference on Pattern Recognition (ICPR)*. 464–468.

Hough, P.V.C. 1962. *Method and Means for Recognizing Complex Patterns*. U.S. Patent #3,069,654.

Huang, T. S. 1979. A Fast Two Dimensional Median Filtering Algorithm. *IEEE Transactions on Acoustics, Speech, and Signal Processing*. Vol. 27. 13–18.

Liang, S., Ahmadi, M., and M. Shridhan. 1993. Segmentation of Touching Characters in Printed Document Recognition. *Second International Conference on Document Analysis and Recognition (ICDAR)*. Tsukuba, Japan. 569–572.

Lu, Y. 1993. On the Segmentation of Touching Characters. *Second International Conference on Document Analysis and Recognition (ICDAR)*. Tsukuba, Japan. 440–443.

O'Gorman, L. 1992. Image and Document Processing Techniques for the RightPages Electronic Library System. *Proc. International Conference on Pattern Recognition*. Los Alimitos, CA: 260–263.

Parker, J. R. 1994. *Practical Computer Vision Using C*. New York, NY: John Wiley & Sons.

Tsujimoto, S. and H. Asada. 1991. Resolving Ambiguity in Segmenting Touching Characters. *First International Conference on Document Analysis and Recognition*. San Malo, CA: 701–709.

Wilkinson, T. and J. Goodman. 1990. Slope Histogram Detection of Forged Signatures. *SPIE Conference on High Speed Inspection, Barcoding, and Character Recognition*. SPIE. Vol. 1384. 293–304.

9

SYMBOL RECOGNITION

9.1 HANDPRINTED CHARACTERS

The major problem encountered when attempting to classify handprinted characters is their inconsistency. It is not possible for a human to print a character in exactly the same way twice. Many matching algorithms, especially those using templates, depend on consistency in order to function, and the further apart the template is from the input glyph, the less likely the correct match is to be located. What is needed are methods that use characterizations of general shape and structure, rather than pixel-level features (which are more likely to vary from glyph to glyph).

In this section a number of methods for classifying images as handprinted digits will be considered, both statistical and structural. In addition to providing an exposure to a diverse collection of methods, it is also possible that all of the algorithms can be applied to the same glyph. The result of using many different techniques is an increased confidence in the result in the cases where they agree, and an increased ability to determine the possibility of error in cases where they do not agree. It is generally considered that an algorithm that can indicate that it cannot classify a glyph is superior to one that performs the classification in error. The goal is to minimize the error rate, even if this increases the number of unclassified characters. An inability to classify is termed a *rejection*, and is not normally counted as an error.

Four methods for handprinted-digit recognition will be examined in this section. The test data, which cannot be included on the CD for reason of copyright, consists of two sets of 1000 digits each, in glyph form. One set was used for training the recognition algorithms, and the other was used for assessing their performance. One should not test a recognizer using the same data on which it was trained.

One way to examine the behavior of a symbol-recognition program is to use the *confusion matrix*. This is a two-dimensional array of classifications; the columns represent the classification of the symbol by the algorithm under scrutiny, and the rows represent the actual value of the symbol.

For example, the following confusion matrix was computed for a program that would recognize the four letters *A*, *B*, *C*, and *D*:

	A	B	C	D
A	96	2	0	2
B	0	98	0	2
C	0	0	100	0
D	0	1	0	99

There were 100 test glyphs of each type used in this example; note that each row sums to 100. This will be true unless there are rejected (unclassifiable) glyphs in the data set. The values in the first row represent the number of classifications of each type for the glyphs that were actually *A*. Most of the *A* glyphs were in fact classified as *A*, but some were not. In the failed cases, we can see what, and how severe, the confusion was.

The columns represent the data as classified. For example, in the last column we can see that for the glyphs that were classified as *D*, 99 of them were correct, and four were in error. There is a lot of useful information in a confusion matrix, as will be seen in later sections.

Properties of the Character Outline

In a collection of interesting articles, Shridhar et al. (Shridhar 1986; Shridhar 1987; Kimura 1991) describe a collection of topological features that can be used to classify handprinted numerals. Most of these features are properties of the outline, or *profile*, of the numeral. For instance, a digit *8* might be described as having a smooth profile on both the left and the right sides, and as having the width at a minimum in the center region. Not all handprinted *8* digits would be recognized by this description, and certainly some other digits might also have this description; the idea is to provide a sufficient number of descriptions for each digit that a high recognition rate can be achieved.

Figure 9.1 shows how the left and right profiles are defined and calculated for a sample digit *9*. After the digit is isolated and thresholded, the number of background pixels between the left side of the character's bounding box and the first black pixel is counted and saved for each row in the bounding box. This gives a sampled version of the left profile (LP), which is then scaled to a standard size;

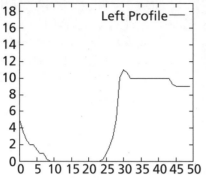 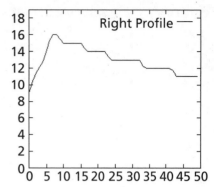

Figure 9.1 Simple properties of the Left and Right profiles. These are the profiles for a 9 glyph.

in this case, 52 pixels. A similar process gives the right profile (RP); the difference is that the last black pixel on each row is saved.

Having the profiles, the next step is to measure some of their properties. For example, one important property is the location of the extrema: L_{min} is the location of the minimum value on the left profile, and L_{max} is the location of the maximum value. There are similar properties R_{min} and R_{max} on the right profile. For a *9* digit, it would be expected that L_{min} would occur in the top half of the character, as seen in Figure 9.1, but for a *6*, L_{min} would be in the lower half. Using these measures alone can often distinguish between some of the digits.

At this stage some other simple measures can also be useful, such as:

❑ $W(k)$ = width at position k = $RP(k) - LP(k)$.
❑ W_{max}, the maximum width of the digit; this is $W(k)$ at some point k where $RP(k) - LP(k)$ is a maximum.
❑ R, the ratio of height to maximum width.

The use of R alone can identify a large majority of the *1* digits; an *1* has a very large R value compared with all other digits.

Now another set of features can be defined on the left and right profiles based on first differences. Let $LDIF(k) = LP(k) - LP(k-1)$ and $RDIF(k) = RP(k) - RP(k-1)$. Large values of LDIF imply a large change in the profile at the specified point, and this can assist in classification. For example, the change in the profile of the *9* in Figure 9.1 near position 30 would give a large value of LDIF at this point, and that fact is characteristic of the digits *3* and *9*. The locations of the actual peaks in LDIF and RDIF and their values happen to be quite important in characterizing numerals, and the peaks are located using a range rather than a single position. Thus, a digit *5* would have the RDIF peak near the top of the digit,

Feature #	Feature calculation	Feature #	Feature calculation
1	$L_{peak} < 10; 2 <= R_2 <= 50$	31	$RP(R_{min}) = RP(R_{max})$ where R_{min} in the range $5 <= R_1 <= 25$, and R_{max} in $1 <= R_1 <= R_{min}$
2	$L_{peak} < 5; 2 <= R_2 <= 10$		
3	$L_{peak} > 5; 2 <= R_2 <= 15$		
4	$L_{peak} > 10; 2 <= R_2 <= 15$	32	$RP(R_{min}) = RP(R_{max})$, R_{min} in the range $5 <= R_1 <= 25$ and R_{max} in the range $1 <= R_1 <= R_{min}$
5	$L_{peak} > 10; 2 <= R_2 <= 20$		
6	$L_{peak} > 5; 2 <= R_2 <= 25$		
7	$L_{peak} > 5; 5 <= R_2 <= 15$	33	$RP(R_{min}) = RP(R_{max})$, R_{min} in $5 <= R1 <= 25$; R_{max} in $R_{min} <= R_1 <= 40$
8	$L_{peak} > 5; 5 <= R_2 <= 35$		
9	$L_{peak} > 10; 5 <= R_2 <= 40$	34	$L_{max} < L_{min}$; L_{max} in $1 <= R_2 <= 30$; L_{min} in $1 <= R_2 <= L_{max}$
10	$L_{peak} > 10; 10 <= R_2 <= 30$		
11	$L_{peak} > 10; 15 <= R_2 <= 40$	35	$L_{max} < L_{min}$; L_{max} in $10 <= R_2 <= 30$; L_{min} in $10 <= R_2 <= L_{max}$
12	$L_{peak} < 5; 25 <= R_2 <= 50$		
13	$L_{peak} > 10; 30 <= R_2 <= 50$	36	$L_{max} < L_{min}$; L_{max} in $10 <= R_1 <= 30$; L_{min} in $10 <= R_1 <= L_{max}$
14	$L_{peak} < 5; 30 <= R_2 <= 50$		
15	$L_{peak} < 5; 35 <= R_2 <= 50$	37	$L_{max} < L_{min}$; L_{max} and L_{min} in range $15 <= R_1 <= 45$
16	$L_{peak} > 10; 35 <= R_2 <= 50$		
17	$L_{peak} > 5; 40 <= R_2 <= 50$	38	$L_{max} < L_{min}$; L_{max} and L_{min} in range $20 <= R_1 <= 50$
18	$R_{peak} > 10; 2 <= R_2 <= 50$	39	$L_{max} < L_{min}$; L_{max} and L_{min} in range $20 <= R_1 <= 50$
19	$R_{peak} > 10; 2 <= R_2 <= 15$		
20	$R_{peak} < 10; 2 <= R_2 <= 30$	40	$R_{min} < R_{max}$; R_{min} in $1 <= R_1 <= 30$ and R_{max} in $1 <= R_1 <= R_{min}$
21	$R_{peak} < 5; 2 <= R_2 <= 45$		
22	$R_{peak} < 10; 25 <= R_2 <= 45$	41	$R_{min} < R_{max}$; R_{min}, R_{max} in range $20 <= R_1 <= 35$
23	$R_{peak} > 10; 25 <= R_2 <= 50$		
24	$R_{peak} < 5; 25 <= R_2 <= 50$	42	$R_{min} < R_{max}$; R_{min}, R_{max} in range $35 <= R_1 <= 50$
25	$R_{peak} > 10; 30 <= R_2 <= 50$		
26	$R_{peak} > 5; 35 <= R_2 <= 50$	43	$W(20) >= W(40)$
27	$R_{peak} > 10; 35 <= R_2 <= 50$	44	$W(25) >= W(10)$
28	$R_{peak} > 5; 40 <= R_2 <= 50$	45	$W(25) >= W(40)$
		46	$W(25) >= W(45)$
29	$R_{min}(1 <= R_1 <= 30)$ is less than $R_{max2}(R_{min} <= R_1 <= 30)$ and greater than $R_{max1}(1 <= R_1 <= R_{min})$	47	Ratio > 2.5
30	$R_{min}(10 <= R_1 <= 40)$ is less than $R_{max2}(R_{min} <= R_1 <= 40)$ and greater than $R_{max1}(1 <= R_1 <= R_{min})$	48	$W_{min} < W_{max1}$ and $W_{min} < W_{max2}$ where $W_{min} = W(L_{min})$ between 10 and 40; W_{max1} is max of W between 1 and L_{min}; W_{max2} is max of W from L_{min} to 50.

Figure 9.2 The 48 profile features used to recognize digits.

and the peak would have a relatively large value. This set of features is not comprehensive. In all, 48 features are used and others could be defined. The features used in the recognizer described here (Shridhar 1986) are listed in Figure 9.2.

In the training phase, all 48 features are computed for each sample numeral and a feature vector is created in each case. The features are binary, being either TRUE or FALSE; for example, feature number 43 is TRUE if the width of the character at row 20 is greater than or equal to the width at row 40 (W(20) >= W(40)). Then all of the resulting bit strings for each digit are searched for common elements, and the features in common for each digit class are stored in a library. Matching is performed by extracting the profiles of the input image and measuring and saving the bit string (feature vector) that results. This string is matched against the common elements of the templates—this is obviously very fast since only bit operations are involved. A perfect match of a library bit string against an input string results in the corresponding digit class being assigned to the input digit.

The bit strings identified for the sample data (1000 digits) used for this purpose are:

```
1234567890123456789012345678901234567890123456789012345678
*******0**0**********1******0**0******0****1*1**0
***************0******1*******************1*1
***************0********1*************0****0**2
0****1*******0*****1*1****0****000*******0*****13
***********0*******0**********0***00*******10*4
0*0*********0*****0*********************1******15
1*****0*********************0******0*1**1***16
*****1*1*****1*******1****0****0*0************7
***00***000*0**0***1************0****0**0****18
**0*0*********0****1****0****00******0*1*****9
```

where * represents a "don't care" situation. The results from this method are, again, only acceptable at this stage, with an overall rate of 94.2%. The recognition rates for our samples are outlined in Table 9.1.

Table 9.1 Object Outline Method—Recognition Rates

	0	1	2	3	4	5	6	7	8	9
% Right	94	95	96	100	95	100	84	94	90	94
% Error	1	4	1	0	5	0	10	5	4	6
% Reject	5	1	3	0	0	0	6	1	6	0

The recognition rates could be improved by using multiple features sets for each digit. However, identifying optimal feature sets automatically is a computationally hard problem. One other option would be to specify the features in subsets: For example, a *6* may be classified by the fact that one of the features {2,6,7,21} is true, one of {5,43} is true, and all but one of {1,32,33,41} are true. Again, the number of possible combinations makes identification of optimal feature groupings a very difficult task.

Since an optimal template or set of templates is hard to find, one other possibility is to use a set of 1000 digits as training data and build a library or database of bit strings having known classifications. These are used to identify unknown glyphs using the standard statistical method: the bit string in the database that is closest, in a Euclidean sense, to the bit string obtained from the unknown glyph provides the classification.

The purely statistical method above does give a slightly higher recognition rate at 94.7%, but takes significantly longer to execute. In addition, some digits are recognized very well (100% of the *2*, *3*, and *5* samples) while others are quite poor (86% of *7*s). The program recp.c (on the CD) is an implementation of this algorithm. It uses the file prof.db as the database of bit strings, obtained by processing the test digits.

Convex Deficiencies

A digitized character image consists of pixels, usually black on a background of white. Structural character-recognition techniques attempt to collect the black, or object, pixels into sets that represent a feature in a model of an object to be recognized. Features may be lines or curves, for example. Then an effort is made to determine the relationships between the features and to compare these against the relationships in the model, hoping to find a match. Statistical techniques involve the determination of statistical relationships between properties of object pixels. For example, the character image could be divided into nine equal areas and the average grey level or number of set pixels in each area could be measured. This gives nine values that can be stored in a feature vector and matched against existing template feature vectors by using a distance function.

There are numerous problems with existing methods, the basic one being that none of them work well enough in all situations. This suggests a slightly different approach—why not use the more numerous background pixels as a basis for classification? Noise, in the structural sense, ought to have less influence, but similar methods to the ones applied to object pixels should still yield results.

While most character-recognition systems are concerned with the pixels belonging to the characters themselves, there are good arguments to be made for analyzing the size, shape, and position of the background regions surrounding the character image. Certainly the number and position of the *holes* has been used—

an *8*, for example, has two holes, one in the upper part and one in the lower part of the character image, and a *0* has one in the middle. However, there are other such features that might be used to classify images—for example, a numeral *2* has a left-facing concave region in the top half of the image and a right-facing one in the bottom half. A more complete analysis of these *convex deficiencies* may permit the development of a classification scheme based on the background regions.

For use with digital character images, a relatively crude but effective scheme has been developed. From each background pixel in an input image an attempt is made to draw a line in each of the four major directions (up, down, left, right). If at least three of these lines encounter an object pixel, then the original pixel is labelled with the direction in which an object pixel was *not* encountered—this is called the *open* direction. If none of the four directions are open then the pixel concerned is part of a hole, and is labelled with a zero. Figure 9.3 shows the direction labels, and illustrates the process of locating and labelling the convex deficiencies.

Some of the holes identified in this way are not holes at all, but are part of a convoluted region in the image. A real hole will have boundary pixels that all belong to the object—if this is not true then the hole is false, and it is converted into a region labeled by its most common nonobject neighbor. Figure 9.4 shows the C code needed to locate and classify the basic convex deficiencies in the raster image.

After all the regions are labelled, they are counted and measured. Very small regions, relative to the number of pixels in the object, are ignored, and the largest four regions are used to classify the image. Sometimes a relatively simple relationship exists. For example, 99% of all zeros can be identified by the large central

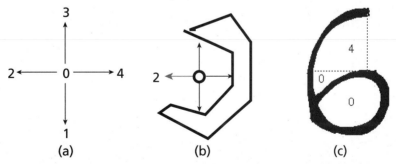

Figure 9.3 Locating convex deficiencies. (a) Codes for the directions. (b) Background pixels are tested to find the open directions (this one is 2). (c) Regions found for a 6—one of the holes (connected to the 4 region) is not real, and will be connected to another region.

```
int czones (struct image *x)
{
    int i,j,k,left,right,up,down;
    struct image *z=0;

    copy (x, &z, &k);
    for (i=0; i<z->info->nr; i++)
        for (j=0; j<z->info->nc; j++)
        {
            if (x->data[i][j] == 0) z->data[i][j] = 255;
            else
            {
                up = 0; down = 0; left = 0; right = 0;

                for (k=i-1; k>=0; k--)/* Check upwards */
                    if (x->data[k][j] == 0)
                    {
                        up = 1; break;
                    }
                for (k=i+1; k<x->info->nr; k++)/* Check
                        down */
                    if (x->data[k][j] == 0)
                    {
                        down = 1; break;
                    }
                for (k=j; k>=0; k--)/* Check left */
                    if (x->data[i][k] == 0)
                    {
                        left = 1; break;
                    }
                for (k=j+1; k<x->info->nc; k++)/*Check
                        right*/
                    if (x->data[i][k] == 0)
                    {
                        right = 1; break;
                    }
/* Consolidate these directions */
                if (left && up && right && down)
                z->data[i][j] = 0;
```

Figure 9.4 Sample C code for finding and classifying convex deficiencies.

```
                else if (left && up && right)
                z->data[i][j] = 1;/* Open down */
                else if (up && right && down)
                z->data[i][j] = 2;/* Open left */
                else if (right && down && left)
                z->data[i][j] = 3;/* Up */
                else if (down && left && up)
                z->data[i][j] = 4;
                else z->data[i][j] = 255;
        }
    }
}
```

Figure 9.4 (continued)

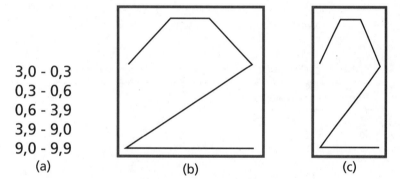

```
3,0 - 0,3
0,3 - 0,6
0,6 - 3,9
3,9 - 9,0
9,0 - 9,9
  (a)                    (b)                    (c)
```

Figure 9.5 An example vector template. (a) The coordinates of the vector endpoints for a 2 template. (b) Vectors drawn on a 10 × 10 grid. (c) Vectors drawn on 20 × 20 grid.

hole and lack of other convex deficiencies. The next more complex scheme uses relative positions of the regions; for example, an *8* has two holes, one above the other, a left-facing region on the left of the two holes, and a right-facing region on the right of the holes. The most complex schemes require shape information in addition to size and position. As an example, some *7* digits and some *3* digits both have a large left-facing region on the left side of the image. However, this region is convex for the *7* but nonconvex for the *3*, as seen in Figure 9.5. This fact can be used to discriminate between some *7*s and *3*s.

An important aspect of the method involves not being too specific about the sizes of the regions. The algorithm discards as unimportant any region that has an area less than 10% of the object. Then regions are classified as large or small. In addition, the regions are sorted according to size and only the largest, whatever the actual area, are used. For example, when looking for a 2, only the largest two regions are examined: one is expected to be a left-facing region at the top, and the other is expected to be a right-facing region at the bottom. Position, too, is intentionally classified in only a crude manner as top, bottom, left, or right, with a special flag set for those regions that are sufficiently close to the center (either horizontally or vertically or both). This provides an overall description of the background geometry that provides enough information to classify the image according to digit type, but is not overly affected by the usual variations in line thickness, orientation, size, and shape found in handprinted character images.

Table 9.2 provides a sample set of digit descriptions in terms of convex deficiencies. It is not complete; sometimes a dozen different descriptions are needed for a single digit. Still, it should serve to give the flavor of the kind of description that will work.

The recognition rate achieved using this method is acceptable, averaging about 94%. Table 9.3 details the recognition rate for convex deficiencies.

This approach has the advantage of not requiring a thinning step (Holt 1987;

Table 9.2 Convex Deficiencies Digit Descriptions

Digit	Open Direction	Size	Location	Shape
0	0	middle	center	convex
1	None	—	—	—
2	2	middle	upper left	—
	4	middle	lower right	—
3	2	large	left-of	nonconvex
	4	small	right	—
4	3	middle	upper	—
5	4	middle	upper right	—
	2	middle	lower left	—
6	4	middle	above	—
	0	middle	lower	—
7	2	middle	left	—
8	0	middle	upper	—
	0	middle	lower	—
	2	small	left	—
	4	small	right	—
9	0	middle	not-center, above	—
	4	middle	lower	—

Table 9.3 Recognition Rate—Convex Deficiencies

0	1	2	3	4	5	6	7	8	9
99%	94%	98%	96%	94%	90%	90%	93%	95%	92%

Zhang 1984), although smoothing the outline does help, and a morphological closing step might improve the rates for *8, 6,* and *9.*

The 94% recognition figure could be improved with the addition of more feature sets, or sets that discriminated more thoroughly. Once the obvious features are included, what remains is essentially a matter of common sense and trial-and-error to find the features that discriminate the best. recc.c is the sample implementation of this method. If run as:

```
recc digit.pbm
```

the classification of the digit seen in the image will be printed at the console screen.

Vector Templates

Template-matching techniques in many forms have been applied to the problem of recognizing handprinted digits using a computer. The basic idea is that each digit has a particular shape that can be captured in a small set of models, usually stored as raster images. An incoming (unknown) digit, also in raster form, is compared against each template, and the one that matches most closely is selected as belonging to the same digit class as the unknown. The system that performs template matching can be "taught" new forms by simply adding new templates to its sets. This is often done when an incoming digit can't be identified well enough; a human classifies it, and the unknown image can be added as a new template if desired.

Once the learning phase is complete, template-based recognition methods work quite well for machine-printed characters. These are uniform in size, shape, and orientation, and preprocessing methods can be devised that produce quite recognizable characters for any particular document or set of documents that were created in the same way. On the other hand, characters printed by a human show a large degree of variation in shape, size, orientation, and grey-level intensity, even in sets of characters printed by the same person. This variation mitigates against the use of templates.

One likely solution is to represent the template digits as vectors. This is commonly done in computer typography systems, where the fonts are stored in vector form. This permits easy scaling and rotation, allowing one set of characters to be used for all sizes, plus bold and italic forms. The fonts were originally produced, painstakingly and with human assistance, so as to be of high visual quality when scaled to large sizes and thick line widths. Although fonts are often stored as outlines, it seems that the vector form generally has the properties needed of a good template.

For applications in digit recognition, vectors that form the skeleton of the characters are used rather than those that form the outline. This yields a good abstraction of the shape, and permits the lines to be thickened in an arbitrary way. The templates are stored as sets of four integers, those being the starting and ending row and column on a standard grid. All templates have the same size, 10 by 10; this means that all coordinates in any template have an integer value between 0 and 9 inclusive. Given a scale and rotation, then, all templates in the collection would be modified in a consistent way.

There have been some efforts to normalize handprinted characters, but these are only successful for certain types of variation. Orientation, slant, and scale can be accounted for to some extent, but other aspects, such as line thickness, have not been. Thus, either an enormous number of raster templates are needed to account for all possible variations, or standard template-matching techniques fail. There is enough difference in shape between different digits to permit human recognition at high rates of success; perhaps the templates should abstract the shape more accurately than possible using a raster model, which depends on individual pixel-to-pixel correspondence and not more global shape properties.

A vector template can be produced using only a pencil and perhaps some graph paper, and indeed, the first set of templates was generated in just this way. An example appears in Figure 9.5, which shows a template for the digit 2. Figure 9.5 shows the vector coordinates that were obtained manually from a line drawing of a 2 on a 10 $\times$ 10 grid. This is drawn as lines (Figure 9.5b) using the original scale, and also using a new scale: 20 $\times$ 10 (Figure 9.5c). This particular template is, by itself, able to match over 80% of the sample 2 images encountered in the test data set, when the matching method described below was used.

It is also possible to create a template from a data image, and this might be desirable when starting to process data from a new source. The first step in this process is to threshold and then thin the input image. Thinning can be done using any competent algorithm: we have used both Holt's variation on Zhang-Suen and the (Section 2.2) force-based method to yield acceptable sets of skeletal pixels. The result is a binary image in which only skeletal pixels have a value of 0; all others are 1. Figure 9.6 gives an example of this process, showing the original input image, the thresholded version, and the skeleton as located by both thinning methods.

At this point the pixels are collected into sets, each representing a curve. An end pixel is found (either a pixel connected only to one other, or an arbitrary

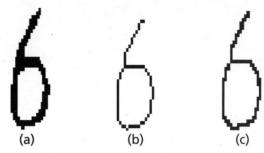

(a)   (b)   (c)

Figure 9.6 Converting a raster digit image into a vector template. (a) The original digit image. (b) Thinned version, using Zhang-Suen. (c) Thinned version using force-based thinning (Parker et al).

starting point if no such pixel exists) and the set of pixels connected to it are saved, taking care to trace only one curve. The method described in Lam and Suen works very well here. Finally, a set of vectors is extracted from each curve using a recursive splitting technique, a relatively simple and common method for vectorizing small, simple images. Briefly, the endpoints of the curve are presumed initially to be the start and endpoints of a line, and the distances between all pixels in the curve and the mathematical line are computed. If the maximum distance for this set of pixels exceeds a predetermined threshold, then the curve is broken into two curves at the pixel having that maximum distance, and the same procedure is applied again (recursively) to each of the two curve sections. Alternatively, if the maximum distance is less than the threshold, then the curve is presumed to be an approximation to a line, and the endpoint coordinates are saved as one of the vectors in the template. The coordinates are scaled down to the standard 10×10 grid after the extent of all of the vectors has been determined. Figure 9.7 shows this vectorization process applied to the skeleton of Figure 9.6b, and shows its final appearance after being scaled. This particular template matched over half of all of the *6* images in the test data set. The program that creates templates from images actually generates C code for the initialization of the template data array in the matching program.

Once all of the templates have been generated and there are multiple templates for each digit, the system is ready to recognize digits. An incoming image is first preprocessed in any desired fashion and is then thresholded. The width of the lines in the image is then estimated using horizontal and vertical scans. A histogram containing the widths of the black portions of the image on all slices is produced, and the mode of this histogram has been found to be a close enough approximation to the actual line width. A better approximation can be had by computing the

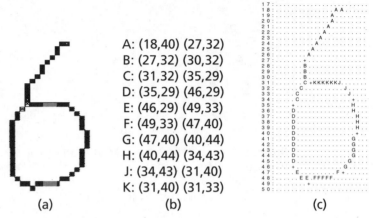

A: (18,40) (27,32)

B: (27,32) (30,32)

C: (31,32) (35,29)

D: (35,29) (46,29)

E: (46,29) (49,33)

F: (49,33) (47,40)

G: (47,40) (40,44)

H: (40,44) (34,43)

J: (34,43) (31,40)

K: (31,40) (31,33)

(a) (b) (c)

Figure 9.7 Finding vectors in the thinned image. (a) The curves encountered (2 of them). (b) Extracted vector coordinates. (c) Vectors (linear features) marked in the thinned image.

gradient at each pixel on the outline of the digit and finding the width of a slice through the digit in a direction perpendicular to the outline at that point, but this rarely gives a result sufficiently better to be worth the extra computation time. While the line width is being computed, the actual extent of the digit image is also found so that the templates can be scaled. This is saved as the coordinates of the upper left and the lower right pixels.

At this point the scaling factors for the templates can be computed. The templates will be scaled in the x and the y directions independently, and the same scale factors can be applied to all templates. The factors include an adjustment that results in a correct scaling accounting for the thickness of the line. Now the template vectors are drawn into an otherwise clear image the same size as the input image, producing an initial raster template that represents the scaled skeleton. Finally, each pixel is "grown" equally on all sides to give a line width comparable to that found in the input image. The result is a raster template with some similar properties to those found in the input image. Figure 9.8 illustrates the process of generating a raster template from a vector one.

The matching process is somewhat different from that used in other template matching systems, but the goal is still to produce a measure of distance between the template and the image. The first step is to locate those pixels that are black in both images. These have a distance between them of zero, and are ignored in future processing. Next, each black pixel in the image has its nearest corresponding pixel in the template located and marked. The 8-distance between these pixels is noted, and a sum of these distances is computed. After all image pixels have been assigned corresponding pixels in the template the total distance is an initial measure of similarity. Efforts have been made to reduce the distance total by looking at pairs of corresponding pixels and swapping those having a smaller distance after being swapped. This is a very time-consuming process, and does not greatly improve the distance.

At this point a numeric value that can be used as a goodness of match metric has been found. It is normalized to a per-pixel distance and stored as a measure for the digit having the same class as the template. The class having the smallest such measure over all templates is chosen as the class of the input digit image. Figure 9.9 shows the overlapping pixels and a distance map for the example begun in Figure 9.8.

There is a problem with using this method to match a *1*, or any other object that has an extreme ratio of height to width. The problem is that the vectors for

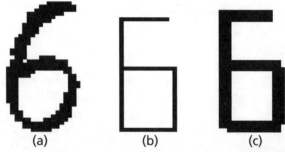

(a)   (b)   (c)

Figure 9.8 Matching using a vector template. (a) Input digit image (to be matched). (b) Scaled vector template. (c) Thickened vector template (not a good match here).

(a)   (b)

Figure 9.9 The final stages of the template match. (a) Pixels that overlap between the template and the image. (b) Distance map between template and image. Darker pixels are farther away.

almost any template will match after having been scaled to fit. For example, the sides of a *0* will be brought together and the central hole will be filled in due to the width of the two lines. When recognizing *1* digits, we used one template for those cases where the image is sufficiently wide (2% of the sample) and a combination of aspect ratio and line width vs. image width for the rest of the cases. Once the *1* digits were recognized, templates were used in all of the remaining cases.

The software implementing this method is called recv.c. It has been executed on both a Sun SPARC II workstation and an IBM PC. The time needed for preprocessing varies depending on the kind of image acquired, but the template scaling and drawing takes 0.019 seconds per template on the Sun. Since there are 28 different templates, the total time needed to create the raster templates is 0.55 seconds. This could easily be done in parallel, which would reduce the real time needed. Pixel pairing and matching takes an average of 0.015 seconds per template, or 0.84 seconds per input image. The average time to recognize a digit without using parallel processing is 4.4 seconds on a Sun SPARCstation 2, and about twice as long on the PC.

Recognition rates are relatively good, at least on the 1000 digits of test data. The overall rate of recognition was 94.3%; Table 9.4 details the results.

There are multiple templates for each digit, but not necessarily the same number. Table 9.5 outlines the number of templates per digit.

The vector template method has been applied to symbols extracted from maps, and to music recognition. For an example of this, Figure 9.10 shows a quarter rest, the vectors, and a scaled template. Experiments have shown that scale is still an issue in that there is a better rate of recognition when the template and the data are about the same size. The method works best when large glyphs are vectorized into templates.

Table 9.4 Vector Template Digit Recognition Rates

	0	1	2	3	4	5	6	7	8	9
Correct	99%	94%	98%	96%	94%	92%	90%	93%	95%	92%

Table 9.5 Number of Templates per Digit

0	1	2	3	4	5	6	7	8	9
1	1	3	1	5	3	2	4	4	4

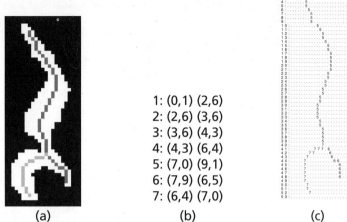

1: (0,1) (2,6)
2: (2,6) (3,6)
3: (3,6) (4,3)
4: (4,3) (6,4)
5: (7,0) (9,1)
6: (7,9) (6,5)
7: (6,4) (7,0)

(a)   (b)   (c)

Figure 9.10 Vector templates applied to music symbol recognition. (a) A quarter rest. (b) The vectors extracted, in template creation. (c) The final template.

Neural Nets

The use of artificial neural systems (ANS) for various recognition tasks is well-founded in the literature (Aarts 1989; Ansari 1993; Carpenter 1988; Fukushima 1983; Mui 1994; Shang 1994; Touretzky 1989; Yong 1988). The advantage of using *neural nets*, as they are commonly called, is not that the solution they provide is especially elegant or even fast; it is that the system ''learns'' its own algorithm for the classification task, and does so on actual samples of data. Indeed, the same basic neural net program that recognizes digits can also be used to recognize squares, circles, and triangles.

To thoroughly explore the use of neural nets is not the goal of this section; instead, the goal is to provide a summary of neural nets for the uninitiated, to show the utility of the method, and to provide pointers to more detailed information.

A Simple Neural Net

Before devising a neural net for recognizing digits, let's look at a simple example in an effort to explain the basic ideas. What is commonly called a neural net is an interconnected set of processing elements (PEs), each of which performs a very simple calculation. A single processing element, as seen in Figure 9.11, has some number of *inputs*, a *weight value* for each input, and an *output value*, which can be fanned out and used as inputs by other elements. Each of these values is numeric. The value associated with any node is called its *activation*, and is simply the sum of each input value multiplied by its respective weight value. The output

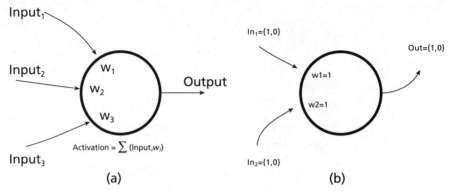

Figure 9.11 Neural net basics. (a) A single processing element with three inputs. (b) A processing element configured to operate as an AND function with two inputs.

of the PE may be simply the activation value, but is most often a function of the activation: the *activation function*, sometimes called the *output function*.

A processing element is a primitive model of a neuron. Like a real neuron, there are many input values that interact (are summed) to produce an output. The response of a neuron is to *fire*, or to send a pulse-like signal to its output. In a real neuron some of the inputs actually inhibit the firing; these would correspond to PE inputs having a negative weight value. Other neuronal inputs encourage the neuron to fire, which corresponds to a positive weight. Often a single input is not sufficient to cause firing, which is why a PE sums all of the weighted inputs.

The activation function ensures that the PE output values fall into a predefined legal range. For example, the PE in Figure 9.11b accepts binary input values and generates a binary output value. Since there are two inputs and both weights are 1, the four possible activations for this PE are:

Inputs		Activation
In1	In2	
0	0	0
0	1	1
1	0	1
1	1	2

Since the output is supposed to be binary some thresholding must be performed, and this is done by the activation function. Suppose that this PE is to respond in the same way as a Boolean AND; in that case, the output should be 0 unless both inputs are 1, in which case the output should be 1. An activation function that performs in this manner is:

$$f(A) = \begin{cases} 0 & \text{if } a < 1.5 \\ 1 & \text{if } a > 1.5 \end{cases} \qquad \text{(EQ 9.1)}$$

That is, if the activation is 1 or less the output is 0; otherwise it is 1.

Processing elements are not used alone, but are connected as a *graph*, more commonly called a *network*. The output from a set of PEs can be used as inputs to another, or to many. There can be as many stages (*layers*) as is desired, and as many elements in each layer as needed.

Figure 9.12 shows two quite simple nets. The first (9.12a) is a combination of three of the two-input AND elements configured to act as a four-input AND. The interconnections are done in the obvious way, which is basically the same way we would wire up AND gates in a logic circuit. The second example (9.12b) shows a two-input AND that has a TRUE output and a FALSE output. The first layer of processing elements (to the left, and called the *input layer*) simply distribute their inputs over two outputs. The second layer of elements (to the right, called the output layer) each computes one of the AND values of their inputs. One responds if the inputs are both 1 (TRUE), while the other responds in all other situations. A simple way to accomplish this is to set the input weights of the input elements to 1 and pass this value through to the output. The TRUE element of the output layer is an AND element from Figure 9.11b, and the FALSE element is a TRUE element but with the thresholding in the activation function reversed (i.e., return 0 if the activation is > 1, and 1 otherwise).

Pleased with our success at this task, we now try to implement other logic functions. An OR is easy enough, but problems are encountered with the exclusive OR function (XOR). No matter what weights or activation functions we try, the

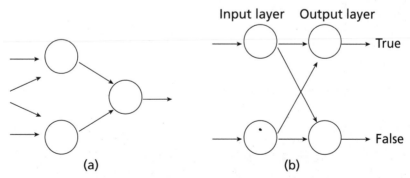

(a)   (b)

Figure 9.12 Simple neural nets. (a) A four-input AND, built from three two-input ANDs. (b) A two-input AND having discrete TRUE/FALSE output values.

XOR cannot be implemented. Why not? Let's take a closer look at what the PE for AND is actually doing.

In Figure 9.13a, the four possible inputs for the AND element are plotted in two dimensions; they can, in fact, be thought of as vectors. The line $1.5 = w_1\text{Input}_1 + w_2\text{Input}_2$ has been plotted in the same graph; note that the line divides the input values into two sets: one set corresponding to an output of 1 (which is circled in the figure), and one set with an output of 0. This is what neural nets do in general: divide N-dimensional space into regions, each corresponding to an output value.

Now examine the problem of simulating an XOR in this light, as in Figure 9.13b. Note that there is no single straight line that can be drawn that has the input values that correspond to a 1 output in one region without also including at least one of the other inputs. This means that it is not possible to find a neural net of this type that can solve the XOR problem.

This is not to say that the problem cannot be solved. The solution entails straight lines, as seen in Figure 9.14. The middle region (the one between the two lines) corresponds to an output of 1, while the other two regions result in an output of 0. This partitioning of the input space is accomplished by adding an extra layer of processing elements (the *hidden layer*) between the input and output layers. Indeed, the use of hidden layers permits a neural net to solve quite complex problems.

An advantage of neural networks over more traditional computational methods

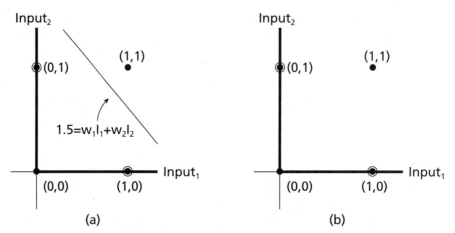

Figure 9.13 What the neural net actually computes. (a) The division of 2-space for the AND element. All inputs on one side of the line correspond to TRUE outputs (which are circled), and all inputs on the other side correspond to FALSE. (b) For the XOR function, there is no single line that can divide the TRUE (circled) points from the FALSE.

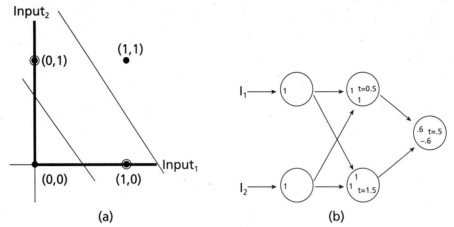

Figure 9.14 Solution to the XOR problem. (a) Dividing the solution space into three regions allows the middle region (the one containing the TRUE outputs) to be isolated from the other (FALSE) region. (b) The neural net that corresponds to this has a hidden layer of PEs that permits the extra subdivision. The numbers beside each input are the weights, and the values of t are the thresholds applied to the activation to get the output. Outputs greater than the activation yield a 1; otherwise the output is 0.

is the fact that a net can *learn* to solve a particular problem. Learning, in a neural net sense, means the determination of the weights for each processing element. The nets that have been discussed to this point have been simple, and have had the weights already determined. In common use a net is trained by presenting a sample of the data with known properties to the inputs, and then adjusting the weights until the outputs are correct. This process is repeated many times with different classes of data until the weights appear to stabilize, at which point the learning process is complete, and the net can be used to classify the inputs for unknown cases.

There are various ways in which a net can be "taught" a set of weights. The method that will be used for handprinted character recognition is known as *backpropagation*, and is commonly used for this sort of problem. It is based on a feedback of the outputs to the previous layers, and uses a least-squares/gradient-descent optimization method.

A Backpropagation Net for Digit Recognition

With the previous discussion on neural nets in mind, a three-layer backpropagation net (BPN) such as the one shown in Figure 9.15 is proposed. There are 48 nodes in the input layer, one node for each pixel in an image of 8 rows × 6 columns.

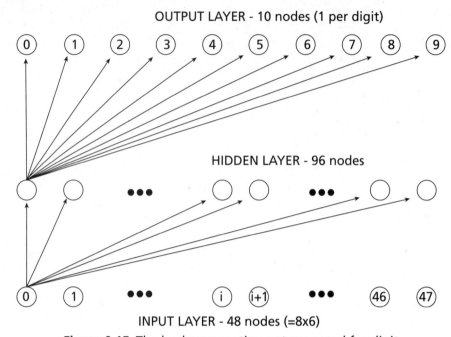

Figure 9.15 The backpropagation net proposed for digit recognition. Only some of the many connections between nodes are illustrated here.

The raster input digits are scaled to this size as a first step. The bounding box for each character is used rather than image size so that the scaling effect is consistent over all of the data images.

Initially the weights are unknown. After the net is trained, the pixels of a digit image are used as the 48 input values; the output PE corresponding to the correct digit will have a 1 output, with the remaining output PEs being 0.

Training proceeds by applying the pixels of a known glyph to the inputs of the net. Once a scaled image is applied to the input layer, each input node sends its value to all of the hidden nodes. The output associated with a hidden node is the weighted sum of all of the input values:

$$H_i = \sum_{j=0}^{48} W_{ij}I_j \qquad \text{(EQ 9.2)}$$

where H_i is the value associated with hidden node i, I_j is the value of input node j, and W_{ij} is the weight associated with the link between input node j and hidden node i. The output from hidden node i may simply be this value H_i or, in the case where a binary output is needed, it may be a *logistic* function $f(H_i)$

$= (1 + e^{-H_i})^{-1}$. In either case, a similar situation now exists between the hidden layer and the output layer; each output node has a value associated with it that is the weighted sum of all of the hidden nodes:

$$O_k = \sum_{i=0}^{96} f(H_i)X_{ki} \qquad \text{(EQ 9.3)}$$

where O_k is the value associated with output node k, $f(H_i)$ is the output from hidden node i, and X_{ki} is the weight applied between hidden node i and output node k. The binary output from this output node is $f(O_k)$, and since there is one output node per digit, it is to be hoped that the largest output response will be from the node associated with the actual input digit class.

Before the net can be expected to correctly classify any digits it must be trained. This amounts to determining the weight W_{ij} and X_{ki} that lead to a correct classification. Initially these weights were initially set to random values between -0.5 and $+0.5$, which should lead to random classifications. The net is trained by applying known data to the inputs; that is, glyphs whose classification is known. The output values for all output nodes are computed, and the result is compared against the correct result. For example, when a three is used as input data, all of the output nodes should have the output value 0 except output node 3, which should be 1. The error at each output node k can therefore be represented by:

$$\delta_k = (D_k - O_k) \qquad \text{(EQ 9.4)}$$

where D_k is the correct output value for output node k and O_k is the output value computed for output node k. The error of node O_k can be thought to have been contributed to by all of the hidden nodes through the weights X_k, and so δ_k can be used to modify those weights to bring them closer to those needed to produce a correct classification. Minimizing the error E in the least-squares sense means minimizing:

$$E = \frac{1}{2} \sum_{k=1}^{10} \sigma_k^2 \qquad \text{(EQ 9.5)}$$

Due more to tradition than function, most BPN systems minimize this expression using the method of *steepest descent*, which has some serious shortcomings: it is slow, inefficient, and does not always converge to the overall (*global*) minimum. While there are much better schemes around (Masters 1995), we will stick to the most commonly encountered method and notation.

The method of steepest descent attempts to find the minimum of a function F of some number of variables N. The parameters to F can be thought of as a vector $\bar{x}$, for convenience. The process is iterative, consisting of the following steps:

1. Select a starting point in N space; this will be the vector $\bar{x}_0$.

2. Compute the gradient $\nabla F(\bar{x}_i)$ for the parameter vector $\bar{x}_i$; initially $i=0$, and is incremented each iteration.

3. Pick an appropriate step size d_s. This is a factor by which each component of the gradient will be multiplied.

4. Compute the next set of parameters (the next point in N-space) by:

$$\bar{x}_{i+1} = \bar{x}_i - d_s \, \nabla F(\bar{x}_i) \qquad \text{(EQ 9.6)}$$

5. Continue from step 2 until the error $F(\bar{x}_i) - F(\bar{x}_{i+1}) < \epsilon$, for some predetermined value ϵ.

The backpropagation learning algorithm uses this scheme to minimize the error (Equation 9.5) by adjusting the weights on all of the processing elements following the presentation of a known glyph to the input nodes. First the weights on the output nodes are adjusted, then the hidden nodes, and finally the input nodes. This is where the name *backpropagation* comes from: the changes to the weights propagates back from the output to the input.

After the mathematics of the gradient descent has been done (Freeman 1991) the weights on the output nodes are updated by:

$$X'_{ki} = X_{ki} + \eta \delta_k f'(O_k) f(H_i) \qquad \text{(EQ 9.7)}$$

and the hidden node weights are updated by:

$$W'_{ij} = W_{ij} + \eta \delta_i^h I_j \qquad \text{(EQ 9.8)}$$

where the error term for the hidden node i is:

$$\sigma_i^h = f'(H_i) \sum_k \sigma_k X_{ki} \qquad \text{(EQ 9.49)}$$

The value η in the expressions above is called the *learning rate parameter*, and controls the rate of convergence. A value near 0.25 is not unusual, but this can vary according to the type of problem being studied. A very nice discussion of this entire procedure, and of backpropagation nets in general, can be found in Freeman (1991).

Each application of a new training image to the input layer amounts to an iteration of the steepest-descent minimization of the error in the weights. After each known glyph (training data) is applied to the neural net inputs, the weights are updated and a new error term E is computed. When E reaches an acceptably small value, training can be stopped.

This three-layer net was trained using 1000 digits (100 drawn from each class) presented alternately to the inputs; that is, one sample of each class 0 through 9 produced by a single writer was presented, followed by another set 0–9, and so on. If all of the 0 digits were presented first, then the 1s and so on, the net would tend to forget the earlier digits and recognize only the later ones trained. After the training phase, a second set of 1000 digits from 100 different writers was used to test the recognition rate. The results were initially not very good, at least for nines (Table 9.6).

What was even more interesting was that when the same net was trained using the second set of data and used to recognize the first set (i.e., the opposite of the situation above) the results improved (Table 9.7).

An explanation for this may be that the digits in the second set are in some way more consistent, and do not provide a sufficiently diverse training set. The error found after training was not as good in the second case either, and perhaps more training data is needed. One common means of dealing with this problem (Gaines 1995) is to introduce noise into the training data. For example, when black training pixels are changed to white with a probability of 0.2, the recognition rate for nines in Table 9.5 increases to 88%. However, it may be useful to have one or two low-rate digits in the multiple classifier to note the effect on overall recognition, so the rates of Table 9.5 will be used.

The logistic function gives an almost binary output that can be used as a ranking, so that a neural net of this type can provide both a simple classification and a ranking of likely classifications that can be ordered according to likelihood. This will become important in the next chapter.

The neural-net software on the CD consists of two programs. The first, named nnlearn.c, trains the net on sample data. The weights resulting from this process are saved on a file named weights.dat. The second program is nnclass.c and this reads the weights from the file and attempts to recognize a glyph, which is in the form of a PBM image file. The file weights.dat contains weights obtained by training the net on the set of 1000 digits, and can be used in conjunction with the net software to perform actual recognitions. The program nncvt.c can be used to

Table 9.6 Backpropagation Net—Digit Recognition Rates (%)

	0	1	2	3	4	5	6	7	8	9
Correct	99	93	99	95	100	95	99	100	95	74

Table 9.7 Backpropagation Net—2nd Digit Recognition Rates (%)

	0	1	2	3	4	5	6	7	8	9
Correct	100	99	100	94	99	99	94	98	99	98

create a neural net input file (i.e., one suitable for nnclass.c) from a PBM/PGM image of a digit.

9.2 THE USE OF MULTIPLE CLASSIFIERS

There exists quite a variety of methods for handprinted-character recognition, and it may very well be that there is no one method that can be thought of as the ''best'' under all circumstances. Each algorithm has strengths and weaknesses, good ideas and bad. There is a way to take advantage of this variety: Apply many methods to the same recognition task, and have a scheme to merge the results; this should be successful over a wider range of inputs than would any individual method (Parker 1994). The weaknesses should, in an ideal situation, more or less cancel out rather than reinforcing each other, giving high recognition rates under many sets of conditions. This situation can be encouraged by discarding methods that are the same, at least as far as the classifications of the data are concerned.

In the previous section, four methods for classifying handprinted digits were discussed. Now the output from these will be combined to form a single classification.

Merging Multiple Methods

A classifier can produce one of three kinds of output. The simplest and probably the most common is a simple, unqualified expression of the class determined for the data object. For a digit-classification scheme, this would mean that the classifier might simply state ''this is a six,'' for example; this will be called a *type 1* response (Xu 1992). A classifier might also produce a ranking of the possible classes for a data object. In this case, the classifier may say: ''This is most likely a five, but could be a three, and is even less likely to be a two.'' The number of classes ranked need not be ten even in the case of digits, as some classes will be discarded as impossible. Probabilities are not associated with the ranking. This will be called a *type 2* response. Finally, a classifier may give a probability or other such confidence rating to each of the possible classes. This is the most specific case of all, since either a ranking or a classification can be produced from it. In this case, each possible digit would be given a confidence number that can be normalized to any specific range. This will be called a *type 3* response.

Any reasonable scheme for merging the results from multiple classifiers must deal with three important issues:

❏ The response of the multiple classifier must be the best one given the results of the individual classifiers. It should in some logical way represent the most likely true classification, even when presented with contradictory individual classifications.

❑ The classifiers in the system may produce different types of response. These must be merged into a coherent single response.

❑ The multiple classifier must yield the correct result more often than any of the individual classifiers, or there is no point to it.

The first problem above has various potential solutions for each of the possible type of response, and these will be dealt with first.

Merging Type 1 Responses

Given that the output of each of the classifiers is a single, simple classification value, the obvious way to combine them is by using a voting strategy. A majority voting scheme can be expressed as follows: let $C_i(x)$ be the result produced by classifier i for the digit image x, where that are k different classifiers in the system; then let $H(d)$ be the number of classifiers giving a classification of d for the digit image x, where d is one of $\{0,1,2,3,4,5,6,7,8,9\}$. H can be thought of as a histogram, and could be calculated in the following manner:

```
for (i=0; i<k; i++)
        H[ Ci(x) ] += 1;
```

The overall classification E, expressing the opinions of all of the k classifiers, could be:

$$
E(x) = \begin{cases} j & \text{if max(H(i))} = \text{H(j) and H(j)} > \dfrac{k}{2} \\ 10 & \text{otherwise} \end{cases} \quad \text{(EQ 9.10)}
$$

This is called a *simple majority vote* (SMV). For comparison, a *parliamentary majority vote* would simply select j so that $H(j)$ was a maximum. An easy generalization of this scheme replaces the constant $k/2$ in the above expression with $k \times \alpha$ for $0 <= \alpha <= 1$ (Xu 1992). This permits a degree of flexibility in deciding what degree of majority will be sufficient, and will be called a *weighted majority vote* (WMV). This scheme can be expressed as:

$$
E(x) = \begin{cases} j & \text{if max(H(i))} = \text{H(j) and H(j)} > \alpha k \\ 10 & \text{otherwise} \end{cases} \quad \text{(EQ 9.11)}
$$

For example, many important votes in government and administrative committees require a ⅔ majority in order to pass. This would be equivalent to a value of $\alpha = ⅔$ in Equation 9.9.

Neither of these two equations takes into account the possibility that all of the dissenting classifiers agree with each other. Consider the following cases: In case A, there are ten classifiers, with six of them supporting a classification of *6*, one supporting *5*, one supporting *2*, and two classifiers rejecting the input digit. In case B, using the same ten classifiers, six of them support the classification *6* and the other four all agree that it is a *5*. Do cases A and B both support a classification of *6*, and do they do so equally strongly?

One way to incorporate dissent into the decision is to let *max1* be the number of classifiers that support the majority classification *j* (*max1* = H(*j*), and to let *max2* be the number supporting the second most popular classification *h*(*max2*=H(*h*)). The classification becomes:

$$E(x) = \begin{cases} j & \text{if } \max(\text{H(i)}) = \text{H(j) and } \max 1 - \max 2 \geq \alpha k \\ 10 & \text{Otherwise} \end{cases} \qquad \text{(EQ 9.12)}$$

where α is between 0.0 and 1.0. This is called a *dissenting-weighted majority vote* (DWMV).

For the four classifier system being discussed, the SMV strategy gave the following results:

Correct: 994   Incorrect: 2   Rejected: 4

This is in spite of poor results (76% recognition) from the neural net classifier (#4) on nines—indeed, 100% of the nines are recognized by the multiple classifier. This begs the question "what is the contribution of any one classifier to the overall result?" To determine this for the SMV case is simple. The multiple classifier can be run using any three of the four individual classifiers, and the results can be compared against the five classifier case above to determine whether the missing classifier assisted in the classification. If omitting a classifier does not improve the results, it *can* be removed from consideration; if omitting a classifier improves the results, then that classifier *must* not be used at all.

Evaluation of WMV is a little more difficult, requiring an assessment of the effect of the value of α on the results. A small program was written that varied α from 0.05 to 0.95, classifying all sample digits on each iteration. This process was then repeated five more times, omitting one of the classifiers each time to again test the relative effect of each classifier on the overall success. With this much data, a numerical value is needed than can be used to assess the quality of the results. The recognition rate could be used alone, but this does not take into account that a rejection is much better than a misclassification; both would count against the recognition rate. A measure of *reliability* can be computed as:

$$\text{Reliability} = \frac{\text{Recognition}}{100\% - \text{Rejection}} \qquad \text{(EQ 9.13)}$$

The reliability value will be low when few misclassifications occur. Unfortunately, it will be high if recognition is only 50%, with the other 50% being rejections. This would not normally be thought of as acceptable performance. A good classifier will combine high reliability with a high recognition rate; in that case, why not simply use the product *reliability* $\times$ *recognition* as a measure of performance? In the 50/50 example above, this measure would have the value 0.5: reliability is 100% (1.0) and recognition is 50% (0.5). In a case where the recognition rate was 50%, with 25% rejections and 25% misclassifications, this measure will have the value 0.333, indicating that the performance is not as good. The value *reliability* $\times$ *recognition* will be called *acceptability*. The first thing that should be done is to determine which value of α gives the best results, and this is more accurately done when the data is presented in tabular form (Table 9.8).

Duplicate rows are not shown in the table. From this information it can be concluded that α should be between 0.25 and 0.5, for in this range the acceptability peaks without causing a drop in recognition rate.

DWMV also uses the α parameter, and can be evaluated in a fashion identical to what has just been done for WMV. The optimal value of α, obtained from Table 9.8, was found to be 0.25 (Table 9.9).

Table 9.8 Acceptability of the Multiple Classifier Using a Weighted Majority Vote

Alpha	Acceptability
0.05	0.992
0.25	0.993
0.50	0.978
0.75	0.823

Table 9.9 Acceptability of the Multiple Classifier Using a Dissenting Weighted Majority Vote

Alpha	Acceptability
0.05	0.994
0.25	0.994
0.30	0.983
0.45	0.983
0.55	0.877
0.65	0.877
0.80	0.823
0.85	0.823

Converting Between Response Types

Before proceeding to analyze methods for merging type 2 responses (ranks), it would be appropriate to discuss means of converting one response type to another. In particular, not all of the classifiers yield a rank ordering, and this will be needed before merging the type 2 responses with those of types 1 and 3:

Type 3 to Type 1: Select the class having the maximum confidence rating as the response.

Type 3 to Type 2: Sort the confidence ratings in descending order. The corresponding classes are in rank order.

Type 2 to Type 1: Select the class having the highest rank as the type 1 response.

Converting a type 1 response to a type 3 cannot be done in a completely general and reliable fashion. However, an approximation can be had based on the measured past performance of the particular algorithm. Each row in the confusion matrix represents the classifications actually encountered for a particular digit with that classifier expressed as a probability, and the columns represent the other classifications possible for a specified classification; this latter could be used as the confidence rating. The conversions from type 1 can be expressed as:

Type 1 to Type 3: Compute the confusion matrix K for the classifier. If the classification in this case is j, then first compute:

$$s = \sum_{i=0}^{9} K(i,j) \qquad \text{(EQ 9.14)}$$

Now compute the type 3 response as a vector V, where

$$V(i) = \frac{K(i,j)}{s} \qquad \text{(EQ 9.15)}$$

Type 1 to Type 2: Convert from type 1 to type 3 as above, then convert to type 2 from type 3.

Merging Type 2 Responses

The problem encountered when attempting to merge type 2 responses is as follows: Given M rankings, each having N choices, which choice has the largest degree of support? For example, consider the following 3-voter/4-choice problem (Straffin 1980):

Voter 1: a b c d   **Voter 2**: c a b d   **Voter 3**: b d c a

This case has no majority winner; a, b and c each get one first-place vote. Intuitively, it seems reasonable to use the second-place votes in this case to see if the situation resolves itself. In this case b receives two second-place votes to a's one, which would tend to support b as the overall choice. In the general case there are a number of techniques for merging rank-ordered votes, four of which will be discussed here.

The *Borda count* (Borda 1781; Black 1958) is a well-known scheme for resolving this kind of situation. Each alternative is given a number of points depending on where in the ranking it has been placed. A selection is given no points for placing last, one point for placing next to last, and so on up to $N-1$ points for placing first. In other words, the number of points given to a selection is the number of classes below it in the ranking. For the 3-voter/4-choice problem described above, the situation is:

Voter 1: a(3) b(2) c(1) d(0)
Voter 2: c(3) a(2) b(1) d(0)
Voter 3: b(3) d(2) c(1) a(0)

where the points received by each selection appears in parentheses behind the choice. The overall winner is the choice receiving the largest total number of points:

$$a = 3 + 2 + 0 = 5$$

$$b = 2 + 1 + 3 = 6$$

$$c = 1 + 3 + 1 = 5$$

$$d = 0 + 0 + 2 = 2$$

This gives choice b as the *Borda winner*. However, the Borda count does have a problem that might be considered serious. Consider the following 5-voter/3-choice problem:

Voter 1: a b c   **Voter 2**: a b c   **Voter 3**: a b c
Voter 4: b c a   **Voter 5**: b c a

The Borda counts are a=6, b=7, c=2, which selects b as the winner. However, a simple majority of the first-place votes would have selected a! This violates the so-called *majority criterion* (Straffin 1980):

If a majority of voters have an alternative X as their first choice, a voting rule should choose X.

This is a weaker version of the *Condorcet Winner Criterion* (Condorcet 1785):

If there is an alternative X which could obtain a majority of votes in pair-wise contests against every other alternative, a voting rule should choose X as the winner.

This problem may have to be taken into account when assessing performance of the methods.

A procedure suggested by Thomas Hare (Straffin 1980) falls into the category of an *elimination* process. The idea is to repeatedly eliminate undesirable choices until a clear majority supports one of the remaining choices. Hare's method is as follows: If a majority of the voters rank choice X in first place, then X is the winner; otherwise, the choice with the *smallest number of first-place votes* is removed from consideration, and the first-place votes are recounted. This elimination process continues until a clear majority supports one of the choices.

The Hare procedure satisfies the majority criterion, but fails the Condorcet winner criterion as well as the *monotonicity criterion*:

If X is a winner under a voting rule, and one or more voters change their preferences in a way favorable to X without changing the order in which they prefer any other alternative, then X should still be the winner.

No rule that violates the monotonicity criterion will be considered as an option for the multiple classifier. This decision will eliminate the Hare procedure, but not the Borda count. With the monotonicity criterion in mind, two relatively simple rank merging strategies become interesting. The first is by Black (1958), and chooses the winner by the Condorcet criterion if such a winner exists; if not, the Borda winner is chosen. This is appealing in its simplicity, and can be shown to be monotonic. Another strategy is the so-called Copeland rule (Straffin 1980): For each option, compute the number of pairwise wins of that option with all other options, and subtract from that the number of pairwise losses. The overall winner is the class for which this difference is the greatest. In theory this rule is superior to the others discussed so far, but it has a drawback in that it tends to produce a relatively large number of tie votes in general.

The Borda, Black, and Copeland rules were implemented as described and applied to the five classifier problem, and the results are summarized in Table 9.10. From this table it would appear that the Borda scheme is tied with Black, followed by Copeland. It is important to temper this view with the fact that this result was obtained from basically one observation. Confirmation would come from applying these schemes to a large number of sets of characters.

Another consideration is that a voting scheme may err in favor of the correct classification when it should, in fact, be rejected. Upon careful analysis this was found to have happened for the Borda method applied to digit #267. The rankings were:

Classifier 1:   2
Classifier 2:   1 7 4 2 9

Table 9.10 Results of the Voting Rules for Rank Ordering (Omit #4)

Rule	Recognition	Error	Rejection	Reliability	Acceptability
Borda	99.9	0.1	0.0	0.999	0.998
Black	99.9	0.1	0.0	0.999	0.998
Copeland	99.6	0.2	0.2	0.998	0.994

Classifier 3:   2
Classifier 4:   1 9 6 3 2 7 8 5
Classifier 5:   1 2 9

The Borda count for the one digit is 27, and for the two digit is 37, giving a classification of two even though the majority winner and the Condorcet winner is one! Thus, the Black scheme classifies this digit (correctly according to the votes, in my opinion) as a one. Given this problem, and the fact that Black and Borda are otherwise equally acceptable, my conclusion is that the Black classifier is slightly superior to the others.

Merging Type 3 Responses

The five-classifier system under discussion has no single classifier that gives a proper type 3 response, and only one that yields a reliable set of weights for each digit (#5, the neural net). Because of this, the problem of merging type 3 responses was not pursued with as much vigor as were the type 1 and 2 problems. Indeed, the solution may be quite simple. Suen (Xu 1992) decides that any set of type 3 classifiers can be combined using an averaging technique. That is,

$$P_E(x \in C_i|x = \frac{1}{k} \sum_{j=1}^{k} P_j(x \in C_i|x), \ i = 1, \ldots, M \qquad \text{(EQ 9.16)}$$

where P_E is the probability associated with a given classification for the multiple classifier, and P_k is the probability associated with a given classification for each individual classifier k. The overall classification is the value j for which $P_E(x \in C_j|x)$ is a maximum.

There is little actual type 3 data, but it could be approximated by using the *a posteriori* method described previously, where it is used to convert type 1 responses to type 3 responses. Using this approximate data set, the result obtained by merging type 3 responses using averaging is given by:

Correct: 997   **Incorrect**: 3   **Rejected**: 0
Acceptability is 0.994.

Table 9.11 Multiple Classifier Performance

Name	Type	Acceptability
SMV	1	0.994
Black	2	0.998
Average	3	0.994

Results from the Multiple Classifier

Using the acceptability measure to assess each of the merging methods discussed, we need to look only at the best method in each of the three groups; that is, the best multiplier type 1 classifier, the best type 2, and the best type 3. The best three are given in Table 9.11.

From the table above it can be seen that the best classifier uses the Black scheme for merging rank ordered responses.

9.3 PRINTED MUSIC RECOGNITION—A STUDY

In order to provide a second example of symbol recognition, a problem has been selected that is familiar to most—that of reading printed music. Like handprinted-character recognition, optical music recognition (OMR) is a problem that has yet to be solved in a satisfactory manner. There is a considerable commercial interest in doing so, and it should be concluded from this that the problem is a difficult one.

One reason OMR is hard is that most of the symbols are connected to one another. The staff lines touch most of the symbols in a score, connecting them into one large region. Since the problem of touching characters was a major reason that the character recognition system of Chapter 8 was not a great success, the importance of the staff lines cannot be overestimated. This, it would appear, is the first problem in the OMR system: to locate the staff lines and remove them without seriously affecting the remainder of the score.

Having isolated at least the majority of the symbols, the next step is to recognize them. For machine-printed scores the symbols should be uniform enough to permit a template-matching scheme to be used. This may classify enough of the symbols so that the number of possibilities for the remaining ones is significantly decreased.

Finally, the use of context will be used to detect errors and resolve ambiguities. This step is rather like the use of a spelling checker to ensure that the words extracted by an OCR system are, in fact, words. The final system will be compared against some commercially available programs to see how it stacks up.

Staff Lines

Figure 9.16 shows a sample piece of music notation. The staff lines are the five long horizontal lines that provide a framework for the symbols. Each line and each space between lines represents a musical note on the scale, and so the position of the notes vertically indicates tone, whereas the horizontal position indicates the order in which they are played.

Horizontal projections have been used to locate the staff lines (Bulis 1992; Kato 1992), but even relatively small skew angles can lead to problems (Figure 9.16b). A large set of angles could be tried in an attempt to find a best angle, but for images the size of a scanned page of sheet music (10 megabytes and larger) this could require a great deal of time. However, the Hough transform was used with some success to identify the skew angle of printed text, and should work here. In fact, the Hough transform can be thought of as a calculation of all of the projections that are possible.

Since the Hough transform is generally slow too, the structure of the staff lines can be used to speed things up. Instead of transforming all black pixels, collect pixels into short horizontal line segments and transform the coordinates of the center of the segment. While this will actually work for a perfect image, even a small amount of curvature in the lines will prevent success (Figure 9.17a). Curvature can result from the page not being flat against the scanner (such as when a book is being scanned). A better approach would be to break up the staff horizontally into sections small enough so that any reasonable curvature in the entire staff can be ignored in the section (Figure 9.17b). The smaller pieces are *effectively* straight. This actually does work very well, but requires about 90 seconds per page, and is quite complex to implement correctly.

One method that works well and is fast enough uses the fact that the staff lines

(a)   (b)

Figure 9.16 Examples of scanned music notation (a) A portion of Mozart, showing the horizontal and vertical projections. (b) The same portion rotated five degrees. The horizontal projection is virtually useless for locating the staff lines.

are equally spaced. Simply look at columns of pixels and look for five equally spaced and sized runs of black pixels, as seen in Figure 9.17c. A large-enough collection of these staff samples will collect into groups, each having similar spacing, thickness, and vertical position. Within each group, the angles between all of the samples can be calculated, and samples that disagree wildly with the median angle can be discarded. Now that the angle has been found, a Hough transform can be computed quickly to find ρ. This method find the staff lines in about 15 seconds per page, or four times as fast as the best alternative Hough-based method.

Now the staff lines can be removed by travelling along each line, deleting the black pixels except where the vertical run length (thickness) exceeds a specified threshold which is dependent on the staff line thickness. This simple precaution prevents the removal of pixels belonging to note heads, sharps, flats, and other

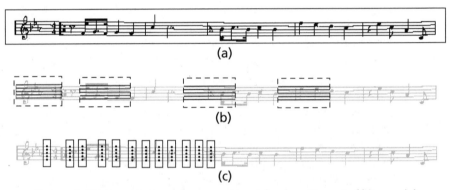

Figure 9.17 Hough transform method for locating staff lines. (a) A music staff with a slight curve—place a ruler along the top staff line. (b) Breaking the staff into small horizontal sections. The sections can be relinked later. (c) The use of vertical samples.

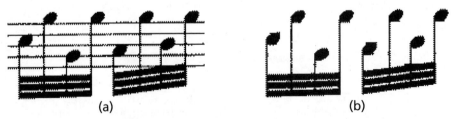

Figure 9.18 Staff line removal, using staff samples. (a) Before. (b) After.

symbols that may touch a staff line. Figure 9.18 shows an image before and after staff line removal.

Segmentation

In this instance, segmentation refers to the process of identifying the regions of the image that contain music, text, and artwork. The regions containing music can then be addressed, leaving the rest as ''noise.'' Segmentation begins on an image in which the staff lines have been removed by identifying the connected components. These are simply sets of pixels in which any pixel can be reached from any other by traveling on black pixels only.

While the connected components can be found in a recursive tracing strategy, one efficient way to find and represent them uses *line adjacency graphs* (LAG). When scanning the image along either rows or columns, each run of black pixels becomes a node, the coordinates of which are those of the center pixel in the run. An edge is placed between two nodes if the runs associated with the nodes overlap, and the runs are on adjacent rows (columns). The basic idea is illustrated in Figure 9.19.

Now the LAG can be compressed, so as to occupy less space. This is accomplished by merging nodes A and B that have the following properties (assume horizontal run lengths):

1. A is above B (is on the preceding row).
2. A has *degree* (A, 1) and B has *degree* (1, B).
3. A and B have nearly the same run length.
4. The resulting amalgamated node can be represented approximately by a straight line.

The degree of a node is the number of edges on each side (above and below). A node has degree (2,3) if there are two edges connecting to it from above (the previous row) and three edges connecting below (the next row). Figure 9.19 attempts to make this situation more clear.

When the overall connected component analysis is complete, we have a LAG for each component in the score. Since the LAG is found after the staff lines are removed, there is a good chance that each represents a symbol, or set of related symbols. Indeed, any that would intersect a staff are considered to be music symbols. However, there are many other symbols on a score, most notably text (e.g., lyrics), and these symbols clutter the scene significantly. Text should therefore be removed, if possible.

One algorithm for doing this (Fletcher 1988) was actually designed for distinguishing between regions of text and graphics on a document page. The basic idea is that text consists of connected components that are oriented along a straight

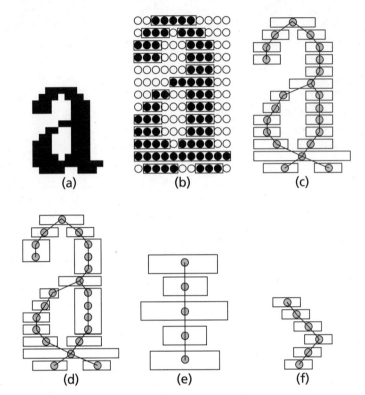

Figure 9.19 Line adjacency graphs. (a) Sample glyph.
(b) Horizontal runs that are used to create the LAG. (c) The LAG
found from (b). (d) The compressed version of the LAG. (e) In
the compression method, different-sized runs are not merged.
(f) Even if the runs have identical lengths, the set of nodes must
form a linear collection, not a curve or corner.

line. A set of colinear objects having a regular spacing forms a word, and may be removed since text is of no interest to the OMR system. The centroids of each connected region are fed into a Hough transform to determine colinearity. Then any LAG sets that are words, based on their spacing, are marked as such for later deletion.

This is an oversimplification of a fairly complex algorithm. The result of this segmentation process is exemplified by Figure 9.20, in which a page from a simple score has had the text and nontext regions identified very accurately. This means that the recognition of music symbols can proceed, concentrating on the nontext regions. Some text may remain in the score, and can later be discarded by the matching process.

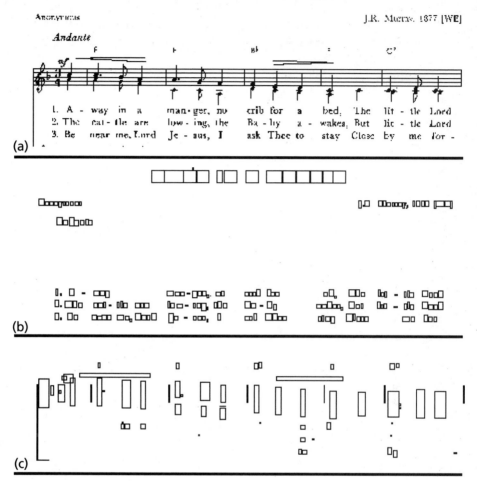

Figure 9.20 Results of segmentation. (a) Original score image. (b) The text regions identified by the Fletcher algorithm. (c) The nontext (music?) regions. Note that a little of the text remains with the music.

Music Symbol Recognition

Music notation is unusual in that there are a great many horizontal and vertical straight line segments within a score. For example, measures are separated by a vertical line, and most notes consist of a vertical stem and an elliptical note head. This is convenient, because the LAG representation lends itself to the identification of lines: every node in the compressed LAG represents a line segment, and adjacent line segments can be merged into a single, longer one if their slopes are nearly the same.

Because of this, the recognition of symbols is split into three parts: horizontal lines, vertical lines, and others; this final part can be further split into note heads and symbols. Figure 9.21 shows the kind of result to be expected from the use of LAGs for the location of horizontal and vertical lines. This method is accurate enough to provide a means for identifying the other features; specifically, note heads are to be found near the end of a stem, which is a vertical line segment.

For recognizing symbols (such as sharps, flats, and rests) that are often isolated by staff line removal, the method of character outlines (see the section titled ''Properties of the Character Outline'') was used with great success. The features used in the recognition were found by measuring a collection of known symbols, and the resulting database of features was used to recognize the unknown glyphs.

Note heads, on the other hand, are almost never isolated, being connected to stems. The method used to locate note heads is the template-matching scheme, last seen in Section 8.2. The hierarchical matching scheme was used to speed up the process, since the vast majority of the processing time of the entire OMR system was used in matching templates.

Many variations of the note heads were used as templates. This is essential, since the staff line removal is not perfect, and often leaves small stems where they intersect note heads. Also, in the case of whole and half-notes (which have a hole),

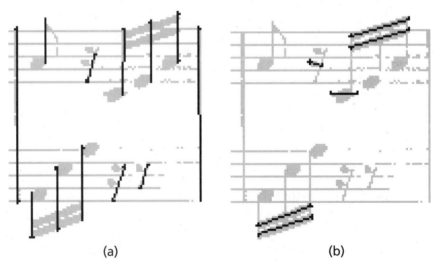

(a)   (b)

Figure 9.21 The identification of line segments using Line Adjacency Graphs. (a) Vertical lines. (b) Horizontal lines. Note that the beams are found consistently.

the staff line can be seen running through the center of the note. Figure 9.22 shows a few of the templates needed to recognize the head of a half-note.

Once the individual symbols have been found, they are synthesized into more complex forms by using context. Structures are represented in the form of *graph grammars* (Claus 1978; Ehig 1990). For example, a sharp symbol, two note heads, two stems, and a beam can, if the situation is right, be combined into a single high-level symbol (as illustrated in Figure 9.23). Graphs are created from the low-level symbols in the score, and are parsed by a *graph parser* to perform the high-level match (Fahmy 1993; Reed 1995).

The OMR system described here, which is called Lemon, was tested on multiple scores and the results compared against those obtained from two commercially available systems, which will be referred to as A and B to avoid embarrassment. While Lemon almost always requires a longer time than the others (about 15 minutes per page on a 486/33 PC running OS/2), the overall recognition rate was 95.2% on 10 samples containing over 2500 symbols. System A had a recognition rate of 9.27%, and was better than Lemon on $\frac{4}{10}$ of the sample scores. System B had a recognition rate of 83.2%, and performed better than Lemon on only one score.

An executable version of Lemon is provided on the CD as a bonus, although the source cannot be made available. It runs under OS/2 only.

(a)   (b)   (c)   (d)

Figure 9.22 Templates for the head of a half-note. (a) Basic template. (b) A template for a half-note on a staff line. (c) Half-note between staff lines. (d) Half note below a ledger line.

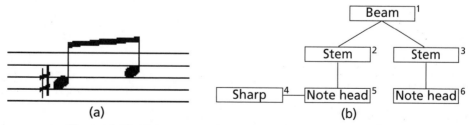

(a)   (b)

Figure 9.23 Using a graph representation to incorporate context. (a) A small sample, containing six primitive symbols. (b) The graph representation of the sample.

9.4 SOURCE CODE FOR NEURAL NET RECOGNITION SYSTEM

```c
/* Backpropagation network + character recognition */

/* TRIAL I: Test data is a binary to decimal conversion */
#include <stdio.h>
#include <math.h>
#include <malloc.h>

int NO_OF_INPUTS = 0;
int NO_OF_HIDDEN = 0;
int NO_OF_OUTPUTS = 0;

float *inputs;/* Input values in the first layer */

float **hweights;/* Weights for hidden layer. HWEIGHTS[i][j]
*/
                /* is the weight for hidden node i from
*/
                /* input node j.      */
float *hidden;/* Outputs from the hidden layer    */
float *vhidden;
float *err_hidden;/* Errors in hidden nodes */

float **oweights;/* Weights for the output layer, as before
*/
float *outputs;/*Final outputs */
float *voutputs;
float *err_out;/* Errors in output nodes */

float *should;/* Correct output vector for training datum */
float learning_rate = 0.3;
FILE *training_data=0;/* File with training data */
FILE *test_data=0;/* File with unknown data */
FILE *infile;    /* One of the two files above */
int actual;      /* Actual digits — tells us the output */

void compute_hidden (int node);
void compute_output (int node);
float output_function (float x);
void compute_all_hidden ();
void compute_all_outputs ();
float weight_init (void);
void initialize_all_weights ();
float compute_output_error ();
```

```
float compute_hidden_node_error (int node);
void compute_hidden_error ();
void update_output ();
void update_hidden (void);
float * fvector (int n);
float **fmatrix (int n, int m);
void setup (void);
void get_params (int *ni, int *nh, int *no);
int get_inputs (float *x);

int printf();
int scanf ();

/*   Compute the output from hidden node NODE*/
void compute_hidden (int node)
{
    int i = 0;
    float x = 0;

    for (i=0; i<NO_OF_INPUTS; i++)
      x += inputs[i]*hweights[node][i];
    hidden[node] = output_function (x);
    vhidden[node] = x;
}

/*   Compute the output from output node NODE*/
void compute_output (int node)
{
    int i = 0;
    float x = 0;

    for (i=0; i<NO_OF_HIDDEN; i++)
      x += hidden[i]*oweights[node][i];
    outputs[node] = output_function (x);
    voutputs[node] = x;
}

/*   Output function for hidden node — linear or sigmoid*/
float output_function (float x)
{
    return 1.0/(1.0 + exp((double)(−x)));

    return x; /* Linear */
}
```

```
/*     Derivative of the output function*/
float of_derivatives (float x)
{
      float a = 0.0;

      a = output_function(x);

      return 1.0; /* Linear */
      return a*(1.0-a);
}

/*    Compute all hidden nodes*/
void compute_all_hidden ()
{
      int i = 0;

      for (i=0; i<NO_OF_HIDDEN; i++)
        compute_hidden (i);
}

/*    Compute all hidden nodes*/
void compute_all_outputs ()
{
      int i = 0;

      for (i=0; i<NO_OF_OUTPUTS; i++)
        compute_output (i);
}
/*    Initialize a weight*/
float weight_init (void)
{
      double drand48();

      return (float)(drand48() - 0.5);
}

/*    Initialize all weights*/
void initialize_all_weights ()
{
      init i = 0; j = 0;

      for (i=0; i<NO_OF_INPUTS; i++);
        for (j=0; j<NO_OF_HIDDEN; j++)
          hweights[j][i] = weight_init();
```

```
      for (i=0; i<NO_OF_HIDDEN; i++)
        for (j=0; j<NO_OF_OUTPUTS; j++)
          oweights[j][i] = weight_init ();
}

/*   Calculate the error in the output nodes*/
float compute_output_error ()
{
     int i = 0;
     int x = 0;

     for (i=0; i<NO_OF_OUTPUTS; i++)
     {
        err_out[i] = (should[i]−outputs[i]) *
of_derivative(voutputs[i]);
        x += err_out[i];
     }
     return x;
}

/*   What SHOULD the output vector be?*/
compute_training_outputs()
{
     int i;

     printf ("Output SHOULD be:\n");
     printf (" 0 1 2 3 4 5 6 7 8 9\n");
     for (i=0; i<NO_OF_OUTPUTS; i++)
     {
       if (i==actual) should[i] = 1.0;
         else should[i] = 0.0;
       printf ("%5.1f ", should [i]);
     }
     printf ("\n");
}

/*   Compute the error term for the given hidden node*/
float compute_hidden_node_error (int node)
{
     int i = 0;
     float x = 0.0;

     for (i=0; i<NO_OF_OUTPUTS; i++)
       x += err_out[i]*oweights[i][node];
```

```
        return of_derivative(vhidden[node]) * x;
}

/*    Compute all hidden node error terms*/
void compute_hidden_error ()
{
    int i = 0;

    for (i=0; i<NO_OF_HIDDEN; i++)
      err_hidden[i] = compute_hidden_node_error(i);
}

/*    Update the output layer weights*/
void update_output ()
{
    int i=0, j=0;

    for (i=0; i<NO_OF_OUTPUTS; i++)
      for (j=0; j<NO_OF_HIDDEN; j++)
        oweights[i][j] +=
learning_rate*err_out[i*hidden[j];
}

/*    Update the hidden layer weights*/
void update_hidden (void)
{
    int i=0; j=0;

    for (i=0; i<NO_OF_HIDDEN; i++)
      for (j=0; j<NO_OF_INPUTS; j++)
        hweights[i][j] +=
learning_rate*err_hidden[i]*inputs[j];
}

float compute_error_term ()
{
    int i = 0;
    float x = 0.0;

    for (i=0; i<NO_OF_OUTPUTS; i++)
      x += (err_out[i]*err_out[i]);
    return x/2.0;
}

float * fvector (int n)
{
```

```
        return (float *)malloc(sizeof(float)*n);
}

float **fmatrix (int n, int m)
{
        int i = 0;
        float *x, **y;

/*Allocate rows */
        y = float **)malloc (size of(float)*n);

/* Allocate NXM array of floats */
        x = (float *)malloc (size of(float)*n*m);
/*Set pointers in y to each row in x */
        for (i=0; i<n; i++)
          y[i] = &(x[i*m]);

        return y;
}

/*   Allocate all arrays and matrices*/
void setup (void)
{
        inputs      = fvector (NO_OF_INPUTS);

        hweights    = fmatrix (NO_OF_HIDDEN, NO_OF_INPUTS);
        hidden      = fvector (NO_OF_HIDDEN);
        vhidden     = fvector (NO_OF_HIDDEN);
        err_hidden  = fvector (NO_OF_HIDDEN);

        oweights    = fmatrix (NO_OF_OUTPUTS, NO_OF_HIDDEN);
        outputs     = fvector (NO_OF_OUTPUTS);
        voutputs    = fvector (NO_OF_OUTPUTS);
        err_out     = fvector (NO_OF_OUTPUTS);

        should      = fvector (NO_OF_OUTPUTS);
}

void get_params (int *ni, int *nh, int *no)
{
        printf ("How many input nodes: ");
        scanf ("%d", ni);
        printf ("How many hidden nodes: ");
        scanf ("%d", nh);
        printf ("How many output nodes: ");
        scanf ("%d", no);
```

```
}

int get_inputs (float *x)
}
    int i, k;

    for (i=0; i<NO_OF_INPUTS; i++)
    {
      k = fscanf (infile, "%f", &(x[i]));
      if (k<1) return 0:
    }
    if (infile == training_data)
      fscanf (infile, "%d", &actual);

    return 1;
}

void print_outputs ()
{
    int i, j;

    j = 0;
    for (i=0; i<NO_OF_OUTPUTS; i++)
    {
      printf ("%f ", outputs[i]);
      if (outputs[i] > outputs[j]) j = i;
    }
    printf ("Actual %d NN classified as %d\n", actual, j);
}

int main(int argc, char *argv[])
{
    int k = 0;
    float x = 0.0;
    int dset = 1;
/* Look for data files */
    if (argc < 3)
    {
        printf ("bpn <training set> <data set>\n");
        exit(1);
    }

    training_data = fopen (argc[1], "r");
    if (training_data == NULL)
```

```
        {
            printf ("Can't open training data '%s'\n",
argv[1]);
            exit(2);
        }
        infile = training_data;

/* Get the size of the net */
        get_params (&NO_OF_INPUTS, &NO_OF_HIDDEN,
&NO_OF_OUTPUTS);

/* Initialize */
        setup ();
        initialize_all_weights();

/* Train */

        k = get_inputs (inputs);
        while (k)
        {
          printf ("Training on set %d\n", dset);
          compute_all_hidden();
          compute_all_outputs();

/* Weight errors propagate backwards */
          compute_training_outputs();
          compute_output_error();
          compute_hidden_error();

          update_output();
          update_hidden();

          x = compute_error_term();
          printf ("Set %d error term is %f\n", dset, x);
          k = get_inputs(inputs);
          dset++;
        }
        fclose (training_data);
        training_data = NULL;infile = NULL;

        test_data = fopen (argv[2], "r");
        if (test_data == NULL)
        {
          printf ("Can't open data '%s'\n", argv[2]);
          exit(3);
```

```
        }
     infile = test_data;

/* Now apply the NN to the remaining inputs */
     k = get_inputs (inputs);
     while (k)
     {
       compute_all_hidden();
       compute_all_outputs();
       print_outputs();
       k = get_inputs (inputs);
     }
     fclose (test_data);
}
```

9.5   BIBLIOGRAPHY

Aarts, A. and J. Korst. 1989. *Simulated Annealing and Boltzmann Machines: A Stochastic Approach to Combinatorial Optimization and Neural Computing.* New York: John Wiley & Sons.

Ansari, N. and K. Li. 1993. Landmark Based Shape Recognition by a Modified Hopfield Neural Network. *Pattern Recognition.* Vol. 26. 531–542.

Baird, H. S. 1987. The Skew Angle of Printed Documents. *Proceedings of the Conference of the Society of Photographic Scientists and Engineers.* SPIE. Bellingham, WA: 14–21.

Black, D. 1958. *The Theory of Committees and Elections.* Cambridge: Cambridge University Press.

de Borda, J. 1781. Memoire sur les Elections au Scrutin. *Histoire de l'Academie Royale des Sciences.* Paris.

Brams, S. J. and P. C. Fishburn. 1983. *Approval Voting.* Boston: Birkhauser.

Bulis, A., Almog, R., Gerner, M., and U. Shimony. 1992. Computerized Recognition of Hand-Written Music Notes. *Proceedings of the International Computer Music Conference.* 110–112.

Carpenter, G. A. and S. Grossberg. 1988. The Art of Adaptive Pattern Recognition by Self-Organizing Neural Network. *Computer.* Vol. 21 3:77–88.

Claus, V., Ehrig, H., and G. Rozenberg. (Eds.). 1978. Graph Grammars and Their Applications to Computer Science and Biology. International Workshop No. 73 in *Lecture Notes in Computer Science.* Berlin: Springer-Verlag.

de Condorcet, M. 1785. *Essai sur l'application de l'analyse a la probabilite des decisions rendues a la pluralite des voix.* Paris.

Ehrig, H., Kreowski, H., and G. Rozenberg. (Eds.). 1990. Graph Grammars and Their

Applications to Computer Science: 4th International Workshop no. 291 in *Lecture Notes in Computer Science*. Berlin: Springer-Verlag.

Enelow, J. M. and M. J. Hinich. 1984. *The Spatial Theory of Voting: An Introduction.* Cambridge: Cambridge University Press.

Fahmy, H. and D. Blostein. 1993. A Graph Grammar Programming Style for Recognition of Music Notation. *Machine Vision and Applications*. Vol. 6. 83–89.

Farquharson, R. 1969. *Theory of Voting*. New Haven, CT: Yale University Press.

Fletcher, L. A. and R. Kasturi. 1988. A Robust Algorithm for Text String Separation from Mixed Text/Graphics Image. *IEEE Transactions on Pattern Analysis and Machine Intelligence*. Vol. 10. 6:910–918.

Freeman, J. and D. Skarpura. 1991. *Neural Networks—Algorithms, Applications, and Programming Techniques*. Reading, MA: Addison-Wesley.

Fukushima, K., Miyake, S. and T. Ito. 1983. Neocognitron: A Neural Model for a Mechanism of Pattern Recognition. *IEEE Transactions on Systems, Man, and Cybernetics*. Vol. T-SMC13. 826–834.

Ho, T. K., Hull, J. J., and S. N. Srihari. 1994. Decision Combination in Multiple Classifier Systems. *IEEE Transactions on Pattern Analysis and Machine Intelligence*. Vol. 16.

Holt, C. M., Stewart, A., Clint, M., and R. Perrot. 1987. An Improved Parallel Thinning Algorithm. *Communications of the ACM*. Vol. 30. 2:156–160.

Kato, H. and S. Inokuchi. 1992. A Recognition System for Printed Piano Music Using Musical Knowledge and Constraints. *Structured Document Image Analysis*. Baird et al. (Eds.). Berlin: Springer-Verlag.

Kimura, F. and M. Shridhar. 1991. Handwritten Numeral Recognition Based on Multiple Algorithms. *Pattern Recognition*. Vol. 24.

Masters, T. 1995. *Advanced Algorithms for Neural Networks—A C++ Sourcebook*. New York: John Wiley & Sons.

Mui, L., Agarwal, A., and P.S.P. Wang. 1994. An Adaptive Modular Neural Network with Application to Unconstrained Character Recognition. *International Journal of Pattern Recognition*. Vol. 8. 5:1189.

Parker, J. R. 1994. Recognition of Hand Printed Digits Using Multiple Parallel Methods. *Third Golden West International Conference on Intelligent Systems*. Las Vegas. June 6–9.

Reed, T. 1995. *Optical Music Recognition*. University of Calgary Department of Computer Science MSc Thesis.

Shang, C. and K. Brown. 1994. Principal Features Based Texture Classification with Neural Networks. *Pattern Recognition*. Vol. 27. 675–687.

Shridhar, M. and A. Badrelin. 1986. Recognition of Isolated and Simply Connected Handwritten Numerals. *Pattern Recognition*. Vol. 19. No. 1.

Shridhar, M. and A. Badrelin. 1987. Context-Directed Segmentation Algorithm for Handwritten Numeral Strings. *Image and Vision Computing*. Vol. 5. No. 1.

Straffin, P. D. Jr. 1980. *Topics in the Theory of Voting*. Boston: Birkhauser.

Touretzky, D. (Ed.). 1989. *Advances in Neural Information Processing Systems*. San Mateo, CA: Morgan-Kaufmann.

Xu, L., Krzyzak, A., and C. Y. Suen. Methods of Combining Multiple Classifiers and Their Application to Handwriting Recognition. *IEEE Transactions on Systems, Man, and Cybernetics*. Vol. 22. No. 3.

Yong, Y. 1988. Handprinted Chinese Character Recognition via Neural Network. *Pattern Recognition Letters*. Vol. 7. 19–25.

Zhang, Y. Y. and C. Y. Suen. 1985. A Fast Parallel Algorithm for Thinning Digital Patterns. *Communications of the ACM*. Vol. 27. 3:236–239.

10

GENETIC ALGORITHMS AND EVOLUTIONARY COMPUTING

A genetic algorithm is a technique for optimization; that is, it can be used to find the minimum or maximum of some arbitrary function. While there are a large number of mathematical techniques for accomplishing this, both in general and for specific circumstances, a genetic algorithm is unique. It is a stochastic method, and it will find a global minimum, neither property being singular. The approach is remarkable because it is based on the way that a population of living organisms grows and evolves, fitting into their ecological niche better with each generation.

10.1 OPTIMIZATION IN IMAGE PROCESSING AND VISION

Optimization methods have been used in most of the preceding chapters. Wherever the phrase *least-squares fit* has been used, an optimization process is implied. Now, a least-squares best fit is not really an algorithm. It is a statement of a criterion for fitness or optimality. Specifically, if a function F is to be fit to a set of data D, then the least-squares best fit satisfies

$$\text{MIN} = \sum (F - D)^2 \qquad \text{(EQ 10.1)}$$

for all function values in the domain involved. There are many other ways in which an optimality criterion can be specified, but the least squares measure is probably the most common.

In Chapter 3, for example, the use of least squares in an optimization was used twice. The Chow-Kaneko thresholding algorithm requires that a pair of Gaussian (normal) curves be fit to the grey-level histogram of a portion of an image. The edge level thresholding (ELT) algorithm fits a surface to the two-dimensional image data of an edge-enhanced image. Both of these optimizations could be performed using a genetic algorithm and (especially in the two-dimensional case) the result would probably be better.

The matching of two-dimensional shapes can be expressed as a minimization or maximization problem, and so can be done using genetic methods too. One special case of this is the fitting of particular surfaces (such as spheres, cones, and cylinders) to objects in an image. In two dimensions this has been done with some success for star images and for DNA sequencing gels (Parker 1993a; b). Indeed, genetic methods can be applied to many diverse areas within the image-analysis spectrum, from locating image areas that may contain a particular object to outline identification. Even learning applications can have a GA component.

The general concepts of this relatively new area of study will be discussed first, followed by some generic applications, and concluding with a few vision-specific applications. Of course, some software has been provided for experimentation.

10.2   AN INTRODUCTION TO GENETIC ALGORITHMS

The way that an optimization algorithm works is, in principle, quite simple: The parameters of the objective function are varied in some structured fashion until an optimum value (either minimum or maximum) is found. Usually the interesting result is the location of the minimum (let's use a minimum from now on) value, rather than the value of the function itself. For example, consider the simple polynomial appearing in Figure 10.1.

There are two minima, one global minimum at $x=-8$ and one other (local) minimum knowing the location of the minimum, it is a simple matter to plug that value into the equation of the polynomial for x and find the minimum function value; the reverse is much more difficult.

Now let's consider the process by which an optimization method can find the location of the minimum. Starting at some initial point $x=x_0$, the value of x is changed to a new one and the value of the function is computed again. The x value is altered by adding some value δx to it. If the new value is less than the old, then we are moving in the right direction. If not, the direction is changed, or the increment added to x is changed. The process repeats until the function value changes by an amount less than some predetermined ϵ.

This process is generic, but there are many specific methods, each with its own way to determine δx, ϵ, and sometimes x_0. For example, the steepest-descent method, discussed in Chapter 9 with respect to minimizing the error in the output of a neural net, uses a value for δx that is in the direction of steepest descent of the curve (perpendicular to the gradient).

The approach used in genetic algorithm is *stochastic*, which is to say, based on probabilities, and so has a random component. It also models the process by which

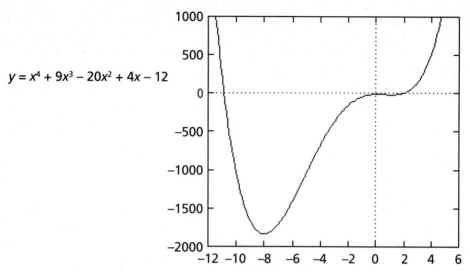

$$y = x^4 + 9x^3 - 20x^2 + 4x - 12$$

Figure 10.1 A polynomial. The problem: Find the location of the global (overall) minimum value.

living organisms are said to evolve to suit their environment. In these ways it is like *simulated annealing*, which is also stochastic, and which is also based on a model from the physical world. To really appreciate the method, the analogy to biological systems must be understood. Indeed, the genetic algorithms literature uses many of the same terms as do biologists when discussing genetics, ecology, and natural selection. A very brief summary of the related material from these areas is therefore in order.

The nature of a living organism is described by the specific structure of the DNA molecules that reside in every cell of that organism. From the DNA, a complete new organism can be created. The DNA is really information coded chemically, and can be thought of as a very long string of bits in a memory. In actual fact, the DNA is divided into a number of sets, each belonging to a *chromosome*. A gene can be thought of as the specific segment of DNA that is responsible for a particular feature; for example, eye color or blood type. There may be many genes on a single chromosome, and any particular organism can have any number of chromosomes. However, each member of a particular species has the same number of chromosomes as each other member.

When a cell in an organism reproduces, it first duplicates its DNA. A cell reproduces by dividing into two, and each half gets a complete copy of the DNA. *Variation* in organisms is introduced in many ways, but two are of major importance. The first is by *mutation*, in which a small portion of the DNA is changed in a random manner; in nature this can be caused by random effects such as radiation exposure (ultraviolet, x-rays, etc.), high-energy subatomic particles, or by exposure to certain chemicals (*mutagens*). This is illustrated in Figure 10.2b. The second major way to introduce variation is by a physical process called *crossover*. Two chromosomes can come into physical contact and reconnect, one to the other. The result is that part of the first chromosome becomes connected to part of the second, producing a new chromosome, as seen in Figure 10.2c. Whatever the cause of the variation, whether mutation or crossover or otherwise, the result is a new code sequence on the DNA, which in turn results in a slightly different organism.

Now consider a *population* of organisms, consisting of many distinct individuals. The process of mutation and crossover would be occurring all of the time, producing many variations of the individuals. Some of these variations will be less fit to survive; for example, a mutation that resulted in an organism not being able to eat would be *lethal*, and that organism would die before reproducing. On the other hand, some variations are advantageous: A mutation that allowed an organism to become faster, stronger, or smarter than the others would permit that

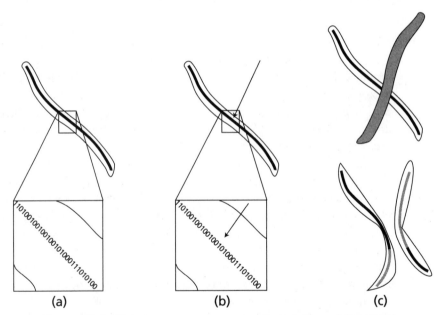

Figure 10.2 Chromosomes, genes, and variation. (a) A single chromosome, containing some number of genes. In real life, genes are not sequences of binary numbers. (b) A mutation can be caused by radiation, and results in a change in the sequence on the chromosome. In this case only a single bit is altered. (c) Two chromosomes that come into contact can "cross over" and exchange parts of themselves with each other. Then entire sequences move from one chromosome to another.

organism to escape from predators, allowing it to pass on its mutation to its children. They, too, would possess the advantage, and would be more fit to survive. This is called a *selective advantage*.

This very simplified model of genetics and natural selection is the basis of the genetic approach to optimization. The analogy is rather plain: The optimization of a function of N parameters is likened to the survival of organisms in a population. A chromosome is one possible set of N parameters, each of which is a gene. A set of parameters (chromosome) is more fit to survive if it results in a better (smaller, for a minimization problem) result of the objective function. A mutation is a single-bit change in the value of a gene, and a crossover results in a copying of bits from one set of parameters to another. A population is a collection of parameter sets, and a new generation is created each iteration of the process; each iteration selects only the most fit (i.e., closest to optimal) parameters sets to be carried into the next iteration.

Volumes have been written on this subject, and it would be unreasonable to expect that this simple explanation would be sufficient. Let's look at a specific example, and see how the analogy would apply to finding the minimum of the function seen in Figure 10.1. The polynomial to be minimized is:

$$y = x^4 + 9x^3 - 20x^2 + 4x - 12 \qquad \text{(EQ 10.2)}$$

This is the objective function, and has but a singe parameter x. When using a genetic algorithm, the parameters are represented as bit strings, and so the length of the string as well as the possible bounds on the parameter must be specified. A length of 10 bits will be assumed, and x will be allowed to range between -10 and $+10$. This means, for example, that the bit string "0000000000" will correspond to the value -10. Some function to perform the mapping between integer and bit string must exist: It will be called encode.

The encode function assigns parameter values to bit strings in an obvious way. If the parameter is an integer, its value is simply the bit string interpreted as such. If the parameter is real a fixed-point representation is used, wherein each increment to the bit string corresponds to a real increment in the parameter. In this case, as an example, the range is 20.0, which is to be stored in 10 bits. The number of different bit strings of 10 bits is 2^{10}, or 1024; thus, the increment is 20.0/1024, or 0.01953125. The space of real values allowed by this representation is:

0000000000	-10.0
0000000001	-9.980469
0000000010	-9.960938
...	
100000000	0.00
1000000001	0.019531
...	
1111111111	9.980469

Note that 10.0 is not a representable value. Parameters cannot have a value between two consecutive increments, because the representation does not permit it. Therefore the choice of chromosome size limits the accuracy of the final result.

The next step is the creation of a population. Initially, a population consisting of randomly generated bit strings is used. The size of the population (which is the number of randomly generated bit strings) is also a parameter to the algorithm. Now each bit-string parameter (gene) is passed as a parameter to the objective function, and the result is a measure of the gene's fitness; in this case, large values correspond to poor fitness, and vice versa. The best P percent of the parameters can reproduce, where a value for P must also be specified to the genetic algorithm, and the remainder of the parameters will not be propagated into the next generation (iteration).

Reproduction

Reproduction begins by selecting one of the best parameters at random. One method of doing this, called *roulette wheel selection*, chooses the parameters in proportion to how fit they are: More-fit members of the population have a higher chance of being selected than their less-fit brethren.

Since reproduction only takes place using the best P percent of the chromosomes, the remainder are discarded. Then the total fitness of the remaining population is found: F is the sum of the fitness values of the best P percent of the chromosomes. Because of the objective function, and because the minimum is being found, the small fitness values are to be given a selective advantage over the larger ones. Hence, the probability of selecting a particular chromosome c_i to reproduce is

$$\frac{F - Y(c_i)}{F} \qquad \text{(EQ 10.3)}$$

where Y is the objective function. The resulting probability is in proportion to the fitness of the chromosome.

It is during reproduction that variation is introduced into the population. There are many ways to do this, but we will examine only the most important two: mutation and crossover. Mutation is implemented as a single-bit change to the chromosome, which occurs with a predefined probability. For each bit in a chromosome, we ask "should this bit be mutated?" by drawing a random number; if this number is less than the probability of a mutation, then the corresponding bit in the chromosome is changed.

For example, consider the problem of minimizing the function seen in Equation 10.2. As discussed previously, the chromosome will be 10 bits in length, and will span the range -10 to $+10$. One of the chromosomes has the value:

1001001000

which corresponds to the real value 1.40625. The algorithm determines that bit 3 (as counted from the left) is to be mutated, so it will become 0. The result is:

    1000001000

which corresponds to a real value of 0.15625.

The second (and more important) way that variation is added to the population is by crossover. When applied to two bit strings, the crossover operation first selects a location at which to cut the two chromosomes involved. A new chromosome is then created by copying the first part of the first chromosome (from the beginning to the cut location) into a bit string, followed by a copy of the last part of the second chromosome (from the cut location to the end) into the same bit string. The remaining, uncopied parts of the chromosomes are also copied into a second new chromosome.

Using the same example as before, consider the chromosomes:

10000 10010	**10001 00110**
0.351562	0.742188

If the crossover occurs at bit 5, then the first five bits of the first chromosome will be connected to the last five bits of the second, and vice versa. This gives two new bit strings, with their associated and also new real values:

10000 00110	**10001 10010**
0.117188	0.976562

Crossover increases in usefulness when there are many parameters. The idea is to be able to mix and match the best individual parameters in the set, and combine them to form a single excellent set. The use of crossover permits multiple parameters to be moved from one chromosome to another, so that this recombination may take place.

The process of selecting a chromosome to reproduce and introducing variation is repeated until the population reaches its normal size, at which time all chromosomes are evaluated and the process repeats itself. Not all of the chromosomes need to be replaced each time, but if they are the process is referred to as *complete generational replacement*. More often the best chromosomes from the previous generation (iteration) are retained, so that the most useful values from the previous generation are not lost to the next (*partial generational replacement*).

A diagrammatic view of the process of generational replacement appears in Figure 10.3.

*PcGen: A Simple Genetic Algorithm Package

The genetic algorithm software that is provided on the CD is a simple yet functional package that provides the ability to optimize either real (FPcGen) or integer

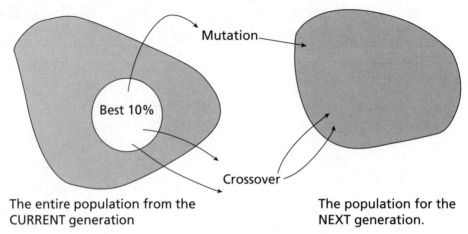

Figure 10.3 An abstract view of generational replacement in a genetic algorithm. This process is repeated many times, once for each iteration requested. It should be that each generation is better than the previous one, or at least no worse.

(IPcGen) functions. The programs are written in C for a PC, but should be easily converted to other systems.

*PcGen stores bit strings as sequences of unsigned characters (bytes), and provides operators for packing and unpacking bits. A global array named population stores all of the bit strings (chromosomes) in the population, whose size is the variable chromlen.

Each parameter to the objective function corresponds to some contiguous set of bits in the chromosome. A parameter has an entry in the parameter table specifying the number of bits it requires, and the minimum and maximum values that are possible. The starting bit position will be stored too; the first argument is given the first bits of the chromosome, and so on until all have been defined by the user. The result is a very flexible system allowing arbitrary chromosome sizes and number of parameters, although default maximum sizes are enforced (these can be changed as memory limits allow).

The main program of *PcGen prompts the user for the following values:

1. Population size (<2000)
2. Number of arguments to the objective function (<20)
3. For each argument: Size (#bits), minimum value, maximum value.
4. The percentage of chromosomes that can reproduce.
5. The number of generations.

Two important values are hard-coded into the system: the probability of a single bit mutation (sbm_rate = 0.01, or 1%) and the probability of a crossover (sc_rate

= 0.65, or 65%). In addition, there are three methods for the selection of new populations each generation: the roulette wheel method (as described), the use of the best few percent drawn at random, or roulette wheel selection after linear normalization. These can be experimented with; the global variable select_method can be set to either *bestpct*, *roulette*, or *linear*.

The functions provided by IPcGen are described here:

char *bit2str (bits b, int s)
Convert the bit string *b*, having length *s*, into a character string, which has a *1* or *0* in each position. Return a pointer to the string.

unsigned long bextract (bits b, int s, int n)
Extract a portion of the bit string *b*: start at bit *s*, and extract a string of *n* bits. The resulting bit string is converted into a long integer.

void binsert (bits b, int s, int n, unsigned long val)
Insert a sequence of bits into the bit string *b*. The value of *val* is converted into a bit string and inserted into *b* starting at bit location *s*; the number of bits being replaced is *n*.

void b1mut (bits b, int n)
Perform a single bit mutation on the *n* bit long string *b*. Probability of a single bit mutation is given by the global variation *sbm_rate*.

void bcopy (bits source, bits dest, int n)
Copy the bit string *source* into the bit string *dest*; they are *n* bits long.

bits bnew (int n)
Allocate a new bit string having length *n*.

void ceval (int n)
Calculate the evaluation value (objective function) for the chromosome numbered *n*; save it in the global evaluation array.

void cross1 (bits s1, bits s2, int n)
Perform a single point crossover of the two chromosomes *s1* and *s2*. This function is called only when it has been decided to do a crossover; it selects the location at random, and the strings will have been altered when the function returns. Strings are *n* bits long.

int decode (bits b, int s, int n)
Convert the bit string at bit number *s* in string *b* having length *n* bits into an integer. This is used to decode a parameter from a bit string.

double drange (double x1, double x2)
Return a random double precision number between *x1* and *x2*.

void encode (bits b, *int* s, *int* n, *int* val)
val is a parameter to be made into a bit string and placed into a chromosome. This function converts val into a bit string n bits long, and places it into the bit string b starting at location s.

int getarg (int n, *bits* thisc)
Return encoded parameter n from the bit string *thisc*.

int getbit (bits b, *int* n)
Extract bit n of bit string b, and return it as an integer.

double irange (int i1, *int* i2)
Return a random integer in the range *i1* to *i2*.

void iterate()
Perform all iterations (*generations*) of the genetic algorithm. It basically calls select, then reprod, then ceval (for all chromosomes).

void outbit (bits b, *int* n)
Print the bit string b, having size n, to standard output as characters.

void putbit (bits b, *int* n, *int* val)
Set bit n of bit string b to the value *val*, which must be either 1 or 0.

void reinit ()
Replace the entire population with random bit strings.

void reprod ()
Create a new generation. Select the top percentage of the existing chromosomes to reproduce. Apply mutation and crossover to these, and then replace the old population with the new.

int rbit ()
Return a random single bit value (0 or 1).

bits rbits (int n)
Return a random bit string n bits in length.

void select (int p *f)*
Sort the chromosomes based on fitness (ascending order). Print a table if the parameter *pf* is true.

bits str2bit (char s, *int* n)
Convert a character string to a bit string. The character string s must contain only *1* or *0* characters, and has length n. The resulting bit string is returned.

A user can write a main program and a bunch of other code, and link to these functions as a library. However, the intent is to have a user write as little code as possible. Therefore, the IPcGen system has a main program that acquires the basic parameters interactively, and calls a few user-defined functions to do critical operations.

To use IPcGen this way requires that the user write the following functions:

double ieval (unsigned char *b, int n)
The user's objective function. The bit string *b* is the chromosome, and *n* is the size of the chromosome. The value returned by this function is the raw objective function value, used for evaluating chromosomes.

void user_init ()
This is a user defined initialization function, called by the system at the beginning. It can be used to define data arrays, read input files, or can simply print a message in some cases.

FPcGen is only slightly different, and will be described later. The usage of IPcGen will be illustrated by the following two sections, each containing one important example.

Discrete Optimizations

In the case of a discrete (or *combinatorial*) optimization, the objective function accepts an argument that is a bit string. Situations in which this is useful include the optimization of the order in which things are done (e.g., scheduling). A classical problem of this type is the *travelling salesman problem*.

Imagine that a salesman must visit *N* cities on his route. It makes sense as a matter of cost and time to visit each city only once; the geographical position of each city is known, and the trip is to be as short as possible. This problem has been studied extensively, and is known to be costly to solve for large N[1]. It also tends to contain a number of local minima.

Each city can be given a unique number, an integer that identifies the city. The path that the salesman takes can then be represented as a permutation of the numbers from 1 to *N*. For instance, the string 1,3,2,4 means that city 1 would be visited first, followed by cities 3, 2, and 4 in that order. Since the list of cities contains each city only once, the rule that a city may be visited only once is automatically enforced by the standard algorithms. The objective function is simply the expression for the total distance travelled for a particular ordering (permutation) *P*; that is,

---

1. The travelling salesman problem is, in fact, NP complete.

$$F(P) = \sum_{i=1}^{N} \sqrt{(Px_i - Px_{i+1}) + (Py_i - Py_{i+1})} \qquad \text{(EQ 10.4)}$$

where Px_i is the x coordinate for city i, and city $N+1$ is the same as city 1.

Solving this problem using a genetic algorithm does not seem the obvious approach, mainly because a city cannot appear in the list more than once. There is no genetic operator that will enforce this. However, since we have complete control over the objective function, a penalty can be attached to a duplicate. As the objective function accumulates the total distance travelled, it can also set flags to indicate which of the cities have been visited. Any unvisited cities correspond to a duplicate elsewhere in the route, and results in a value of 1000 being added to the distance.

The program tsset is a genetic algorithm solution to the Travelling Salesman Problem, and an example of the input to the program can be found in the file tsdata2. The problem specified by this data corresponds to the situation seen in Figure 10.4; there are eight cities placed on a simple grid. The user-defined code needed to solve this problem using IPcGen is shown in Figure 10.5; note that the penalty for duplication is added to the distance. This is the only place where the ''no duplicates'' rule is enforced, yet after the initial iterations there are no entries in the top few percent of evaluations that contain a duplicate. Also note that the

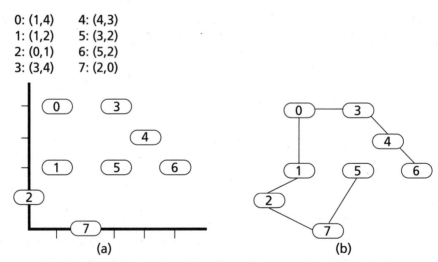

0: (1,4)	4: (4,3)
1: (1,2)	5: (3,2)
2: (0,1)	6: (5,2)
3: (3,4)	7: (2,0)

(a)   (b)

Figure 10.4 Solving the Travelling Salesman Problem. (a) The initial layout of 8 cities. We must find a route connecting all cities, none more than once, having a minimum total distance. (b) The solution found using the genetic algorithm (total distance = 17.714776). This happens to be optimal.

```
/* User-defined functions for the Travelling Salesman
Problem: TSSET.C */
#include <math.h>
#define MAXARGS 100
extern int nargs;
float cityx[MAXARGS], cityy[MAXARGS];

void user_init ()
{
 int i;

 printf ("This GA solves the Travelling Salesman Problem.
         The\n");
 printf ("of arguments is the number of cities.\n");
 printf ("Now enter the (x,y) coordinates of each
             city.\n");
 for (i=0; i<nargs; i++)
 {
  printf("Coordinates for city #%d: ", i);
    scanf ("%f", &(cityx[i])); printf ("%f ", cityx[i]);
    scanf ("%f", &(cityy[i])); printf ("%f\n", cityy[i]);
 }
}

double distance (int a, int b)
{
 float x1, y1, x2, y2;

x1 = cityx[a]; y1 = cityy[a]; x2 = cityx[b]; y2 =
            cityy[b];
 return sqrt( (double)( (x1-x2)*(x1-x2) + (y1-y2)*(y1-y2)
) );
}

/* Evaluate chromosome N and store result in EVALS array
*/
double ieval (unsigned char *b, int n)
{
 int rout[MAXARGS], i,j,k, visited[MAXARGS];
 double total_distance=0.0;
```

Figure 10.5 Source code for the objective function (function to be minimized) and the user-defined initialization for the Travelling Salesman Problem.

```
for (i=0; i<nargs; i++)         /* Extract the route from
            this chromosome */
{
  route[i] = getarg (i, b);
  visited[i] = 0;
}

for (i=0; i<nargs-1; i++)        /* Compute the distance
            for this route */
{
  j = route[i]; k = route[i+1];
  total_distance += distance (j, k);
  visited[j] = 1; visited[k] = 1;
}
total_distance += distance (route[0], route[nargs-1]);
visited[route[nargs-1]] = 1;

for (i=0; i<nargs; i++) /* Compute penalties for cities
            not on the route. */
  if (visited[i] == 0) total_distance += 1000.0;
return total_distance;
}
```

Figure 10.5 (continued)

position of the cities is read in by the user-defined function user_init, and that an extra function (distance) is included to be used only by eval.

There is a wide variety of such rules that can be enforced using the objective function alone. For example, penalties can be attached to certain routes to simulate the existence of toll booths or river crossings (Press 1988); both should be kept to a minimum.

There are some direct applications of this type of organization to computer vision: specifically, subgraph isomorphism for matching graph representations of objects against templates. This is but one illustration of the overall power of the technique.

Binary (Integer) Optimizations

Solving a set of equations in such a way that the solution is a set of integers is much more difficult than finding a real solution. Since raster coordinates are integers, this sort of problem pops up relatively often in image analysis and computer vision. The traditional approach (integer programming) finds correct solutions, but is thought to be difficult to understand, and can be tricky when the time comes to write the programs. We have an optimization system that does seem to work (at least for the Travelling Salesman Problem) and it should be possible to apply it to integer programming as well.

Consider the problem of finding the minimum of the objective function (Wolfe 1973):

$$M = 1600x_1 + 3200x_2 + 2300x_3 \qquad \text{(EQ 10.5)}$$

subject to the following constraints:

$$3x_1 + x_2 + 6x_3 = 2000$$
$$2x_1 + 5x_2 + x_3 \geq 1000 \qquad \text{(EQ 10.6)}$$
$$x_1 + 2x_2 + 4x_3 \leq 3000$$

and where x_1, x_2, and x_3 are all positive integers. This can be formulated as a genetic algorithm by first realizing that there are only two variables: once x_1 and x_2 are known, the first constraint determines x_3. Next, the objective function is formulated so that the inequality constraints become penalties that, when violated, add a value to the objective function that is in proportion to the amount by which the constraint is missed.

The formulation of the objective function appears in Figure 10.5, and includes the penalties for constraint violation. The program that implements the solution, ipset, uses IPcGen, and so is basically the same as tsset except for the objective function and the obvious differences in the expected input. This is why IPcGen is structured the way it is: The differences in the way two problems are solved can be found by examining only the user-defined code. The code for ipset appears in Figure 10.6.

The input data that resulted in the best solution can be found in the file lpdata. One important consideration is that the range for each parameter (which is specified to the genetic algorithm in advance) should place the expected or reasonable parameter values in the middle, rather than at one end of the range.

The best solution to this problem occurs at $x_1=438$, $x_2=2$ and $x_3=114$, and the value of the objective function at this point is 969400. While the program ipset did arrive at this solution, failure to do so can be the result of using a population that is too small, or of too few iterations. This raises the question of termination: How do we know when the solution has been found? A standard method involves observing the objective function. When no progress has been made for some number of consecutive iterations, the computation can be halted. This will not

```
/* User-defined functions for the Integer Programming
Problem : IPSET.C */

#include <match.h>
extern int nargs;

void user_init ()
{
    int i;

    printf ("This GA solves the Integer Programming
            Problem :\n");
    printf (" 1600X1 + 3200X2 + 2300X3 = MIN\n");

}

/* Evaluate chromosome N and store result in EVALS array
*/
double ieval (unsigned char *b, int n)
{
    float total_distance;
    int i,j,k, M, 1;
    int x1, x2, x3;
/* Extract the parameters */
    x1 = getarg(0, b);
    x3 = getarg(1, b);
    x2 = 2000 - 6*x3 - 3*x1; /* X2 is a function of X1
                and X3 */

    if (x2 < 0) 1 = abs(x2) * 10000;
     else 1 = 0;
    M = 1600*x1 + 3200*x2 + 2300*x3;

/* Compute penalties for violating the constraints */
/* Constraint 2: */
    k = 2*x1 + 5*x2 + x3;
    if (k < 1000) k = (1000 - k) * 3000;
    else k = 0;

/* Constraint 3: */
    j = x1 + 2*x2 + 4*x3;
    if (j > 3000) j = (j-3000) * 3000;
    else j = 0;

    return (double)( M + k + j + 1);
}
```

Figure 10.6 The user-defined code (ipset) for the integer
programming problem.

always be correct, and so multiple runs using the same data but different random-number seeds can be performed. If they terminate with the same values, we can conclude that the optimum has probably been achieved.

Real Optimizations

When discussing the Chow-Kaneko thresholding algorithm (Section 3.2), recall that one of the steps involved fitting a Gaussian curve (normal distribution) to a histogram. This is a good example of a real (floating-point) optimization problem, and one that has application to computer vision. The parameters to the Gaussian curve are real, as is the function value itself. What is more, the problem is typical of a generally useful technique (curve fitting) that can be used to find the best curve of other types (such as polynomial or exponential) that can be used to describe a set of pixels found in an image.

In order to solve this problem, we must use floating-point parameters. This means using the FPcGen program, which works in the same way as IPcGen except for those functions that access the real parameters. However, the user interface is the same as before.

The functions in FPcGen that differ from those in IPcGen are:

double decode (bits data, *int* sb, *int* n, *double* dmin, *double* dmax)
  Like decode in IPcGen, but returns a double precision floating point result. Also, the variables *dmin* and *dmax* define the legal range of values for this parameter; these are used for scaling.

void encode (bits data, *int* sb, *int* n, *double* dmin, *double* dmax, *double* val)
  Like the previous encode, but the value being converted into a bit string is a double. As in decode, *dmin* and *dmax* are used to create a fixed point value to be stored as a bit string.

double getarg (int n, *bits* thisc)
  Return encoded parameter *n* from the bit string *thisc*.

The procedure for fitting Gaussians to data should look familiar. First, the data, to which the Gaussian is to be fit, is read in (*user_init*). The objective function is defined to be the sum of the squares of the distances between the Gaussian function, sampled at the same points as is the data, and the data values. This is to be minimized (*feval*).

Figure 10.7 gives the C source code for the user-defined portion of the solution to this problem. Note that the evaluation function is called feval, rather than ieval; otherwise the use of FPcGen is identical to that of IPcGen. The program works quite well on the data samples tested (for example, the file gdata on the CD), but might well be too slow for use with the Chow-Kaneko thresholding algorithm.

```c
/* User-defined functions for the Gaussian fit problem */
#include <math.h>
#include <stdio.h>
extern int nargs;
float datax[256], datay[256];
int NPTS = 0;
double getarg (int n, unsigned char *this);

void user_init ()
{
    int i,j, k;
    FILE *f;
    char fn[128];

    printf ("This GA fits a Gaussian to a set of data
            values.\n");
    printf ("The name of the data file is: "); scanf
            ("%s", fn);
    f = fopen (fn, "r");
    if (f == NULL)
    { printf ("Can't open the file '%s' for input\n", fn);
            exit(1); }
    for (i=0; i<256; i++)
    {
      printf ("Coordinates for point #%d: ", i);
      k = fscanf (f, "%f", &(datax[i])); printf ("%f ",
            datax[i]);
      if (k<1) break;
      k = fscanf (f, "%f", &(datay[i])); printf ("%f\n",
            datay[i]);
      if (k<1) break;
      j = 1;
    }
    fclose (f); NPTS = j;
}

double gauss (double a, double b, double c, double d)
{
    double x;
    x = -(d-a)*(d-a)/(b*b);
    return c*exp(x);
}
```

Figure 10.7 C Source for the user-defined portion of the fit of a Gaussian to a set of data points.

374

```
/* Evaluate chromosome N and store result in EVALS array
*/
double feval (unsigned char *bs, int n)
{
    double a, b, x[5];
    int, i,j,k;

    x[0] = getarg(0, bs);
    x[1] = getarg(1, bs);
    x[2] = getarg(2, bs);

    for (i=0; i<NPTS; i++)
    }
      a = gauss (x[0], x[1], x[2], datax[i]);
      b += (a—datay[i])*(a—datay[i]);
    }
    return sqrt(b);
}
```

Figure 10.7 (continued)

10.3 PERFORMANCE IMPROVEMENTS FOR FLOATING POINT

The two operations that could be called the basis of genetic algorithms are the single-bit mutation and the one-point crossover. Together they provide the bulk of the variability in the parameter sets that is needed for the selection process to do its work. Both operations are applied to bit strings, which are the encoded form of the actual parameter. In the case where the parameters are symbolic, integer, or even fixed points, this representation makes a great deal of sense, and is evocative of the original biological analogy.

For floating point (real) parameters, the bit string representation requires a good deal of time spent converting to and from bit string form. Each time the objective function is evaluated the parameter must be decoded (converted into real form). Initially, each parameter must be encoded (converted to bit string form) so that the operators can be applied. In addition, some flexibility is lost—some work has been done with dynamic changing of the ranges and size of the bit string as the optimization proceeds, and this also requires encoding and decoding.

The idea of using real numbers directly has been discussed, but generally in the context of hybrid algorithms, and the operators used are not the same—they are statistical analogies. For example, Davis (Davis 1991) suggests *real number mutation*, which is the replacing of a real number in a chromosome with a randomly selected real number. This is not a single-bit mutation; indeed, it could change all of the bits in that number. *Real number creep* is also not a traditional operator; it is an additional method that can prove useful in some circumstances, but which many purists eschew as being not general or robust. A creep operator examines all of the parameters on a chromosome and, with a known probability, will change them by a random small amount.

What is proposed here are two operators that are precise analogs of the bit string operations, but which apply to real numbers. Some of the advantages are obvious for continuous optimization problems; there are also some interesting by-products.

Single-Bit Mutation

Without loss of generality the single-bit mutation operator will be defined as one that reverses a specified bit in the encoded representation. Consider a four-bit representation of the range 0.0–1.0; the values it is possible to represent are:

```
0.0 = 00   0.25 = 01   0.50 = 10   0.75 = 11
```

A bit in the low bit position has a value $V=0.25$ associated with it; more generally,

$$V = \frac{Dmax - Dmin}{2^n}$$

(EQ 10.7)

where *Dmax* is the largest value in the range, *Dmin* is the smallest, and n is the number of bits in the representation. In the example, $V=(1.0-0.0)/2^2$.

Each bit in the encoded bit string representation corresponds to a power of two multiplied by V. The low bit is $2^0 \times V$, the next is $2^1 \times V$ and so on. It seems apparent that to do a single-bit reversal on a parameter X at bit position n is to subtract $2^n \times V$ from X if bit n is set (1), or to add $2^n \times V$ to X if bit n is clear (0).

Bit n of the fixed-point bit-string representation of X is set if the bit string that is shifted right n bits has the low bit set; the corresponding floating point expression is to consider the expression $(X-Dmin)/(v \times 2^n)$. If this result has the low bit set then the bit corresponding to $v \times 2^n$ is set in the encoding.

This argument leads to the single-bit mutation function seen in Figure 10.8. Note that the calculation of V would normally be done globally only once, and all values of $V \times 2^n$ could also be precomputed. This leaves the operation count at one floating divide, one floating multiply, two floating subtractions, and an integer division.

One-Point Crossover

The crossover operation is a little more complex, but is based on the same ideas. Consider the situation where an argument has a size of 10 bits and a range from

```
/* Implement a single-bit mutation */
void fmut (float *b, int n, float xmax, float xmin, int size)
{
double m, v, d3;
        v = (double)(xmax-xmin)/(double)(1<<size);
        m = (double)(1<<(size-n-1));
        if ( (int)((*b-xmin)/(v*m)) % 2 )
                *b = *b - v*m;
        else
                *b = *b + v*m;
}
```

Figure 10.8 C code to perform a single-bit mutation on a real argument b.

0.0 to 1.0. Two instances of this argument, X and Y, are to be crossed over at bit 4; this situation is:

```
Argument Bit Value Real Value Crossed Bit Value Resulting
Real

X 0110101010 .416016 0110010011 .393555

Y 0010010011 .143555 0010101010 .166016
```

This is accomplished by taking the high four bits of X and adding to it the low six bits of Y (and vice versa). In real terms, the low six bits can represent values up to $(2^7-1) \times V$, and the high four bits represent values from $2^7 \times V$ upwards. Thus, the high four bits of the real value X is given by:

$$X_h = \left[\frac{X - Dmin}{V \times 2^n} \right] \times V \times 2^n \qquad \text{(EQ 10.8)}$$

for $n=4$, which effectively masks out the low six bits by truncation and then shifts the value left by the proper amount. The low six bits are obtained by simply subtracting this from X:

$$X_l = X - X_h \qquad \text{(EQ 10.9)}$$

Now do the same for Y, and finally let $X = X_h + Y_l$ and $Y = Y_h + X_l$, as seen in the code for fcross1 in Figure 10.9.

Evaluation of the Methods

The single-bit mutation function has been tested on tens of thousands of mutations using various experimental protocols. For an example, a program has been written that generates random whole-number ranges, bit string sizes, and values, and then creates a bit string from the generated values. All possible one-bit mutations were carried out, both on the bit string and the real value, and the results were compared. The worst-case error (the difference between the two values) was 0. For this same experiment the worst-case error for the one-point crossover was 5%; this occurred

```
/* Perform a 1 point crossover */
void fcross1 (float *s1, float *s2, int n, float xmin, float xmax, int size)
{
    int i, k, cl;
    double xl, xh, yl, yh;
    double v,j;
    v = (double)(xmax-xmin)/(double)(1<<size);
    j = (double)(1 << (size-n));
    xh = (int)((*s1-xmin)/(j*v)) * (j*v);
    xl = (*s1) - xh;
    yh = (int)((*s2-xmin)/(j*v)) * (j*v);
    yl = (*s2) - yh;
    xh = xh + yl ;
    yh = yh + xl ;
    *s1 = (float)xh;
    *s2 = (float)yh;
}
```

Figure 10.9 Code to perform a one-point crossover on real arguments s1 and s2.

Table 10.1 Crossover Execution Performance

Method	Time for Mutation	Time for Crossovers
Real numbers	0.25	0.02
Bit strings	0.365	0.09

in one case out of 1000. Two more cases had an error of 2%, and all of the rest were under 1%, with the average error being 0.0082%.

Speed of execution is another important issue, but a more difficult one to evaluate. There is a very good chance that someone else could code a faster bit-string module than the one used in the evaluation. Still, some evaluation must be done and, after all, all of the code was written by the same person. For the execution profile done on a SPARCstation 2, an example that performed 2000 crossovers and 30,000 mutations is illustrated in Table 10.1.

This experiment is flattering to the bit-string representation in that some of the global overhead is not included, and the Sun workstation does not have floating-point acceleration.

When one is using real arguments in the way described thus far, the notion of chromosome length is a fiction. The size and range associated with any argument is only of importance when a mutation or crossover is being performed. It is therefore a simple task to change these, or possibly even make them parameters themselves. Increasing the size of the bit string has the effect of decreasing V, which means that the precision of the search is improved. There is no significant implementation overhead involved in using large sizes up the maximum precision of a floating point number.

Changing the ranges while performing an optimization can be done if it can be determined with some reliability that the argument involved does not have an optimal value in the outlying regions of the range. Decreasing the average while maintaining a constant size has the effect of refining the step size (decreasing V again) and increasing the precision of the result while improving the speed with which the optimal value can be achieved. To modify the range in a bit string implementation requires a decoding of the argument, a modification of the range, and then an encoding at the new range. The real implementation does not require a change in the encoding, and achieves high-accuracy simulation of the bit string results provided that the ranges have acceptable numerical properties. Integral ranges and powers of two are best, while repeating fractions and irrational numbers are worst.

The method could be easily applied to multiple mutations and crossovers and to other operators used in genetic algorithms.

10.4 GENETIC METHODS FOR VISION

As the number of dimensions (parameters) increases, an optimization problem becomes much more complex. Since images possess two spatial dimensions, it is to be expected that an optimization problem involving an image would take much longer than the corresponding problem using simple 1D data points. Still, the use of genetic algorithms in computer vision has begun to flower, partly because of the robust nature of the method.

A part of the application of genetic algorithm to a vision problem is a good choice of representation, and the careful use of what we know or can easily find out about an image. This is a common thread in the discussion of the practical and interesting methods in this section.

Finding a Target Contour

One interesting application of genetic algorithm to vision involves the identification of a primitive object contour in a larger image (Toet 1995). This could be a first step in a recognition system, since it is important to know where in the image to look for objects. The contour, in this case, is rather like a bounding box, but it has six sides and can therefore convey more detailed information on orientation and area—this will be called a *six-point contour*.

Consider the objects seen in Figure 10.10. The difference between a simple bounding box and a six-point contour is clear enough. What is not quite as clear is the precise nature of the best six-point contour, or how to find it. The problem can be expressed as an optimization problem in the following way: Rather than thinking of the contour as six *edges*, we can think in terms of the six *vertices*. Each vertex can be expressed in polar coordinates as a pair (r,h), given some coordinate system. Specifically, if the coordinate system is at the center of the

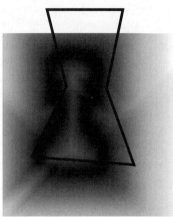

Figure 10.10 The six-point contour of a simple object, in this case a black pawn.

contour (i.e., where lines through opposite vertices intersect), then the representation is even simpler. The distance between the center and the two opposing vertices is the same, and the angles sum to 180 degrees. Thus, only three distances and three angles are needed (provided that the coordinates of the center are parameters also).

The notation to be used is defined in Figure 10.11. The parameter vector consists of the radii, the angles, and the coordinates of the center point, giving an eight-parameter optimization problem. This representation constrains the contours to be symmetrical, but this does not seem like a severe problem.

What is needed now is to identify the objective function. In what sense is the contour to be an optimal one? What is being measured? The total distance of the

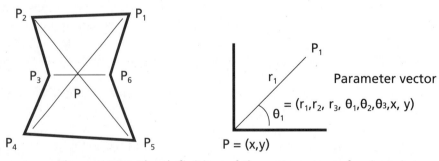

Figure 10.11 The definition of the parameters of a six-point contour.

contour from the object pixels could be minimized, as could the maximum distance, or the distance of the midpoints of each edge to the object. In any case, only the outline of the object is required, and a distance calculation is performed. There is a fast way to do this.

The first step is edge detection, which can be done by any of the methods from Chapter 1. The second step is the calculation of the distance values in advance using the distance transform. Basically, an image is created in which the pixel values are integers representing the distance between that pixel and the nearest edge pixel. This reduces the distance calculation in the objective function to a table lookup, and makes the use of a genetic algorithm possible. Calculation of the vast number of floating-point distances needed would otherwise demand some other solution.

Figure 10.12 shows both the edge-enhanced image resulting from applying the Sobel edge detector to Figure 10.10a, and the image consisting of distance values between each pixel and the nearest edge. SInce the distance can be calculated using a simple lookup in the distance map, the objective function is coded as an *average* of the distances of the pixels along each polygon edge, rather than as the sum; minimizing the sum would encourage very small contours to be located. In addition, a penalty should be imposed for polygons that cross over themselves (self-intersection), and for polygons having two adjacent vertices with less than a five-degree difference in angle. These penalties are somewhat expensive to compute.

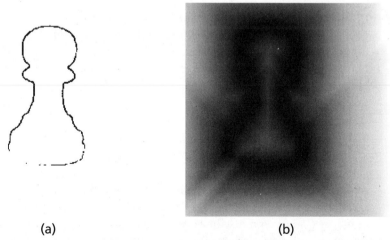

(a)   (b)

Figure 10.12 (a) The pawn image, after application of the Sobel edge detector. (b) Distance map: The pixel value is the distance to the nearest edge pixel.

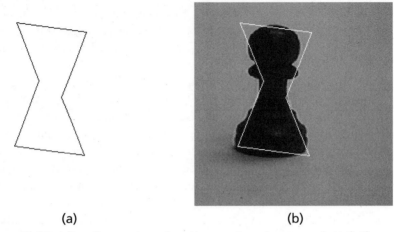

(a)   (b)

Figure 10.13 After the contour location process has completed, the result is a simple polygon. (a) The six-point contour found for the pawn image. (b) The contour superimposed on the original image.

The calculation of the edge-enhanced image and the distance map is performed in user_init, which prompts for the name of the image file. The feval function decodes the parameters and checks the constraints, then calculates the average distance for each edge in the polygon. The program conset contains all of the user-defined code for the contour identification process. The result for the pawn image, which uses the input file named condata, appears in Figure 10.13.

Identifying Simple Shapes

Simple geometric shapes occur frequently in real-world scenes of interest in computer vision. Since vision applications tend to involve artificial constructions (such as mechanical and electronic parts, characters, symbols, and tools) (Agin 1980; Horn 1975; Perkins 1978), the identification of simple shapes would appear to be useful in practice. Actually, it is common practice to approximate more complex objects by simple ones like cones and cylinders (Nevatia 1977; Soroka 1981).

Efforts to extract geometric primitives from acquired images have met with some success (Roth 1994), and are an interesting application of genetic algorithm. The algorithm uses the idea of a minimal subset of a curve; that is, the smallest number of points required to unambiguously describe the curve. For a line, a minimal subset consists of two points, for a circle three points, and for a general conic section five points. In principle any points will do, but a sample of widely separated points gives better results in practice.

There are many ways in which a genetic algorithm can be employed to locate simple curves in an image. In particular, the example to be discussed will involve finding circles, and the paper by Roth locates ellipses. An approach that uses IPcGen in this context begins by assigning a number (or *index*) to each black pixel. A minimal subset for a circle has three points, so a chromosome will consist of three parameters, namely the indices of each of the three pixels.

The objective function should be some measure of how well the circle defined by the specified minimal subset fits the black pixels in the image. The ieval function used in this case checks each of the pixels that should be set in the specified circle. It counts black pixels as *1* values, and it counts white pixels as *−1* values. The problem is to *maximize* the objective function rather than to minimize it, as has been done in all of the previous examples. A penalty is applied for radii that are too small or too large, for circle centers that fall outside the image, and for colinear data pixels.

Initialization of the chromosomes is not random, as it has been in the past. After edge-detection is applied to the input image, each connected region is found and numbered. The initial set of chromosomes is obtained by sampling among the identified regions at three points each, selected at random. Because of this novel initialization scheme, the IPcGen program could not be used as it was intended. Instead, it was modified to do the required initializations, and the new program was named geoset.

A random mutation could result in a new point, one from a different connected region, replacing one of the existing points in the chromosome. A crossover could unite two connected regions into one large one, permitting circles of various sizes to be identified.

The example data shown in Figure 10.14 was artificially generated, although the original paper used a real image containing partly occluded ellipses. Figure 10.14 pretends to show an image of a collection of red blood cells, which are

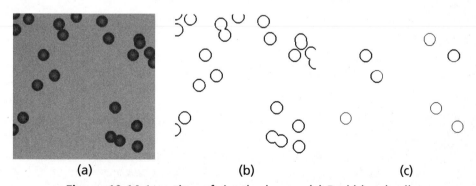

(a)	(b)	(c)

Figure 10.14 Location of simple shapes. (a) Red blood cell image. (b) Edges enhanced. (c) Some of the circles found by the genetic algorithm described here.

clearly circular in outline. After a very few iterations, many of the cells have been located and can be removed and counted.

Of course, more complex shapes can be found by this method, and the source code for geoset was provided for the purpose of experimenting with different objective functions, methods for parameter encoding, and shape parameterization.

Chromosome Classification

As a final specific example of the use of genetic methods in the processing of images, a genetic algorithm has been used for classifying real chromosomes from microscopic images (Piper 1995). The terminology is bound to get confusing here, because the objects in the image are chromosomes and the data structure for holding the parameters is also called a chromosome. (Sorry about that.)

A human has 46 chromosomes, which are really 23 pairs—each chromosome has another like it, called a *homologue*; one was obtained from each parent. A chart showing each pair of chromosomes identified is called a *karyogram*, and creating such a chart is a useful step in locating structurally abnormal chromosomes and corresponding medical problems. The chromosome images show a characteristic banding pattern that can be used in their identification: Homologues are closer to each other in this pattern than they are to other chromosomes.

Figure 10.15 shows a couple of chromosomes that display the characteristic banding patterns. This pattern has not commonly been used in chromosome classification procedures, which instead concentrate on the relative length of the chro-

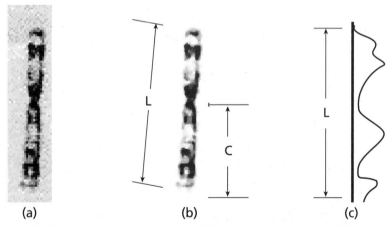

(a) (b) (c)

Figure 10.15 Human chromosome classification. (a) A digitized chromosome image. (b) A second instance of the same chromosome, showing two measurements used in classification. (c) The grey levels seen on a linear traversal of the chromosome, showing a characteristic profile.

mosomes and the position of the constriction that invariably appears somewhere along the length of the chromosomes, and some general properties of the bands.

A genetic algorithm chromosome (called a *ga-chromosome*) consists of a single classification of the objects in the image; that is, it is a labelling of the chromosomes as belonging to one of the 23 classes. Associated with each chromosome label is a likelihood, and the objective function is the sum of the likelihood of all of the classifications specified by the ga-chromosomes (all 46 of them). Maximizing these likelihoods is the job of the genetic algorithm.

A crossover operation will result in a reclassification of the last k chromosomes in the image, given that a ga-chromosome contains an ordered set of classifications, whereas a mutation will change just one classification. For the purposes of this algorithm, as with the previous one, a nonrandom initial population yielded the best results. A preliminary pass of a simple classifier was used as an initial guess, which the genetic algorithm refined.

Applications in Statistical Pattern Recognition

One final note on the use of genetic algorithms in computer vision concerns applications in statistical pattern recognition. The general method involves the creation of a feature vector in N dimensions, and then classifying unknown images according to their relative position (in N-dimensional space) to that of known objects. A genetic algorithm has been used for identifying a set of reference (template) vectors (Kuncheva 1995); for identifying the boundaries between regions in feature space (Bandyopadyay 1995); and for searching for clusters automatically (Srikanth 1995).

Other applications are mentioned in the bibliography, including a very interesting use of genetic method for matching objects in a stereo image pair so that a distance to the objects can be computed (Saito 1995).

10.5 BIBLIOGRAPHY

Agin, G. J. 1980. Computer Vision Systems for Industrial Inspection and Assembly. *IEEE Computer*. 11–20.

Bandyopadhyay, S., Murthy, C. A., and S. K. Pal. 1995. Pattern Classification with Genetic Algorithms. *Pattern Recognition Letters*. Vol. 16. 801–808.

Davis, L. (Ed.). 1991. Handbook of Genetic Algorithms. New York: Van Nostrand Reinhold.

Goldberg, D. E. 1989. *Genetic Algorithms, Optimization, and Machine Learning*. Reading, MA: Addison-Wesley.

Holland, J. H. 1975. *Adaptation in Natural and Artificial Systems*. Ann Arbor, MI: University of Michigan Press.

Horn, B. K. P. 1975. A Problem in Computer Vision: Orienting Silicon Integrated Circuit Chips for Lead Bonding. *Computer Graphics and Image Processing*. Vol 4. 3:294–303.

Katz, A. J. and P. R. Thrift. 1994. Generating Image Filters for Target Recognition by Genetic Learning. *IEEE Transactions on Pattern Analysis and Machine Intelligence*. Vol. 16. 9:906–910.

Kuncheva, L. I. 1995. Editing for the k-Nearest Neighbors Rule by a Genetic Algorithm. *Pattern Recognition Letters*. Vol. 16. 809–814.

Maio, D., Maltoni, D., and S. Rizzi. 1995. Topological Clustering of Maps Using a Genetic Algorithm. *Pattern Recognition Letters*. Vol. 16. 89–96.

Parker, J. R. 1995. A Genetic Algorithm for Stellar Photometry. University of Calgary Department of Computer Science Research Report #95/565/17.

Perkins, W. A. 1978. A Model Based Vision System for Industrial Parts. *IEEE Transactions on Computers*. Vol. 27. 126–143.

Piper, J. 1995. Genetic Algorithm for Applying Constraints in Chromosome Classification. *Pattern Recognition Letters*. Vol. 16. 857–864.

Prakash, M. and M. N. Murty. 1995. A Genetic Approach for Selection of Near Optimal Subsets of Principal Components for Discrimination, *Pattern Recognition Letters*. Vol. 16. 781–787.

Press, W. H., Flannery, B. P., Teukolsky, S. A., and W. T. Vettering. 1988. *Numerical Recipes in C: The Art of Scientific Computing*. Cambridge: Cambridge University Press.

Nevatia, R. and T. O. Binford. 1977. Description and Recognition of Curved Objects. *Artificial Intelligence*. Vol. 8. 1:77–98.

Roth, G. and M. D. Levine. 1994. Geometric Primitive Extraction Using a Genetic Algorithm. *IEEE Transactions on Pattern Analysis and Machine Intelligence*. Vol. 16. 9:901–905.

Saito, H. and M. Mori. 1995. Application of Genetic Algorithm to Stereo Matching of Image. *Pattern Recognition Letters*. Vol. 16. 815–821.

Schraudolph, N. N. and R. K. Belew. 1990. Technical Report. #LAUR 90-2795. Los Alamos National Laboratory.

Snyers D. and Y. Petillot. 1995. Image Processing Optimization by Genetic Algorithm with a New Coding Scheme. *Pattern Recognition Letters*. Vol. 1. 843–848.

Soroka, B. I. 1981. Generalized Cones from Serial Sections. *Computer Graphics and Image Processing*. Vol. 15. 2:154–166.

Srikanth, R. et al. 1995. A Variable-length Genetic Algorithm for Clustering and Classifications. *Pattern Recognition Letters*. Vol. 16. 789–800.

Toet, A., and W. P. Hajema. Genetic Contour Matching. *Pattern Recognition Letters*. Vol. 16. 849–856.

Wolfe, C. S. 1973. *Linear Programming with FORTRAN*. Glenview, IL: Scott, Foresman and Company.

Appendix

THE CD—WHERE DO I START?

A.1 BASIC DIRECTORY STRUCTURE

The accompanying CD is organized into ten directories; there is one for each chapter, plus special directories that contain code and images that are included as a special bonus. The chapter directories are named chap1 through chap10, and each one contains the relevant C source code and test images for the corresponding chapter. These directories have no subdirectories.

Most of the programs must be compiled with one of the libraries provided. The most important one, lib.c, contains basic operations on images, such as allocation, input, output, display, and low-level computations. Most of the programs must be compiled with this library.

When writing code to be compiled on a PC there is always a problem in deciding what compiler to us. Code that works using Turbo C might not work when using other compilers, and the choice of one compiler limits the use of the book for those who do not possess it. I therefore decided to include a C compiler with the book!

The GNU C compiler, while not well known in the PC world, is a command-line compiler that is in common use on workstations that run the operating system UNIX. The port of the compiler that is included here includes the source code, a debugger, simple VGA graphics, and (most importantly) a 32-bit DOS extender that allows programs compiled using this system to take advantage of all of the memory on the system. As you likely know, many compilers are restricted to using 640K of memory, and can only allocate 64K at a time. Not so with the GNU C (gcc) compiler.

In addition, this compiler can handle a dialect called C++, which is an object-oriented version of C.

Documentation for this system resides on the CD. The entire system is stored in the hierarchy starting with the directory gnu. All of the code for this book will compile using gcc, and those functions marked with * can also be compiled using Borland Turbo C.

A.2 CHAPTER DIRECTORIES

Chapter 1—Edge Detection

C Source Code

canny.c   Canny edge detector.

Usage:

```
canny <input>
```

This command uses a setup file named canny.par for default parameters; this file contains three values: the low-hysteresis threshold, the high threshold, and the standard deviation of the smoothing Gaussian. The edge-enhanced image will be written to a file named canny.pbm.

Example:

```
canny et1.pgm
```

*eval1.c   Pratt edge-detector evaluation.

Usage:

```
eval1 <edge image> <edge pixel file> { M }
```

This program evaluates an edge detector by comparing the position of located edge pixels against known edges. The known edges are placed in a file named *.edg in the following form:

N	Number of coordinates in this file.
$x^1 y^1$	Coordinates of an edge pixel.
. . .	
$x^n y^n$	Coordinates of the last edge pixel.

The optional third parameter M indicates the number of rows and columns to be ignored on the margin of the image. This would be specified for edge detectors that use a convolution mask, and which cannot properly deal with pixels in the first and last rows and columns (e.g., Canny, ISEF).

Example:

```
eval1 canny.pgm et1.edg 8
```

   *eval2.c   Rosenfeld edge-detector evaluation.

Usage:

```
eval2 <edge image>
```

This routine evaluates an edge detector based on how well the located edge pixels form a coherent edge set. No .edg file is needed.
   Example:

```
eval2 canny.pgm
```

   gnoise.c   Generate Gaussian note, in image form.

Usage:

```
gnoise <image> <standard deviation>
```

Generate Gaussian noise with the specified standard deviation. A PGM image consisting of noise only will be written to the file gnoise.pgm. The noise will be added to the specified image file (argument 1) and written to the file named noisy.pgm.
   Example:

```
gnoise et1.pgm
```

   *grad1.c   Gradient edge detection, method 1.

Usage:

```
grad1 <input>
```

Edge detection using the ∇_1 algorithm. The edge-enhanced image is written to the file grad1.pgm.
   Example:

```
grad1 et1.pgm
```

   *grad2.c   Gradient edge detection, method 2.

Usage:

```
grad 2 <input>
```

Edge detection using the ∇_2 algorithm. The edge-enhanced image is written to the file grad2.pgm.
   Example:

```
grad2 et1.pgm
```

    *kirsch.c   Kirsch edge detector.

    Usage:

```
kirsch <input>
```

Edge detection using the Kirsch algorithm. The edge-enhanced image is written to the file kirsch.pgm.
    Example:

```
kirsch et1.pgm
```

    maketmpl.c   Create standard images.

    Usage:

```
maketmpl
```

Creates the files et1.pgm . . et5.pgm.
    Example:

```
maketmpl
```

    marr.c   Marr edge detector.

    Usage:

```
marr <image> {SD}
```

Edge detection using the Marr-Hildreth algorithm. The edge-enhanced image is written to the file marr.pgm. Uses a setup file called marr.par, that contains a value for the standard deviation of the Gaussian used for smoothing. This value might optionally be specified as the second argument. The edge detector will use two standard deviation values ($SD-0.8$ and $SD+0.8$) and merges the results into a single edge-enhanced image.
    Example:

```
marr et1.pgm
```

    *measure.c   Measure/estimate noise levels in an image.

    Usage:

```
measure <image>
```

Measure the noise in the specified image. The image should represent an area of constant intensity. The noise is assumed to have zero mean and to be Gaussian in nature.

Example:

```
measure gnoise.pgm
```

    shen.c   Shen-Castan edge detector.

Usage:

```
shen <input>
```

Edge detection using the Shen-Castan (SEF) algorith. The edge-enhanced image is written to the file shen.pgm. Uses a setup file called shen.par that contains: the percentage of pixels to be above the hysteresis threshold; the smoothing factor, between 0 and 1; the window size for the adaptive gradient calculation; a thinning factor (number of pixels); and a flag (1 or 0) indicating whether hysteresis thresholding should be done.
    Example:

```
shen et1.pgm
```

    *sobel.c   Sobel edge detector.

Usage:

```
sobel <image>
```

Applies to the Sobel edge detector to the specified image file. The result is written to the file sobel.pgm.
    Example:

```
sobel et1.pgm
```

Images

chess.pgm	The test image of an occupied chess board.
chess_18.pgm	The chess image with noise ($\sigma = 18$)
chess_3.pgm	The chess image with noise ($\sigma = 3$)
chess_9.pgm	The chess image with noise ($\sigma = 9$)
et1.pgm	The ET1 test image. A step edge.
et1_18.pgm	The ET1 image with noise ($\sigma = 18$)
et1_3.pgm	The ET1 image with noise ($\sigma = 3$)
et1_9.pgm	The ET1 image with noise ($\sigma = 9$)
et2.pgm	The ET2 test image.
et2_18.pgm	The ET2 image with noise ($\sigma = 18$)
et2_3.pgm	The ET2 image with noise ($\sigma = 3$)
et2_9.pgm	The ET2 image with noise ($\sigma = 9$)

et3.pgm	The ET3 test image.
et3_18.pgm	The ET3 image with noise ($\sigma = 18$)
et3_3.pgm	The ET3 image with noise ($\sigma = 3$)
et3_9.pgm	The ET3 image with noise ($\sigma = 9$)
et4.pgm	The ET3 image with noise ($\sigma = 9$)
et4_18.pgm	The ET3 image with noise ($\sigma = 9$)
et4_3.pgm	The ET3 image with noise ($\sigma = 9$)
et4_9.pgm	The ET3 image with noise ($\sigma = 9$)
et5.pgm	The ET3 image with noise ($\sigma = 9$)
et5_18.pgm	The ET3 image with noise ($\sigma = 9$)
et5_3.pbm	The ET3 image with noise ($\sigma = 9$)
et5_9.pgm	The ET3 image with noise ($\sigma = 9$)
n20b.pgm	An image with Gaussian noise, $\sigma = 20$.
n20w.pgm	An image with Gaussian noise, $\sigma = 20$.
wood.pgm	Woodgrain (Teak). Figure 1.2a.

Other Files

compile.bat	DOS script for compiling all of the C source code.
et1.edg	Edges in the image et1.pgm. Used by the evaluation program eval1 to calculate a metric that can be used to compare the edge detection methods.

The files et*.edg are the edge pixel files for the et*.pgm test image.

canny.par	A sample argument set for the Canny edge detector.
marr.par	A sample arument set for the Marr edge detector.
shen.par	A sample argument set for the ISEF edge detector.
disp.exe	Display utility for PBM/PGM files.
lib.c,lib.h	Standard library for use with most source files.
*.exe	gcc compiled versions of the C source code.

Chapter 2—Morphology

C Source Code

This chapter discusses the MAX language, for which a compiler is provided in this directory. The file containing a MAX program must end with *.max*; the compiler converts this file into a C program that can then be compiled along with the morphology library MAXLIB.

If you have the Turbo C compiler then MAX is very easy to use. To compile the program t1.max, do the following:

```
max t1.max
```

The MAX compiler will create a file called t1.c, and one called t1.h. It will then automatically call the Turbo C compiler and create a file t1.exe. The maxlib.c library must be in the working directory for this to succeed.

Using the GNU compiler means performing the last step by hand. The MAX compiler will still create the .c and .h files; the user must then compile using

```
gcc —o t1 t1.c maxlib.c —lm
```

and then use coff2exe to create an .exe file, if desired.

*bindil.c	Source code for binary dilation (uses mlib.c).
*binero.c	Source code for binary erosion (uses mlib.c).
*grey.c	Grey level MAX library.
*max.c	Compiler for the MAX programming language.
*max.h	Include file for MAX.
*maxg.c	Grey level MAX compiler.
*maxg.h	Include file for maxg (grey level MAX).
*maxlib.c	The source code for the MAX library.
*mlib.c	Some morphological operations in library form.
*morph.h	Include file for mlib.c.

MAX Source Code

and.max	AND of two binary images.
bindil.max	Binary dilation.
binerode.max	Binary erosion.
boundary.max	Morphological boundary extraction.
close.max	Closing.
conditio.max	Conditional dilation.
count.max	Count 8-connected regions.
dil.max	Perform a dilation the hard way—using the definition.
dilg.max	Grey level dilation.
dual.max	MAX illustration of the dual nature of erosion/dilation.
erog.max	Grey level erosion.

fill.max	Conditional dilation—fill a polygonal region.
gclose.max	Grey-level *close* operation.
gopen.max	Grey-level *open* operation.
gradient.max	Morphological gradient.
hitmiss.max	Example of the hit and miss transform.
hitmiss2.max	Hit and miss with one SE reversed.
iotest.max	Test of MAX input/output.
open.max	Perform an open operation; depth is read from the keyboard.
smooth.max	Morphological smoothing.
t1.max	Test of input and output of images in MAX. Read in images named a and b; create copya, which is a copy of image a, and copyb, a copy of image b.
t2.max	Test of the ++ (dilation) operator, and of image constructors. Dilate a simple image, printing it before and after.
t3.max	Test of the—(erosion) operator. Like t2.max above.
t4.max	A dilation then an erosion. Also test of equality and subset (=, <>, <=) operators.
t5.max	Test of simple integer and pixel expressions.
t6.max	Test of translation (—>) operator.
t7.max	Test of membership operator (@).
t8.max	Test of subset (<= and >=).
t9.max	Test of union operator (+).
t10.max	Nested loop statements.
t11.max	Test of image constructor.
t12.max	Test of intersection (*) operator.
t13.max	Test of pixel + image.
t14.max	Test of isolated pixel operator (#).
t15.max	Multiple expression in a message statement.
tophat.max	Tophat transform.

Images

2_7a.pbm	Test image (Figure 2.7a).
2_7se1.pbm	Structuring elements used in Figure 2.7.
2_7se2.pbm	
2_7se3.pbm	
2_7se4.pbm	
2_7se5.pbm	
2_7se6.pbm	

a1.pbm	Figure 2.3a.
b1.pbm	Figure 2.3b.
circ.pbm	Test image—a circuit board.
circr.pbm	Bigger image of a circuit board.
circle4.pgm	Circles of various radii—for use as structuring elements in any bilevel application.

. . .

circle14.pgm	
coin3.pgm	Image of a set of coins.
coins.pgm	Image of a set of coins.
countme.pbm	Test image for count.max.
disk1.pgm	Sample image of a clean disk guard.
disk2.pgm	Sample image of scored diskette guard.
elise.pbm	Music image (Figure 2.8a).
elisese.pbm	SE for staff line removal (Figure 2.8b).
keys.pgm	Grey level image of keys on a carpet.
knight.pgm	Image of a chess piece.
noisy.pgm	Noisy image of a diskette guard.
qrest.pbm	A quarter rest (music notation).
rod.pgm	One version of a rod-shaped structuring element.
scans.pgm	Sample of scan-line noise.
se1.pbm	Another name for simple.pbm.
simple.pbm	Simple structuring element; all 1 in 3×3 pattern.
simple.pgm	Grey-level version of simple.pbm.
squares.pbm	Bilevel image of two squares. (2.17a).
texture.pgm	Image of two textures (2.30a).

Other Files

compile.bat	DOS script—compiles all of the source using gcc.
max.doc	Summary of MAX
turbomax.exe	MAX compiler created using Turbo C
turbomg.exe	Grey level MAX compiler created using Turbo C
disp.exe	Display utility for PBM/PGM files.
*.exe	gcc compiled versions of the C source code.

All other .exe files are gcc compiled versions of the corresponding C.

Chapter 3—Thresholding

Code for Chapter 3

*relax.c	Relaxation thresholding (Eqs. 3.46–3.50; Figure 3.11).
*relax2.	Relaxation with small regions (Fig. 3.12).
*relax3.c	Relaxation using grey-level differences (Fig. 3.13).
*thrdd.c	Adaptive thresholding for text images.

Usage:

```
thrdd <input image> <outout image>
```

Use the adaptive thresholding algorithm (section 3.4) to threshold the input image. The output image is the thresholded version, and is bilevel.

    *thrfuz.c   Thresholding by minimizing fuzziness. Two methods can be used; using Equation 3.23:

Usage:

```
thrfuz sky.pgm thr.pgm ENTROPY
```

Using Equation 3.24:
Usage:

```
thrfuz sky.pgm thr.pgm YAGER
```

    *thrglh.c   Method of grey-level histograms (thresholding).

Usage:

```
thrglh<input image> <output image>
```

Threshold the input image by the method of grey-level histograms (Section 3.1).

    *thris.c   Thresholding by iterative selection (Section 3.1).

Usage:

```
thris <input image> <output image>
```

    *thrjoh.c   Johanson's thresholding algorithm (Section 3.1).

Usage:

```
thrjob <input image> <output image>
```

    *thrkapur.c   Kapur's algorithm (Section 3.1)

Usage:

```
thrkapur <input image> <output image>
```

*thrlap.c   Thresholding using the Laplacian (Section 3.1)

Usage:

```
thrlap <input image> <output image> <percent>
```

*thrme.c   Minimum error thresholding (Section 3.1).
*thrmean.c   Threshold using the mean grey level (Section 3.1)

Usage:

```
thrmean <input image> <output image>
```

*thrmultis.c   Iterative selection on subimages.

Usage:

```
thrmulis <input image> <output image>
```

Use the method of iterative selection on subimages of the input image, so as to compute one threshold per region.

*thrpct.c   Select a specific percentage of the pixels as black.

Usage:

```
thrpct <input image> <output image> <percent>
```

*thrpun.c   Pun's thresholding algorithm (Section 3.1).

Usage:

```
thrpun <input image> <output image>
```

*twopeaks.c   Locate two peaks in the histogram (Section 3.1)

Usage:

```
twopeaks <input image> <output image>
```

Images

face.pgm	Basic face image from a CCD video camera.
faceg.pgm	Face image with imposed Gaussian illumination.
facel.pgm	Face image with imposed linear illumination.
faces.pgm	Face image with imposed sine-wave illumination.
pascal.pgm	Basic image of a Pascal program (text).
pascals.pgm	Pascal text with imposed sine-wave illumination.
sky.pgm	Basic image of a building, trees, and sky.

| skyg.pgm | Sky image with imposed Gaussian illumination. |
| skyl.pgm | Sky image with imposed linear illumination. |

Other Files

compile.bat	DOS script—compiles all of the source using gcc.
thrchow2.exe	Experimental Chow-Kaneko method. (Uses code that is not public domain).
disp.exe	Display utility for PBM/PGM files.
lib.c,lib.h	Standard library for use with most source files.
*.exe	gcc-compiled versions of the C source code.

Chapter 4—Texture

C Source Code

fast.c

The fast versions of the texture segmentation algorithms discussed in Section 4.3. Keywords specified as the second argument specifies which of the grey-level co-occurrence matrix measures will be calculated. The keyword must be one of:

average	Mean of the window.
stddev	Standard deviation.
pmax	Max probability.
contrast	Contrast.
homo	Homogeneity
energy	as defined in Section 4.3.

text.c

The texture segmentation program discussed throughout most of Chapter 4. This one program contains 13 basic algorithms, each possibly having many variations that can be specified using the parameters; the one desired is specified by a keyword in the second argument position, which must be one of:

grey_level	Grey level in a region (Section 4.2).
sd_level	Regional standard deviation (Section 4.2).
kurtosis	Section 4.2—3rd moment.
skewness	Section 4.2—4th moment.
pmax	Co-occurrence/max probability (Section 4.3).
moments	kth geometric moment (Section 4.3).
contrast	Expected value of delta (Section 4.3).
homo	Homogeneity (Section 4.3).
entropy	Information content (Section 4.3).

E5E5,E5L5,
E5R5 . . .

R5R5	Energy measures (Fig. 4.7).
vd	Vector dispersion (Section 4.6).
dx,dy	Edge direction proper
nx,ny	Edge direction; the number of edges in a general direction.
sang	Angle of Sobel edges; GLCM
sobel	Magnitude of Sobel edges; GLCM.

k1,
k2,
k3,
k4,
k5,
k6, elliptic,
parabolic,

saddle	Curvature (Section 4.6).
fractal	Fractal dimension (Section 4.7).

Examples of calls to this program can be found in the listed section.

Images

sky.pgm	Sky/building/trees—see ch3\sky.pgm.
t1.pgm	Test image #1—artificial pattern.
t2.pgm	Test image #2—artificial pattern.
t3.pgm	Test image #3—two types of cardboard.
t4.pgm	Test image #4—two types of cardboard.
t5.pgm	Test image #5–Two types of cloth.

Other texture images (brick, card*, cloth*, conc, grass, tree) can be found in the images directory.

Other Files

compile.bat	DOS script—compiles all of the source using gcc.
disp.exe	Display utility for PBM/PGM files.
lib.c,lib.h	Standard library for use with most source files.
*.exe	gcc compiled version of the C source code.

Chapter 5—Thinning

C Source Code

*bestzs.c	Best Zhang-Suen combined method.
*contourh.c	Contour-based thinning.

dist.c	Distance transform.
lap.c	Find discontinuities in the derivative of the medial axis, transform; uses the Laplacian.
*mat.c	Medial axis.
*thnstent.c	Stentiford's algorithm.
*thnstpp.c	Stentiford's algorithm, with preprocessing.
*thnz.c	Standard Zhang-Suen.
thnzh.c	Zhang-Suen-Holt.

Images:

5.pbm	Image of the digit *5*.
8.pbm	Image of the digit *8*.
b.pbm	Image of the letter *B*.
h.pbm	Image of the letter *H*.
t.pbm	Image of the letter *T*.
test2a.pbm	Smaller image of the letter *T*.
test3.pbm	Rectangle with a one-pixel flaw on the outline.
tsp.pbm	The letter *T* with a one-pixel flaw.
v.pbm	The letter *V*.
x.pbm	The letter *X*.

Other Files:

compile.bat	DOS script—compiles all of the source using gcc.
disp.exe	Display utility for PBM/PGM files.
lib.c,lib.h	Standard library for use with most source files.
*.exe	gcc compiled versions of the C source code.

Chapter 6—Restoration

The majority of the C programs here (those described as modules) are described at the end of Chapter 6.

C Source Code

align.c	Module 2—image alignment.
blur.c	Module 3—artifical blur.
fftlib.c	Fourier transform library—used by almost all of the restoration programs, in addition to lib.c.
fftlib.h	Include file for the Fourier transform library.
hiemph.c	Module 15—high-frequency emphasis filter.

hipass.c	Module 13—high-frequency pass filter.
homo.c	Module16—homomorphic filter.
inverse.c	Module 4—inverse filter.
lopass.c	Module 14—low-frequency pass filter.
makepsf.c	Creates a Gaussian point-spread function image.
mblur.c	Module 10—artifical motion blur.
motion.c	Module 11—remove motion blur.
notch.c	Module 9—notch filter for structured-noise removal.
shuffle.c	Module 7—shuffle the quadrants of an image.
slow1.c	Fourier transform—stage 1 implementation.
slow2.c	Fourier transform—stage 2 implementation.
slow3.c	Fourier transform—stage 3 implementation.
slow4.c	Fourier transform—stage 4 implementation (FFT).
snoise.c	Module 6—introduce structured noise.
snr.c	Module 8—structured-noise removal.
transfor.c	Module 12—Fourier transform of an image.
wiener.c	Module 5—simple Wiener filter.

Images

face.pbm	128×128 face image.
faces.pgm	Face image with sine-wave illumination.
faceb.pgm	Face image with blur.
fsn.pgm	Face image with structured noise (Fig. 6.11a).
four.pbm	*The Fourier Transform* image (Fig. 6.8a).
four.pgm	Grey-level version of four.pbm.
foura.pbm	Level reserved version of four.pbm.
fourbl.pgm	Blurred version of fourpgm.
grid.pgm	Hand printing on graph paper (Fig. 6.12a).
psf1.pgm	Sample point-spread function.
psf1a.pgm	Sample point-spread function.
psf2.pgm	Sample point-spread function.
psf2a.pgm	Sample point-spread function.
skym.pgm	Sky image (Fig. 6.13b) with motion blur.

Other Files

compile.bat	DOS script for compiling all of the C source code.
disp.exe	Display utility for PBM/PGM files.

lib.c,lib.h	Standard library for use with most source.
*.exe	gcc compiled versions of the C source code.

Chapter 7—Wavelets

C Source Code

bfwt.c	Brute-force wavelet transform.

Usage:

```
bfwt
```

Using Equation 7.7, transforms an impulse (as in Figure 7.3).

bfwtr.c	As BFWT, but transforms a rectangle (Fig. 7.4).
daub2d.c	2D Daubechies wavelet transform.
dfilter.c	Filter Daubechies wavelet image by level,quad.
dthres.c	Thresholded Daubechies wavelets.
fwt1d.c	Fast Haar wavelet transform, 1D.
fwt2d.c	Fast 2D Haar wavelent transform.
recur.c	Recursive wavelet transform.
showdaub.c	Display a daubechies wavelet transform (2D).
unwalsh.c	Inverse Walsh transform.
walsh2d.c	Walsh transform.
wthresh.c	Thresholded 2D Haar wavelet transform.

Images

face.pgm	The face image.
keys.pgm	The original KEYS image (Figure 7.10).
square.pbm	The image of a square (Figure 7.13).
sq128.pgm	Square image, 128×128.

Other Files

compile.bat	DOS script for compiling all of the C source code.
disp.exe	Display utility for PBM/PGM files.
lib.c,lib.h	Standard library for use with most source.
*.exe	gcc-compiled versions of the C source code.

Chapter 8—Optical Character Recognition

C Source Code

baird.c	Skew detection. This program finds bounding boxes for each of the characters seen in the image, and plots the position. A Hough transform can then be used to find the skew angle.

Usage:

```
baird image.pbm
```

This yields an output file called baird.pgm, which can be used as input to hskew.c below.

dists.c   Compute distances between feature vectors. A sample set of vectors is provided, representing slope histograms for the characters *C*, *D* (3 variations), and *B*. The matrix printed shows distances between each of the vectors.

hough.c   Hough transform procedure with a simple main program. This can be adapted easily for other specific uses.

hskew.c   Reads an image, such as created by baird.c, having single pixels in some arrangement. Assumes that each pixel represents a character and computes the skew angle.

Usage:

```
nskew baird.pgm
```

Prints the skew angle to the screen.

kfill.c   Noise-reduction algorithm for text.

Usage:

```
kfill kftest.pbm 5 out.pbm
```

learn.c   Read the standard template image and learn the character set, creating a database of templates. This version assumes perfect samples.

Usage:

```
learn testpage.pbm zzz
```

This creates a database file called zzz.

learn2.c   Read a standard template image and learn the characters, creating a database. This version assumes scanned, and therefore imperfect, samples.

Usage:

```
learn pagec.pbm zzz
```

This creates a database file called zzz.

learn3.c   Read a standard template image and learn the characters, creating a database. This version assumes scanned samples, and creates a database of feature vectors for statistical recognition. The purpose is to permit you to experiment with measurements and statistical recognition. *This code is to be modified by the user!*

Usage:

```
learn3 test14.pbm zzz
```

ocr1.c   Recognizes a page of perfect text. Uses the database created by learn.c above.

Usage:

```
ocr1 sample.pbm out.dat
```

The file out.dat will contain the extracted text (ASCII).

ocr2.c   Recognizes a page of scanned text. Uses the database created by learn2.c above.

Usage:

```
ocr2 paged.pbm out.dat
```

The file out.dat will contain the extracted text (ASCII).

ocr3.c   Primitive statistical recognizer. Useful for experimentation with statistical methods. The learn3.c program must create the same vectors for templates as those found by ocr3.c.

segpro.c   Segments a line of glyphs into individual characters by using profiles. Outputs the profiles to standard output.

Usage:

```
segpro smalla.pbm
```

segcost.c   Segments a line of glyphs into individual characters by using break cost. Outputs the profiles to standard output.

Usage:

```
segcost smalla.pbm
```

sig.c   Calculate and draw the signature of a glyph image.

Usage:

```
sig b.pbm
```

The signature is plotted on the screen, and the sampled values are printed.

slhist.c	Compute the slope histogram for a glyph. Can be used as a feature vector, or as part of one.

Usage:

```
slhist b.pbm
```

This prints the slope histogram to the screen.

vect.c	Simple vectorizer, for use of glyphs. Creates a set of line segments that corresponds to the boundary of the glyph.

Usage:

```
vect b.pbm
```

The vectors are written to the screen, and the vector outline is plotted.

Images

b.pbm	The character 'B'.
c.pbm	The character 'C'.
d.pbm	One version of the character 'D'.
d2.pbm	Another version of the character 'D'.
d3.pbm	Yet another version of the character 'D'.
kftest.pbm	Noisy version of a 'B' for testing the kFill algorithm.
pagec.pbm	Image having the scanned template for learn2.c.
paged.pbm	Image having sample text for ocr2.c.
sample.pbm	Sample data for ocr1.c.
sample14.pgm	Sample ocr image, 14 point type.
sk10.pbm	Text image having the lines of text at a 10-degree angle to the horizontal. For testing of the skew-detection methods.
sk10.pgm	Grey-level version of sk10.pbm.
sk15.pbm	Text image having the lines of text at a 15-degree angle.
sk15.pgm	Grey-level version of sk15.pbm.
smalla.pbm	Small text image for experimenting with isolation of characters.
smallb.pbm	Another image like smalla.pbm.
testpage.pbm	Perfect image of the template date (for learn.c)

Other Files

compile.bat	DOS script for compiling all of the C source code.
helv.db	Database for recognition of perfect characters.
tr.db	Database for recognition of scanned characters.

disp.exe	Display utility for PBM/PGM files.
lib.c,lib.h	Standard library for use with most source.
*.exe	gcc compiled versions of the C source code.

Chapter 9—Symbol Recognition

C Source Code

recc.c   Handprinted digit recognition using convex deficiencies.

Usage:

```
recc <input image>
```

The input image is expected to be a single-digit glyph. The program will print some intermediate results, followed by a classification for this digit.

recv.c   Handprinted digit recognition using vector templates.

Usage:

```
recv <input image>
```

The input image is expected to be a single-digit glyph. The program will print some intermediate results, followed by a classification for this digit.

recp.c   Handprinted digit recognition using character profiles.

Usage:

```
recpt <input image>
```

The input image is expected to be a single-digit glyph. The program will print some intermediate results, followed by a classification for this digit.

*nnlearn.c   Neural net—learn a set of digits (or other input data).

Usage:

```
nnlearn <input file>
```

The input file is a collection of classified records. For the digit example, we rescale the digit to a size of 8×6, or 48 pixels. Each entry in the input file consists of 48 floating point numbers between 0 and 1, which represent the pixel levels. The final (49th) value is the classification, which is an integer between 0–9. This program creates an output file called weights.dat containing the weights for each node; this file is used as input to nnclass.c.

*nnclass.c   Neural net—classify a digit image.

Usage:

```
nnclass<input file >
```

The input file is a single unclassified record, of the type described for nnlearn.c above. It represents a simple rescaling of a digit image (See nncvt.c). This program will print the classification to the screen.

*nncvt.c	Neural net—convert a digit image into input data for the neural net programs.

Usage:

```
nncvt<input pbm image><output file>
```

Rescales the image to 8×6 pixels after finding the bounding box and rescaling the values. Writes levels as floats between 0.0 and 1.0

Classification of a digit image dig0.pbm requires:

```
nncvt dig0.pbm xx
nnclass xx
```

Images
dig0.pbm	
. . .	
dig9.pbm	Sample handprinted digit images in PBM format.

Other FIles
compile.bat	DOS script for compiling all of the C source code.
datapc1,	
datapc2	Precomputed neural net training input—each should contain data for 1000 classified handprinted digits. Compute a weights.dat file by:

```
nnlearn datapc1
```

nndata0	
. . .	
ndata9	Sample input files for nnclass.c; these were produced using nncvt (e.g., nncvt dig0.pbm nndata0).
prof.db	Profiles used by recp.c to recognize digits.
weights.dat	A precomputed set of weights for use by nnclass.c
disp.exe	Display utility for PBM/PGM files.

lib.c,lib.h	Standard library for use with nncvt.c.
*.exe	gcc-compiled versions of the C source code.

Chapter 10—Genetic Algorithms

C Source Code

conset.c	User portion of the code needed for 6-point contour generation.

Usage:

```
conset < condata
```

drawncon.c	Program for drawing the 6-point contour found by conset.c.
fpcgen.c	The genetic algorithm library for floating point.
gafloat.c	The fast procedures for floating-point mutation and crossover.
gapoly.c	GA program for finding the minimum of a polynomial.
gauset.c	User portion of code needed for fitting Gaussians to data.

Usage:

```
gauset < gaudata
```

geoset.c	GA program to locate circles in an image.

Usage:

```
geoset < geodata
```

ipcgen.c	The genetic algorithm library for integers.
ipset.c	The user portion of the integer programming solution.

Usage:

```
ip < ipdata
```

trysol.c	Program to find x^2 given x^1 and x^3 (for geoset.c)
tsset.c	User portion of the Travelling Salesman Problem.

Usage:

```
ts< tsdata
```

Images

c256.pgm	Chess piece image, 256×256. (Fig. 10.10).
cell.pgm	Synthetic image of red blood cells (for geoset.c).
contour1.pgm	Chess image, for contour generation.

contour2.pgm   Chess image, for contour generation.

contour3.pgm   Chess image, for contour generation.

Other Files

compile.bat	DOS script for compiling all of the C source code.
condata	Data file for conset.exe.
disp.exe	Display utility for PBM/PGM files.
gaudata	Data file for gauset.exe.
gdata	Sample 1D Gaussian, sampled. For use with gauset.exe.
geodata	Data file for geoset.exe.
lib.c,lib.h	Standard library for use with most source.
lpdata	Data file for ipset.exe.
tsdata	Data file for ts.exe.
lib.c,lib.h	Standard library.
*.exe	gcc-compiled versions of the C source code.

A.3 SPECIAL DIRECTORIES

The IMAGES Directory

A variety of digitized scenes that you are free to use in any way that you like. No fee, just mention the source, please.

bc1.pbm	Business card
bc2.pbm	Business card, Japanese
brick.pgm	Brick and floor tile (CCD video camera).
card1.pgm	Card stock (scanned).
card2.pgm	Corrugated cardboard (scanned).
card3.pgm	Manilla folder (scanned).
cloth1.pgm	Fleece fabric.
cloth2.pgm	Coarse weave wool/polyester (scanned).
conc.pgm	Concrete and floor tile (CCD video camera).
dolp.pgm	A dolphin.
grass.pgm	Grass/sidewalk interface.
kang.pgm	A kangaroo.
princ1.pgm	A page from *Principia*, by Isaac Newton.
princ2.pgm	. . . and the following page.
rott.pgm	A dog (a Rottweiler, actually).

templ.pgm	A building in a park in Tokyo.
tokyo.pgm	Part of Tokyo seen from the Emperor's palace.
tree.pgm	Tree bark and grass.
tree2.pgm	Another tree.
williams.pgm	A page from *A History Of Computing Technology*, by M.R. Williams, Prentice-Hall 1985.

The GNU Directory

The source and executable for the gnu C compiler, libraries, and utilities.

There is far too much stuff to list it all here. The important thing to know is the the documentation is there (gnu\doc*, gnu\readme*.*), including installation instructions. In addition, the complete directory set is present *PLUS* the compressed archives, from which the entire directory tree can be re-created. The archives are in gnu/zip in pkzip format.

The LEMON Directory

No source code here, but the executable version of the Lemon optical music recognition system can be found here, and some sample images on which to try it. Just for variety, Lemon runs under OS/2 only (the OS/2 guys seem to get left out all of the time). What documentation we have is online. If you have a scanner, you can convert your own sheet music into computer-readable form.

lemon.doc	Documentation for the system.
lemon.exe	Executable version (OS/2 only).
moz.tif	An example of sheet music input to Lemon.
omr.ini	Initalization file.
templs	A directory containing the templates used to match the music symbols during the recognition process.

A.4   INSTALLING THE GNU C COMPILER

From the ZIP files:

Create a directory named c:\gnu and copy the .zip files into it. Run PKUNZIP (Version 2 or better) on all .zip files except those of the form dj112m*.zip—these are fixes, and must be left until the end. Then unzip the fixes in numerical order: dj112m1.zip . . . dj112m4.zip.

From the CD/gnu directory:

Simply copy the cd\gnu directory into c:\gnu, which you must create.

In either case, now create a directory for temprary files named c:\tmp.

Setting up the compiler:
Add to CONFIG.SYS:

```
files=15
shell=c:\command.com c:\ /e:1000 /p
```

Add to AUTOEXEC.BAT:

```
set DJGPP=c:/gnu/djgpp.env
set TMPDIR=c:/tmp
SET PATH= . . . ;c:\gnu\bin
```

IF YOU DO NOT HAVE AN 80387 FLOATING POINT CHIP:
Type:

```
SET 387=NO
```

at the command line.

Many more details can be found in the files readme.1st and readme.dj as well as in the other online documentation files in the gnu directory.

A.5   USING THE GNU C COMPILER

A simple compilation can be done using:

```
gcc -0 xx xx.c -lm
```

which places the object code in a file called xx, and which loads the match library. The input file (C source code) is xx.c. The compile.bat files give examples of how to compile the source code on the CD.

The 32-bit emulator is called go32. When a program is compiled, as was done for xx.c above, the object file is NOT directly executable. It is, instead, used as input to go32, which "executes" it. It is not an interpreter, but is an extender that allows full 32-bit addresses to be used.

For the above example, there are two options. To execute the program xx a single time, simply type:

```
go32xx . . . . . args for xx . . . .
```

To enable the go32 extender to be permanently associated with the program xx, type:

```
coff2exe -s c:\gnu\bin\go32.exe xx
```

which will create a file named xx.exe that can be run directly. Again, examples of this can be seen in the compile.bat files.

A.6 ON THE INTERNET

The Intel version of the GNU C compiler is a port, by D. J. Delorie, to whom many thanks go for the effort. The compiler can be found at:

oak.oakland.edu in *pub/msdos/djgpp*

There is a version of the pkzip compression utility there, too.

There is an electronic mailing list that is used to trade information on this compiler. To join it, try the following:

```
mail listserv@sun.soe,clarkson.edu
Subject:
help
add <e-mail address> djgpp
^ D
```

To send an article to the mailing list (you should join it first, and read the messages for a while) send mail to: *djgpp@sun.soe.clarkson.edu*. It will be sent to all members of the list.

There is a vast array of software on the net that uses PBM or PGM format images. This package is becoming standard on academic UNIX systems. Because locations move about, I would suggest the use of a browser such as archie for the location of source code. In particular, Mike Castle has ported the standard PGM system to run using DOS on a PC—search for *pbmp191d.zip*.

Finally, as I stated in the preface, I will maintain a ''bug list'' and fixes to the code on the CD. FTP access to this is through the host

ftp.cpsc.ucalgary.ca

in the directory

pub/images/vision/book.

If you plan to send me an error you have found, please look in this directory first to make sure that it has not been reported already.

INDEX

CUSTOMER NOTE: IF THIS BOOK IS ACCOMPANIED BY SOFT-WARE, PLEASE READ THE FOLLOWING BEFORE OPENING THE PACKAGE.

This software contains files to help you utilize the models described in the accompanying book. By opening the package, you are agreeing to be bound by the following agreement:

This software product is protected by copyright and all rights are reserved by the author, John Wiley & Sons, Inc., or their licensors. You are licensed to use this software on a single computer. Copying the software to another medium or format for use on a single computer does not violate the U.S. Copyright Law. Copying the software for any other purpose is a violation of the U.S. Copyright Law.

This software product is sold as is without warranty of any kind, either express or implied, including but not limited to the implied warranty of merchantability and fitness for a particular purpose. Neither Wiley nor its dealers or distributors assumes any liability for any alleged or actual damages arising from the use of or the inability to use this software. (Some states do not allow the exclusion of implied warranties, so the exclusion may not apply to you.)